perspectives

ᴉ the philosophy

of

language

a concise anthology

perspectives

in the philosophy

of

language

a concise anthology

edited by

robert j. stainton

 broadview

Canadian Cataloguing in Publication Data

Stainton, Robert J., 1964-
        Perspectives in the philosophy of language : a concise anthology

ISBN 1-55111-253-1

1. Language and languages – Philosophy. 2. Analysis (Philosophy).
I. Title.

P106.S73 1999   401   C99-930466-6

Broadview Press Ltd., is an independent, international publishing house, incorporated in 1985.

North America:
Post Office Box 1243, Peterborough, Ontario, Canada K9J 7H5
3576 California Road, Orchard Park, NY 14127
Tel: (705) 743-8990; Fax: (705) 743-8353;
e-mail: customerservice@broadviewpress.com

United Kingdom:
Turpin Distribution Services Ltd.
Blackhorse Rd., Letchworth, Hertfordshire SG6 1HN
Tel: (1462) 672555; Fax: (1462) 480947; e-mail: turpin@rsc.org

Australia:
St. Clair Press, P.O. Box 287, Rozelle, NSW 2039
Tel: (02) 818-1942; Fax: (02) 418-1923

www.broadviewpress.com

Broadview Press gratefully acknowledges the financial support of the Book Publishing Industry Development Program, Ministry of Canadian Heritage, Government of Canada.

Cover design and book layout: Alvin Choong, Calgary, Canada

PRINTED IN CANADA

*I dedicate my work on this anthology to
my wife, Anita R. Kothari, and to
my mother, Mary Liz Stainton,
with much love.*

Contents

Acknowledgements

I am grateful to Don Lepan for suggesting this anthology, and to the Social Sciences and Humanities Research Council of Canada for supporting my research.

I should also note my debt to A.P. Martinich's *The Philosophy of Language*, which was a very handy resource. I would have preferred to have less duplication between this text and his, but the latter includes so many of the classics that it would be difficult to do a collection of canonical readings in philosophy of language which did not overlap with it.

Finally, I am very grateful to Derrick Lacelle and Jennifer Schellinck for proofreading portions of the typescript.

Preface

This anthology is designed to accompany my *Philosophical Perspectives on Language*, also published by Broadview Press.

It is intended to serve two audiences. On the one hand, the anthology can be used by instructors who have adopted PPL as a required text. Many philosophers of language understandably want their students to read the original articles, and not just my secondary commentary. This is all to the good. The problem is, current anthologies are so expensive that two texts is a real financial burden for students. This collection is therefore intended to make it affordable for students to purchase both a sampling of readings in philosophy of language, as well as a secondary source. On the other hand, as my publisher has impressed upon me, there is room for a concise anthology in this area, at an affordable price, even for students who are not using my text. That's the second audience.

The result of these conflicting aims – to produce a companion to PPL versus publishing a truly stand-alone volume – is a compromise: A concise and inexpensive anthology which closely maps onto PPL, but does not precisely ape its contents. Thus I have included one or two papers which I do not explicitly discuss in PPL. And I have not attempted to provide a reading to go along with every section of my book. (In particular, there is no selection on nativism, prescriptive grammar, the Empiricist Idea Theory of meaning, possible worlds semantics, indexicals, or connectionism.) The choice of what to leave out depended upon factors like: how clear PPL is on the issue; whether there exists a truly canonical paper on the topic; whether the selection would possibly be read in a course which wasn't using PPL, etc. If in doubt, I left the paper out, on the grounds that one or two papers could be made available on library reserve – whereas trying to anticipate every possible desirable paper would result in another expensive text which was anything but concise.

I

Syntax and Semantics
(The System Perspective)

KNOWLEDGE OF LANGUAGE: ITS NATURE, ORIGIN AND USE

Noam Chomsky

1. KNOWLEDGE OF LANGUAGE AS A FOCUS OF INQUIRY

The study of language has a long and rich history, extending over thousands of years. This study has frequently been understood as an inquiry into the nature of mind and thought on the assumption that "languages are the best mirror of the human mind" (Leibniz). A common conception was that "with respect to its substance grammar is one and the same in all languages, though it does vary *accidentally*" (Roger Bacon). The invariant "substance" was often taken to be the mind and its acts; particular languages use various mechanisms – some rooted in human reason, others arbitrary and adventitious – for the expression of thought, which is a constant across languages. One leading eighteenth century rational grammarian defined "general grammar" as a deductive science concerned with "the immutable and general principles of spoken or written language" and their consequences; it is "prior to all languages," because its principles "are the same as those that direct human reason in its intellectual operations" (Beauzée). Thus, "the science of language does not differ at all from the science of thought." "Particular grammar" is not a true "science" in the sense of this rationalist tradition because it is not based solely on universal necessary laws; it is an "art" or technique that shows how given languages realize the general principles of human reason. As John Stuart Mill later expressed the same leading idea, "The principles and rules of grammar are the means by which the forms of language are made to correspond with the universal forms of thought.... The structure of every sentence is a lesson in logic." Others, particularly during the Romantic period, argued that the nature and content of thought are determined in part by the devices made available for its expression in particular languages. These devices may include contributions of individual genius that affect the "character" of a language, enriching its means of expression and the thoughts expressed without affecting its "form," its sound system and rules of word and sentence formation (Humboldt).

With regard to the acquisition of knowledge, it was widely held that the mind is not "so much to be filled therewith from without, like a vessel, as to be kindled and awaked" (Ralph Cudworth); "The growth of knowledge ... [rather resembles] ... the growth of Fruit; however external causes may in some degree cooperate, it is the internal vigour, and virtue of the tree, that must ripen the juices to their just maturity" (James Harris).[1] Applied to language, this essentially Platonistic conception would suggest that knowledge of a particular language grows and matures along a course that is in part intrinsically determined, with modifications reflecting observed usage, rather in the manner of the visual system or other bodily "organs" that develop along a course determined by genetic instructions under the triggering and shaping effects of environmental factors.

With the exception of the relativism of the Romantics, such ideas were generally regarded with much disapproval in the mainstream of linguistic research by the late nineteenth century and on through the 1950s. In part, this attitude developed under the impact of a rather narrowly construed empiricism and later behaviorist and operationalist doctrine. In part, it resulted from the quite real and impressive successes of historical and descriptive studies conducted within a narrower compass, specifically, the discovery of "sound laws" that provided much understanding of the history of languages and their relationships. In part, it was a natural consequence of the investigation of a much richer variety of languages than were known to earlier scholars, languages that appeared to violate many of the allegedly *a priori* conceptions of the earlier rationalist tradition.[2] After a century of general neglect or obloquy, ideas resembling those of the earlier tradition re-emerged (initially, with virtually no awareness of historical antecedents) in the mid-1950s, with the development of what came to be called "generative grammar" – again, reviving a long-lapsed and largely forgotten tradition.[3]

The generative grammar of a particular language (where "generative" means nothing more than "explicit") is a theory that is concerned with the form and meaning of expressions of this language. One can imagine many different kinds of approach to such questions, many points of view that might be adopted in dealing with them. Generative grammar limits itself to certain elements of this larger picture. Its standpoint is that of individual psychology. It is concerned with those aspects of form and meaning that are determined by the "language faculty," which is understood to be a particular component of the human mind. The nature of this faculty is the subject matter of a general theory of linguistic structure that aims to discover the framework of principles and elements common to attainable human languages; this theory is now often called "universal grammar" (UG), adapting a traditional term to a new context of inquiry. UG may be regarded as a characterization of the genetically determined language faculty. One may think of this faculty as a "language acquisition device," an innate component of the human mind that yields a particular language through interaction with presented experience, a device that converts experience into a system of knowledge attained: knowledge of one or another language.

The study of generative grammar represented a significant shift of focus in the approach to problems of language. Put in the simplest terms, to be elaborated below, the shift of focus was from behavior or the products of behavior to states of the mind/brain that enter into behavior. If one chooses to focus attention on this latter topic, the central concern becomes knowledge of language: its nature, origins, and use.

The three basic questions that arise, then, are these:
(1)
(i) What constitutes knowledge of language?
(ii) How is knowledge of language acquired?
(iii) How is knowledge of language put to use?

The answer to the first question is given by a particular generative grammar, a theory concerned with the state of the mind/brain of the person who knows a particular language. The answer to the second is given by a specification of UG along with an account of the ways in which its principles interact with experience to yield a particular language; UG is a theory of the "initial state" of the language faculty, prior to any linguistic experience. The answer to the third question would be a theory of how the knowledge of language attained enters into the expression of thought and the understanding of presented specimens of language, and derivatively, into communication and other special uses of language.

So far, this is nothing more than the outline of a research program that takes up classical questions that had been put aside for many years. As just described, it should not be particularly controversial, since it merely expresses an interest in certain problems and offers a preliminary analysis of how they might be confronted, although as is often the case, the initial formulation of a problem may prove to be far-reaching in its implications, and ultimately controversial as it is developed.

Some elements of this picture may appear to be more controversial than they really are. Consider, for example, the idea that there is a language faculty, a component of the mind/brain that yields knowledge of language given presented experience. It is not at issue that humans attain knowledge of English, Japanese, and so forth, while rocks, birds, or apes do not under the same (or indeed any) conditions. There is, then, some property of the mind/brain that differentiates humans from rocks, birds, or apes. Is this a distinct "language faculty" with specific structure and properties, or, as some believe, is it the case that humans acquire language merely by applying generalized learning mechanisms of some sort, perhaps with greater efficiency or scope than other organisms? These are not topics for speculation or *a priori* reasoning but for empirical inquiry, and it is clear enough how to proceed: namely, by facing the questions of (1). We try to determine what is the system of knowledge that has been attained and what properties must be attributed to the initial state of the mind/brain to account for its attainment. Insofar as these properties are language-specific, either individually or in the way they are organized and composed, there is a distinct language faculty.

Generative grammar is sometimes referred to as a theory, advocated by this or that person. In fact, it is not a theory any more than chemistry is a theory. Generative grammar is a topic which one may or may not choose to study. Of course, one can adopt a point of view from which chemistry disappears as a discipline (perhaps it is all done by angels with mirrors). In this sense, a decision to study chemistry does stake out a position on matters of fact. Similarly, one may argue that the topic of generative grammar does not exist, although it is hard to see how to make this position minimally plausible. Within the study of generative grammar there have been many changes and differences of opinion, often reversion to ideas that had been abandoned and were later reconstructed in a different light. Evidently, this is a healthy phenomenon indicating that the discipline is alive, although it is sometimes, oddly, regarded as a serious deficiency, a sign that something is wrong with the basic approach. I will review some of these changes as we proceed.

In the mid-1950s, certain proposals were advanced as to the form that answers to the questions of (1) might take, and a research program was inaugurated to investigate the adequacy of these proposals and to sharpen and apply them. This program was one of the strands that led to the development of the cognitive sciences in the contemporary sense, sharing with other approaches the belief that certain aspects of the mind/brain can be usefully construed on the model of computational systems of rules that form and modify representations, and that are put to use in interpretation and action. From its origins (or with a longer perspective, one might say "its reincarnation") about 30 years ago, the study of generative grammar was undertaken with an eye to gaining some insight into the nature and origins of systems of knowledge, belief, and understanding more broadly, in the hope that these general questions could be illuminated by a detailed investigation of the special case of human language.

This research program has since been running its course, along a number of different paths. I will be concerned here with only one of these, with the problems it faced and the steps that were taken in an effort to deal with them. During the past 5-6 years, these efforts have converged in a somewhat unexpected way, yielding a rather different conception of the nature of language and its mental representation, one that offers interesting answers to a range of empirical questions and opens a variety of new ones to inquiry while suggesting a rethinking of the character of others. This is what accounts for an unmistakable sense of energy and anticipation – and also uncertainty – which is reminiscent of the period when the study of generative grammar in the modern sense was initiated about 30 years ago. Some of the work now being done is quite different in character from what had previously been possible as well as considerably broader in empirical scope, and it may be that results of a rather new kind are within reach, or at least within sight. I would like to try to explain why this may be so, beginning with some remarks about goals, achievements, and failures of the past years.

To avoid misunderstanding, I am not speaking here about all of the study of language but rather of generative grammar, and even here I will not attempt anything like a real history of the course of research but rather will give a somewhat idealized picture that is in part clearer in retrospect than it was at the time. Furthermore, what I am describing has represented a minority position throughout, and probably still does, although in my view it is the correct one. A number of different current approaches share properties of the sort discussed here and may be intertranslatable to a considerable extent. I will not consider this important topic here and will also make no effort to survey the range of ideas, often conflicting, that fall within the particular tendency that I will discuss – what is now sometimes called "government-binding (GB) theory."

I want to consider, then, two major conceptual shifts, one that inaugurated the contemporary study of generative grammar, and a second, more theory-internal, that is now in process and that offers some new perspectives on traditional problems.[4]

Traditional and structuralist grammar did not deal with the questions of (1), the former because of its implicit reliance on the unanalyzed intelligence of the reader, the latter because of its narrowness of scope. The concerns of traditional and generative grammar are, in a certain sense, complementary: a good traditional or pedagogical grammar provides a full list of exceptions (irregular verbs, etc.), paradigms and examples of regular constructions, and observations at various levels of detail and generality about the form and meaning of expressions. But it does not examine the question of how the reader of the grammar uses such information to attain the knowledge that is used to form and interpret new expressions, or the question of the nature and elements of this knowledge: essentially the questions of (1), above. Without too much exaggeration, one could describe such a grammar as a structured and organized version of the data presented to a child learning a language, with some general commentary and often insightful observations. Generative grammar, in contrast, is concerned primarily with the intelligence of the reader, the principles and procedures brought to bear to attain full knowledge of a language. Structuralist theories, both in the European and American traditions, did concern themselves with analytic procedures for deriving aspects of grammar from data, as in the procedural theories of Nikolay Trubetzkoy, Zellig Harris, Bernard Bloch, and others, but primarily in the areas of phonology and morphology. The procedures suggested were seriously inadequate and in any event could not possibly be understood (and were not intended) to provide an answer to question (1ii), even in the narrower domains where most work was concentrated. Nor was there an effort to determine what was involved in offering a comprehensive account of the knowledge of the speaker/hearer.

As soon as these questions were squarely faced, a wide range of new phenomena were discovered, including quite simple ones that had passed unnoticed, and severe problems arose that had previously been ignored or seriously misunderstood. A standard belief 30 years ago was that language acquisition is a case of "overlearning." Language was regarded as a habit system, one that was assumed to be much overdetermined by available evidence. Production and interpretation of new forms was taken to be a straightforward matter of analogy, posing no problems of principle.[5] Attention to the questions of (1) quickly reveals that exactly the opposite is the case: language poses in a sharp and clear form what has sometimes been called "Plato's problem," the problem of "poverty of stimulus," of accounting for the richness, complexity, and specificity of shared knowledge, given the limitations of the data available. This difference of perception concerning where the problem lies – overlearning or poverty of evidence – reflects very clearly the effect of the shift of focus that inaugurated the study of generative grammar.

A great many examples have been given over the years to illustrate what clearly is the fundamental problem: the problem of poverty of evidence. A familiar example is the structure-dependence of rules, the fact that without instruction or direct evidence, children unerringly use computationally complex structure-dependent rules rather than computationally simple rules that involve only the predicate "leftmost" in a linear sequence of words.[6] To take some other examples, to which we will return, consider sentences (2)-(7):

(2) I wonder who [the men expected to see them]
(3) [the men expected to see them]
(4) John ate an apple

(5) John ate
(6) John is too stubborn to talk to Bill
(7) John is too stubborn to talk to

Both (2) and (3) include the clause bounded by brackets, but only in (2) may the pronoun *them* be referentially dependent on the antecedent *the men*; in (3) the pronoun is understood as referring in some manner indicated in the situational or discourse context, but not to the men. Numerous facts of this sort, falling under what is now generally called "binding theory," are known without relevant experience to differentiate the cases. Such facts pose a serious problem that was not recognized in earlier work: How does every child know, unerringly, to interpret the clause differently in the two cases? And why does no pedagogic grammar have to draw the learner's attention to such facts (which were, in fact, noticed only quite recently, in the course of the study of explicit rule systems in generative grammar)?

Turning to examples (4)-(7), sentence (5) means that John ate something or other, a fact that one might explain on the basis of a simple inductive procedure: ate takes an object, as in (4), and if the object is missing, it is understood as arbitrary. Applying the same inductive procedure to (6) and (7), it should be that (7) means that John is so stubborn that he (John) will not talk to some arbitrary person, on the analogy of (6). But the meaning is, in fact, quite different: namely, that John is so stubborn that some arbitrary person won't talk to him (John). Again, this is known without training or relevant evidence.[7]

The situation is, in fact, more complex. Although plausible, the inductive procedure suggested for the relatively straightforward examples (4)-(5) does not seem correct. As noted by Howard Lasnik, the word eat has a somewhat different meaning in its intransitive usage, something like *dine*. One can say "John ate his shoe," but "John ate" cannot be understood to include this case. The observation is general for such cases. The intransitive forms differ from normal intransitives in other respects; for example, we can form "the dancing bear" (corresponding to "the bear that dances"), but not "the eating man" (corresponding to "the man who eats").[8] Such facts pose further problems of poverty of stimulus.

Children do not make errors about the interpretation of such sentences as (6)-(7) past a certain stage of development, and if they did, the errors would largely be uncorrectable. It is doubtful that even the most compendious traditional or teaching grammar notes such simple facts as those illustrated in (2)-(7), and such observations lie far beyond the domain of structural grammars. A wide variety of examples of this sort immediately come to attention when one faces the questions formulated in (1).

Knowledge of language is often characterized as a practical ability to speak and understand, so that questions (1i) and (1iii) are closely related, perhaps identified. Ordinary usage makes a much sharper distinction between the two questions, and is right to do so. Two people may share exactly the same knowledge of language but differ markedly in their ability to put this knowledge to use. Ability to use language may improve or decline without any change in knowledge. This ability may also be impaired, selectively or in general, with no loss of knowledge, a fact that would become clear if injury leading to impairment recedes and lost ability is recovered. Many such considerations support the commonsense assumption that knowledge cannot be properly described as a practical ability. Furthermore, even if this view could somehow be maintained, it would leave open all of the serious questions. Thus, what is the nature of the "practical ability" manifested in our interpretation of the sentences (2)-(7), how is it properly described, and how is it acquired?

Often it is not immediately obvious what our knowledge of language entails in particular cases, a fact illustrated even with short and simple sentences such as (8)-(10):

(8) his wife loves her husband
(9) John is too clever to expect us to catch Bill
(10) John is too clever to expect us to catch

In the case of (8), it takes some thought to determine whether *his* can be referentially dependent on *her husband* if *her* is dependent on *his wife* – that is, if the reference of either *he* or *she* is not somehow contextually indicated.[9] Examples (9) and (10) are, in fact, analogous to (6) and (7), respectively, but again, it takes some thought to discover that (10) means that John is so clever that an arbitrary person cannot expect us to catch him (John), although it is clear at once that it does not mean that John is so clever that he (John) cannot catch some arbitrary person, on the analogy of (9) (and (4), (5)). Our abilities seem limited somehow in such cases (and there are far more complex ones), but it would make little sense to speak of our knowledge of language as "limited" in any comparable way.

Suppose we insist on speaking of knowledge of language as a practical ability to speak and understand. Then normal usage must be revised in numerous cases such as those just discussed. Suppose that Jones takes a public speaking course and improves his ability to speak and understand without any change in his knowledge of English, as we would describe the situation in normal usage. We must now revise this commonsense usage and say, rather, that Jones has improved his ability$_1$ to use his ability$_2$ to speak and understand; similar translations are required in the other cases. But the two occurrences of "ability" in this description are hardly more than homonyms. Ability$_1$ is ability in the normal sense of the word: it can improve or decline, can be inadequate to determine consequences of knowledge, and so on. Ability$_2$, however, remains stable while our ability to use it changes, and we have this kind of "ability" even when we are unable to detect what it entails in concrete cases. In short, the neologism "ability$_2$" is invested with all the properties of knowledge. Note that there are cases when we do speak of abilities that we cannot put to use: for example, the case of swimmers who cannot swim because their hands are tied, although they retain the ability to swim. The cases in question are not of this sort, however.

The purpose of the attempt to reduce knowledge to ability is, presumably, to avoid problematic features that seem to inhere in the concept of knowledge, to show that these can be explained in dispositional or other terms more closely related to actual behavior (whether this is possible even in the case of ability$_1$, the normal sense, is another question). But nothing of the sort is achieved by this departure from ordinary usage; the problems remain, exactly as before, now embedded in terminological confusion. The task of determining the nature of our knowledge (= ability$_2$), and accounting for its origins and use, remains exactly as challenging as before, despite the terminological innovations.

Other examples similar to (8)-(10) raise further questions. Consider the following sentences:

(11) John is too stubborn to expect anyone to talk to Bill
(12) John is too stubborn to visit anyone who talked to Bill

Suppose we delete *Bill* from (11) and (12), yielding (13) and (14), respectively:

(13) John is too stubborn to expect anyone to talk to
(14) John is too stubborn to visit anyone who talked to

Sentence (13) is structurally analogous to (10), and is understood in the same manner: it means that John is so stubborn that an arbitrary person would not expect anyone to talk to him (John). "By analogy," then, we would expect sentence (14) to mean that John is so stubborn that an arbitrary person would not visit anyone who talked to him (John). But it does not have that meaning; in fact, it is gibberish. Here we have a double failure of analogy. Sentence (14) is not understood "on the analogy" of (4), (5), (6), (9), and (12) (hence meaning that John is so stubborn that he (John) would not visit anyone who talked to some arbitrary person), nor is it understood "on the analogy" of (7), (10), and (13); rather, it has no interpretation at all. And while the status of (11), (12), and (14) is immediately obvious, it takes some thought or preparation to see that (13) has the interpretation it does have, and thus to determine the consequences of our knowledge in this case.

Again, these are facts that we know, however difficult it may be to determine that our system of knowledge has these consequences. We know these facts without instruction or even direct evidence, surely without correction of error by the speech community. It would be absurd to try to teach such facts as these to people learning English as a second language, just as no one taught them to us or even presented us with evidence that could yield this knowledge by any generally reliable procedure. This is knowledge without grounds, without good reasons or support by reliable procedures in any general or otherwise useful sense of these notions. Were we to insist that knowledge is a kind of ability, we would have to claim that we lack the ability to understand "John is too stubborn to talk to" as meaning "John is too stubborn to talk to someone or other" (on the analogy of "John ate an apple" – "John ate"), and that we lack the ability to understand (14) on the analogy of "John ate an apple" – "John ate" (so that it means that John is too stubborn to visit anyone who talked to someone or other) or on the analogy of "John is too stubborn to talk to," with the "inversion strategy" that we somehow use in this case (so that (14) means that John is too stubborn for someone or other to visit anyone who talked to him, John). But these would be odd claims, to say the least. These are not failures of ability. It is not that we are too weak, or lack some special skill that could be acquired. We are perfectly capable of associating the sentence (14), for example, with either of the two meanings that would be provided "by analogy" (or others), but we know that these are not the associations that our knowledge of the language provides; ability is one thing, knowledge something quite different. The system of knowledge that has somehow developed in our minds has certain consequences, not others; it relates sound and meaning and assigns structural properties to physical events in certain ways, not others.

It seems that there is little hope in accounting for our knowledge in terms of such ideas as analogy, induction, association, reliable procedures, good reasons, and justification in any generally useful sense, or in terms of "generalized learning mechanisms" (if such exist). And it seems that we should follow normal usage in distinguishing clearly between knowledge and ability to use that knowledge. We should, so it appears, think of knowledge of language as a certain state of the mind/brain, a relatively stable element in transitory mental states once it is attained; furthermore, as a state of some distinguishable faculty of the mind – the language faculty – with its specific properties, structure, and organization, one "module" of the mind.[10]

2. CONCEPTS OF LANGUAGE

2.1 The Commonsense Concept and Departures From It

Let us turn now to the questions of (1) of Chapter 1. [Reprinted here as Section 1. – Ed.] To begin with, let us distinguish the intuitive, pretheoretic commonsense notion of language from various technical concepts that have been proposed with the intent of developing an eventual science of language. Let us call the latter "scientific approaches" to language, with an eye directed more toward a possible future than a present reality, some might argue. The scientific approaches, I believe without exception, depart from the commonsense notion in several ways; these departures also affect the concepts of knowledge or understanding of language, use of language, rule of language, rule-guided linguistic behavior, and others.

In the first place, the commonsense notion of language has a crucial sociopolitical dimension. We speak of Chinese as "a language," although the various "Chinese dialects" are as diverse as the several Romance languages. We speak of Dutch and German as two separate languages, although some dialects of German are very close to dialects that we call "Dutch" and are not mutually intelligible with others that we call "German." A standard remark in introductory linguistics courses is that a language is a dialect with an army and a navy (attributed to Max Weinreich). That any coherent account can be given of "language" in this sense is doubtful; surely, none has been offered or even seriously attempted. Rather, all scientific approaches have simply abandoned these elements of what is called "language" in common usage.[11]

The commonsense notion also has a normative-teleological element that is eliminated from scientific approaches. I do not refer here to prescriptive grammar but to something else. Consider the way we describe a child or a foreigner learning English. We have no way of referring directly to what that person knows: It is not English, nor is it some other language that resembles English. We do not, for example, say that the person has a perfect knowledge of some language L, similar to English but still different from it. What we say is that the child or foreigner has a "partial knowledge of English," or is "on his or her way" toward acquiring knowledge of English, and if they reach the goal, they will then know English. Whether or not a coherent account can be given of this aspect of the commonsense terminology, it does not seem to be one that has any role in an eventual science of language.

I will follow standard practice in disregarding these aspects of the commonsense notions of language and the associated notions of rule-following and so forth, although the departure should be noted, and one may ask whether it is entirely innocent.

Modern linguistics commonly avoided these questions by considering an idealized "speech community" that is internally consistent in its linguistic practice.[12] For Leonard Bloomfield, for example, a language is "the totality of utterances that can be made in a speech community," regarded as homogeneous (Bloomfield, 1928/1957). In other scientific approaches, the same assumption enters in one or another form, explicitly or tacitly, in identification of the object of inquiry. No attempt is made to capture or formulate any concept with the sociopolitical or normative-teleological aspects of informal usage of the term "language." The same is true of approaches that understand language to be a social product in accordance with the Saussurean concept of "langue."

Of course, it is understood that speech communities in the Bloomfieldian sense – that is, collections of individuals with the same speech behavior[13] – do not exist in the real world. Each individual has acquired a language in the course of complex social interactions with people who vary in the ways in which they speak and interpret what they hear and in the internal representations that underlie their use of language. Structural linguistics abstracted from these facts in its attempts at theory construction: we also abstract from these facts in posing questions (1) of Chapter 1, considering only the case of a person presented with uniform experience in an ideal Bloomfieldian speech community with no dialect diversity and no variation among speakers.

We should also make note of a more subtle theory-internal assumption: the language of the hypothesized speech community, apart from being uniform, is taken to be a "pure" instance of UG in a sense that must be made precise, and to which we will return. We exclude, for example, a speech community of uniform speakers, each of whom speaks a mixture of Russian and French (say, an idealized version of the nineteenth-century Russian aristocracy). The language of such a speech community would not be "pure" in the relevant sense, because it would not represent a single set of choices among the options permitted by UG but rather would include "contradictory" choices for certain of these options.

Questions (1) of Chapter 1, then, arise initially under these idealizations, and the same is true, in effect, of other approaches to language, although the fact is often not explicitly recognized and may even sometimes be denied.

The legitimacy of these idealizations has sometimes been questioned, but on dubious grounds.[14] Indeed, they seem indispensable. Surely there is some property of mind P that would enable a person to acquire a language under conditions of pure and uniform experience, and surely P (characterized by UG) is put to use under the real conditions of language acquisition. To deny these assumptions would be bizarre indeed: it would be to claim either that language can be learned only under conditions of diversity and conflicting evidence, which is absurd, or that the property P exists – there exists a capacity to learn language in the pure and uniform case – but the actual learning of language does not involve this capacity. In the latter case, we would ask why P exists; is it a "vestigial organ" of some sort? The natural approach, and one that I think is tacitly adopted even by those who deny the fact, is to attempt to determine the real property of mind P, and then ask how P functions under the more complex conditions of actual linguistic diversity. It seems clear that any reasonable study of the nature, acquisition, and use of language in real life circumstances must accept these assumptions and then proceed on the basis of some tentative characterization of the property of mind P. In short, the idealizations made explicit in more careful work are hardly controversial; they isolate for examination a property of the language faculty the existence of which is hardly in doubt, and which is surely a crucial element in actual language acquisition.

By making these idealizations explicit and pursuing our inquiry in accordance with them, we do not in any way prejudice the study of language as a social product. On the contrary, it is difficult to imagine how such studies might fruitfully progress without taking into account the real properties of mind that enter into the acquisition of language, specifically, the properties of the initial state of the language faculty characterized by UG.

Note also that the study of language and UG, conducted within the framework of individual psychology, allows for the possibility that the state of knowledge attained may itself include some kind of reference to the social nature of language. Consider, for example, what Putnam (1975) has called "the division of linguistic labor." In the language of a given individual, many words are semantically indeterminate in a special sense: the person will defer to "experts" to sharpen or fix their reference. Suppose, for example, that someone knows that yawls and ketches are sailing vessels but is unsure of the exact reference of the words "yawl" and "ketch," leaving it to specialists to fix this reference. In the lexicon of this person's language, the entries for "yawl" and "ketch" will be specified to the extent of his or her knowledge, with an indication that details are to be filled in by others, an idea that can be made precise in various ways but without going beyond the study of the system of knowledge of language of a particular individual. Other social aspects of language can be regarded in a like manner – although this is not to deny the possibility or value of other kinds of study of language that incorporate social structure and interaction. Contrary to what is sometimes thought, no conflicts of principle or practice arise in this connection.

We are also assuming another idealization: that the property of mind described by UG is a species characteristic, common to all humans. We thus abstract from possible variation among humans in the language faculty. It is plausible to suppose that apart from pathology (potentially an important area of inquiry), such variation as there may be is marginal and can be safely ignored across a broad range of linguistic investigation. Again, in scientific approaches. Weaker assumptions than strict identity would suffice for the discussion below, but this stronger assumption seems a reasonable one, to a very good approximation, and I will keep to it here.

2.2 Externalized Language

Scientific approaches to language, in the sense of the term used earlier, have developed various technical notions of language to replace the common-sense notion. The term "grammar" has also been used in a variety of ways. In conventional usage, a grammar is a description or theory of a language, an object constructed by a linguist. Let us keep to this usage. Then associated with the various technical notions of language there are corresponding notions of grammar and of universal grammar (UG).

Structural and descriptive linguistics, behavioral psychology, and other contemporary approaches tended to view a language as a collection of actions, or utterances, or linguistic forms (words, sentences) paired with meanings, or as a system of linguistic forms or events. In Saussurean structuralism, a language (*langue*) was taken to be a system of sounds and an associated system of concepts; the notion of sentence was left in a kind of limbo, perhaps to be accommodated within the study of language use. For Bloomfield, as noted earlier, a language is "the totality of utterances that can be made in a speech community." The American variety of structural-descriptive linguistics that was heavily influenced by Bloomfield's ideas furthermore concentrated primarily on sound and word structure, apart from various proposals, notably those of Zellig Harris, as to how larger units (phrases) could be constructed by analytic principles modelled on those introduced for phonology and morphology.[15] Many researchers today adopt a position of the sort lucidly developed by David Lewis, who defines a language as a pairing of sentences and meanings (the latter taken to be set-theoretic constructions in terms of possible worlds) over an infinite range, where the language is "used by a population" when certain regularities "in action or belief" hold among the population with reference to the language, sustained by an interest in communication.[16]

Let us refer to such technical concepts as instances of "externalized language" (E-language), in the sense that the construct is understood independently of the properties of the mind/brain. Under the same rubric we may include the notion of language as a collection (or system) of actions or behaviors of some sort. From a point of view such as this, a grammar is a collection of descriptive statements concerning the E-language, the actual or potential speech events (perhaps along with some account of their context of use or semantic content). In technical terms, the grammar may be regarded as a function that enumerates the elements of the E-language. Sometimes, grammar has been regarded as a property of E-language, as in Bloomfield's remark that a grammar is "the meaningful arrangement of forms in a language" (Bloomfield, 1933). Despite appearances, the problem of accounting for the unbounded character of the E-language and the person's knowledge of language including this fundamental property is not squarely addressed in such approaches, a matter to which we will return.

The E-language is now understood to be the real object of study. Grammar is a derivative notion; the linguist is free to select the grammar one way or another as long as it correctly identifies the E-language. Apart from this consideration, questions of truth and falsity do not arise. Quine, for example, has argued that it is senseless to take one grammar rather than another to be "correct" if they are extensionally equivalent, characterizing the same E-language, for him a set of expressions (Quine, 1972). And Lewis doubts that there is any way "to make objective sense of the assertion that a grammar G is used by a population P whereas another grammar G¹, which generates the same language as G, is not."

The notion of E-language is familiar from the study of formal systems, as is the conclusion just cited: in the case of the "language of arithmetic," for example, there is no objective sense to the idea that one set of rules that generates the well-formed formulas is correct and another wrong.

As for UG, to the extent that such a study was recognized as legitimate, this theory would consist of statements that are true of many or all human languages, perhaps a set of conditions satisfied by the E-languages that count as human languages. Some appeared to deny the possibility of the enterprise, for example, Martin Joos, who put forth what he called the "Boasian" view that "languages could differ from each other without limit and in unpredictable ways," echoing William Dwight Whitney's reference to "the infinite diversity of human speech" and Edward Sapir's notion that "language is a human activity that varies without assignable limit."[17] Such statements reflect a fairly broad consensus of the time. Although they could hardly have been intended literally, they did express a relativistic impulse that denigrated the study of UG. More precisely, it cannot be that human language varies without assignable limit, although it might be true that it is "infinitely diverse"; it is an empirical question of some interest whether UG permits an infinite variety of possible languages (or a variety that is infinite in more than structurally trivial respects, say, with no bound on vocabulary), or only a finite diversity.[18]

Nevertheless, significant contributions were made to UG in our sense within these traditions. For example, the theory of distinctive features in phonology, which greatly influenced structuralist studies in other fields, postulated a fixed inventory of "atomic elements" from which phonological systems could be drawn, with certain general laws and implicational relations governing the choice. And it was generally assumed that such notions as topic and comment, or subject and predicate, were universal features of language, reflecting the fact that a declarative sentence is about something and says something about it. Later, important work on linguistic universals was conducted by Joseph Greenberg and others, yielding many generalizations that require explanation, for example, the fact that if a language has subject-object-verb order, it will tend to have postpositions rather than prepositions, and so on.

Along these lines, then, we may develop a certain technical concept of language (E-language), and an associated concept of grammar and UG, as a basis for a scientific study of language. Many different specific ideas fall roughly within this general framework.

2.3 Internalized Language

A rather different approach was taken, for example, by Otto Jespersen, who held that there is some "notion of structure" in the mind of the speaker "which is definite enough to guide him in framing sentences of his own," in particular, "free expressions" that may be new to the speaker and to others.[19] Let us refer to this "notion of structure" as an "internalized language" (I-language). The I-language, then, is some element of the mind of the person who knows the language, acquired by the learner, and used by the speaker-hearer.

Taking language to be I-language, the grammar would then be a theory of the I-language, which is the object under investigation. And if, indeed, such a "notion of structure" exists, as Jespersen held, then questions of truth and falsity arise for grammar as they do for any scientific theory. This way of approaching the questions of language is radically different from the one sketched above and leads to a very different conception of the nature of the inquiry.

Let us return now to the point of view outlined in Chapter 1. Knowing the language L is a property of a person H; one task of the brain sciences is to determine what it is about H's brain by virtue of which this property holds. We suggested that for H to know the language L is for H's mind/brain to be in a certain state; more narrowly, for the language faculty, one module of this system, to be in a certain state S_L.[20] One task of the brain sciences, then, is to discover the mechanisms that are the physical realization of the state S_L.

Suppose we analyze the notion "H knows language L" in relational terms, that is, as involving a relation R (knowing, having, or whatever) holding between H and an abstract entity L. One might question this move; we speak of a person as knowing U.S. history without assuming that there is an entity, U.S. history, that the person knows, or knows in part. Let us, however, assume the move to be legitimate in this case. The assumption will be justified to the extent that this move contributes to providing insight into the questions that primarily concern us, those of (1) of Chapter 1; this would be the case, for example, if there are significant principles governing the set of postulated entities L. Suppose that we proceed further to regard talk of mind as talk about the brain undertaken at a certain level of abstraction at which we believe, rightly or wrongly, that significant properties and explanatory principles can be discovered. Then statements about R and L belong to the theory of mind, and one task of the brain sciences will be to explain what it is about H's brain (in particular, its language faculty) that corresponds to H's knowing L, that is, by virtue of which R (H, L) holds and the statement that R (H, L) is true.

It is natural to take L to be I-language, Jespersen's "notion of structure," regarding this as an entity abstracted from a state of the language faculty, the latter being one component of the mind. Then, for H to know L is for H to have a certain I-language. The statements of grammar are statements of the theory of mind about the I-language, hence statements about structures of the brain formulated at a certain level of abstraction from mechanisms. These structures are specific things in the world, with their specific properties. The statements of a grammar or the statement that R (H, L) are similar to statements of a physical theory that characterizes certain entities and their properties in abstraction from whatever may turn out to be the mechanisms that account for these properties: say, a nineteenth-century theory about valence or properties expressed in the periodic table. Statements about I-language or the statement that R (H, L) (for various choices of H and L) are true or false, much in the way that statements about the chemical structure of benzene, or about the valence of oxygen, or about chlorine and fluorine being in the same column of the periodic table are true or false. The I-language L may be the one used by a speaker but not the I-language L', even if the two generate the same class of expressions (or other formal objects) in whatever precise sense we give to this derivative notion; L' may not even be a possible human I-language, one attainable by the language faculty.

UG now is construed as the theory of human I-languages, a system of conditions deriving from the human biological endowment that identifies the I-languages that are humanly accessible under normal conditions. These are the I-languages L such that R (H, L) may be true (for normal H, under normal conditions).[21]

Of course, there is no guarantee that this way of approaching the problems of (1) in chapter 1 is the correct one. This approach may turn out to be thoroughly misguided, even if it achieves substantial success – just as a theory of valence, etc. might have turned out to be completely off the track, despite its substantial success in nineteenth-century chemistry. It is always reasonable to consider alternative approaches, if they can be devised, and this will remain true no matter what successes are achieved. The situation does not seem different in principle from what we find in other areas of empirical inquiry. I will suggest directly that in certain fundamental respects early ideas about I-language were misguided and should be replaced by a rather different conception, although one formulated in the same general framework. The reasons, however, do not derive from any incoherence or flaw in the general approach but rather from empirical considerations of description and explanation.

2.4 The Shift of Focus from E-language to I-language

2.4.1 On the Reasons for the Shift of Focus

In chapter 1, we saw that the study of generative grammar shifted the focus of attention from actual or potential behavior and the products of behavior to the system of knowledge that underlies the use and understanding of language, and more deeply, to the innate endowment that makes it possible for humans to attain such knowledge. The shift in focus was from the study of E-language to the study of I-language, from the study of language regarded as an externalized object to the study of the system of knowledge of language attained and internally represented in the mind/brain. A generative grammar is not a set of statements about externalized objects constructed in some manner. Rather, it purports to depict exactly what one knows when one knows a language: that is, what has been learned, as supplemented by innate principles. UG is a characterization of these innate, biologically determined principles, which constitute one component of the human mind – the language faculty.

With this shift of focus, we at once face the questions (1) of Chapter 1. In the earliest work, the answer to (1i) was taken to be that knowledge of language is knowledge of a certain rule system; the answer to (1ii), that this knowledge arises from an initial state S_0 that converts experience to a "steady state" S_s, which incorporates an I-language. Acquisition of language is, then, a matter of adding to one's store of rules, or modifying this system, as new data are processed. Question (1iii) breaks down into two parts: a "perception problem" and a "production problem." The perception problem would be dealt with by construction of a parser that incorporates the rules of the I-language along with other elements: a certain organization of memory and access (perhaps a deterministic pushdown structure with buffer of a certain size; see Marcus, 1980), certain heuristics, and so forth. A parser should not map expressions into their structures in the way that these are associated by the I-language. For example, a parser should fail to do so in the case of so-called "garden-path sentences"[22] or sentences that over-load memory for left-to-right pass, it should mirror the difficulties experienced with sentences such as (8)-(14) of Chapter 1 and so forth. The production problem is considerably more obscure; we will return to that.

The E-language that was the object of study in most of traditional or structuralist grammar or behavioral psychology is now regarded as an epiphenomenon at best. Its status is similar to that of other derivative objects, say, the set of rhyming pairs, which is also determined by the I-language that constitutes the system of knowledge attained. One might argue that the status of the E-language is considerably more obscure than that of the set of rhyming pairs, since the latter is determined in a fairly definite way by the I-language whereas the bounds of E-language can be set one way or another, depending on some rather arbitrary decisions as to what it should include.

Summarizing, then, we have the following general picture. The language faculty is a distinct system of the mind/brain, with an initial state S_0 common to the species (to a very close first approximation, apart from pathology, etc.) and apparently unique to it in essential respects.[23] Given appropriate experience, this faculty passes from the state S_0 to some relatively stable steady state S_s, which then undergoes only peripheral modification (say, acquiring new vocabulary items). The attained state incorporates an I-language (it is the state of having or knowing a particular I-language). UG is the theory of S_0; particular grammars are theories of various I-languages. The I-languages that can be attained with S_0 fixed and experience varying are the attainable human languages, where by "language" we now mean I-language. The steady state has two components that can be distinguished analytically, however, they may be merged and intertwined: a component that is specific to the language in question and the contribution of the initial state. The former constitutes what is "learned" – if this is the appropriate concept to employ in accounting for the transition from the initial to the mature state of the language faculty; it may well not be.[24]

The system of knowledge attained – the I-language – assigns a status to every relevant physical event, say, every sound wave. Some are sentences with a definite meaning (literal, figurative or whatever). Some are intelligible with, perhaps, a definite meaning, but are ill-formed in one way or another ("the child seems sleeping"; "to whom did you wonder what to give?" in some dialects; "who do you wonder to whom gave the book?" in all dialects). Some are well formed but unintelligible. Some are assigned a phonetic representation but no more; they are identified as possible sentences of some language, but not mine. Some are mere noise. There are many possibilities. Different I-languages will assign status differently in each of these and other categories. The notion of E-language has no place in this picture. There is no issue of correctness with regard to E-languages, however characterized, because E-languages are mere artifacts. We can define "E-language" in one way or another or not at all, since the concept appears to play no role in the theory of language.

The shift of focus from E-to I-language, reviving and modifying much older traditions, was very much in order. The technical concept of E-language is a dubious one in at least two respects. In the first place, as just observed, languages in this sense are not real-world objects but are artificial, somewhat arbitrary, and perhaps not very interesting constructs. In contrast, the steady state of knowledge attained and the initial state S_0 are real elements of particular mind/brains, aspects of the physical world, where we understand mental states and representations to be physically encoded in some manner. The I-language is abstracted directly as a component of the state attained. Statements about I-language, about the steady state, and about the initial state S_0 are true or false statements about something real and definite, about actual states of the mind/brain and their components (under the idealizations already discussed). UG and theories of I-languages, universal and particular grammars, are on a par with scientific theories in other domains; theories of E-languages, if sensible at all, have some different and more obscure status because there is no corresponding real-world object. Linguistics, conceived as the study of I-language and S_0, becomes part of psychology, ultimately biology. Linguistics will be incorporated within the natural sciences insofar as mechanisms are discovered that have the properties revealed in these more abstract studies; indeed, one would expect that these studies will be a necessary step toward serious investigation of mechanisms.[25] To put it differently, E-language, however construed, is further removed from mechanisms than I-language, at a higher order of abstraction. Correspondingly, the concept raises a host of new problems, and it is not at all clear whether they are worth addressing or trying to solve, given the artificial nature of the construct and its apparent uselessness for the theory of language.

The shift of focus is also, arguably, a shift toward the commonsense notion of language. This matter is less important than the move toward realism and also much less clear, because, as noted, all of these approaches deviate from the commonsense concept in certain respects. But it seems that when we speak of a person as knowing a language, we do not mean that he or she knows an infinite set of sentences, or sound-meaning pairs taken in extension, or a set of acts or behaviors; rather, what we mean is that the person knows what makes sound and meaning relate to one another in a specific way, what makes them "hang together," a particular characterization of a function, perhaps. The person has "a notion of structure" and knows an I-language as characterized by the linguist's grammar. When we say that it is a rule of English that objects follow verbs, as distinct from the rule of Japanese that verbs follow objects, we are not saying that this is a rule of some set of sentences or behaviors, but rather that it is a rule of a system of rules, English, an I-language. The rules of the language are not rules of some infinite set of formal objects or potential actions but are rules that form or constitute the language, like Articles of the Constitution or rules of chess (not a set of moves, but a game, a particular rule system). Of the various technical notions that have been developed in the study of language, the concept of I-language seems closer to the commonsense notion than others.

The shift of perspective from the technical concept E-language to the technical concept I-language taken as the object of inquiry is therefore a shift toward realism in two respects: toward the study of a real object rather than an artificial construct, and toward the study of what we really mean by "a language" or "knowledge of language" in informal usage (again, abstracting from sociopolitical and normative-teleological factors).

Of these two considerations, the first is the clearer and more important. It is not to be expected that the concepts that are appropriate for the description and understanding of some system of the physical world (say, I-language and S_0) will include the sometimes similar concepts of normal discourse, just as the physicist's concepts of energy or mass are not those of ordinary usage. Furthermore, many questions arise about the usage of the intuitive concepts that have no obvious relevance to the inquiry into the nature of the real objects, I-language and S_0. Suppose, for example, that a Martian with a quite different kind of mind/brain were to produce and to understand sentences of English as we do, but as investigation would show, using quite different elements and rules – say, without words, the smallest units being memorized phrases, and with a totally different rule system and UG. Would we then say that the Martian is speaking the same language? Within what limits would we say this? Similar questions arise as to whether an artificial system is exhibiting some form of intelligence or understanding. These may be reasonable questions concerning the intuitive concepts of language and the like in colloquial usage, but it is not clear that they have much bearing on the inquiry into the real-world objects, I-language and the initial state S_0.[26]

The conceptual shift from E-language to I-language, from behavior and its products to the system of knowledge that enters into behavior, was in part obscured by accidents of publishing history, and expository passages taken out of context have given rise to occasional misunderstanding.[27] Some questionable terminological decisions also contributed to misunderstanding. In the literature of generative grammar, the term "language" has regularly been used for E-language in the sense of a set of well-formed sentences, more or less along the lines of Bloomfield's definition of "language" as a "totality of utterances." The term "grammar" was then used with systematic ambiguity, to refer to what we have here called "I-language" and also to the linguist's theory of the I-language; the same was true of the term UG, introduced later with the same systematic ambiguity, referring to S_0 and the theory of S_0. Because the focus of attention was on I-language, E-language being a derivative and largely artificial construct, we find the paradoxical situation that in work devoted to language, the term "language" barely appears. In my 1965 book *Aspects of the Theory of Syntax*, for example, there is no entry for "language" in the index, but many entries under "grammar," generally referring to I-language.

It would have been preferable to use the term "language" in something closer to the intuitive sense of informal usage; that is, to use the term "language" as a technical term in place of "(generative) grammar" (in the sense of I-language) while adopting some technical term (perhaps "E-language") for what was called "language." The term "(generative) grammar" would then have naturally been used for the linguist's theory of the (I-) language, along the lines of the preceding discussion. Much confusion might have been spared in this way. I suspect that the debate in past years over the alleged problems concerning the concepts grammar and knowledge of grammar may in part be traced to these unfortunate terminological choices, which reinforced inappropriate analogies to the formal sciences and gave rise to the erroneous idea that the study of grammar poses new, complex, and perhaps intractable philosophical issues compared with the study of E-language.[28]

The misleading choice of terms was, in part, a historical accident. The study of generative grammar developed from the confluence of two intellectual traditions: traditional and structuralist grammar, and the study of formal systems. Although there are important precursors, it was not until the mid-1950s that these intellectual currents truly merged, as ideas adapted from the study of formal systems came to be applied to the far more complex systems of natural language in something approaching their actual richness, and in subsequent years, their actual variety, thus making it possible, really for the first time, to give some substance to Humboldt's aphorism that language involves "the infinite use of finite means," the "finite means" being those that constitute the I-language.

But the study of formal languages was misleading in this regard. When we study, say, the language of arithmetic, we may take it to be a "given" abstract object: an infinite class of sentences in some given notation. Certain expressions in this notation are well-formed sentences, others are not. And of the well-formed sentences, some express arithmetical truths, some do not. A "grammar" for such a system is simply some set of rules that specifies exactly the well-formed sentences. In this case, there is no further question of the correct choice of grammar, and there is no truth or falsity to the matter of choosing among such grammars. Much the same is true of alternative axiomatizations, although in this case we know that none of them will capture exactly the truths. It is easy to see how one might take over from the study of formal languages the idea that the "language" is somehow given as a set of sentences or sentence-meaning pairs, while the grammar is some characterization of this infinite set of objects, hence, it might be thought, a construct that may be selected one way or another depending on convenience or other extraneous concerns. The move is understandable, but misguided, and it has engendered much pointless discussion and controversy.

Recall Quine's conclusion, cited above [p. 17], that it is senseless to take one grammar rather than another to be "correct" if they are extensionally equivalent, and Lewis's doubts that there is any way "to make objective sense of the assertion that a grammar G is used by a population P whereas another grammar G', which generates the same language as G, is not." It is quite true that for every E-language, however we choose to define this notion, there are many grammars (i.e., many grammars, each of which is a theory of a particular I-language that, under some convention that one has adopted, determines this E-language). But this is a matter of no consequence. In the case of some formal system, say arithmetic (presumably the model in mind), we assume the class of well-formed formulas in some notation to be "given," and we select the "grammar" (the rules of formation) as we please. But the E-language is not "given." What is "given" to the child is some finite array of data, on the basis of which the child's mind (incorporating S_0) constructs an I-language that assigns a status to every expression, and that we may think of as generating some E-language under one or another stipulated convention (or we may dispense with this apparently superfluous step). What is given to the linguist are finite arrays of data from various speech communities, including much data not available to the language learner, on the basis of which the linguist will attempt to discover the nature of S_0 and of the particular I-languages attained. The account presented by Quine, Lewis, and others has the story backwards: E-languages are not given, but are derivative, more remote from data and from mechanisms than I-languages and the grammars that are theories of I-languages; the choice of E-language therefore raises a host of new and additional problems beyond those connected with grammar and I-language. Whether it is worthwhile addressing or attempting to solve these problems is not at all clear, because the concept of E-language, however construed, appears to have no significance. The belief that E-language is a fairly clear notion whereas I-language or grammar raises serious, perhaps intractable philosophical problems, is quite mistaken. Just the opposite is true. There are numerous problems concerning the notions I-language and grammar, but not the ones raised in these discussions.

It should be noted that familiar characterizations of "language" as a code or a game point correctly toward I-language, not the artificial construct E-language. A code is not a set of representations but rather a specific system of rules that assigns coded representations to message-representations. Two codes may be different, although extensionally identical in the message-code pairings that they provide. Similarly, a game is not a set of moves but rather the rule system that underlies them. The Saussurean concept of *langue*, although far too narrow in conception, might be interpreted as appropriate in this respect. The same is true of Quine's definition of a language as a "complex of present dispositions to verbal behavior" insofar as it focuses on some internal state rather than E-language, although it is unacceptable for other reasons: thus, two individuals who speak the same language may differ radically in their dispositions to verbal behavior, and if dispositions are characterized in terms of probability of response under given conditions, then it is impossible to identify languages in these terms; and again, the fundamental question of the use and understanding of new sentences is left without any explanation. Perhaps the clearest account is Jespersen's in terms of the "notion of structure" that guides the speaker "in framing sentences of his own ...," these being "free expressions."

As we have seen, these ideas became the focus of attention in the study of generative grammar, although not without controversy. Saussurean structuralism had placed Jespersen's observation about "free expressions" outside of the scope of the study of language structure, of Saussure's *langue*. Bloomfield (1933) held that when a speaker produces speech forms that he has not heard, "we say that he utters them *on the analogy* of similar forms which he has heard," a position later adopted by Quine, C.F. Hockett, and the few others who even attempted to deal with the problem. This idea is not wrong but rather is vacuous until the concept of analogy is spelled out in a way that explains why certain "analogies" are somehow valid whereas others are not, a task that requires a radically different approach to the whole question. Why, for example, are sentences (6) and (7) of Chapter 1 [p. 9] not understood "on the analogy" of (4) and (5)? Why is sentence (14) not understood "on the analogy" of *any* of the earlier examples, in fact given no interpretation at all? We can give substance to the proposal by explaining "analogy" in terms of I-language, a system of rules and principles that assigns representations of form and meaning to linguistic expressions, but no other way to do so has been proposed; and with this necessary revision in the proposal, it becomes clear that "analogy" is simply an inappropriate concept in the first place.

I have been freely using various commonsense notions such as "knowledge," "rule-following," and so forth in this account. Various questions have been raised about the legitimacy of this usage. I will put these questions off for now, returning to them in Chapter 4, but meanwhile continuing to use the terms. I think the usage here is reasonably in accord with common usage, but nothing of great moment is at stake, and one could introduce technical terms for our purposes, giving them the meaning required for this discussion.

Sometimes it has been suggested that knowledge of language should be understood on the analogy of knowledge of arithmetic, arithmetic being taken to be an abstract "Platonic" entity that exists apart from any mental structures.[29] It is not in question here that there does exist what we have called an internalized language (described by what Thomas Bever calls "a psychogrammar") and that it is a problem of the natural sciences to discover it. What is claimed is that apart from particular I-languages, there is something else additional, what we might call "P-languages" (P-English, P-Japanese, etc.), existing in a Platonic heaven alongside of arithmetic and (perhaps) set theory, and that a person who we say knows English may not, in fact, have complete knowledge of P-English, or, indeed, may not know it at all. Similarly, the best theory of the I-language, of what this person actually knows, might not be the best theory of what is selected on some grounds to be P-English.[30]

The analogy to arithmetic is, however, quite unpersuasive. In the case of arithmetic, there is at least a certain initial plausibility to a Platonistic view insofar as the truths of arithmetic are what they are, independent of any facts of individual psychology, and we seem to discover these truths somewhat in the way that we discover facts about the physical world. In the case of language, however, the corresponding position is wholly without merit. There is no initial plausibility to the idea that apart from the truths of grammar concerning the I-language and the truths of UG concerning S_0 there is an additional domain of fact about P-language, independent of any psychological states of individuals. Knowing everything about the mind/brain, a Platonist would argue, we still have no basis for determining the truths of arithmetic or set theory, but there is not the slightest reason to suppose that there are truths of language that would still escape our grasp. Of course, one can construct abstract entities at will, and we can decide to call some of them "English" or "Japanese" and to define "linguistics" as the study of these abstract objects, and thus not part of the natural sciences, which are concerned with such entities as I-language and S_0, with grammar and universal grammar in the sense of the earlier discussion. But there seems little point to such moves.

A somewhat similar conception is advanced by Soames (1984). He distinguishes between two disciplines, psychology and linguistics, each defined by certain "Leading Questions," which are different for the two disciplines. The study of I-language and S_0, as described above, is part of psychology. However, "If one's goal is to answer the Leading Questions of linguistics, one will abstract away from psycholinguistic data that are not constitutive of languages" (and similarly, from neurophysiological data, etc.). The "Leading Questions" of linguistics include, for example, the questions, "In what ways are English and Italian alike?," "In what ways has English changed" in the course of its history? and so forth. The concepts English and Italian are taken to be clear enough pretheoretically to give these Leading Questions content, a highly dubious assumption for reasons already discussed, and surely not one made in actual linguistic research. Again, no question is raised here about the legitimacy of the investigation of I-language and S_0; rather, the question is whether this study falls under what we will decide to call "linguistics" and whether there is, as Soames urges, "a theoretically sound, empirically significant conception of linguistics" that restricts itself to a certain stipulated domain of evidence, to facts that are "constitutive of language."

One might point out that the terminological proposals that Soames advances are a bit eccentric. It seems odd, to say the least, to define "linguistics" so as to exclude many of its major practitioners – for example, Roman Jakobson and Edward Sapir, who would surely not have agreed that what Soames regards as extralinguistic data are irrelevant to the questions of linguistics as they understood them, including the "Leading Questions," and who, in support of their analyses, adduced evidence of a sort that Soames places outside of that "constitutive of language." But putting aside terminology, the real question that arises is whether there is any reason to establish a discipline of "linguistics" that restricts itself on *a priori* grounds to some particular data and constructs a concept of "language" that can be studied within this choice of relevant data.

To clarify what is at stake, suppose that two proposed grammars G_1 and G_2 differ in the choice of phonological features postulated: G_1 postulates the system F_1, and G_2, the system F_2. Suppose that G_1 and G_2 are not distinguishable with respect to a data base consisting of what Soames stipulates to be the "linguistically relevant" facts. Suppose that perceptual experiments of the sort Sapir conducted in his classic work, or other more sophisticated ones, yield results that can be explained in terms of the features of F_1 but not F_2. Imagine further that studies of aphasia and child language show that language breakdown and growth can be explained along Jakobsonian lines in terms of F_1 but not F_2, and that the choice of F_1 but not F2 provides an account for speech production and recognition, again along Jakobsonian lines. Soames agrees that there is a field of inquiry, call it "C(ognitive)-linguistics," which would use this evidence to select G_1 over G_2 as the theory of language that is represented in the mind/brains of the members of this speech community. But he proposes that there is another discipline, call it "A(bstract)-linguistics," which dismisses this evidence and regards G_1 and G_2 as equally well supported by "relevant" empirical evidence; in fact, a practitioner of A-linguistics would choose G_2 over G_1 if it were "simpler" on some general grounds. There is no doubt that Sapir and Jakobson, among many others, would have followed the path of C-linguistics in such a case, selecting G_1 as the grammar and applying this conclusion to the study of "Leading Questions" concerning the historical evolution of languages, and so on.[31]

The burden of proof clearly falls on those who believe that alongside C-linguistics, the status of which is not here in question, there is some point in developing the new discipline of A-linguistics, which not only differs from linguistics as it has actually been practised by major figures in the field but also is radically different from anything known in the sciences: it would be regarded as strange indeed to restrict biology or chemistry in some *a priori* fashion to questions and concepts defined so as to delimit in advance the category of relevant evidence. In the sciences, at least, disciplines are regarded as conveniences, not as ways of cutting nature at its joints or as the elaboration of certain fixed concepts; and their boundaries shift or disappear as knowledge and understanding advance.[32] In this respect, the study of language as understood in the discussion above is like chemistry, biology, solar physics, or the theory of human vision. Whether the burden of proof faced by advocates of A-linguistics can be borne, I will not speculate, except to observe that even if it can, the fact would have no consequences with regard to the legitimacy or character of the enterprise we are discussing, as Soames makes clear.

Note that the issue is not the legitimacy of abstraction. It is perfectly proper to develop the subject of rational mechanics, a branch of mathematics abstracted from physics that treats planets as mass points obeying certain laws, or to develop theories that consider aspects of I-language in abstraction from their physical realization or other properties; indeed, that is the standard practice, as outlined earlier. But one is not misled thereby into believing that the subject matter of rational mechanics is an entity in a Platonic heaven, and there is no more reason to suppose that that is true in the study of language.[33]

2.4.2 The Empirical Basis for the Study of I-language

In actual practice, linguistics as a discipline is characterized by attention to certain kinds of evidence that are, for the moment, readily accessible and informative: largely, the judgments of native speakers. Each such judgment is, in fact, the result of an experiment, one that is poorly designed but rich in the evidence it provides. In practice, we tend to operate on the assumption, or pretense, that these informant judgments give us "direct evidence" as to the structure of the I-language, but, of course, this is only a tentative and inexact working hypothesis, and any skilled practitioner has at his or her disposal an armory of techniques to help compensate for the errors introduced. In general, informant judgments do not reflect the structure of the language directly; judgments of acceptability, for example, may fail to provide direct evidence as to grammatical status because of the intrusion of numerous other factors. The same is true of other judgments concerning form and meaning. These are, or should be, truisms.[34]

In principle, evidence concerning the character of the I-language and initial state could come from many different sources apart from judgments concerning the form and meaning of expressions: perceptual experiments, the study of acquisition and deficit or of partially invented languages such as creoles,[35] or of literary usage or language change, neurology, biochemistry, and so on. It was one of the many contributions of the late Roman Jakobson to have emphasized this fact, in principle, and in his own work in practice. As in the case of any inquiry into some aspect of the physical world, there is no way of delimiting the kinds of evidence that might, in principle, prove relevant. The study of language structure as currently practiced should eventually disappear as a discipline as new types of evidence become available, remaining distinct only insofar as its concern is a particular faculty of the mind, ultimately the brain: its initial state and its various attainable mature states.

To be sure, the judgments of native speakers will always provide relevant evidence for the study of language, just as perceptual judgments will always provide relevant evidence for the study human vision, although one would hope that such evidence will eventually lose its uniquely privileged status. If a theory of language failed to account for these judgments, it would plainly be a failure; we might, in fact, conclude that it is not a theory of language, but rather of something else. But we cannot know in advance just how informative various kinds of evidence will prove to be with regard to the language faculty and its manifestations, and we should anticipate that a broader range of evidence and deeper understanding will enable us to identify in just what respects informant judgments are useful or unreliable and why, and to compensate for the errors introduced under the tentative working assumption, which is indispensable, for today, and does provide us with rich and significant information.

It is important to bear in mind that the study of one language may provide crucial evidence concerning the structure of some other language, if we continue to accept the plausible assumption that the capacity to acquire language, the subject matter of UG, is common across the species. This conclusion is implicit in the research program outlined earlier. A study of English is a study of the realization of the initial state S_0 under particular conditions. Therefore, it embodies assumptions, which should be made explicit, concerning S_0. But S_0 is a constant; therefore, Japanese must be an instantiation of the same initial state under different conditions. Investigation of Japanese might show that the assumptions concerning S_0

derived from the study of English were incorrect; these assumptions might provide the wrong answers for Japanese, and after correcting them on this basis we might be led to modify the postulated grammar of English. Because evidence from Japanese can evidently bear on the correctness of a theory of S_0, it can have indirect – but very powerful – bearing on the choice of the grammar that attempts to characterize the I-language attained by a speaker of English. This is standard practice in the study of generative grammar. For this reason alone it is quite wrong to suppose that there are no grounds to choose among "extensionally equivalent grammars" for a "given language" [...] One of these might, for example, require a theory of S_0 that is demonstrably inadequate for some other language.

On the highly relativistic assumptions of certain varieties of descriptive linguistics that held that each language must be studied in its own terms, this research program may seem to be senseless or illegitimate, although one should note that this point of view was, in part, an ideology that was not observed in practice. If we are interested in discovering the real properties of the initial state of the language faculty and of its particular realizations as potential or actual I-languages, the ideology must be abandoned, and we must regard a theory of one language as subject to change on the basis of evidence concerning other languages (mediated through a theory of UG), or evidence of other sorts.

We observed that it is a task for the brain sciences to explain the properties and principles discovered in the study of mind. More accurately, the interdependency of the brain sciences and the study of mind is reciprocal. The theory of mind aims to determine the properties of the initial state S_0 and each attainable state S_L of the language faculty, and the brain sciences seek to discover the mechanisms of the brain that are the physical realizations of these states. There is a common enterprise: to discover the correct characterization of the language faculty in its initial and attained states, to discover the truth about the language faculty. This enterprise is conducted at several levels: an abstract characterization in the theory of mind, and an inquiry into mechanisms in the brain sciences. In principle, discoveries about the brain should influence the theory of mind, and at the same time the abstract study of states of the language faculty should formulate properties to be explained by the theory of the brain and is likely to be indispensable in the search for mechanisms. To the extent that such connections can be established, the study of the mind – in particular, of I-language – will be assimilated to the mainstream of the natural sciences.

So little is now known about the relevant aspects of the brain that we can barely even speculate about what the connections might be. We can, however, imagine how they might be established in principle, however remote the goal. Suppose that the study of I-language establishes certain general principles of binding theory that explain facts of the sort discussed in Chapter 1. Then a task of the brain sciences is to determine what mechanisms are responsible for the fact that these principles hold. Suppose that we have two grammars – two theories of the state of knowledge attained by a particular person – and suppose further that these theories are "extensionally equivalent" in the sense that they determine the same E-language in whatever sense we give to this derivative notion. It could in principle turn out that one of these grammars incorporates properties and principles that are readily explained in terms of brain mechanisms whereas the other does not. Similarly, two theories of UG that are equivalent in that they specify exactly the same set of attainable I-languages might be distinguishable in terms of properties of the brain. For example, one might contain certain principles and possibilities of variation that can be readily explained in terms of brain mechanisms, and the other not.

It is easy enough to imagine cases of this sort. Suppose that theory I contains the principles P_1, ..., P_n and theory II contains the principles Q_1, ..., Q_m, and that the two theories are logically equivalent: the principles of each can be deduced from the principles of the other so that any description of behavior or potential behavior in terms of one of these theories can be reformulated in terms of the other. It could be that the brain sciences would show that each P_i corresponds to some determinate complex of neural mechanisms, whereas there is no such account of the Q_i's; some brain injury, for example, might selectively modify the P_i's but not the Q_i's. In such a case, facts about the brain would select among theories of the mind that might be empirically indistinguishable in other terms. Although results of this sort are remote in the current state of understanding, they are possible. The relation of brain and mind, so conceived, is a problem of the natural sciences.

2.4.3 Some Consequences of the Shift of Focus

To summarize, we may think of a person's knowledge of a particular language as a state of the mind, realized in some arrangement of physical mechanisms. We abstract the I-language as "what is known" by a person in this state of knowledge. This finite system, the I-language, is what the linguist's generative grammar attempts to characterize. If I say that this system has such-and-such properties, what I say is true or false. I am, in short, proposing a theoretical account of the properties of certain mechanisms, an account presented at a level of abstraction at which we believe that significant properties of these mechanisms can be expressed and principles governing these mechanisms and their functions elucidated. The study is in some ways similar to what Gunther Stent has called "cerebral hermeneutics," referring to the abstract investigation of the ways in which the visual system constructs and interprets visual experience (Stent, 1981). Similarly,

UG is the study of one aspect of biological endowment, analogous to the study of the innate principles that determine that we will have a human rather than an insect visual system. The technical concept "knowledge of I-language" is a reasonably close approximation to what is informally called "knowledge of language," abstracting from several aspects of the common-sense notion as discussed earlier, although this consideration is a secondary one for reasons already mentioned.

The shift of point of view to a mentalist interpretation of the study of language was, as noted earlier, one factor in the development of the contemporary cognitive sciences, and constituted a step toward the incorporation of the study of language within the natural sciences, because it helps pave the way to an inquiry into the mechanisms with the properties exhibited in the study of rules and representations. This shift also led at once to a recasting of many of the traditional questions of language study. Many new and challenging problems arose, while a number of familiar problems dissolved when viewed from this perspective.

Consider the study of sound structure, the primary focus of attention in structural and descriptive linguistics. Taking E-language as the topic of inquiry, the problem is to discover the elements into which the stream of speech is subdivided and their properties and structural arrangements: phonemes and features, regarded as segments of an acoustic wave form or of a series of articulatory motions. Much of phonological theory consisted of analytic procedures for accomplishing this task. Focusing on the I-language, however, the problem is a rather different one: to find the mental representations that underlie the production and perception of speech and the rules that relate these representations to the physical events of speech. The problem is to find the best theory to account for a wide variety of facts, and we do not expect that analytic procedures exist to accomplish this task, just as there are no such procedures in other fields.

Consider, for example, the words listed below, where column I is the conventional orthography, column II appears

I	II	III
bet	bet	bet
bent	bent	bẽt
bend	bend	bend
knot	nat	nat
nod	nad	nAd
write	rayt	rayt
ride	rayd	rAyd
writer	rayt+r	rayDr
rider	rayd+r	rAyDr

to be the correct phonological representation, and column III, the approximate phonetic representations in one dialect of English, taking [a] to be a short vowel and [A] a corresponding long vowel (their exact phonetic character is irrelevant here), [ẽ] a nasalized counterpart to [e], and D a tongue flap rather like a trilled [r].

We may assume that the phonetic representations of column III correspond to actual speech events by universal principles of interpretation that essentially preserve linearity; that is, the sequence of phonetic symbols corresponds to the sequence of sounds (the matter is not this simple, as is well known). The phonological representations of the second column, not the phonetic representations of the third, correspond to the way that we intuitively "hear" these words. Although phonetic analysis reveals that *bet* and *bent* differ only in nasalization of the medial vowel, and that each has three phonetic segments as distinct from the four-segment word *bend*, this does not correspond to the intuitive perception; we hear *knot* and *nod* as differing only in one feature, voicing of the final consonant, not in both the vowel and the consonant (as, e.g., *knot* versus *Ned*). The representations of *writer* and *rider* that we intuitively perceive and that clearly relate to lexical and syntactic structure are as indicated in the second column (with + standing for the break between the lexical item and the agentive affix), not the third, although the latter expresses the phonetic fact that the words differ only in vowel quality. Examples such as these posed difficult problems for an approach to phonology that sought to determine phonological units by analytic procedures applying to actual speech events. The question is the status of the representations of column II, which were always recognized to be "correct" in some sense although their elements do not correspond point-by-point to the actual sounds of speech, the subparts of the actual specimens of E-language.

Shifting the focus of attention to I-language, the problems quickly dissolve. The representations of column II are essentially the mental representations of the lexicon, which enter into the syntax and semantics. The phonetic representations of column III derive from these by straightforward rules, most of them quite general: vowels assume a particular quality before voiced and unvoiced consonants and become nasalized before nasal consonants, the nasal consonant drops before an unvoiced dental, and (in this dialect) the dental stops merge as [D] medially under this stress contour. Applying these rules, we derive the phonetic forms (III) from the lexical-phonological representations (II). The latter representations are not derived from the speech sounds by analytic procedures of segmentation, classification, extraction of physical features, and so forth, but are established and justified as part of the best theory for accounting ultimately for the general relation between sound and meaning of the I-language. Further syntactic and semantic rules apply to the representations of (II) in the expressions in which these words appear. The I-language, incorporating the rules that form the representations (II) and the rules that relate them to (III), is acquired by the child by applying the principles incorporated in the initial state S_0 to the presented facts; the problem for the grammarian is to discover these principles and show how they lead to the choice of the representations (II) (assuming these to be correct). The failure of taxonomic procedures is of no significance, because there is no reason to believe that such procedures play any role in language acquisition or have any standing as part of UG.

As these very simple examples illustrate, even at the level of sound structure, mental representations may be relatively abstract – i.e., not related in a simple way to actual specimens of linguistic behavior (in fact, this is even true of the phonetic representations, as a closer analysis would show). As we move to other levels of inquiry into the I-language, we find increasing evidence that mental representations are abstract in this sense. The systems of rules and principles that form and modify them are fairly simple and natural, although they interact to yield structures of considerable complexity and to determine their properties in quite a precise fashion. In short, the language faculty appears to be, at its core, a computational system that is rich and narrowly constrained in structure and rigid in its essential operations, nothing at all like a complex of dispositions or a system of habits and analogies. This conclusion seems reasonably well established and has been given considerable substance; there is no known alternative that even begins to deal with the actual facts of language, and empirically meaningful debate takes place largely within the framework of these assumptions.

Nevertheless, it should be observed that the conclusion is in many ways a rather surprising one. One might not have expected that a complex biological system such as the language faculty would have evolved in this fashion, and if indeed it has, that discovery is of no small significance.[36]

The scope of the shift to a mentalist or conceptualist interpretation, to internalized rather than externalized language, is broader than has been sometimes appreciated. Quite explicitly, it included the study of syntax, phonology, and morphology. I think it also includes much of what is misleadingly called "the semantics of natural language" – I say "misleadingly" because I think that much of this work is not semantics at all, if by "semantics" we mean the study of the relation between language and the world – in particular, the study of truth and reference. Rather, this work deals with certain postulated levels of mental representation, including representations of syntactic and lexical form and others called "models" or "pictures" or "discourse representations" or "situations," or the like. But the relation of these latter systems to the world of objects with properties and relations, or to the world as it is believed to be, is often intricate and remote, far more so than one might be led to believe on the basis of simple examples. The relation cannot, for example, be described as "incorporation" or element-by-element association.

Consider, for example, the principles of pronominal reference, which have been central to these quasisemantic investigations. If I say "John thinks that he is intelligent," *he* may refer to John, but not if I say "he thinks that John is intelligent."[37] We can account for such facts by a theory of the structural configurations in which a pronoun can acquire its "reference" from an associated name that binds it. The same principles, however, apply to such sentences as "the average man thinks that he is intelligent" "he thinks that the average man is intelligent," (or "John Doe thinks that he is intelligent," where "John Doe" is introduced as a designation for the average man). But no one assumes that there is an entity, the average man (or John Doe), to which the pronoun is permitted to refer in one but not the other case. If I say "John took a look at him, but it was too brief to permit a positive identification," *it* can refer to the look that John took; but the near synonym "John looked at him" cannot be extended in this way with the same interpretation, although no one believes that there are looks that a person can take, to one of which the pronoun *it* in the first sentence refers. Or, consider such widely discussed examples as "everyone who owns a donkey beats it," problematic because the pronoun *it* does not appear to be formally within the scope of the quantified noun phrase *a donkey* that binds it. One might try to approach the analysis of such sentences by constructing a representation with the property that for every pair (man, donkey), if *own* holds of the pair, then so does *beat*. Then we should say the same about "everyone who has a chance wastes it," without, however, committing ourselves to the belief that among the things in the world there are chances. Even if we restrict ourselves to the context "there are ...," we can hardly assume that there are entities in the world, or in the world as we believe it to be, that correspond to the terms that appear ("there are looks that injure and others that charm," "there are chances that are too risky to take," "there are opportunities that should not be passed up," etc.).

One can think of many still more extreme examples. Although there has been much concern over the status of fictional and abstract objects, the problem, in fact, cuts far deeper. One can speak of "reference" or "coreference" with some intelligibility if one postulates a domain of mental objects associated with formal entities of language by a relation with many of the properties of reference, but all of this is internal to the theory of mental representations; it is a form of syntax. There seems no obvious sense in populating the extra-mental world with corresponding entities, nor any empirical consequence or gain in explanatory force in doing so. Insofar as this is true, the study of the relation of syntactic structures to models, "pictures," and the like, should be regarded as pure syntax, the study of various mental representations, to be supplemented by a theory of the relation these mental objects bear to the world or to the world as it is conceived or believed to be. Postulation of such mental representations is not innocuous but must be justified by empirical argument, just as in the case of phonological or other syntactic representations. Thus, the shift toward a computational theory of mind encompasses a substantial part of what has been called "semantics" as well, a conclusion that is only fortified if we consider more avowedly "conceptualist" approaches to these topics.

To proceed, we are now concerned with I-language and the initial state of the language faculty, with the linguist's grammars and UG. As a tentative empirical hypothesis, we might take the I-language to be a rule system of some sort, a specific realization of the options permitted by UG, fixed by presented experience. The rule system assigns to each expression a structure, which we may take to be a set of representations, one on each linguistic level, where a linguistic level is a particular system of mental representation. This structure must provide whatever information about an expression is available to the person who knows the language, insofar as this information derives from the language faculty; its representations must specify just what the language faculty contributes to determining how the expression is produced, used, and understood.

A linguistic level is a system consisting of a set of minimal elements (primes), an operation of concatenation that forms strings of primes, as much mathematical apparatus as is necessary to construct appropriate formal objects from these elements, the relevant relations that hold of these elements, and a class of designated formal objects (markers) that are assigned to expressions as their representations on this level. The rule system expresses the relations among the various levels in the language in question and determines the elements and properties of each level. At the level of phrase structure, for example, the primes are the minimal elements that enter into syntactic description (*John, run, past-tense*, N, V, S, etc.), the basic relation *is-a* (*John* is an N, *John ran* is an S, etc.), and the phrase-markers will be certain formal objects constructed out of primes that express completely the relation *is-a*. The phrase-marker for the string *John ran* will indicate that the full string is an S (sentence), that *John* is an N (noun) and an NP (noun phrase), and that *ran* is a V (verb) and a VP (verb phrase) ...

The theory of linguistic structure (UG) will have the task of specifying these concepts precisely.[38] The theory must provide grammars for the I-languages that can, in principle, be attained by a human mind/brain, given appropriate experience,[39] and it must furthermore be so constrained that just the right I-language is determined, given the kind of evidence that suffices for language acquisition. We turn next to these questions.

38   Noam Chomsky

NOTES

1. On these and many other discussions, primarily in the seventeenth-nineteenth centuries, see Chomsky (1966). For discussion of some misinterpretation of this work, see Bracken (1984).

2. The alleged *a priorism* of work in this tradition has often been exaggerated. See Chomsky (1966) and more recent work for discussion of this point.

3. The tradition, in this case, is a different one, represented in its most advanced form in the early work of the Indian grammarians 2,500 years ago. See Kiparsky (1982). A modern counterpart is Bloomfield (1939), which was radically different in character from the work of the period and inconsistent with his own theories of language, and remained virtually without influence or even awareness despite Bloomfield's great prestige.

4. See Newmeyer (1980) for one view of the history of this period prior to the second major conceptual shift; and for some more personal comments, the introduction to Chomsky (1975a), a somewhat abbreviated version of a 1956 revision of a 1955 manuscript, both unpublished. See Lightfoot (1982) and Hornstein and Lightfoot (1981) for discussion of the general backgrounds for much current work, and Radford (1981) for an introduction to the work that led to the second conceptual shift. See Chomsky (1981) for a more technical presentation of some of the ideas that entered into this conceptual shift and van Riemsdijk and Williams (1985) for an introductory study of this current work.

5. Although basically adopting this point of view, W.V. Quine, however, argued that there is a very severe, in fact insuperable problem of underdetermination affecting all aspects of language and grammar, and much of psychology more generally (Quine, 1960, 1972). I do not think that he succeeded in showing that some novel form of indeterminacy affects the study of language beyond the normal underdetermination of theory by evidence, his own formulations of the thesis furthermore involve internal inconsistency (see Chomsky, 1975b, 1980b). There seems no reason on these grounds, then, to distinguish linguistics or psychology in principle from the natural sciences in accordance with what Hockney (1975) calls Quine's "bifurcation thesis." A similar conclusion is reached by Putnam (1981) in his abandonment of metaphysical realism on Quinean grounds. His step also abandons the bifurcation thesis, although in the opposite direction.

6. See Chomsky (1975a). See Crain and Nakayama (1984) for empirical study of this question with 3-5 year-old children.

7. The reaction to such phenomena, also unnoticed until recently, again illustrates the difference of outlook of structuralist-descriptive and generative grammar. For some practitioners of the former, the statement of the facts, which is straightforward enough once they are observed, is the answer – nothing else is necessary; for the latter, the statement of the facts poses the problem to be solved. Cf. Ney (1983), particularly, his puzzlement about the "peculiar view of grammar [that] unnecessarily complicates the whole matter" by seeking an explanation for the facts. Note that there is no question of right or wrong here, but rather of topic of inquiry.

8. In early work, such facts were used to motivate an analysis of intransitives such as *eat* as derived from corresponding transitives by a system of ordered rules that excluded the unwanted cases; see Chomsky (1962).

9. On structures of this type, and problems of binding theory, more generally, see Higginbotham (1983a), among much other work.

10. See Fodor (1983). But it is too narrow to regard the "language module" as an input system in Fodor's sense, if only because it is used in speaking and thought. We might consider supplementing this picture by adding an "output system," but plainly this must be linked to the input system; we do not expect a person to speak only English and understand only Japanese. That is, the input and output systems must each access a fixed system of knowledge. The latter, however, is a central system which has essential problems of modularity, a fact that brings the entire picture into question. Furthermore, even regarded as an input system, the language module does not appear to have the property of rapidity of access that Fodor discusses, as indicated by (8)-(14). Note also that even if Fodor is right in believing that there is a sharp distinction between modules in his sense and "the rest," which is holistic in several respects, it does not follow that the residue is unstructured. In fact, this seems highly unlikely, if only because of the "epistemic boundedness" that he notes. Many other questions arise concerning Fodor's very intriguing discussion of these issues, which I will not pursue here.

11. These observations, generally considered truisms, are rejected by Katz (1981, pp. 79-80) on the grounds that to recognize the fact that the concepts language and dialect of colloquial usage involve a sociopolitical dimension would be "like claiming that the concept of number is not a concept of mathematics but a sociopolitical one." There is no reason to accept this curious conclusion.

12. However, there were exceptions, for example, the theory of "overall patterns," of which each English dialect was held to be a subsystem. See Trager and Smith (1951). Note that the question of "variable rules," as discussed by some sociolinguists, is not relevant here.

13. We put aside here just what this term would mean in Bloomfieldian or any other variety of "behaviorist" linguistics. Pursuing such an approach, one would have to explain just what it means to say that people speak the very same language although they do not tend to say the same things in given circumstances. The same question arises if language is defined as a "complex of present dispositions to verbal behavior" (Quine, 1960), as do other problems that seem insoluble if the technical constructed concept "language" is to be a useful term for the investigation of language, to have any relation to what we call "language." On this matter, see Chomsky (1975b, pp. 192-195).

14. One might also note some unintentionally comical objections, such as the charge by Oxford professor of linguistics Roy Harris (1983) that the standard idealization (which he ascribes to Saussure-Bloomfield-Chomsky) reflects "a fascist concept of language if ever there was one" because it takes the "ideal" speech community to be "totally homogeneous."

15. For some discussion, see Chomsky (1964) and Postal (1964). For comparison of transformational generative grammar with Harris's early theory of transformations, regarded as an analytic procedure applying beyond the sentence level of "structural grammar," see the introduction to Chomsky (1975a).

16. Lewis (1975). Lewis provides one of the clearest presentations of an "extensional" approach to language and also a critique of studies of "internalized language" in the sense described below. For critical discussion, see Chomsky (1980b).

17. Editorial comments in Joos (1957); Whitney (1872); Sapir (1921). Whitney, who exerted a major influence on Saussure and American linguistics, was criticizing Steinthal's Humboldtian approach, which I believe, falls naturally into the earlier tradition referred to above. Humboldt, who is widely regarded (e.g., by Bloomfield) as an extreme relativist, in fact held that "all languages with regard to their grammar are very similar, if they are investigated not superficially, but deeply in their inner nature." See Chomsky (1966), p. 90, and references cited, for further discussion.

18. This question, however, was surely not what Whitney had in mind.

19. Jespersen (1924). On Jespersen's notions as compared to those of contemporary generative grammar, see Reynolds (1971); Chomsky (1977), Chapter 1.

20. One might argue that the systems we are considering constitute only one element of the faculty of language, understood more broadly to encompass other capacities involved in the use and understanding of language, for example, what is sometimes called "communicative competence," or parts of the human conceptual system that are specifically related to language. See Chomsky (1980b). I will put such questions aside here, continuing to use the term "language faculty" in the narrower sense of the previous discussion.

21. For a related but somewhat different way of viewing these questions, see Higginbotham (1983b).

22. Those that tend to yield a false parse, such as Thomas Bever's example "the horse raced past the barn fell," where the first six words are generally taken to constitute a full clause, leaving no interpretation for the final word, although on reflection it is clear that the expression is a well-formed sentence stating that a certain horse fell, namely, the one that was raced past the barn.

23. Obviously, the questions of innateness and species-specificity are distinct. It has been alleged that I and others have taken "innate" and "species-specific" to be "synonyms" (Cartmill, 1984). I am unaware of any examples of such confusion, although there are a number of articles refuting it.

24. See Chomsky (1980b), pp. 134-139.

25. On this matter, see Marr (1982). Note that the question of the legitimacy or sense of a realist interpretation of science in general is not at issue here; rather, nothing new in principle seems to arise in the case of the study of I-language and its origins. If one wants to consider the question of realism, psychology and linguistics seem poor choices; the question should be raised with regard to the more advanced sciences, where there is much better hope of gaining insight into the matter. See Chomsky (1980b) for further discussion.

26. For some commentary on the general issue, see Enc (1983).

27. On some misunderstandings, which are repeated in subsequent work that I will not discuss here, see Chomsky (1980b), pp. 123-128. As for the publishing history, the earliest publications on generative grammar were presented in a framework suggested by certain topics in automata theory (e.g., my *Syntactic Structures*, 1957 – actually course notes for an undergraduate course at MIT and hence presented from a point of view related to interests of these students). Specifically linguistic work, such as Chomsky (1975a), was not publishable at the time. In the latter, considerations of weak generative capacity (i.e., characterizability of E-languages), finite automata and the like were completely absent, and emphasis was on I-language, although the term was not used.

28. For further discussion of this matter, see Chomsky (1980b).

29. See Katz (1981) and Bever (1983).

30. This would follow if the evidence stipulated to be relevant to identifying a certain Platonic language as P-English is distinct from the evidence that bears on the theory of the I-language actually represented in the mind/brain of speakers of English, or if some novel canons are adopted for interpreting evidence. By a similar procedure, we could establish "Platonistic biology," concerned, for example, with what Katz call the "essential property" of a heart (that it is a pump) and thus abstracting from the physical laws that make it beat (a nonessential property). We might then find that the best biological theory is distinct from the best theory of Platonistic biology just as the best (ultimately, biological) theory of I-language might be distinct from the best theory of Platonistic language (however it is specified; for Katz, by analysis of "our concept of the abstract object natural language").

31. For some recent discussion of the matter in connection with historical linguistics, see Lightfoot (1979).

32. Katz insists that disciplines such as chemistry, biology, and so forth have inherent, conceptually determined boundaries. Indeed, he regards the claim as uncontroversial, the alternative being a form of "nihilism" that "would turn the spectrum of well-focused academic disciplines into chaos" (*op.cit.*).

33. Arguments that have been offered to the contrary seem to me question-begging or otherwise flawed. Thus, Katz argues against Hilary Putnam that if what we call "cats" were discovered to be robots controlled from outer space, then they would not be cats, because the meaning of "cat" in the Platonic entity P-English is "feline animal"; this would remain true even if it were determined that in the I-language of each speaker of English, "cat" is understood in accordance with Putnam's analysis, which takes cats to be of the same natural kind (a concept of science) as particular exemplars. The argument goes through, trivially, with regard to P-English as Katz stipulates its properties. But Putnam was proposing a theory concerning human languages and conceptual systems, concerning English, not P-English as Katz defines it, and Katz offers no reason to believe that his Platonic object merits the name "English" any more than an equally legitimate abstract object that would incorporate Putnam's assumptions. Throughout, the arguments are of this sort. Katz also presents an account of the history of generative grammar and of documents he cites that is seriously inaccurate, as is often evident even on internal grounds. See also Chomsky (1981), pp. 314-315.

34. For discussion of some common misunderstandings about these and related matters, see Newmeyer (1983).

35. On the relevance of this material, see Bickerton (1984) and references cited, and discussion in the same issue of the journal.

36. For some discussion, see Chomsky (1980b, 1981); and Chomsky, Huybregts, and van Riemsdijk (1982).

37. The matter is more complex. See Evans (1980) and Higginbotham (1983a). But we can put aside the required sharpening of these notions here.

38. For an early effort, see Chomsky (1975a) dating from 1955-56.

39. A stronger requirement would be that UG specify exactly the I-langauges attainable under normal conditions. It is not obvious, however, that UG meets these conditions. The attainable languages are those that fall in the intersection of those determined by UG and the humanly learnable systems, and conditions on learnability might exclude certain grammars permitted by UG. Similar remarks hold with regard to parsing. For background on these matters, see Wexler and Culicover (1980) and Berwick and Weinberg (1984).

REFERENCES

Berwick, R. & Weinberg, A. (1984). *The Grammatical Basis of Linguistic Performance*, Cambridge, MIT Press.

Bever, T.G. (1983). "The Nonspecific Bases of Language," in E. Wanner & L. Gleitman (eds.) *Language Acquisition: The State of the Art*, Cambridge, Harvard.

Bickerton, D. (1984). "The Language Biogram Hypothesis," *Behavioral and Brain Sciences*, 7.2.

Bloomfield, L. (1928). "A Set of Postulates for the Science of Language," *Language* 2, reprinted by M. Joos (ed.) *Readings in Linguistics*, Washington, American Council of Learned Sciences, 1957.

Bloomfield, L. (1933). *Language*, New York, Holt.

Bloomfield, L. (1939). "Menomini Morphophonemics," *Travaux du cercle linguistique de Prague*.

Bracken, H. (1984). *Mind and Language*, Dordrecht, Foris.

Cartmill, M. (1984). "Innate Grammars and the Evolutionary Presumption," *Behavioral and Brain Sciences*, 7.2.

Chomsky, N. (1957). *Syntactic Structures*, The Hague, Mouton.

Chomsky, N. (1962). "A Transformational Approach to Syntax," in A.A. Hill (ed.) *Proceedings of the Third Texas Conference on Problems of Linguistic Analysis in English* (1958), Austin, University of Texas Press.

Chomsky, N. (1964). *Current Issues in Linguistic Theory*, The Hague, Mouton.

Chomsky, N. (1965). *Aspects of the Theory of Syntax*, Cambridge, MIT Press.

Chomsky, N. (1966). *Cartesian Linguistics*, New York, Harper & Row.

Chomsky, N. (1975a). *Logical Structure of Linguistic Theory*, New York, Plenum, drawn from an unpublished 1955-56 manuscript.

Chomsky, N. (1975b). *Reflections on Language*, New York, Pantheon.

Chomsky, N. (1977). *Essays on Form and Interpretation*, Amsterdam, North-Holland.

Chomsky, N. (1980b). *Rules and Representations*, New York, Columbia University Press.

Chomsky, N. (1981). *Lectures on Government and Binding*, Dordrecht, Foris.

Chomsky, N. (1982). *Some Concepts and Consequences of the Theory of Government and Binding*, Cambridge, MIT Press.

Chomsky, N., Huybregts, R., & Riemsdijk, H. van. (1982). *The Generative Enterprise*, Dordrecht, Foris.

Crain, S. & Nakayama, M. (1984). "Structure Dependence in Grammar Formation," ms., University of Connecticut.

Enc, B. (1983). "In Defense of the Identity Theory," *J. of Philosophy*, 80.5.

Evans, G. (1980). "Pronouns," *Linguistic Inquiry*, 11.2.

Harris, R. (1983). "Theoretical Ideas," *Times Literary Supplement*, 14 October.

Higginbotham, J. (1983a). "Logical Form, Binding and Nominals," *Linguistic Inquiry*, 14.3.

Higginbotham, J. (1983b). "Is Grammar Psychological?" in *How Many Questions?* L.S. Cauman, I. Levi, C. Parsons, & R. Schwartz, Indianapolis, Hackett.

Hockney, D. (1975). "The Bifurcation of Scientific Theories and Indeterminacy of Translation," *Philosophy of Science*, 42.4.

Hornstein, N. & Lightfoot, D. (eds.), (1981). *Explanation in Linguistics*, London, Longman.

Jespersen, O. (1924). *The Philosophy of Grammar*, London, Allen & Unwin.

Joos, M., (ed.). (1957). *Readings in Linguistics*, Washington, American Council of Learned Societies.

Katz, J. (1981). *Language and Other Abstract Objects*, Totowa, NJ, Rowman & Littlefield.

Kiparsky, P. (1982). *Some Theoretical Problems in Panini's Grammar*, Poona, Bhandarkar Oriental Research Institute.

Lewis, D. (1975). "Languages and Language," in *Language, Mind and Knowledge*, K. Gunderson (ed.), Minneapolis, University of Minnesota Press.

Lightfoot, D. (1979). *Principles of Diachronic Syntax*, London, Cambridge University Press.

Lightfoot, D. (1982). *The Language Lottery*, Cambridge, MIT Press.

Marcus, M. (1980). *A Theory of Syntactic Recognition for Natural Language*, Cambridge, MIT Press.

Marr, D. (1982). *Vision*, San Francisco, Freeman.

Newmeyer, F.J. (1980). *Linguistic Theory in America*, New York, Academic Press.

Newmeyer, F.J. (1983). *Grammatical Theory*, Chicago, University of Chicago Press.

Ney, J. (1983). "Review of Chomsky (1982)," *Language Sciences*, 5.2.

Postal, P. (1964). *Constituent Structure*, The Hague, Mouton.

Postal, P. (1971). *Cross-Over Phenomena*, New York, Holt, Rinehart & Winston.

Putnam, H. (1975). "The Meaning of 'Meaning'," in *Language, Mind and Knowledge*, K. Gunderson (ed.), Minneapolis, University of Minnesota Press.

Putnam, H. (1981). *Reason, Truth and History*, Cambridge, Cambridge University Press.

Quine, W.V. (1960). *Word and Object*, Cambridge, MIT Press.

Quine, W.V. (1972). "Methodological Reflections on Current Linguistic Theory," in G. Harman & D. Davidson (eds.) *Semantics of Natural Language*, New York, Humanities Press.

Radford, A. (1981). *Transformational Syntax*, Cambridge, Cambridge University Press.

Reynolds, A.L. (1971). "What Did Otto Jespersen Say?" *Papers of the Chicago Linguistic Society*.

Riemsdijk, H. van & Williams, E. (1985). *Introduction to the Theory of Grammar*, Cambridge: MIT Press.

Sapir, E. (1921). *Language*, New York, Harcourt, Brace.

Soames, S. (1984). "Linguistics and Psychology," *Linguistics and Philosophy*, 7.2

Stent, G. (1981). "Cerebral Hermeneutics," *J. Social Biol. Struct.*, 4.107-124.

Trager, G. & Smith, H.L. (1951). *An Outline of English Structure*, Studies in Linguistics Occasional Papers 3.

Wexler, K. & Culicover, P. (1980). *Formal Principles of Language Acquisition*, Cambridge, MIT Press.

Whitney, W.D. (1872). "Steinthal and the Psychological Theory of Language," *North American Review*.

UEBER SINN UND BEDEUTUNG (ON SENSE AND REFERENCE)

Gottlob Frege

Equality[1] gives rise to challenging questions which are not altogether easy to answer. Is it a relation? A relation between objects, or between names or signs of objects? In my *Begriffsschrift*[2] I assumed the latter. The reasons which seem to favour this are the following: $a = a$ and $a = b$ are obviously statements of differing cognitive value; $a = a$ holds a priori and, according to Kant, is to be labelled analytic, while statements of the form $a = b$ often contain very valuable extensions of our knowledge and cannot always be established *a priori*. The discovery that the rising sun is not new every morning, but always the same, was one of the most fertile astronomical discoveries. Even to-day the identification of a small planet or a comet is not always a matter of course. Now if we were to regard equality as a relation between that which the names "a" and "b" designate, it would seem that $a = b$ could not differ from $a = a$ (i.e. provided $a = b$ is true). A relation would thereby be expressed of a thing to itself, and indeed one in which each thing stands to itself but to no other thing. What is intended to be said by $a = b$ seems to be that the signs or names "a" and "b" designate the same thing, so that those signs themselves would be under discussion: a relation between them would be asserted. But this relation would hold between the names or signs only in so far as they named or designated something. It would be mediated by the connexion of each of the two signs with the same designated thing. But this is arbitrary. Nobody can be forbidden to use any arbitrary producible event or object as a sign for something. In that case the sentence $a = b$ would no longer refer to the subject matter, but only to its mode of designation; we would express no proper knowledge by its means. But in many cases this is just what we want to do. If the sign "a" is distinguished from the sign "b" only as object (here, by means of its shape), not as sign (i.e. not by the manner in which it designates something), the cognitive value of $a = a$ becomes essentially equal to that of $a = b$, provided $a = b$ is true. A difference can arise only if the difference between the signs corresponds to a difference in the mode of presentation of that which is designated. Let a, b, c, be the lines connecting the vertices of a triangle with the midpoints of the opposite sides. The point of intersection of a and b is then the same as the point of intersection of b and c. So we have different designations for the same point, and these names ("point of intersection of a and b," "point of intersection of b and c") likewise indicate the mode of presentation; and hence the statement contains actual knowledge.

It is natural, now, to think of there being connected with a sign (name, combination of words, letter), besides that to which the sign refers, which may be called the reference of the sign, also what I should like to call the sense of the sign, wherein the mode of presentation is contained. In our example, accordingly, the reference of the expressions "the point of intersection of a and b" and "the point of intersection of b and c" would be the same, but not their senses. The reference of "evening star" would be the same as that of "morning star" but not the sense.

It is clear from the context that by "sign" and "name" I have here understood any designation representing a proper name, which thus has as its reference a definite object (this word taken in the widest range), but not a concept or a relation, which shall be discussed further in another article.[3] The designation of a single object can also consist of several words or other signs. For brevity, let every such designation be called a proper name.

The sense of a proper name is grasped by everybody who is sufficiently familiar with the language or totality of designations to which it belongs;[4] but this serves to illuminate only a single aspect of the reference, supposing it to have one. Comprehensive knowledge of the reference would require us to be able to say immediately whether any given sense belongs to it. To such knowledge we never attain.

The regular connexion between a sign, its sense, and its reference is of such a kind that to the sign there corresponds a definite sense and to that in turn a definite reference, while to a given reference (an object) there does not belong only a single sign. The same sense has different expressions in different languages or even in the same language. To be sure, exceptions to this regular behaviour occur. To every expression belonging to a complete totality of signs, there should certainly correspond a definite sense; but natural languages often do not satisfy this condition, and one must be content if the same word has the same sense in the same context. It may perhaps be granted that every grammatically well-formed expression representing a proper name always has a sense. But this is not to say that to the sense there also corresponds a reference. The words "the celestial body most distant from the Earth" have a sense, but it is very doubtful if they also have a reference. The expression "the least rapidly convergent series" has a sense; but it is known to have no reference, since for every given convergent series, another convergent, but less rapidly convergent, series can be found. In grasping a sense, one is not certainly assured of a reference.

If words are used in the ordinary way, what one intends to speak of is their reference. It can also happen, however, that one wishes to talk about the words themselves or their sense. This happens, for instance, when the words of another are quoted. One's own words then first designate words of the other speaker, and only the latter have their usual reference. We then have signs of signs. In writing, the words are in this case enclosed in quotation marks. Accordingly, a word standing between quotation marks must not be taken as having its ordinary reference.

In order to speak of the sense of an expression "A" one may simply use the phrase "the sense of the expression 'A.'" In reported speech one talks about the sense, e.g., of another person's remarks. It is quite clear that in this way of speaking words do not have their customary reference but designate what is usually their sense. In order to have a short expression, we will say: In reported speech, words are used *indirectly* or have their *indirect* reference. We distinguish accordingly the customary from the *indirect* reference of a word; and its *customary* sense from its *indirect* sense. The indirect reference of a word is accordingly its customary sense. Such exceptions must always be borne in mind if the mode of connexion between sign, sense, and reference in particular cases is to be correctly understood.

The reference and sense of a sign are to be distinguished from the associated idea. If the reference of a sign is an object perceivable by the senses, my idea of it is an internal image,[5] arising from memories of sense impressions which I have had and acts, both internal and external, which I have performed. Such an idea is often saturated with feeling; the clarity of its separate parts varies and oscillates. The same sense is not always connected, even in the same man, with the same idea. The idea is subjective: one man's idea is not that of another. There result, as a matter of course, a variety of differences in the ideas associated with the same sense. A painter, a horseman, and a zoologist will probably connect different ideas with the name "Bucephalus." This constitutes an essential distinction between the idea and the sign's sense, which may be the common property of many and therefore is not a part of a mode of the individual mind. For one can hardly deny that mankind has a common store of thoughts which is transmitted from one generation to another.[6]

In the light of this, one need have no scruples in speaking simply of the sense, whereas in the case of an idea one must, strictly speaking, add to whom it belongs and at what time. It might perhaps be said: Just as one man connects this idea, and another that idea, and another that idea, with the same word, so also one man can associate this sense and another that sense. But there still remains a difference in the mode of connexion. They are not prevented from grasping the same sense; but they cannot have the same idea. *Si duo idem faciunt, non est idem.* If two persons picture the same thing, each still has his own idea. It is indeed sometimes possible to establish differences in the ideas, or even in the sensations, of different men; but an exact comparison is not possible, because we cannot have both ideas together in the same consciousness.

The reference of a proper name is the object itself which we designate by its means; the idea, which we have in that case, is wholly subjective; in between lies the sense, which is indeed no longer subjective like the idea, but is yet not the object itself. The following analogy will perhaps clarify these relationships. Somebody observes the Moon through a telescope. I compare the Moon itself to the reference: it is the object of the observation, mediated by the real image projected by the object glass in the interior of the telescope, and by the retinal image of the observer. The former I compare to the sense, the latter is like the idea or experience. The optical image in the telescope is indeed one-sided and dependent upon the standpoint of observation; but it is still objective, inasmuch as it can be used by several observers. At any rate it could be arranged for several to use it simultaneously. But each one would have his own retinal image. On account of the diverse shapes of the observers' eyes, even a geometrical congruence could hardly be achieved, and an actual coincidence would be out of the question. This analogy might be developed still further, by assuming A's retinal image made visible to B; or A might also see his own retinal image in a mirror. In this way we might perhaps show how an idea can itself be taken as an object, but as such is not for the observer what it directly is for the person having the idea. But to pursue this would take us too far afield.

We can now recognize three levels of difference between words, expressions, or whole sentences. The difference may concern at most the ideas, or the sense but not the reference, or, finally, the reference as well. With respect to the first level, it is to be noted that, on account of the uncertain connexion of ideas with words, a difference may hold for one person, which another does not find. The difference between a translation and the original text should properly not overstep the first level. To the possible differences here belong also the colouring and shading which poetic eloquence seeks to give to the sense. Such colouring and shading are not objective, and must be evoked by each hearer or reader according to the hints of the poet or the speaker. Without some affinity in human ideas art would certainly be impossible; but it can never be exactly determined how far the intentions of the poet are realized.

In what follows there will be no further discussion of ideas and experience; they have been mentioned here only to ensure that the idea aroused in the hearer by a word shall not be confused with its sense or its reference.

To make short and exact expressions possible, let the following phraseology be established:

A proper name (word, sign, sign combination, expression) *express-es* its sense, *stands for* or *designates* its reference. By means of a sign we express its sense and designate its reference.

Idealists or sceptics will perhaps long since have objected: "You talk, without further ado, of the Moon as an object; but how do you know that the name 'the Moon' has any reference? How do you know that anything whatsoever has a reference?" I reply that when we say "the Moon," we do not intend to speak of our idea of the Moon, nor are we satisfied with the sense alone, but we presuppose a reference. To assume that in the sentence "The Moon is smaller than the Earth" the idea of the Moon is in question, would be flatly to misunderstand the sense. If this is what the speaker wanted, he would use the phrase "my idea of the Moon." Now we can of course be mistaken in the presupposition, and such mistakes have indeed occurred. But the question whether the presupposition is perhaps always mistaken need not be answered here; in order to justify mention of the reference of a sign it is enough, at first, to point out our intention in speaking or thinking. (We must then add the reservation: provided such reference exists.)

So far we have considered the sense and reference only of such expressions, words, or signs as we have called proper names. We now inquire concerning the sense and reference for an entire declarative sentence. Such a sentence contains a thought.[7] Is this thought, now, to be regarded as its sense or its reference? Let us assume for the time being that the sentence has reference. If we now replace one word of the sentence by another having the same reference, but a different sense, this can have no bearing upon the reference of the sentence. Yet we can see that in such a case the thought changes; since, e.g., the thought in the sentence "The morning star is a body illuminated by the Sun" differs from that in the sentence "The evening star is a body illuminated by the Sun." Anybody who did not know that the evening star is the morning star might hold the one thought to be true, the other false. The thought, accordingly, cannot be the reference of the sentence, but must rather be considered as the sense. What is the position now with regard to the reference? Have we a right even to inquire about it? Is it possible that a sentence as a whole has only a sense, but no reference? At any rate, one might expect that such sentences occur, just as there are parts of sentences having sense but no reference. And sentences which contain proper names without reference will be of this kind. The sentence "Odysseus was set ashore at Ithaca while sound asleep" obviously has a sense. But since it is doubtful whether the name "Odysseus," occurring therein, has reference, it is also doubtful whether the whole sentence has one. Yet it is certain, nevertheless, that anyone who seriously took the sentence to be true or false would ascribe to the name "Odysseus" a reference, not merely a sense; for it is of the reference of the name that the predicate is affirmed or denied. Whoever does not admit the name has reference can neither apply nor withhold the predicate. But in that case it would be super-fluous to advance to the reference of the name; one could be satisfied with the sense, if one wanted to go no further than the thought. If it were a ques-tion only of the sense of the sentence, the thought, it would be unnecessary to bother with the reference of a part of the sentence; only the sense, not the reference, of the part is relevant to the sense of the whole sentence. The thought remains the same whether "Odysseus" has reference or not. The fact that we concern ourselves at all about the reference of a part of the sen-tence indicates that we generally recognize and expect a reference for the sentence itself. The thought loses value for us as soon as we recognize that the reference of one of its parts is missing. We are therefore justified in not being satisfied with the sense of a sentence, and in inquiring also as to its reference. But now why do we want every proper name to have not only a sense, but also a reference? Why is the thought not enough for us? Because, and to the extent that, we are concerned with its truth value. This is not always the case. In hearing an epic poem, for instance, apart from the euphony of the language we are interested only in the sense of the sentences and the images and feelings thereby aroused. The question of truth would cause us to abandon aesthetic delight for an attitude of scientific investiga-tion. Hence it is a matter of no concern to us whether the name "Odysseus," for instance, has reference, so long as we accept the poem as a work of art.[8] It is the striving for truth that drives us always to advance from the sense to the reference.

We have seen that the reference of a sentence may always be sought, whenever the reference of its components is involved; and that this is the case when and only when we are inquiring after the truth value.

We are therefore driven into accepting the *truth value* of a sentence as constituting its reference. By the truth value of a sentence I understand the circumstance that it is true or false. There are no further truth values. For brevity I call the one the True, the other the False. Every declarative sentence concerned with the reference of its words is therefore to be regard-ed as a proper name, and its reference, if it has one, is either the True or the False. These two objects are recognized, if only implicitly, by everybody who judges something to be true – and so even by a sceptic. The designation of the truth values as objects may appear to be an arbitrary fancy or perhaps a mere play upon words, from which no profound consequences could be drawn. What I mean by an object can be more exactly discussed only in connexion with concept and relation. I will reserve this for another article.[9] But so much should already be clear, that in every judgment,[10] no matter how trivial, the step from the level of thoughts to the level of reference (the objective) has already been taken.

One might be tempted to regard the relation of the thought to the True not as that of sense to reference, but rather as that of subject to predicate. One can, indeed, say: "The thought, that 5 is a prime number, is true." But closer examination shows that nothing more has been said than in the simple sentence "5 is a prime number." The truth claim arises in each from the form of the declarative sentence, and when the latter lacks its usual force, e.g., in the mouth of an actor upon the stage, even the sentence "The thought that 5 is a prime number is true" contains only a thought, and indeed the same thought as the simple "5 is a prime number." It follows that the relation of the thought to the True may not be compared with that of subject to predicate. Subject and predicate (understood in the logical sense) are indeed elements of thought; they stand on the same level for knowledge. By combining subject and predicate, one reaches only a thought, never passes from sense to reference, never from a thought to its truth value. One moves at the same level but never advances from one level to the next. A truth value cannot be a part of a thought, any more than, say, the Sun can, for it is not a sense but an object.

If our supposition that the reference of a sentence is its truth value is correct, the latter must remain unchanged when a part of the sentence is replaced by an expression having the same reference. And this is in fact the case. Leibniz gives the definition: "*Eadem sunt, quae sibi mutuo substitui possunt, salva veritate.*" What else but the truth value could be found, that belongs quite generally to every sentence if the reference of its components is relevant, and remains unchanged by substitutions of the kind in question?

If now the truth value of a sentence is its reference, then on the one hand all true sentences have the same reference and so, on the other hand, do all false sentences. From this we see that in the reference of the sentence all that is specific is obliterated. We can never be concerned only with the reference of a sentence; but again the mere thought alone yields no knowledge, but only the thought together with its reference, i.e. its truth value. Judgments can be regarded as advances from a thought to a truth value. Naturally this cannot be a definition. Judgment is something quite peculiar and incomparable. One might also say that judgments are distinctions of parts within truth values. Such distinction occurs by a return to the thought. To every sense belonging to a truth value there would correspond its own manner of analysis. However, I have here used the word "part" in a special sense. I have in fact transferred the relation between the parts and the whole of the sentence to its reference, by calling the reference of a word part of the reference of the sentence, if the word itself is a part of the sentence. This way of speaking can certainly be attacked, because the whole reference and one part of it do not suffice to determine the remainder, and because the word "part" is already used in another sense of bodies. A special term would need to be invented.

The supposition that the truth value of a sentence is its reference shall now be put to further test. We have found that the truth value of a sentence remains unchanged when an expression is replaced by another having the same reference: but we have not yet considered the case in which the expression to be replaced is itself a sentence. Now if our view is correct, the truth value of a sentence containing another as part must remain unchanged when the part is replaced by another sentence having the same truth value. Exceptions are to be expected when the whole sentence or its part is direct or indirect quotation; for in such cases, as we have seen, the words do not have their customary reference. In direct quotation, a sentence designates another sentence, and in indirect quotation a thought.

We are thus led to consider subordinate sentences or clauses. These occur as parts of a sentence complex, which is, from the logical standpoint, likewise a sentence – a main sentence. But here we meet the question whether it is also true of the subordinate sentence that its reference is a truth value. Of indirect quotation we already know the opposite. Grammarians view subordinate clauses as representatives of parts of sentences and divide them accordingly into noun clauses, adjective clauses, adverbial clauses. This might generate the supposition that the reference of a subordinate clause was not a truth value but rather of the same kind as the reference of a noun or adjective or adverb – in short, of a part of a sentence, whose sense was not a thought but only a part of a thought. Only a more thorough investigation can clarify the issue. In so doing, we shall not follow the grammatical categories strictly, but rather group together what is logically of the same kind. Let us first search for cases in which the sense of the subordinate clause, as we have just supposed, is not an independent thought.

The case of an abstract[11] noun clause, introduced by "that," includes the case of indirect quotation, in which we have seen the words to have their indirect reference coinciding with what is customarily their sense. In this case, then, the subordinate clause has for its reference a thought, not a truth value; as sense not a thought, but the sense of the words "the thought, that ...," which is only a part of the thought in the entire complex sentence. This happens after "say," "hear," "be of the opinion," "be convinced," "conclude," and similar words.[12] There is a different, and indeed somewhat complicated, situation after words like "perceive," "know," "fancy," which are to be considered later.

That in the cases of the first kind the reference of the subordinate clause is in fact the thought can also be recognized by seeing that it is indifferent to the truth of the whole whether the subordinate clause is true or false. Let us compare, for instance, the two sentences "Copernicus believed that the planetary orbits are circles" and "Copernicus believed that the apparent motion of the Sun is produced by the real motion of the Earth."

One subordinate clause can be substituted for the other without harm to the truth. The main clause and the subordinate clause together have as their sense only a single thought, and the truth of the whole includes neither the truth not the untruth of the subordinate clause. In such cases it is not permissible to replace one expression in the subordinate clause by another having the same customary reference, but only by one having the same indirect reference, i.e. the same customary sense. If somebody were to conclude: The reference of a sentence is not its truth value for in that case it could always be replaced by another sentence of the same truth value; he would prove too much; one might just as well claim that the reference of "morning star" is not Venus, since one may not always say "Venus" in place of "morning star." One has the right to conclude only that the reference of a sentence is not *always* its truth value, and that "morning star" does not always stand for the planet Venus, viz. when the word has its indirect reference. An exception of such a kind occurs in the subordinate clause just considered which has a thought as its reference.

If one says "It seems that ..." one means "It seems to me that ..." or "I think that...." We therefore have the same case again. The situation is similar in the case of expressions such as "to be pleased," "to regret," "to approve," "to blame," "to hope," "to fear." If, toward the end of the battle of Waterloo,[13] Wellington was glad that the Prussians were coming, the basis for his joy was a conviction. Had he been deceived, he would have been no less pleased so long as his illusion lasted; and before he became so convinced he could not have been pleased that the Prussians were coming – even though in fact they might have been already approaching.

Just as a conviction or a belief is the ground of a feeling, it can, as in inference, also be the ground of a conviction. In the sentence: "Columbus inferred from the roundness of the Earth that he could reach India by travelling towards the west," we have as the reference of the parts two thoughts, that the Earth is round, and that Columbus by travelling to the west could reach India. All that is relevant here is that Columbus was convinced of both, and that the one conviction was a ground for the other. Whether the Earth is really round, and whether Columbus could really reach India by travelling to the west, are immaterial to the truth of our sentence; but it is not immaterial whether we replace "the Earth" by "the planet which is accompanied by a moon whose diameter is greater than the fourth part of its own." Here also we have the indirect reference of the words.

Adverbial final clauses beginning "in order that" also belong here; for obviously the purpose is a thought; therefore: indirect reference for the words, subjunctive mood.

A subordinate clause with "that" after "command," "ask," "forbid," would appear in direct speech as an imperative. Such a clause has no reference but only a sense. A command, a request, are indeed not thoughts, yet they stand on the same level as thoughts. Hence in subordinate clauses depending upon "command," "ask," etc. words have their indirect reference. The reference of such a clause is therefore not a truth value but a command, a request, and so forth.

The case is similar for the dependent question in phrases such as "doubt whether," "not to know what." It is easy to see that here also the words are to be taken to have their indirect reference. Dependent clauses expressing questions and beginning with "who," "what," "where," "when," "how," "by what means," etc., seem at times to approximate very closely to adverbial clauses in which words have their customary references. These cases are distinguished linguistically [in German] by the mood of the verb. With the subjunctive, we have a dependent question and indirect reference of the words, so that a proper name cannot in general be replaced by another name of the same object.

In the cases so far considered the words of the subordinate clauses had their indirect reference, and this made it clear that the reference of the subordinate clause itself was indirect, i.e. not a truth value but a thought, a command, a request, a question. The subordinate clause could be regarded as a noun, indeed one could say: as a proper name of that thought, that command, etc., which it represented in the context of the sentence structure.

We now come to other subordinate clauses, in which the words do have their customary reference without however a thought occurring as sense and a truth value as reference. How this is possible is best made clear by examples.

Whoever discovered the elliptic form of the planetary orbits died in misery.

If the sense of the subordinate clause were here a thought, it would have to be possible to express it also in a separate sentence. But this does not work, because the grammatical subject "whoever" has no independent sense and only mediates the relation with the consequent clause "died in misery." For this reason the sense of the subordinate clause is not a complete thought, and its reference is Kepler, not a truth value. One might object that the sense of the whole does contain a thought as part, viz. that there was somebody who first discovered the elliptic form of the planetary orbits; for whoever takes the whole to be true cannot deny this part. This is undoubtedly so; but only because otherwise the dependent clause "whoever discovered the elliptic form of the planetary orbits" would have no reference. If anything is asserted there is always an obvious presupposition that the simple or compound proper names used have reference. If one therefore asserts "Kepler died in misery," there is a presupposition that the name "Kepler" designates something; but it does not follow that the sense of the sentence "Kepler died in misery" contains the thought that the name "Kepler" designates something. If this were the case the negation would have to run not

> Kepler did not die in misery

but

> Kepler did not die in misery, or the name "Kepler" has no reference.

That the name "Kepler" designates something is just as much a pre-supposition for the assertion

> Kepler died in misery

as for the contrary assertion. Now languages have the fault of containing expressions which fail to designate an object (although their grammatical form seems to qualify them for that purpose) because the truth of some sentences is a prerequisite. Thus it depends on the truth of the sentence:

> There was someone who discovered the elliptic form of the planetary orbits

whether the subordinate clause

> Whoever discovered the elliptic form of the planetary orbits

really designates an object or only seems to do so while having in fact no reference. And thus it may appear as if our subordinate clause contained as a part of its sense the thought that there was somebody who discovered the elliptic form of the planetary orbits. If this were right the negation would run:

> Either whoever discovered the elliptic form of the planetary orbits did not die in misery or there was nobody who discovered the elliptic form of the planetary orbits.

This arises from an imperfection of language, from which even the symbolic language of mathematical analysis is not altogether free; even there combinations of symbols can occur that seem to stand for something but have (at least so far) no reference, e.g. divergent infinite series. This can be avoided, e.g., by means of the special stipulation that divergent infinite series shall stand for the number 0. A logically perfect language. (*Begriffsschrift*) should satisfy the conditions, that every expression grammatically well constructed as a proper name out of signs already introduced shall in fact designate an object, and that no new sign shall be introduced as a proper name without being secured a reference. The logic books contain warnings against logical mistakes arising from the ambiguity of expressions. I regard as no less pertinent a warning against apparent proper names having no reference. The history of mathematics supplies errors which have arisen in this way. This lends itself to demagogic abuse as easily as ambiguity – perhaps more easily. "The will of the people" can serve as an example; for it is easy to establish that there is at any rate no generally accepted reference for this expression. It is therefore by no means unimportant to eliminate the source of these mistakes, at least in science, once and for all. Then such objections as the one discussed above would become impossible, because it could never depend upon the truth of a thought whether a proper name had a reference.

With the consideration of these noun clauses may be coupled that of types of adjective and adverbial clauses which are logically in close relation to them.

Adjective clauses also serve to construct compound proper names, though, unlike noun clauses, they are not sufficient by themselves for this purpose. These adjective clauses are to be regarded as equivalent to adjectives. Instead of "the square root of 4 which is smaller than 0," one can also say "the negative square root of 4." We have here the case of a compound proper name constructed from the expression for a concept with the help of the singular definite article. This is at any rate permissible if the concept applies to one and only one single object.[14]

Expressions for concepts can be so constructed that marks of a concept are given by adjective clauses as, in our example, by the clause "which is smaller than 0." It is evident that such an adjective clause cannot have a thought as sense or a truth value as reference, any more than the noun clause could. Its sense, which can also be expressed in many cases by a single adjective, is only a part of a thought. Here, as in the case of the noun clause, there is no independent subject and therefore no possibility of reproducing the sense of the subordinate clause in an independent sentence.

Places, instants, stretches of time, are, logically considered, objects; hence the linguistic designation of a definite place, a definite instant, or a stretch of time is to be regarded as a proper name. Now adverbial clauses of place and time can be used for the construction of such a proper name in a manner similar to that which we have seen in the case of noun and adjective clauses. In the same way, expressions for concepts bringing in places, etc., can be constructed. It is to be noted here also that the sense of these subordinate clauses cannot be reproduced in an independent sentence, since an essential component viz. the determination of place or time, is missing and is only indicated by a relative pronoun or a conjunction.[15]

In conditional clauses, also, there may usually be recognized to occur an indefinite indicator, having a similar correlate in the dependent clause. (We have already seen this occur in noun, adjective, and adverbial clauses.) In so far as each indicator refers to the other, both clauses together form a connected whole, which as a rule expresses only a single thought. In the sentence

> If a number is less than 1 and greater than 0, its square is less than 1 and greater than 0

the component in question is "a number" in the conditional clause and "its" in the dependent clause. It is by means of this very indefiniteness that the sense acquires the generality expected of a law. It is this which is responsible for the fact that the antecedent clause alone has no complete thought as its sense and in combination with the consequent clause expresses one and only one thought, whose parts are no longer thoughts. It is, in general, incorrect to say that in the hypothetical judgment two judgments are put in reciprocal relationship. If this or something similar is said, the word "judgment" is used in the same sense as I have connected with the word "thought," so that I would use the formulation: "A hypothetical thought establishes a reciprocal relationship between two thoughts." This could be true only if an indefinite indicator is absent;[16] but in such a case there would also be no generality.

If an instant of time is to be indefinitely indicated in both conditional and dependent clauses, this is often achieved merely by using the present tense of the verb, which in such a case however does not indicate the temporal present. This grammatical form is then the indefinite indicator in the main and subordinate clauses. An example of this is: "When the Sun is in the tropic of Cancer, the longest day in the northern hemisphere occurs." Here, also, it is impossible to express the sense of the subordinate clause in a full sentence, because this sense is not a complete thought. If we say: "The Sun is in the tropic of Cancer," this would refer to our present time and thereby change the sense. Just as little is the sense of the main clause a thought; only the whole, composed of main and subordinate clauses, has such a sense. It may be added that several common components in the antecedent and consequent clauses may be indefinitely indicated.

It is clear that noun clauses with "who" or "what" and adverbial clauses with "where," "when," "wherever," "whenever" are often to be interpreted as having the sense of conditional clauses, e.g. "who touches pitch, defiles himself."

Adjective clauses can also take the place of conditional clauses. Thus the sense of the sentence previously used can be given in the form "The square of a number which is less than 1 and greater than 0 is less than 1 and greater than 0."

The situation is quite different if the common component of the two clauses is designated by a proper name. In the sentence:

Napoleon, who recognized the danger to his right flank, himself led his guards against the enemy position

two thoughts are expressed:

1. Napoleon recognized the danger to his right flank
2. Napoleon himself led his guards against the enemy position.

When and where this happened is to be fixed only by the context, but is nevertheless to be taken as definitely determined thereby. If the entire sentence is uttered as an assertion, we thereby simultaneously assert both component sentences. If one of the parts is false, the whole is false. Here we have the case that the subordinate clause by itself has a complete thought as sense (if we complete it by indication of place and time). The reference of the subordinate clause is accordingly a truth value. We can therefore expect that it may be replaced, without harm to the truth value of the whole, by a sentence having the same truth value. This is indeed the case; but it is to be noticed that for purely grammatical reasons, its subject must be "Napoleon," for only then can it be brought into the form of an adjective clause belonging to "Napoleon." But if the demand that it be expressed in this form be waived, and the connexion be shown by "and," this restriction disappears.

Subsidiary clauses beginning with "although" also express complete thoughts. This conjunction actually has no sense and does not change the sense of the clause but only illuminates it in a peculiar fashion.[17] We could indeed replace the conditional clause without harm to the truth of the whole by another of the same truth value; but the light in which the clause is placed by the conjunction might then easily appear unsuitable, as if a song with a sad subject were to be sung in a lively fashion.

In the last cases the truth of the whole included the truth of the component clauses. The case is different if a conditional clause expresses a complete thought by containing, in place of an indefinite indicator, a proper name or something which is to be regarded as equivalent. In the sentence

If the Sun has already risen, the sky is very cloudy

the time is the present, that is to say, definite. And the place is also to be thought of as definite. Here it can be said that a relation between the truth values of conditional and dependent clauses has been asserted, viz. such that the case does not occur in which the antecedent stands for the True and the consequent for the False. Accordingly, our sentence is true if the Sun has not yet risen, whether the sky is very cloudy or not, and also if the Sun has risen and the sky is very cloudy. Since only truth values are here in question, each component clause can be replaced by another of the same truth value without changing the truth value of the whole. To be sure, the light in which the subject then appears would usually be unsuitable; the thought might easily seem distorted; but this has nothing to do with its truth value. One must always take care not to clash with the subsidiary thoughts, which are however not explicitly expressed and therefore should not be reckoned in the sense. Hence, also, no account need be taken of their truth values.[18]

The simpler cases have now been discussed. Let us review what we have learned.

The subordinate clause usually has for its sense not a thought, but only a part of one, and consequently no truth value as reference. The reason for this is either that the words in the subordinate clause have indirect reference, so that the reference, not the sense, of the subordinate clause is a thought; or else that, on account of the presence of an indefinite indicator, the subordinate clause is incomplete and expresses a thought only when combined with the main clause. It may happen, however, that the sense of the subsidiary clause is a complete thought, in which case it can be replaced by another of the same truth value without harm to the truth of the whole – provided there are no grammatical obstacles.

An examination of all the subordinate clauses which one may encounter will soon provide some which do not fit well into these categories. The reason, so far as I can see, is that these subordinate clauses have no such simple sense. Almost always, it seems, we connect with the main thoughts expressed by us subsidiary thoughts which, although not expressed, are associated with our words, in accordance with psychological laws, by the hearer. And since the subsidiary thought appears to be connected with our words of its own accord, almost like the main thought itself, we want it also to be expressed. The sense of the sentence is thereby enriched, and it may well happen that we have more simple thoughts than clauses. In many cases the sentence must be understood in this way, in others it may be doubtful whether the subsidiary thought belongs to the sense of the sentence or only accompanies it.[19] One might perhaps find that the sentence

Napoleon, who recognized the danger to his right flank, himself led his guards against the enemy position expresses not only the two thoughts shown above, but also the thought that the knowledge of the danger was the reason why he led the guards against the enemy position. One may in fact doubt whether this thought is merely slightly suggested or really expressed. Let the question be considered whether our sentence be false if Napoleon's decision had already been made before he recognized the danger. If our sentence could be true in spite of this, the subsidiary thought should not be understood as part of the sense. One would probably decide in favour of this. The alternative would make for a quite complicated situation: We would have more simple thoughts than clauses. If the sentence

Napoleon recognized the danger to his right flank

were now to be replaced by another having the same truth value, e.g.

Napoleon was already more than 45 years old

not only would our first thought be changed, but also our third one. Hence the truth value of the latter might change – viz. if his age was not the reason for the decision to lead the guards against the enemy. This shows why clauses of equal truth value cannot always be substituted for one another in such cases. The clause expresses more through its connexion with another than it does in isolation.

Let us now consider cases where this regularly happens. In the sentence:

Bebel mistakenly supposes that the return of Alsace-Lorraine would appease France's desire for revenge

two thoughts are expressed, which are not however shown by means of antecedent and consequent clauses, viz.:

(1) Bebel believes that the return of Alsace-Lorraine would appease France's desire for revenge
(2) the return of Alsace-Lorraine would not appease France's desire for revenge

In the expression of the first thought, the words of the subordinate clause have then indirect reference, while the same words have their customary reference in the expression of the second thought. This shows that the subordinate clause in our original complex sentence is to be taken twice over, with different reference, standing once for a thought, once for a truth value. Since the truth value is not the whole reference of the subordinate clause, we cannot simply replace the latter by another of equal truth value. Similar considerations apply to expressions such as "know," "discover," "it is known that."

By means of a subordinate causal clause and the associated main clause we express several thoughts, which however do not correspond separately to the original clauses. In the sentence: "Because ice is less dense than water, it floats on water" we have

1. Ice is less dense than water;
2. If anything is less dense than water, it floats on water;
3. Ice floats on water.

The third thought, however, need not be explicitly introduced, since it is contained in the remaining two. On the other hand, neither the first and third nor the second and third combined would furnish the sense of our sentence. It can now be seen that our subordinate clause

because ice is less dense than water

expresses our first thought, as well as a part of our second. This is how it comes to pass that our subsidiary clause cannot be simply replaced by another of equal truth value, for this would alter our second thought and thereby might well alter its truth value.

The situation is similar in the sentence

If iron were less dense than water, it would float on water.

Here we have the two thoughts that iron is not less dense than water, and that something floats on water if it is less dense than water. The subsidiary clause again expresses one thought and a part of the other.

If we interpret the sentence already considered

After Schleswig-Holstein was separated from Denmark, Prussia and Austria quarrelled

in such a way that it expresses the thought that Schleswig-Holstein was once separated from Denmark, we have first this thought, and secondly the thought that at a time, more closely determined by the subordinate clause, Prussia and Austria quarrelled. Here also the subordinate clause expresses not only one thought but also a part of another. Therefore it may not in general be replaced by another of the same truth value.

It is hard to exhaust all the possibilities given by language; but I hope to have brought to light at least the essential reasons why a subordinate clause may not always be replaced by another of equal truth value without harm to the truth of the whole sentence structure. These reasons arise:

1. when the subordinate clause does not stand for a truth value, inasmuch as it expresses only a part of a thought;
2. when the subordinate clause does stand for a truth value but is not restricted to so doing, inasmuch as its sense includes one thought and part of another.

The first case arises:

1. in indirect reference of words
2. if a part of the sentence is only an indefinite indicator instead of a proper name.

In the second case, the subsidiary clause may have to be taken twice over, viz. once in its customary reference, and the other time in indirect reference; or the sense of a part of the subordinate clause may likewise be a component of another thought, which, taken together with the thought directly expressed by the subordinate clause, makes up the sense of the whole sentence.

It follows with sufficient probability from the foregoing that the cases where a subordinate clause is not replaceable by another of the same value cannot be brought in disproof of our view that a truth value is the reference of a sentence having a thought as its sense.

Let us return to our starting point.

When we found "$a = a$" and "$a = b$" to have different cognitive values, the explanation is that for the purpose of knowledge, the sense of the sentence, viz., the thought expressed by it, is no less relevant than its reference, i.e. its truth value. If now $a = b$, then indeed the reference of "b" is the same as that of "a," and hence the truth value of "$a = b$" is the same as that of "$a = a$." In spite of this, the sense of "b" may differ from that of "a", and thereby the sense expressed in "$a = b$" differs from that of "$a = a$." In that case the two sentences do not have the same cognitive value. If we understand by "judgment" the advance from the thought to its truth value, as in the above paper, we can also say that the judgments are different.

NOTES

1. I use this word strictly and understand "$a = b$" to have the sense of "a is the same as b" or "a and b coincide."

2. Trans. note: The reference is to Frege's *Begriffsschrift, eine der arithmetischen nachge-bildete Formelsprache des reinen Denkens* (Halle, 1879).

3. Trans. Note: See his "Ueber Begriff und Gegenstand," *Vierteljahrsschrift für wissenschaftliche Philosophie*, 16 (1892), 192-205.

4. In the case of an actual proper name such as "Aristotle" opinions as to the sense may differ. It might, for instance, be taken to be the following: the pupil of Plato and teacher of Alexander the Great. Anybody who does this will attach another sense to the sentence "Aristotle was born in Stagira" than will a man who takes as the sense of the name: the teacher of Alexander the Great who was born in Stagira. So long as the reference remains the same, such variations of sense may be tolerated, although they are to be avoided in the theoretical structure of a demonstrative science and ought not to occur in a perfect language.

5. We can include with ideas the direct experiences in which sense-impressions and acts themselves take the place of the traces which they have left in the mind. The distinction is unimportant for our purpose, especially since memories of sense-impressions and acts always help to complete the perceptual image. One can also understand direct experience as including any object, in so far as it is sensibly perceptible or spatial.

6. Hence it is inadvisable to use the word "idea" to designate something so basically different.

7. By a thought I understand not the subjective performance of thinking but its objective content, which is capable of being the common property of several thinkers.

8. It would be desirable to have a special term for signs having only sense. If we name them, say, representations, the words of the actors on the stage would be representations; indeed the actor himself would be a representation.

9. Trans. note: See his "Ueber Begriff und Gegenstand," *Vierteljahrsschrift für wissenschaftliche Philosophie*, 16 (1892), 192-205.

10. A judgment, for me is not the mere comprehension of a thought, but the admission of its truth.

11. Trans. note: A literal translation of Frege's "abstracten Nennsätzen" whose meaning eludes me.

12. In "A lied in saying he had seen B," the subordinate clause designates a thought which is said (1) to have been asserted by A (2) while A was convinced of its falsity.

13. Trans. note: Frege uses the Prussian name for the battle – "Belle Alliance."

14. In accordance with what was said above, an expression of the kind in question must actually always be assured of reference, by means of a special stipulation, e.g. by the convention that 0 shall count as its reference, when the concept applies to no object or to more than one.

15. In the case of these sentences, various interpretations are easily possible. The sense of the sentence, "After Schleswig-Holstein was separated from Denmark, Prussia and Austria quarrelled" can also be rendered in the form "After the separation of Schleswig-Holstein from Denmark, Prussia and Austria quarrelled." In this version, it is surely sufficiently clear that the sense is not to be taken as having as a part the thought that Schleswig-Holstein was once separated from Denmark, but that this is the necessary presupposition in order for the expression "after the separation of Schleswig-Holstein from Denmark" to have any reference at all. To be sure, our sentence can also be interpreted as saying that Schleswig-Holstein was once separated from Denmark. We then have a case which is to be considered later. In order to understand the difference more clearly, let us project ourselves into the mind of a Chinese who, having little knowledge of European history, believes it to be false that Schleswig-Holstein was ever separated from Denmark. He will take our sentence, in the first version, to be neither true nor false but will deny it to have any reference, on the ground of absence of reference for its subordinate clause. This clause would only apparently determine a time. If he interpreted our sentence in the second way, however, he would find a thought expressed in it which he would take to be false, beside a part which would be without reference for him.

16. At times an explicit linguistic indication is missing and must be read off from the entire context.

17. Similarly in the case of "but," "yet."

18. The thought of our sentence might also be expressed thus; "Either the Sun has not risen yet or the sky is very cloudy" – which shows how this kind of sentence connexion is to be understood.

19. This may be important for the question whether an assertion is a lie, or an oath a perjury.

DESCRIPTIONS

Bertrand Russell

We dealt in the preceding chapter with the words *all* and *some*; in this chapter we shall consider the word *the* in the singular, and in the next chapter we shall consider the word *the* in the plural. It may be thought excessive to devote two chapters to one word, but to the philosophical mathematician it is a word of very great importance: like Browning's Grammarian with the enclitic δε, I would give the doctrine of this word if I were "dead from the waist down" and not merely in a prison.

We have already had occasion to mention "descriptive functions," i.e. such expressions as "the father of *x*" or "the sine of *x*." These are to be defined by first defining "descriptions."

A "description" may be of two sorts, definite and indefinite (or ambiguous). An indefinite description is a phrase of the form "a so-and-so," and a definite description is a phrase of the form "the so-and-so," (in the singular). Let us begin with the former.

"Who did you meet?" "I met a man." "That is a very indefinite description." We are therefore not departing from usage in our terminology. Our question is: What do I really assert when I assert "I met a man"? Let us assume, for the moment, that my assertion is true, and that in fact I met Jones. It is clear that what I assert is *not* "I met Jones." I may say "I met a man, but it was not Jones"; in that case, though I lie, I do not contradict myself, as I should do if when I say I met a man I really mean that I met Jones. It is clear also that the person to whom I am speaking can understand what I say, even if he is a foreigner and has never heard of Jones.

But we may go further: not only Jones, but no actual man, enters into my statement. This becomes obvious when the statement is false, since then there is no more reason why Jones should be supposed to enter into the proposition than why anyone else should. Indeed the statement would remain significant, though it could not possibly be true, even if there were

no man at all. "I met a unicorn" or "I met a sea-serpent" is a perfectly significant assertion, if we know what it would be to be a unicorn or a sea-serpent, i.e. what is the definition of these fabulous monsters. Thus it is only
what we may call the *concept* that enters into the proposition. In the case of
"unicorn," for example, there is only the concept: there is not also, somewhere among the shades, something unreal which may be called "a unicorn." Therefore, since it is significant (though false) to say "I met a unicorn," it is clear that this proposition, rightly analyzed, does not contain a
constituent "a unicorn," though it does contain the concept "unicorn."

The question of "unreality," which confronts us at this point, is a
very important one. Misled by grammar, the great majority of those logicians who have dealt with this question have dealt with it on mistaken
lines. They have regarded grammatical form as a surer guide in analysis
than, in fact, it is. And they have not known what differences in grammatical form are important. "I met Jones" and "I met a man" would count traditionally as propositions of the same form, but in actual fact they are of
quite different forms: the first names an actual person, Jones; while the second involves a propositional function, and becomes, when made explicit:
"The function 'I met x and x is human' is sometimes true." (It will be
remembered that we adopted the convention of using "sometimes" as not
implying more than once.) This proposition is obviously not of the form "I
met x," which accounts for the existence of the proposition "I met a unicorn" in spite of the fact that there is no such thing as "a unicorn."

For want of the apparatus of propositional functions, many logicians have been driven to the conclusion that there are unreal objects. It is
argued, e.g. by Meinong,[1] that we can speak about "the golden mountain,"
"the round square," and so on; we can make true propositions of which these
are the subjects; hence they must have some kind of logical being, since
otherwise the propositions in which they occur would be meaningless. In
such theories, it seems to me, there is a failure of that feeling for reality
which ought to be preserved even in the most abstract studies. Logic, I
should maintain, must no more admit a unicorn than zoology can; for logic
is concerned with the real world just as truly as zoology, though with its
more abstract and general features. To say that unicorns have an existence
in heraldry, or in literature, or in imagination, is a most pitiful and paltry
evasion. What exists in heraldry is not an animal, made of flesh and blood,
moving and breathing of its own initiative. What exists is a picture, or a
description in words. Similarly, to maintain that Hamlet, for example, exists
in his own world namely, in the world of Shakespeare's imagination, just as
truly as (say) Napoleon existed in the ordinary world, is to say something
deliberately confusing, or else confused to a degree which is scarcely credi-
ble. There is only one world, the "real" world: Shakespeare's imagination is
part of it, and the thoughts that he had in writing Hamlet are real. So are

the thoughts that we have in reading the play. But it is of the very essence of fiction that only the thoughts, feelings, etc., in Shakespeare and his readers are real, and that there is not, in addition to them, an objective Hamlet. When you have taken account the feelings roused by Napoleon in writers and readers of history, you have not touched the actual man; but in the case of Hamlet you have come to the end of him. If no one thought about Hamlet, there would be nothing left of him; if no one had thought about Napoleon, he would have soon seen to it that some one did. The sense of reality is vital in logic, and whoever juggles with it by pretending that Hamlet has another kind of reality is doing a disservice to thought. A robust sense of reality is very necessary in framing a correct analysis of propositions about unicorns, golden mountains, round squares, and other such pseudo-objects.

In obedience to the feeling of reality, we shall insist that, in the analysis of propositions, nothing "unreal" is to be admitted. But, after all, if there *is* nothing unreal, how, it may be asked, *could* we admit anything unreal? The reply is that, in dealing with propositions, we are dealing in the first instance with symbols, and if we attribute significance to groups of symbols which have no significance, we shall fall into the error of admitting unrealities, in the only sense in which this is possible, namely, as objects described. In the proposition "I met a unicorn," the whole four words together make a significant proposition, and the word "unicorn" by itself is significant, in just the same sense as the word "man." But the *two* words "a unicorn" do not form a subordinate group having a meaning of its own. Thus if we falsely attribute meaning to these two words, we find ourselves saddled with "a unicorn," and with the problem how there can be such a thing in a world where there are no unicorns. "A unicorn" is an indefinite description which describes nothing. It is not an indefinite description which describes something unreal. Such a proposition as "*x* is unreal" only has meaning when "*x*" is a description, definite or indefinite; in that case the proposition will be true if "*x*" is a description which describes nothing. But whether the description "*x*" describes something or describes nothing, it is in any case not a constituent of the proposition in which it occurs; like "a unicorn" just now, it is not a subordinate group having a meaning of its own. All this results from the fact that, when "*x*" is a description, "*x* is unreal" or "*x* does not exist" is not nonsense, but is always significant and sometimes true.

We may now proceed to define generally the meaning of propositions which contain ambiguous descriptions. Suppose we wish to make some statement about "a so-and-so," where "so-and-so's" are those objects that have a certain property ϕ, i.e. those objects x for which the propositional function ϕx is true. (E.g. if we take "a man" as our instance of "a so-and-so," ϕx will be "x is human.") Let us now wish to assert the property ψ

of "a so-and-so," i.e. we wish to assert that "a so-and-so" has that property which x has when ψx is true. (E.g. in the case of "I met a man," ψx will be "I met x.") Now the proposition that "a so-and-so" has the property ψ is not a proposition of the form "ψx." If it were, "a so-and-so" would have to be identical with x for a suitable x; and although (in a sense) this may be true in some cases, it is certainly not true in such a case as "a unicorn." It is just this fact, that the statement that a so-and-so has the property ψ is not of the form ψx, which makes it possible for "a so-and-so" to be, in a certain clearly definable sense, "unreal." The definition is as follows:

> The statement that "an object having the property ø has the property ψ"

means:

> "The joint assertion of $øx$ and ψx is not always false."

So far as logic goes, this is the same proposition as might be expressed by "some ø's are ψ's"; but rhetorically there is a difference, because in the one case there is a suggestion of singularity, and in the other case of plurality. This, however, is not the important point. The important point is that, when rightly analyzed, propositions verbally about "a so-and-so" are found to contain no constituent represented by this phrase. And that is why such propositions can be significant even when there is no such thing as a so-and-so.

The definition of *existence*, as applied to ambiguous descriptions, results from what was said at the end of the preceding chapter [chapter 15 of *Introduction to Mathematical Philosophy*]. We say that "men exist" or "a man exists" if the propositional function "x is human" is sometimes true; and generally "a so-and-so" exists if "x is so-and-so" is sometimes true. We may put this in other language. The proposition "Socrates is a man" is no doubt equivalent to "Socrates is human," but it is not the very same proposition. The *is* of "Socrates is human" expresses the relation of subject and predicate; the *is* of "Socrates is a man" expresses identity. It is a disgrace to the human race that it has chosen to employ the same word "is" for these two entirely different ideas – a disgrace which a symbolic logical language of course remedies. The identity in "Socrates is a man" is identity between an object named (accepting "Socrates" as a name, subject to qualifications explained later) and an object ambiguously described. An object ambiguously described will "exist" when at least one such proposition is true, i.e. when there is at least one true proposition of the form "x is a so-and-so," where "x" is a name. It is characteristic of ambiguous (as opposed to definite) descriptions that there may be any number of true propositions of the above form – Socrates is a man, Plato is a man, etc. Thus "a man exists" follows from Socrates, or Plato, or anyone else. With definite descriptions, on the other hand, the corresponding form of a proposition, namely, "x is the so-and-so" (where "x" is a name), can only be true for one value of x at most. This brings us to the subject of definite descriptions, which are to be defined in a way analogous to that employed for ambiguous descriptions, but rather more complicated.

We come now to the main subject of the present chapter, namely, the definition of the word *the* (in the singular). One very important point about the definition of "a so-and-so" applies equally to "the so-and-so"; the definition to be sought is a definition of propositions in which this phrase occurs, not a definition of the phrase itself in isolation.

In the case of "a so-and-so," this is fairly obvious: no one could suppose that "a man" was a definite object, which could be defined by itself. Socrates is a man, Plato is a man, Aristotle is a man, but we cannot infer that "a man" means the same as "Socrates" means and also the same as "Plato" means and also the same as "Aristotle" means, since these three names have different meanings. Nevertheless, when we have enumerated all the men in the world, there is nothing left of which we can say, "This is a man, and not only so, but it is *the* 'a man,' the quintessential entity that is just an indefinite man without being anybody in particular." It is of course quite clear that whatever there is in the world is definite: if it is a man it is one definite man and not any other. Thus there cannot be such an entity as "a man" to be found in the world, as opposed to specific men. And accordingly it is natural that we do not define "a man" itself, but only the propositions in which it occurs.

In the case of "the so-and-so" this is equally true, though at first sight less obvious. We may demonstrate that this must be the case, by a consideration of the difference between a *name* and a *definite description*. Take the proposition, "Scott is the author of *Waverley*." We have here a name, "Scott," and a description, "the author of *Waverley*," which are asserted to apply to the same person. The distinction between a name and all other symbols may be explained as follows:

A name is a simple symbol whose meaning is something that can only occur as subject, i.e. something of the kind that we defined as an "individual" or a "particular." And a "simple" symbol is one which has no parts that are symbols. Thus "Scott" is a simple symbol, because, though it has parts (namely, separate letters), these parts are not symbols. On the other hand, "the author of *Waverley*" is not a simple symbol, because the separate words that compose the phrase are parts which are symbols. If, as may be the case, whatever *seems* to be an "individual" is really capable of further analysis, we shall have to content ourselves with what may be called "relative individuals," which will be terms that, throughout the context in question, are never analyzed and never occur otherwise than as subjects. And in that case we shall have correspondingly to content ourselves with "relative names." From the standpoint of our present problem, namely, the definition of descriptions, this problem, whether these are absolute names or only relative names, may be ignored, since it concerns different stages in the hierarchy of "types," whereas we have to compare such couples as "Scott" and "the author of *Waverley*," which both apply to the same object, and do not raise the problem of types. We may, therefore, for the moment, treat names as capable of being absolute; nothing that we shall have to say will depend upon this assumption, but the wording may be a little shortened by it.

We have, then, two things to compare: (1) a *name* which is a simple symbol, directly designating an individual which is its meaning, and having this meaning in its own right, independently of the meanings of all other words; (2) a *description*, which consists of several words, whose meanings are already fixed, and from which results whatever is to be taken as the "meaning" of the description.

A proposition containing a description is not identical with what that proposition becomes when a name is substituted, even if the name names the same object as the description describes. "Scott is the author of *Waverley*" is obviously a different proposition from "Scott is Scott": the first is a fact in literary history, the second a trivial truism. And if we put anyone other than Scott in place of "the author of *Waverley*," our proposition would become false, and would therefore certainly no longer be the same proposition. But, it may be said, our proposition is essentially of the same form as (say) "Scott is Sir Walter," in which two names are said to apply to the same person. The reply is that, if "Scott is Sir Walter" really means "the person named 'Scott' is the person named 'Sir Walter,'" then the names are being used as descriptions: i.e. the individual, instead of being named, is being described as the person having that name. This is a way in which names are frequently used in practice, and there will, as a rule, be nothing in the phraseology to show whether they are being used in this way or as names. When a name is used directly, merely to indicate what we are speaking about, it is no part of the *fact* asserted, or of the falsehood if our assertion happens to be false: it is merely part of the symbolism by which we express our thought. What we want to express is something which might (for example) be translated into a foreign language; it is something for which the actual words are a vehicle, but of which they are no part. On the other hand, when we make a proposition about "the person called 'Scott,'" the actual name "Scott" enters into what we are asserting, and not merely into the language used in making the assertion. Our proposition will now be a different one if we substitute "the person called 'Sir Walter.'" But so long as we are using names as names, whether we say "Scott" or whether we say "Sir Walter" is as irrelevant to what we are asserting as whether we speak English or French. Thus so long as names are used as names, "Scott is Sir Walter" is the same trivial proposition as "Scott is Scott." This completes the proof that "Scott is the author of *Waverley*" is not the same proposition as results from substituting a name for "the author of *Waverley*," no matter what name may be substituted.

When we use a variable, and speak of a propositional function, $\emptyset x$ say, the process of applying general statements about x to particular cases will consist in substituting a name for the letter "x," assuming that $\emptyset$ is a function which has individuals for its arguments. Suppose, for example, that $\emptyset x$ is "always true"; let it be, say, the "law of identity," $x=x$. Then we may substitute for "x" any name we choose, and we shall obtain a true proposition. Assuming for the moment that "Socrates," "Plato," and "Aristotle" are names (a very rash assumption), we can infer from the law of identity that Socrates is Socrates, Plato is Plato, and Aristotle is Aristotle. But we shall commit a fallacy if we attempt to infer, without further premises, that the author of *Waverley* is the author of *Waverley*. This results from what we have just proved, that, if we substitute a name for "the author of *Waverley*" in a proposition, the proposition we obtain is a different one. That is to say, applying the result to our present case: if "x" is a name, "$x=x$" is not the same proposition as "the author of *Waverley* is the author of *Waverley*," no matter what name "x" may be. Thus from the fact that all propositions of the form "$x=x$" are true we cannot infer, without more ado, that the author of *Waverley* is the author of *Waverley*. In fact, propositions of the form "the so-and-so is the so-and-so" are not always true: it is necessary that the so-and-so" should *exist* (a term which will be explained shortly). It is false that the present King of France is the present King of France, or that the round square is the round square. When we substitute a description for a name, propositional functions which are "always true" may become false, if the description describes nothing. There is no mystery in this as soon as we realize (what was proved in the preceding paragraph) that when we substitute a description the result is not a value of the propositional function in question.

We are now in a position to define propositions in which a definite description occurs. The only thing that distinguishes "the so-and-so" from "a so-and-so" is the implication of uniqueness. We cannot speak of "*the* inhabitant of London," because inhabiting London is an attribute which is not unique. We cannot speak about "the present King of France," because there is none; but we can speak about "the present King of England." Thus propositions about "the so-and-so" always imply the corresponding propositions about a "so-and-so," with the addendum that there is not more than one so-and-so. Such a proposition as "Scott is the author of *Waverley*" could not be true if *Waverley* had never been written, or if several people had written it; and no more could any other proposition resulting from a propositional function *x* by the substitution of "the author of *Waverley*" for "*x*." We may say that "the author of *Waverley*" means "the value of *x* for which '*x* wrote *Waverley*' is true." Thus the proposition "the author of *Waverley* was Scotch," for example, involves:

(1) "*x* wrote *Waverley*" is not always false
(2) "if *x* and *y* wrote *Waverley*, *x* and *y* are identical" is always true
(3) "if *x* wrote *Waverley*, *x* was Scotch" is always true.

These three propositions, translated into ordinary language, state:

(1) at least one person wrote *Waverley*
(2) at most one person wrote *Waverley*
(3) whoever wrote *Waverley* was Scotch

All these three are implied by "the author of *Waverley* was Scotch." Conversely, the three together (but no two of them) imply that the author of *Waverley* was Scotch. Hence the three together may be taken as defining what is meant by the proposition "the author of *Waverley* was Scotch."

We may somewhat simplify these three propositions. The first and second together are equivalent to: "There is a term *c* such that '*x* wrote *Waverley*' is true when *x* is *c* and is false when *x* is not *c*." In other words, "There is a term *c* such that '*x* wrote *Waverley*' is always equivalent to '*x* is *c*'" (Two propositions are "equivalent" when both are true or both are false.) We have here, to begin with, two functions of *x*, "*x* wrote *Waverley*" and "*x* is *c*," and we form a function of *c* by considering the equivalence of these two functions of *x* for all values of *x*; we then proceed to assert that the resulting function of *c* is "sometimes true," i.e. that it is true for at least one value of *c*. (It obviously cannot be true for more than one value of *c*.) These two conditions together are defined as giving the meaning of "the author of *Waverley* exists."

We may now define "the term satisfying the function *øx* exists." This is the general form of which the above is a particular case. "The author of *Waverley*" is "the term satisfying the function '*x* wrote *Waverley*.'" And "the so-and-so" will always involve reference to some propositional function, namely, that which defines the property that makes a thing a so-and-so. Our definition is as follows:

"The term satisfying the function *øx* exists" means:
"There is a term *c* such that *øx* is always equivalent to '*x* is *c*.'"

In order to define "the author of *Waverley* was Scotch," we have still to take account of the third of our three propositions, namely, "Whoever wrote

Waverley was Scotch." This will be satisfied by merely adding that the *c* in question is to be Scotch. Thus "the author of *Waverley* was Scotch" is:

> "There is a term *c* such that (1) '*x* wrote *Waverley*' is always equivalent to '*x* is *c*,' (2) *c* is Scotch."

And generally: "the term satisfying ϕx satisfies ψx" is defined as meaning:

> "There is a term c such that (1) ϕx is always equivalent to '*x* is *c*,' (2) ψx is true."

This is the definition of propositions in which descriptions occur.

It is possible to have much knowledge concerning a term described, i.e. to know many propositions concerning "the so-and-so," without actually knowing what the so-and-so is, i.e. without knowing any proposition of the form "*x* is the so-and-so," where "*x*" is a name. In a detective story propositions about "the man who did the deed" are accumulated, in the hope that ultimately they will suffice to demonstrate that it was A who did the deed. We may even go so far as to say that, in all such knowledge as can be expressed in words – with the exception of "this" and "that" and a few other words of which the meaning varies on different occasions – no names, in the strict sense, occur, but what seem like names are really descriptions. We may inquire significantly whether Homer existed, which we could not do if "Homer" were a name. The proposition "the so-and-so exists" is significant, whether true or false; but if *a* is the so-and-so (where "*a*" is a name), the words "*a* exists" are meaningless. It is only of descriptions – definite or indefinite – that existence can be significantly asserted: for, if "*a*" is a name, it *must* name something: what does not name anything is not a name, and therefore, if intended to be a name, is a symbol devoid of meaning, whereas a description, like "the present King of France," does not become incapable of occurring significantly merely on the ground that it describes nothing, the reason being that it is a *complex* symbol, of which the meaning is derived from that of its constituent symbols. And so, when we ask whether Homer existed, we are using the word "Homer" as an abbreviated description: we may replace it by (say) "the author of the *Iliad* and the *Odyssey*." The same considerations apply to almost all uses of what look like proper names.

When descriptions occur in propositions, it is necessary to distinguish what may be called "primary" and "secondary" occurrences. The abstract distinction is as follows. A description has a "primary" occurrence when the proposition in which it occurs results from substituting the description for "*x*" in some propositional function ϕx; a description has a "secondary" occurrence when the result of substituting the description for *x* in øx gives only part of the proposition concerned. An instance will make this clearer. Consider "the present King of France is bald." Here "the present King of France" has a primary occurrence, and the proposition is false. Every proposition in which a description which describes nothing has a primary occurrence is false. But now consider "the present King of France is not bald." This is ambiguous. If we are first to take "*x* is bald," then substitute "the present King of France" for "*x*," and then deny the result, the occurrence of "the present King of France" is secondary and our proposition is true; but if we are to take "*x* is not bald" and substitute "the present King of France" for "*x*," then "the present King of France" has a primary occurrence and the proposition is false. Confusion of primary and secondary occurrences is a ready source of fallacies where descriptions are concerned....

The theory of descriptions, briefly outlined in the present chapter, is of the utmost importance both in logic and in theory of knowledge. But for purposes of mathematics, the more philosophical parts of the theory are not essential, and have therefore been omitted in the above account, which has confined itself to the barest mathematical requisites.

NOTES

1. *Untersuchungen zur Gegenstandstheorie und Psychologie,* 1904.

TRUTH AND MEANING

Donald Davidson

It is conceded by most philosophers of language, and recently even by some linguists, that a satisfactory theory of meaning must give an account of how the meanings of sentences depend upon the meanings of words. Unless such an account could be supplied for a particular language, it is argued, there would be no explaining the fact that we can learn the language: no explaining the fact that, on mastering a finite vocabulary and a finitely stated set of rules, we are prepared to produce and to understand any of a potential infinitude of sentences. I do not dispute these vague claims, in which I sense more than a kernel of truth.[1] Instead I want to ask what it is for a theory to give an account of the kind adumbrated.

One proposal is to begin by assigning some entity as meaning to each word (or other significant syntactical feature) of the sentence; thus we might assign Theaetetus to "Theaetetus" and the property of flying to "flies" in the sentence "Theaetetus flies." The problem then arises how the meaning of the sentence is generated from these meanings. Viewing concatenation as a significant piece of syntax, we may assign to it the relation of participating in or instantiating; however, it is obvious that we have here the start of an infinite regress. Frege sought to avoid the regress by saying that the entities corresponding to predicates (for example) are "unsaturated" or "incomplete" in contrast to the entities that correspond to names, but this doctrine seems to label a difficulty rather than solve it.

The point will emerge if we think for a moment of complex singular terms, to which Frege's theory applies along with sentences. Consider the expression "the father of Annette"; how does the meaning of the whole depend on the meaning of the parts? The answer would seem to be that the meaning of "the father of" is such that when this expression is prefixed to a singular term the result refers to the father of the person to whom the singular term refers. What part is played, in this account, by the unsaturated or incomplete entity for which "the father of" stands? All we can think to say is that this entity "yields" or "gives" the father of x as value when the argument is x, or perhaps that this entity maps people onto their fathers. It may not be clear whether the entity for which "the father of" is said to stand performs any genuine explanatory function as long as we stick to individual expressions; so think instead of the infinite class of expressions formed by writing "the father of" zero or more times in front of "Annette." It is easy to supply a theory that tells, for an arbitrary one of these singular terms, what it refers to: if the term is "Annette" it refers to Annette, while if the term is complex, consisting of "the father of" prefixed to a singular term t, then it refers to the father of the person to whom t refers. It is obvious that no entity corresponding to "the father of" is, or needs to be, mentioned in stating this theory.

It would be inappropriate to complain that this little theory uses the words "the father of" in giving the reference of expressions containing those words. For the task was to give the meaning of all expressions in a certain infinite set on the basis of the meaning of the parts; it was not in the bargain also to give the meanings of the atomic parts. On the other hand, it is now evident that a satisfactory theory of the meanings of complex expressions may not require entities as meanings of all the parts. It behooves us then to rephrase our demand on a satisfactory theory of meaning so as not to suggest that individual words must have meanings at all, in any sense that transcends the fact that they have a systematic effect on the meanings of the sentences in which they occur. Actually, for the case at hand we can do better still in stating the criterion of success: what we wanted, and what we got, is a theory that entails every sentence of the form "t refers to x" where "t" is replaced by a structural description[2] of a singular term, and "x" is replaced by that term itself. Further, our theory accomplishes this without appeal to any semantical concepts beyond the basic "refers to." Finally, the theory clearly suggests an effective procedure for determining, for any singular term in its universe, what that term refers to.

A theory with such evident merits deserves wider application. The device proposed by Frege to this end has a brilliant simplicity: count predicates as a special case of functional expressions, and sentences as a special case of complex singular terms. Now, however, a difficulty looms if we want to continue in our present (implicit) course of identifying the meaning of a singular term with its reference. The difficulty follows upon making two reasonable assumptions: that logically equivalent singular terms have the same reference; and that a singular term does not change its reference if a contained singular term is replaced by another with the same reference. But now suppose that "R" and "S" abbreviate any two sentences alike in truth value. Then the following four sentences have the same reference:

(1) R
(2) $\hat{x}(x=x.R)=\hat{x}(x=x)$
(3) $\hat{x}(x=x.S)=\hat{x}(x=x)$
(4) S

For (1) and (2) are logically equivalent, as are (3) and (4), while (3) differs from (2) only in containing the singular term "$\hat{x}(x=x.S)$" where (2) contains "$x(x=x.R)$" and these refer to the same thing if S and R are alike in truth value. Hence any two sentences have the same reference if they have the same truth value.[3] And if the meaning of a sentence is what it refers to, all sentences alike in truth value must be synonymous – an intolerable result.

Apparently we must abandon the present approach as leading to a theory of meaning. This is the natural point at which to turn for help to the distinction between meaning and reference. The trouble, we are told, is that questions of reference are, in general, settled by extralinguistic facts, questions of meaning not, and the facts can conflate the references of expressions that are not synonymous. If we want a theory that gives the meaning (as distinct from reference) of each sentence, we must start with the meaning (as distinct from reference) of the parts.

Up to here we have been following in Frege's footsteps; thanks to him, the path is well known and even well worn. But now, I would like to suggest, we have reached an impasse: the switch from reference to meaning leads to no useful account of how the meanings of sentences depend upon the meanings of the words (or other structural features) that compose them. Ask, for example, for the meaning of "Theaetetus flies." A Fregean answer might go something like this: given the meaning of "Theaetetus" as argument, the meaning of "flies" yields the meaning of "Theaetetus flies" as value. The vacuity of this answer is obvious. We wanted to know what the meaning of "Theaetetus flies" is; it is no progress to be told that it is the meaning of "Theaetetus flies." This much we knew before any theory was in sight. In the bogus account just given, talk of the structure of the sentence and of the meanings of words was idle, for it played no role in producing the given description of the meaning of the sentence.

The contrast here between a real and pretended account will be plainer still if we ask for a theory, analogous to the miniature theory of reference of singular terms just sketched, but different in dealing with meanings in place of references. What analogy demands is a theory that has as consequences all sentences of the form "s means m" where "s" is replaced by a structural description of a sentence and "m" is replaced by a singular term that refers to the meaning of that sentence; a theory, moreover, that provides an effective method for arriving at the meaning of an arbitrary sentence structurally described. Clearly some more articulate way of referring to meanings than any we have seen is essential if these criteria are to be met.[4] Meanings as entities, or the related concept of synonymy, allow us to formulate the following rule relating sentences and their parts: sentences are synonymous whose corresponding parts are synonymous ("corresponding" here needs spelling out of course). And meanings as entities may, in theories such as Frege's, do duty, on occasion as references, thus losing their status as entities distinct from references. Paradoxically, the one thing meanings do not seem to do is oil the wheels of a theory of meaning – at least as long as we require of such a theory that it nontrivially give the meaning of every sentence in the language. My objection to meanings in the theory of meaning is not that they are abstract or that their identity conditions are obscure, but that they have no demonstrated use.

This is the place to scotch another hopeful thought. Suppose we have a satisfactory theory of syntax for our language, consisting of an effective method of telling, for an arbitrary expression, whether or not it is independently meaningful (i.e., a sentence), and assume as usual that this involves viewing each sentence as composed, in allowable ways, out of elements drawn form a fixed finite stock of atomic syntactical elements (roughly, words). The hopeful thought is that syntax, so conceived, will yield semantics when a dictionary giving the meaning of each syntactic atom is added. Hopes will be dashed, however, if semantics is to comprise a theory of meaning in our sense, for knowledge of the structural characteristics that make for meaningfulness in a sentence, plus knowledge of the meanings of the ultimate parts, does not add up to knowledge of what a sentence means. The point is easily illustrated by belief sentences. Their syntax is relatively unproblematic. Yet, adding a dictionary does not touch the standard semantic problem, which is that we cannot account for even as much as the truth conditions of such sentences on the basis of what we know of the meanings of the words in them. The situation is not radically altered by refining the dictionary to indicate which meaning or meanings an ambiguous expression bears in each of its possible contexts; the problem of belief sentences persists after ambiguities are resolved.

The fact that recursive syntax with dictionary added is not necessarily recursive semantics has been obscured in some recent writing on linguistics by the intrusion of semantic criteria into the discussion of purportedly syntactic theories. The matter would boil down to a harmless difference over terminology if the semantic criteria were clear; but they are not. While there is agreement that it is the central task of semantics to give the semantic interpretation (the meaning) of every sentence in the language, nowhere in the linguistic literature will one find, so far as I know, a straightforward account of how a theory performs this task, or how to tell when it has been accomplished. The contrast with syntax is striking. The main job of a modest syntax is to characterize *meaningfulness* (or sentencehood.) We may have as much confidence in the correctness of such a characterization as we have in the representativeness of our sample and our ability to say when particular expressions are meaningful (sentences). What clear and analogous task and test exist for semantics?[5]

We decided a while back not to assume that parts of sentences have meanings except in the ontologically neutral sense of making a systematic contribution to the meaning of the sentences in which they occur. Since postulating meanings has netted nothing, let us return to that insight. One direction in which it points is a certain holistic view of meaning. If sentences depend for their meaning on their structure, and we understand the meaning of each item in the structure only as an abstraction from the totality of sentences in which it features, then we can give the meaning of any sentence (or word) only by giving the meaning of every sentence (and word) in the language. Frege said that only in the context of a sentence does a word have meaning; in the same vein he might have added that only in the context of the language does a sentence (and therefore a word) have meaning.

This degree of holism was already implicit in the suggestion that an adequate theory of meaning must entail *all* sentences of the form "*s* means *m*." But now, having found no more help in meanings of sentences than in meanings of words, let us ask whether we can get rid of the troublesome singular terms supposed to replace "*m*" and to refer to meanings. In a way, nothing could be easier: just write "*s* means that *p*," and imagine "*p*" replaced by a sentence. Sentences, as we have seen, cannot name meanings, and sentences with "that" prefixed are not names at all, unless we decide so. It looks as though we are in trouble on another count, however, for it is reasonable to expect that in wrestling with the logic of the apparently nonextensional "means that" we will encounter problems as hard as, or perhaps identical with, the problems our theory is out to solve.

The only way I know to deal with this difficulty is simple, and radical. Anxiety that we are enmeshed in the intensional springs from using the words "means that" as filling between description of sentence and sentence, but it may be that the success of our venture depends not on the filling but on what it fills. The theory will have done its work if it provides, for every sentence *s* in the language under study, a matching sentence (to replace "*p*") that, in some way yet to be made clear, "gives the meaning" of *s*. One obvious candidate for matching sentence is just *s* itself, if the object language is contained in the metalanguage; otherwise a translation of *s* in the metalanguage. As a final bold step, let us try treating the position occupied by "*p*" extensionally: to implement this, sweep away the obscure "means that," provide the sentence that replaces "*p*" with a proper sentential connective, and supply the description that replaces "*s*" with its own predicate. The plausible result is

(T) *s* is *T* if and only if *p*.

What we require of a theory of meaning for a language L is that without appeal to any (further) semantical notions it place enough restrictions on the predicate "is T" to entail all sentences got from schema T when "s" is replaced by a structural description of a sentence of L and "p" by that sentence.

Any two predicates satisfying this condition have the same extension,[6] so if the metalanguage is rich enough, nothing stands in the way of putting what I am calling a theory of meaning into the form of an explicit definition of a predicate "is T." But whether explicitly defined or recursively characterized, it is clear that the sentences to which the predicate "is T" applies will be just the true sentences of L, for the condition we have placed on satisfactory theories of meaning is in essence Tarski's Convention T that tests the adequacy of a formal semantical definition of truth.[7]

The path to this point has been tortuous, but the conclusion may be stated simply: a theory of meaning for a language L shows "how the meanings of sentences depend upon the meanings of words" if it contains a (recursive) definition of truth-in-L. And, so far at least, we have no other idea how to turn the trick. It is worth emphasizing that the concept of truth played no ostensible role in stating our original problem. That problem, upon refinement, led to the view that an adequate theory of meaning must characterize a predicate meeting certain conditions. It was in the nature of a discovery that such a predicate would apply exactly to the true sentences. I hope that what I am doing may be described in part as defending the philosophical importance of Tarski's semantical concept of truth. But my defense is only distantly related, if at all, to the question whether the concept Tarski has shown how to define is the (or a) philosophically interesting conception of truth, or the question whether Tarski has cast any light on the ordinary use of such words as "true" and "truth." It is a misfortune that dust from futile and confused battles over these questions has prevented those with a theoretical interest in language – philosophers, logicians, psychologists, and linguists alike – from recognizing in the semantical concept of truth (under whatever name) the sophisticated and powerful foundation of a competent theory of meaning.

There is no need to suppress, of course, the obvious connection between a definition of truth of the kind Tarski has shown how to construct, and the concept of meaning. It is this: the definition works by giving necessary and sufficient conditions for the truth of every sentence, and to give truth conditions is a way of giving the meaning of a sentence. To know the semantic concept of truth for a language is to know what it is for a sentence – any sentence – to be true, and this amounts, in one good sense we can give to the phrase, to understanding the language. This at any rate is my excuse for a feature of the present discussion that is apt to shock old hands: my freewheeling use of the word "meaning," for what I call a theory of meaning has after all turned out to make no use of meanings, whether of sentences or of words. Indeed since a Tarski-type truth definition supplies all we have asked so far of a theory of meaning, it is clear that such a theory falls comfortably within what Quine terms the "theory of reference" as distinguished from what he terms the "theory of meaning." So much to the good for what I call a theory of meaning, and so much, perhaps, against my so calling it.[8]

A theory of meaning (in my mildly perverse sense) is an empirical theory, and its ambition is to account for the workings of a natural language. Like any theory, it may be tested by comparing some of its consequences with the facts. In the present case this is easy, for the theory has been characterized as issuing in an infinite flood of sentences each giving the truth conditions of a sentence; we only need to ask, in selected cases, whether what the theory avers to be the truth conditions for a sentence really are. A typical test case might involve deciding whether the sentence "Snow is white" *is* true if and only if snow is white. Not all cases will be so simple (for reasons to be sketched), but it is evident that this sort of test does not invite counting noses. A sharp conception of what constitutes a theory in this domain furnishes an exciting context for raising deep questions about when a theory of language is correct and how it is to be tried. But the difficulties are theoretical, not practical. In application, the trouble is to get a theory that comes close to working; anyone can tell whether it is right.[9] One can see why this is so. The theory reveals nothing new about the conditions under which an individual sentence is true; it does not make those conditions any clearer than the sentence itself does. The work of the theory is in relating the known truth conditions of each sentence to those aspects ("words") of the sentence that recur in other sentences, and can be assigned identical roles in other sentences. Empirical power in such a theory depends on success in recovering the structure of a very complicated ability – the ability to speak and understand a language. We can tell easily enough when particular pronouncements of the theory comport with our understanding of the language; this is consistent with a feeble insight into the design of the machinery of our linguistic accomplishments.

The remarks of the last paragraph apply directly only to the special case where it is assumed that the language for which truth is being characterized is part of the language used and understood by the characterizer. Under these circumstances, the framer of a theory will as a matter of course avail himself when he can of the built-in convenience of a metalanguage with a sentence guaranteed equivalent to each sentence in the object language. Still, this fact ought not to con us into thinking a theory any more correct that entails " 'Snow is white' is true if and only if snow is white" than one that entails instead:

(S) "Snow is white" is true if and only if grass is green,

provided, of course, we are as sure of the truth of (S) as we are of that of its more celebrated predecessor. Yet (S) may not encourage the same confidence that a theory that entails it deserves to be called a theory of meaning.

The threatened failure of nerve may be counteracted as follows. The grotesqueness of (S) is in itself nothing against a theory of which it is a consequence, provided the theory gives the correct results for every sentence (on the basis of its structure, there being no other way). It is not easy to see how (S) could be party to such an enterprise, but if it were – if, that is, (S) followed from a characterization of the predicate "is true" that led to the invariable pairing of truths with truths and falsehoods with falsehoods – then there would not, I think, be anything essential to the idea of meaning that remained to be captured.[10]

What appears to the right of the biconditional in sentences of the form "s is true if and only if p," when such sentences are consequences of a theory of truth, plays its role in determining the meaning of s not by pretending synonymy but by adding one more brush-stroke to the picture which, taken as a whole, tells what there is to know of the meaning of s; this stroke is added by virtue of the fact that the sentence that replaces "p" is true if and only if s is.

It may help to reflect that (S) is acceptable, if it is, because we are independently sure of the truth of "snow is white" and "grass is green"; but in cases where we are unsure of the truth of a sentence, we can have confidence in a characterization of the truth predicate only if it pairs that sentence with one we have good reason to believe equivalent. It would be ill advised for someone who had any doubts about the color of snow or grass to accept a theory that yielded (S), even if his doubts were of equal degree, unless he thought the color of the one was tied to the color of the other.[11] Omniscience can obviously afford more bizarre theories of meaning than ignorance; but then, omniscience has less need of communication.

It must be possible, of course, for the speaker of one language to construct a theory of meaning for the speaker of another, though in this case the empirical test of the correctness of the theory will no longer be trivial. As before, the aim of theory will be an infinite correlation of sentences alike in truth. But this time the theory-builder must not be assumed to have direct insight into likely equivalences between his own tongue and the alien. What he must do is find out, however he can, what sentences the alien holds true in his own tongue (or better, to what degree he holds them true). The linguist then will attempt to construct a characterization of truth-for-the-alien which yields, so far as possible, a mapping of sentences held true (or false) by the alien onto sentences held true (or false) by the linguist. Supposing no perfect fit is found, the residue of sentences held true translated by sentences held false (and vice versa) is the margin for error (foreign or domestic). Charity in interpreting the words and thoughts of others is unavoidable in another direction as well: just as we must maximize agreement, or risk not making sense of what the alien is talking about, so we must maximize the self-consistency we attribute to him, on pain of not understanding *him*. No single principle of optimum charity emerges; the constraints therefore determine no single theory. In a theory of radical translation (as Quine calls it) there is no completely disentangling questions of what the alien means from questions of what he believes. We do not know what someone means unless we know what he believes; we do not know what someone believes unless we know what he means. In radical translation we are able to break into this circle, if only incompletely, because we can sometimes tell that a person accedes to a sentence we do not understand.[12]

In the past few pages I have been asking how a theory of meaning that takes the form of a truth definition can be empirically tested, and have blithely ignored the prior question whether there is any serious chance such a theory can be given for a natural language. What are the prospects for a formal semantical theory of a natural language? Very poor, according to Tarski; and I believe most logicians, philosophers of language, and linguists agree.[13] Let me do what I can to dispel the pessimism. What I can in a general and programmatic way, of course; for here the proof of the pudding will certainly be in the proof of the right theorems.

Tarski concludes the first section of his classic essay on the concept of truth in formalized languages with the following remarks, which he italicizes:

> *The very possibility of a consistent use of the expression "true sentence" which is in harmony with the laws of logic and the spirit of everyday language seems to be very questionable, and consequently the same doubt attaches to the possibility of constructing a correct definition of this expression.*[14]

Late in the same essay, he returns to the subject:

> the concept of truth (as well as other semantical concepts) when applied to colloquial language in conjunction with the normal laws of logic leads inevitably to confusions and contradictions. Whoever wishes, in spite of all difficulties, to pursue the semantics of colloquial language with the help of exact methods will be driven first to undertake the thankless task of a reform of this language. He will find it necessary to define its structure, to overcome the ambiguity of the terms which occur in it, and finally to split the language into a series of languages of greater and greater extent, each of which stands in the same relation to the

next in which a formalized language stands to its metalanguage. It may, however be doubted whether the language of everyday life, after being "rationalized" in this way, would still preserve its naturalness and whether it would not rather take on the characteristic features of the formalized languages.[15]

Two themes emerge: that the universal character of natural languages leads to contradiction (the semantic paradoxes), and that natural languages are too confused and amorphous to permit the direct application of formal methods. The first point deserves a serious answer, and I wish I had one. As it is, I will say only why I think we are justified in carrying on without having disinfected this particular source of conceptual anxiety. The semantic paradoxes arise when the range of the quantifiers in the object language is too generous in certain ways. But it is not really clear how unfair to Urdu or to Hindi it would be to view the range of their quantifiers as insufficient to yield an explicit definition of "true-in-Urdu" or "true-in-Hindi." Or, to put the matter in another, if not more serious way, there may in the nature of the case always be something we grasp in understanding the language of another (the concept of truth) that we cannot communicate to him. In any case, most of the problems of general philosophical interest arise within a fragment of the relevant natural language that may be conceived as containing very little set theory. Of course these comments do not meet the claim that natural languages are universal. But it seems to me this claim, now that we know such universality leads to paradox, is suspect.

Tarski's second point is that we would have to reform a natural language out of all recognition before we could apply formal semantical methods. If this is true, it is fatal to my project, for the task of a theory of meaning as I conceive it is not to change, improve or reform a language, but to describe and understand it. Let us look at the positive side. Tarski has shown the way to giving a theory for interpreted formal languages of various kinds; pick one as much like English as possible. Since this new language has been explained in English and contains much English we not only may, but I think must, view it as part of English for those who understand it. For this fragment of English we have, *ex hypothesi*, a theory of the required sort. Not only that, but in interpreting this adjunct of English in old English we necessarily gave hints connecting old and new. Wherever there are sentences of old English with the same truth conditions as sentences in the adjunct we may extend the theory to cover them. Much of what is called for is just to mechanize as far as possible what we now do by art when we put ordinary English into one or another canonical notation. The point is not that canonical notation is better than the rough original idiom, but rather that if we know what idiom the canonical notation is canonical *for*, we have as good a theory for the idiom as for its kept companion.

Philosophers have long been at the hard work of applying theory to ordinary language by the device of matching sentences in the vernacular with sentences for which they have a theory. Frege's massive contribution was to show how "all," "some," "every" "each," "none," and associated pronouns, in some of their uses, could be tamed; for the first time, it was possible to dream of a formal semantics for a significant part of a natural language. This dream came true in a sharp way with the work of Tarski. It would be a shame to miss the fact that as a result of these two magnificent achievements, Frege's and Tarski's, we have gained a deep insight into the structure of our mother tongues. Philosophers of a logical bent have tended to start where the theory was and work out towards the complications of natural language. Contemporary linguists, with an aim that cannot easily be seen to be different, start with the ordinary and work toward a general theory. If either party is successful, there must be a meeting. Recent work by Chomsky and others is doing much to bring the complexities of natural languages within the scope of serious semantic theory. To give an example: suppose success in giving the truth conditions for some significant range of sentences in the active voice. Then with a formal procedure for transforming each such sentence into a corresponding sentence in the passive voice, the theory of truth could be extended in an obvious way to this new set of sentences.[16]

One problem touched on in passing by Tarski does not, at least in all its manifestations, have to be solved to get ahead with theory: the existence in natural languages of "ambiguous terms." As long as ambiguity does not affect grammatical form, and can be translated, ambiguity for ambiguity, into the metalanguage, a truth definition will not tell us any lies. The trouble, for systematic semantics, with the phrase "believes that" in English is not its vagueness, ambiguity, or unsuitability for incorporation in a serious science: let our metalanguage be English, and all *these* problems will be translated without loss or gain into the metalanguage. But the central problem of the logical grammar of "believes that" will remain to haunt us.

The example is suited to illustrating another, and related, point, for the discussion of belief sentences has been plagued by failure to observe a fundamental distinction between tasks: uncovering the logical grammar or form of sentences (which is in the province of a theory of meaning as I construe it), and the analysis of individual words or expressions (which are treated as primitive by the theory). Thus Carnap, in the first edition of *Meaning and Necessity*, suggested we render "John believes that the earth is round" as "John responds affirmatively to 'the earth is round' as an English sentence." He gave this up when Mates pointed out that John might respond affirmatively to one sentence and not to another no matter how close in meaning. But there is a confusion here from the start. The semantic structure of a belief sentence, according to this idea of Carnap's, is given by a three-place predicate with places reserved for expressions referring to a person, a sentence, and a language. It is a different sort of problem entirely to attempt an analysis of this predicate, perhaps along behavioristic lines. Not least among the merits of Tarski's conception of a theory of truth is that the purity of method it demands of us follows from the formulation of the problem itself, not from the self-imposed restraint of some adventitious philosophical puritanism.

I think it is hard to exaggerate the advantages to philosophy of language of bearing in mind this distinction between questions of logical form or grammar, and the analysis of individual concepts. Another example may help advertise the point.

If we suppose questions of logical grammar settled, sentences like "Bardot is good" raise no special problems for a truth definition. The deep differences between descriptive and evaluative (emotive, expressive, etc.) terms do not show here. Even if we hold there is some important sense in which moral or evaluative sentences do not have a truth value (for example, because they cannot be "verified"), we ought not to boggle at "'Bardot is good' is true if and only if Bardot is good"; in a theory of truth, this consequence should follow with the rest, keeping track, as must be done, of the semantic location of such sentences in the language as a whole – of their relation to generalizations, their role in such compound sentences as "Bardot is good and Bardot is foolish," and so on. What is special to evaluative words is simply not touched: the mystery is transferred from the word "good" in the object language to its translation in the metalanguage.

But "good" as it features in "Bardot is a good actress" is another matter. The problem is not that the translation of this sentence is not in the metalanguage – let us suppose it is. The problem is to frame a truth definition such that "'Bardot is a good actress' is true if and only if Bardot is a good actress" – and all other sentences like it – are consequences. Obviously "good actress" does not mean "good and an actress." We might think of taking "is a good actress" as an unanalyzed predicate. This would obliterate all connection between "is a good actress" and "is a good mother," and it would give us no excuse to think of "good," in these uses, as a word or semantic element. But worse, it would bar us from framing a truth definition at all, for there is no end to the predicates we would have to treat as logically simple (and hence accommodate in separate clauses in the definition of satisfaction): "is a good companion to dogs," "is a good 28-years-old conversationalist," and so forth. The problem is not peculiar to the case: it is the problem of attributive adjectives generally.

It is consistent with the attitude taken here to deem it usually a strategic error to undertake philosophical analysis of words or expressions which is not preceded by or at any rate accompanied by the attempt to get the logical grammar straight. For how can we have any confidence in our analyses of words like "right," "ought," "can," and "obliged," or the phrases we use to talk of actions, events, and causes, when we do not know what (logical, semantical) parts of speech we have to deal with? I would say much the same about studies of the "logic" of these and other words, and the sentences containing them. Whether the effort and ingenuity that has gone into the study of deontic logics, modal logics, imperative and erotetic logics has been largely futile or not cannot be known until we have acceptable semantic analyses of the sentences such systems purport to treat. Philosophers and logicians sometimes talk or work as if they were free to choose between, say, the truth-functional conditional and others, or free to introduce non-truth-functional sentential operators like "Let it be the case that" or "It ought to be the case that." But in fact the decision is crucial. When we depart from idioms we can accommodate in a truth definition, we lapse into (or create) language for which we have no coherent semantical account – that is, no account at all of how such talk can be integrated into the language as a whole.

To return to our main theme: we have recognized that a theory of the kind proposed leaves the whole matter of what individual words mean exactly where it was. Even when the metalanguage is different from the object language, the theory exerts no pressure for improvement, clarification or analysis of individual words, except when, by accident of vocabulary, straightforward translation fails. Just as synonymy, as between expressions, goes generally untreated, so also synonymy of sentences, and analyticity. Even such sentences as "A vixen is a female fox" bear no special tag unless it is our pleasure to provide it. A truth definition does not distinguish between analytic sentences and others, except for sentences that owe their truth to the presence alone of the constants that give the theory its grip on structure: the theory entails not only that these sentences are true but that they will remain true under all significant rewritings of their nonlogical parts. A notion of logical truth thus given limited application, related notions of logical equivalence and entailment will tag along. It is hard to imagine how a theory of meaning could fail to read a logic into its object language to this degree; and to the extent that it does, our intuitions of logical truth, equivalence, and entailment may be called upon in constructing and testing the theory.

I turn now to one more, and very large, fly in the ointment: the fact that the same sentence may at one time or in one mouth be true and at another time or in another mouth be false. Both logicians and those critical of formal methods here seem largely (though by no means universally) agreed that formal semantics and logic are incompetent to deal with the disturbances caused by demonstratives. Logicians have often reacted by downgrading natural language and trying to show how to get along without demonstratives; their critics react by downgrading logic and formal semantics. None of this can make me happy: clearly, demonstratives cannot be eliminated from a natural language without loss or radical change, so there is no choice but to accommodate theory to them.

No logical errors result if we simply treat demonstratives as constants[17]; neither do any problems arise for giving a semantic truth definition. "'I am wise' is true if and only if I am wise," with its bland ignoring of the demonstrative element in "I" comes off the assembly line along with "'Socrates is wise' is true if and only if Socrates is wise" with *its* bland indifference to the demonstrative element in "is wise" (the tense).

What suffers in this treatment of demonstratives is not the definition of a truth predicate, but the plausibility of the claim that what has been defined is truth. For this claim is acceptable only if the speaker and circumstances of utterance of each sentence mentioned in the definition is matched by the speaker and circumstances of utterance of the truth definition itself. It could also be fairly pointed out that part of understanding demonstratives is knowing the rules by which they adjust their reference to circumstance; assimilating demonstratives to constant terms obliterates this feature. These complaints can be met, I think, though only by a fairly far-reaching revision in the theory of truth. I shall barely suggest how this could be done, but bare suggestion is all that is needed: the idea is technically trivial, and quite in line with work being done on the logic of the tenses.[18]

We could take truth to be a property, not of sentences, but of utterances, or speech acts, or ordered triples of sentences, times, and persons; but it is simplest just to view truth as a relation between a sentence, a person, and a time. Under such treatment, ordinary logic as now read applies as usual, but only to sets of sentences relativized to the same speaker and time; further logical relations between sentences spoken at different times and by different speakers may be articulated by new axioms. Such is not my concern. The theory of meaning undergoes a systematic but not puzzling change: corresponding to each expression with a demonstrative element there must in the theory be a phrase that relates the truth conditions of sentences in which the expression occurs to changing times and speakers. Thus the theory will entail sentences like the following:

> "I am tired" is true as (potentially) spoken by p at t if and only if p is tired at t.
> "That book was stolen" is true as (potentially) spoken by p at t if and only if the book demonstrated by p at t is stolen prior to t.[19]

Plainly, this course does not show how to eliminate demonstratives; for example, there is no suggestion that "the book demonstrated by the speaker" can be substituted ubiquitously for "that book" *salva veritate*. The fact that demonstratives are amenable to formal treatment ought greatly to improve hopes for a serious semantics of natural language, for it is likely that many outstanding puzzles, such as the analysis of quotations or sentences about propositional attitudes, can be solved if we recognize a concealed demonstrative construction.

Now that we have relativized truth to times and speakers, it is appropriate to glance back at the problem of empirically testing a theory of meaning for an alien tongue. The essence of the method was, it will be remembered, to correlate held-true sentences with held-true sentences by way of a truth definition, and within the bounds of intelligible error. Now the picture must be elaborated to allow for the fact that sentences are true, and held true, only relative to a speaker and a time. The real task is therefore to translate each sentence by another that is true for the same speakers at the same times. Sentences with demonstratives obviously yield a very sensitive test of the correctness of a theory of meaning, and constitute the most direct link between language and the recurrent macroscopic objects of human interest and attention.[20]

In this paper I have assumed that the speakers of a language can effectively determine the meaning or meanings of an arbitrary expression (if it has a meaning), and that it is the central task of a theory of meaning to show how this is possible. I have argued that a characterization of a truth predicate describes the required kind of structure, and provides a clear and testable criterion of an adequate semantics for a natural language. No doubt there are other reasonable demands that may be put on a theory of meaning. But a theory that does no more than define truth for a language comes far closer to constituting a complete theory of meaning than superficial analysis might suggest; so, at least, I have urged.

Since I think there is no alternative, I have taken an optimistic and programmatic view of the possibilities for a formal characterization of a truth predicate for a natural language. But it must be allowed that a staggering list of difficulties and conundrums remains. To name a few: we do not know the logical form of counterfactual or subjunctive sentences, nor of sentences about probabilities and about causal relations; we have no good idea what the logical role of adverbs is, nor the role of attributive adjectives; we have no theory for mass terms like "fire," "water," and "snow," nor for sentences about belief, perception, and intention, nor for verbs of action that imply purpose. And finally, there are all the sentences that seem not to have truth values at all: the imperatives, optatives, interrogatives, and a host more. A comprehensive theory of meaning for a natural language must cope successfully with each of these problems.[21]

ACKNOWLEDGEMENTS

An earlier version of this paper was read at the Eastern division meeting of the American Philosophical Association in December, 1966; the main theme traces back to an unpublished paper delivered to the Pacific Division of the American Philosophical Association in 1953. Present formulations owe much to John Wallace, with whom I have discussed these matters since 1962. My research was supported by the National Science Foundation.

NOTES

1. Elsewhere I have urged that it is a necessary condition, if a language is to be learn-able, that it have only a finite number of semantical primitives: see "Theories of Meaning and Learnable Language," in *Proceedings of the 1964 International Congress for Logic, Methodology and Philosophy of Science* (North-Holland Publishing Company, Amsterdam: 1965), pp. 383-394.

2. A "structural description" of an expression describes the expression as a concate-nation of elements drawn from a fixed finite list (for example of words or letters).

3. The argument is essentially Frege's. See A. Church, *Introduction to Mathematical Logic*, vol.I (Princeton: 1956), pp. 24-25. It is perhaps worth mentioning that the argument does not depend on any particular identification of the entities to which sentences are supposed to refer.

4. It may be thought that Church, in "A Formulation of the Logic of Sense and Denotation," in *Structure, Method and Meaning: Essays in Honor of H.M. Sheffer*, Henle, Kallen and Langer, eds. (Liberal Arts Press, New York: 1951), pp. 3-24, has given a theory of meaning that makes essential use of meanings as entities. But this is not the case: Church's logics of sense and denotation are interpreted as being about meanings, but they do not mention expressions and so cannot of course be theories of meaning in the sense now under discussion.

5. For a recent and instructive statement of the role of semantics in linguistics, see Noam Chomsky, "Topics in the Theory of Generative Grammar," in *Current Trends in Linguistics*, Thomas A. Sebeok, ed., vol. III (The Hague: 1966). In this article, Chomsky (1) emphasizes the central importance of semantics in linguistic theory, (2) argues for the superiority of transformational grammars over phrase structure grammars largely on the grounds that, although phrase structure grammars may be adequate to define sentencehood for (at least) some natural languages, they are inadequate as a foundation for semantics, and (3) comments repeatedly on the "rather primitive state" of the concepts of semantics and remarks that the notion of semantic interpretation "still resists any deep analysis."

6. Assuming, of course, that the extension of these predicates is limited to the sentences of *L*.

7. Alfred Tarski, "The Concept of Truth in Formalized Languages," in *Logic, Semantics, Metamathematics* (Oxford: 1956), pp. 152-278.

8. But Quine may be quoted in support of my usage: " ... in point of *meaning* ... a word may be said to be determined to whatever extent the truth or falsehood of its contexts is determined." "Truth by Convention," first published in 1936; now in *The Ways of Paradox* (New York: 1966), p. 82. Since a truth definition determines the truth value of every sentence in the object language (relative to a sentence in the metalanguage), it determines the meaning of every word and sentence. This would seem to justify the title Theory of Meaning.

9. To give a single example: it is clearly a count in favor of a theory that it entails "'Snow is white' is true if and only if snow is white." But to contrive a theory that entails this (and works for all related sentences) is not trivial. I do not know a theory that succeeds with this very case (the problem of "mass terms").

10. Critics have often failed to notice the essential proviso mentioned in this paragraph. The point is that (S) could not belong to any reasonably simple theory that also gave the right truth conditions for "That is snow" and "This is white". (See the discussion of indexical expressions below.) [Footnote added in 1982.]

11. This paragraph is confused. What it should say is that sentences of the theory are empirical generalizations about speakers, and so must not only be true but also lawlike. (S) presumably is not a law, since it does not support appropriate counterfactuals. It's also important that the evidence for accepting the (time and speaker relativized) truth conditions for "That is snow" is based on the causal connection between a speaker's assent to the sentence and the demonstrative presentation of snow. For further discussion, see "Reply to Foster", in Davidson, *Inquiries into Truth and Interpretation*, 171-79. [Footnote added in 1982.]

12. This sketch of how a theory of meaning for an alien tongue can be tested obviously owes its inspiration to Quine's account of radical translation in chapter II of *Word and Object* (New York: 1960). In suggesting that an acceptable theory of radical translation take the form of a recursive characterization of truth, I go beyond anything explicit in Quine. Toward the end of this paper, in the discussion of demonstratives, another strong point of agreement will turn up.

13. So far as I am aware, there has been very little discussion of whether a formal truth definition can be given for a natural language. But in a more general vein, several people have urged that the concepts of formal semantics be applied to natural language. See, for example, the contributions of Yehoshua Bar-Hillel and Evert Beth to *The Philosophy of Rudolph Carnap*, Paul A. Schilpp, ed., (La Salle, Ill.: 1963), and Bar-Hillel's "Logical Syntax and Semantics," *Language* 30, 230-237.

14. Tarski, *ibid.*, p. 165.

15. *Ibid.*, p. 267.

16. The rapprochement I prospectively imagine between transformational grammar and a sound theory of meaning has been much advanced by a recent change in the conception of transformational grammar described by Chomsky in the article referred to above (note 5). The structures generated by the phrase-structure part of the grammar, it has been realized for some time, are those suited to semantic interpretation; but this view is inconsistent with the idea, held by Chomsky until recently, that recursive operations are introduced only by the transformation rules. Chomsky now believes the phrase-structure rules are recursive. Since languages to which formal semantic methods directly and naturally apply are ones for which a (recursive) phrase-structure grammar is appropriate, it is clear that Chomsky's present picture of the relation between the structures generated by the phrase-structure part of the grammar, and the sentences of the language, is very much like the picture many logicians and philosophers have had of the relation between the richer formalized languages and ordinary language. (In these remarks I am indebted to Bruce Vermazen.)

17. Quine has good things to say about this in *Methods of Logic* (New York: 1950). See §8.

18. For an up-to-date bibliography, and discussion, see A.N. Prior, *Past, Present, and Future* (Oxford: 1967). [Material added in 1982: This claim has turned out to be naïvely optimistic. For some serious work on the subject, see S. Weinstein, "Truth and Demonstratives", *Nous*, 8 (1974), 179-84.]

19. There is more than an intimation of this approach to demonstratives and truth in Austin's 1950 article "Truth", reprinted in *Philosophical Papers* (Oxford: 1961). See pp. 89-90.

20. These remarks clearly derive from Quine's idea that "occasion sentences" (those with a demonstrative element) must play a central role in constructing a translation manual.

21. For attempted solutions to some of these problems, see Essays 6-10 of *Essays on Actions and Events* (Oxford: Oxford University Press, 1980), and Essays 6-8 of *Inquiries into Truth and Interpretation*. There is further discussion in Essays 3, 4, 9 and 10, and reference to some progress in sect. 1 of Essay 9 in the latter book.

IDENTITY AND NECESSITY

Saul Kripke

A problem which has arisen frequently in contemporary philosophy is: "How are *contingent* identity statements possible?" This question is phrased by analogy with the way Kant phrased his question "How are synthetic a priori judgments possible?" In both cases, it has usually been taken for granted in the one case by Kant that synthetic a priori judgments were possible, and in the other case in contemporary philosophical literature that contingent statements of identity are possible. I do not intend to deal with the Kantian question except to mention this analogy: After a rather thick book was written trying to answer the question how synthetic a priori judgments were possible, others came along later who claimed that the solution to the problem was that synthetic a priori judgments were, of course, impossible and that a book trying to show otherwise was written in vain. I will not discuss who was right on the possibility of synthetic a priori judgments. But in the case of contingent statements of identity, most philosophers have felt that the notion of a contingent identity statement ran into something like the following paradox. An argument like the following can be given against the possibility of contingent identity statements:[1]

First, the law of the substitutivity of identity says that, for any objects x and y, if x is identical to y, then if x has a certain property F, so does y:

$$(1) \qquad (x)(y)[(x=y) \supset (Fx \supset Fy)]$$

On the other hand, every object surely is necessarily self-identical:

$$(2) \qquad (x) \,\square\, (x=x)$$

But

(3) $(x)(y)\ (x=y) \supset [\Box(x=x) \supset \Box\ (x=y)]$

is a substitution instance of (1), the substitutivity law. From (2) and (3), we can conclude that, for every x and y, if x equals y, then, it is necessary that x equals y:

(4) $(x)(y)\ ((x=y) \supset \Box\ (x=y))$

This is because the clause $\Box\ (x=x)$ of the conditional drops out because it is known to be true.

This is an argument which has been stated many times in recent philosophy. Its conclusion, however, has often been regarded as highly paradoxical. For example, David Wiggins, in his paper, "Identity-Statements," says,

> Now there undoubtedly exist contingent identity-statements. Let
> a=b be one of them. From its simple truth and (5) [=(4) above] we
> can derive '$\Box(a=b)$'. But how then can there be any contingent
> identity statements?[2]

He then says that five various reactions to this argument are possible, and rejects all of these reactions, and reacts himself. I do not want to discuss all the possible reactions to this statement, except to mention the second of those Wiggins rejects. This says,

> We might accept the result and plead that provided '*a*' and '*b*' are
> proper names nothing is amiss. The consequence of this is that no
> contingent identity-statements can be made by means of proper
> names.

And then he says that he is discontented with this solution and many other philosophers have been discontented with this solution, too, while still others have advocated it.

What makes the statement (4) seem surprising? It says, for any objects x and y, if x is y, then it is necessary that x is y. I have already mentioned that someone might object to this argument on the grounds that premise (2) is already false, that it is not the case that everything is necessarily self-identical. Well, for example, am I myself necessarily self-identical? Someone might argue that in some situations which we can imagine I would not even have existed and therefore the statement "Saul Kripke is Saul Kripke" would have been false or it would not be the case that I was self-identical. Perhaps, it would have been neither true nor false, in such a world, to say that Saul Kripke is self-identical. Well, that may be so, but really it depends on one's philosophical view of a topic that I will not discuss, that is, what is to be said about truth values of statements mentioning objects that do not exist in the actual world or any given possible world or counterfactual situation. Let us interpret necessity here weakly. We can count statements as necessary if whenever the objects mentioned therein exist, the statement would be true. If we wished to be very careful about this, we would have to go into the question of existence as a predicate and ask if the statement can be reformulated in the form: For every x it is necessary that, if x exists, then x is self-identical. I will not go into this particular form of subtlety here because it is not going to be relevant to my main theme. Nor am I really going to consider formula (4). Anyone who believes formula (2) is, in my opinion, committed to formula (4). If x and y are the same things and we can talk about modal properties of an object at all, that is, in the usual parlance, we can speak of modality *de re* and an object *necessarily* having certain properties as such, then formula (1), I think, has to hold. Where x is any property at all, including a property involving modal operators, and if x and y are the same object and x had a certain property F, then y has to have the same property F. And this is so even if the property F is itself of the form of necessarily having some other property G, in particular that of necessarily being identical to a certain object. Well, I will not discuss the formula (4) itself because by itself it does not assert, of any particular true statement of identity, that it is necessary. It does not say anything about statements at all. It says for every *object* x and *object* y, if x and y are the same object, then it is necessary that x and y are the same object. And this, I think, if we think about it (anyway, if someone does not think so, I will not argue for it here), really amounts to something very little different from the statement (2). Since x, by definition of identity, is the only object identical with x, "$(y)(y{=}x \supset Fy)$" seems to me to be little more than a garralous way of saying 'Fx', and thus $(x)(y)(y{=}x \supset Fx)$ says the same as $(x)Fx$ no matter what 'F' is – in particular, even if 'F' stands for the property of necessary identity with x. So if x has this property (of necessary identity with x), trivially everything identical with x has it, as (4) asserts. But, from statement (4) one may apparently be able to deduce various particular statements of identity must be necessary and this is then supposed to be a very paradoxical consequence.

Wiggins says, "Now there undoubtedly exist contingent identity statements." One example of a contingent identity statement is the statement that the first Postmaster General of the United States is identical with the inventor of bifocals, or that both of these are identical with the man claimed by the *Saturday Evening Post* as its founder (*falsely* claimed, I gather, by the way). Now some such statements are plainly contingent. It plainly is a contingent fact that one and the same man both invented bifocals and took on the job of Postmaster General of the United States. How can we reconcile this with the truth of statement (4)? Well, that, too, is an issue I do not want to go into in detail except to be very dogmatic about it. It was I think settled quite well by Bertrand Russell in his notion of the scope of a description. According to Russell, one can, for example, say with propriety that the author of Hamlet might not have written "Hamlet," or even that the author of Hamlet might not have been the author of "Hamlet." Now here, of course, we do not deny the necessity of the identity of an object with itself; but we say it is true concerning a certain man that he in fact was the unique person to have written "Hamlet" and secondly that the man, who in fact was the man who wrote "Hamlet," might not have written "Hamlet." In other words, if Shakespeare had decided not to write tragedies, he might not have written "Hamlet." Under these circumstances, the man who in fact wrote "Hamlet" would not have written "Hamlet." Russell brings this out by saying that in such a statement, the first occurrence of the description "the author of 'Hamlet'" has large scope.[3] That is, we say "The author of 'Hamlet' has the following property: that he might not have written 'Hamlet.'" We *do not* assert that the following statement might have been the case, namely that the author of "Hamlet" did not write "Hamlet," for that is not true. That would be to say that it might have been the case that someone wrote "Hamlet" and yet did not write "Hamlet," which would be a contradiction. Now, aside from the details of Russell's particular formulation of it, which depends on his theory of descriptions, this seems to be the distinction that any theory of descriptions has to make. For example, if someone were to meet the President of Harvard and take him to be a Teaching Fellow, he might say: "I took the President of Harvard for a Teaching Fellow." By this he does not mean that he took the proposition "The President of Harvard is a Teaching Fellow" to be true. He could have meant this, for example, had he believed that some sort of democratic system had gone so far at Harvard that the President of it decided to take on the task of being a Teaching Fellow. But that probably is not what he means. What he means instead, as Russell points out, is "Someone is President of Harvard and I took him to be a Teaching Fellow." In one of Russell's examples someone says, "I thought your yacht is much larger than it is." And the other man replies, "No, my yacht is not much larger than it is."

Provided that the notion of modality *de re*, and thus of quantifying into modal contexts, makes sense at all, we have quite an adequate solution to the problem of avoiding paradoxes if we substitute descriptions for the universal quantifiers in (4) because the only consequence we will draw,[4] for example, in the bifocals case, is that there is a man who both happened to have invented bifocals and happened to have been the first Postmaster General of the United States, and is necessarily self-identical. There is an object *x* such that *x* invented bifocals, and as a matter of contingent fact an object *y*, such that *y* is the first Postmaster General of the United States, and finally, it is necessary, that *x* is *y*. What are *x* and *y* here? Here, *x* and *y* are both Benjamin Franklin, and it can certainly be necessary that Benjamin Franklin is identical with himself. So, there is no problem in the case of descriptions if we accept Russell's notion of scope.[5] And I just dogmatically want to drop that question here and go on to the question about names which Wiggins raises. And Wiggins says he might accept the result and plead that, provided *a* and *b* are proper names, nothing is amiss. And then he rejects this.

Now what is the special problem about proper names? At least if one is not familiar with the philosophical literature about this matter, one naively feels something like the following about proper names. First, if someone says "Cicero was an orator," then he uses the name 'Cicero' in that statement simply to pick out a certain object and then to ascribe a certain property to the object, namely, in this case, he ascribes to a certain man the property of having been an orator. If someone else uses another name, such as say 'Tully', he is still speaking about the same man. One ascribes the same property, if one says "Tully is an orator," to the same man. So to speak, the fact, or state of affairs, represented by the statement is the same whether one says "Cicero is an orator" or one says "Tully is an orator." It would, therefore, seem that the function of names is *simply* to refer, and not to describe the objects so named by such properties as "being the inventor of bifocals" or "being the first Postmaster General." It would seem that Leibniz' law and the law (1) should not only hold in the universally quantified form, but also in the form "if *a=b* and *Fa*, then *Fb*," wherever '*a*' and '*b*' stand in the place of names and '*F*' stands in place of a predicate expressing a genuine property of the object:

$$(a=b \bullet Fa) \supset Fb$$

We can run the same argument through again to obtain the conclusion where '*a*' and '*b*' replace any names, "If *a=b*, then necessarily *a=b*." And so, we could venture this conclusion: that whenever '*a*' and '*b*' are proper names, if *a* is *b*, that it is necessary that *a* is *b*. Identity statements between proper names have to be necessary if they are going to be true at all. This view in fact has been advocated, for example, by Ruth Barcan Marcus in a paper of hers on the philosophical interpretation of modal logic.[6] According to this view, whenever, for example, someone makes a correct statement of identity between two names, such as, for example, that Cicero is Tully, his statement has to be necessary if it is true. But such a conclusion *seems* plainly to be false. (I, like other philosophers, have a habit of understatement in which "it seems plainly false" means "it is plainly false." Actually, I think the view is true, though not quite in the form defended by Mrs. Marcus.) At any rate, it seems plainly false. One example was given by Professor Quine in his reply to Professor Marcus at the symposium: "I think I see trouble anyway in the contrast between proper names and descriptions as Professor Marcus draws it. The paradigm of the assigning of proper names is tagging. We may tag the planet Venus some fine evening with the proper name 'Hesperus'. We may tag the same planet again someday before sun rise with the proper name 'Phosphorus'." (Quine thinks that something like that actually was done once.) "When, at last, we discover that we have tagged the same planet twice, our discovery is empirical, and not because the proper names were descriptions." According to what we are told, the planet Venus seen in the morning was originally thought to be a star and was called "the Morning Star," or (to get rid of any question of using a description) was called 'Phosphorus'. One and the same planet, when seen in the evening, was thought to be another star, the Evening Star, and was called "Hesperus." Later on, astronomers discovered that Phosphorus and Hesperus were one and the same. Surely no amount of a priori ratiocination on their part could conceivably have made it possible for them to deduce that Phosphorus is Hesperus. In fact, given the information they had, it might have turned out the other way. Therefore, it is argued, the statement 'Hesperus is Phosphorus' has to be an ordinary contingent, empirical truth, one which might have come out otherwise, and so the view that true identity statements between names are necessary has to be false. Another example which Quine gives in *Word and Object* is taken from Professor Schrödinger, the famous pioneer of quantum mechanics: A certain mountain can be seen from both Tibet and Nepal. When seen from one direction it was called 'Gaurisanker'; when seen from another direction, it was called 'Everest'; and then, later on, the empirical discovery was made that Gaurisanker *is* Everest. (Quine further says that he gathers the example is actually geographically incorrect. I guess one should not rely on physicists for geographical information.)

Of course, one possible reaction to this argument is to deny that names like 'Cicero', 'Tully', 'Gaurisanker', and 'Everest' really are proper names. Look, someone might say (someone has said it: his name was 'Bertrand Russell'), just because statements like "Hesperus is Phosphorus" and "Gaurisanker is Everest" are contingent, we can see that the names in question are not really purely referential. You are not, in Mrs. Marcus' phrase, just 'tagging' an object; you are actually describing it. What does the contingent fact that Hesperus is Phosphorus amount to? Well, it amounts to the fact that *the* star in a certain portion of the sky in the evening is *the* star in a certain portion of the sky in the morning. Similarly, the contingent fact that Gaurisanker is Everest amounts to the fact that the mountain viewed from such and such an angle in Nepal is the mountain viewed from such and such another angle in Tibet. Therefore, such names as 'Hesperus' and 'Phosphorus' can only be abbreviations for descriptions. The term 'Phosphorus' *has* to mean "the star seen ...," or (let us be cautious because it actually turned out not to be a star), "the *heavenly body* seen from such and such a position at such and such a time in the morning," and the name 'Hesperus' has to mean "the heavenly body seen in such and such a position at such and such a time in the evening." So, Russell concludes, if we want to reserve the term "name" for things which really just name an object without describing it, the only real proper names we can have are names of our own immediate sense data, objects of our own 'immediate acquaintance'. The only such names which occur in language are demonstratives like "this" and "that." And it is easy to see that this requirement of necessity of identity, understood as exempting identities between names from all imaginable doubt, can indeed be guaranteed only for demonstrative names of immediate sense data; for only in such cases can an identity statement between two different names have a general immunity from Cartesian doubt. There are some other things Russell has sometimes allowed as objects of acquaintance, such as one's self; we need not go into details here. Other philosophers (for example, Mrs. Marcus in her reply, at least in the verbal discussion as I remember it – I do not know if this got into print, so perhaps this should not be 'tagged' on her[7]) have said, "If names are really just tags, genuine tags, then a good dictionary should be able to tell us that they are names of the same object." You have an object *a* and an object *b* with names 'John' and 'Joe'. Then, according to Mrs. Marcus, a dictionary should be able to tell you whether or not 'John' and 'Joe' are names of the same object. Of course, I do not know what ideal dictionaries should do, but ordinary proper names do not seem to satisfy this requirement. You certainly *can*, in the case of ordinary proper names, make quite empirical discoveries that, let's say, Hesperus is Phosphorus, though we thought otherwise. We can be in doubt as to whether Gaurisanker is Everest or Cicero is in fact Tully. Even now, we could conceivably discover that we were wrong in supposing that Hesperus was Phosphorus. Maybe the astronomers made an error. So it seems that this view is wrong and that if by a name we do not mean some artificial notion of names such as Russell's, but a proper name in the ordinary sense, then there can be contingent identity statements using proper names, and the view to the contrary seems plainly wrong.

In recent philosophy a large number of other identity statements have been emphasized as examples of contingent identity statements, different, perhaps, from either of the types I have mentioned before. One of them is, for example, the statement "Heat is the motion of molecules." First, science is supposed to have discovered this. Empirical scientists in their investigations have been supposed to discover (and, I suppose, they did) that the external phenomenon which we call "heat" is, in fact, molecular agitation. Another example of such a discovery is that water is H_2O, and yet other examples are that gold is the element with such and such an atomic number, that light is a stream of photons, and so on. These are all in some sense of "identity statement" identity statements. Second, it is thought, they are plainly contingent identity statements, just because they were scientific discoveries. After all, heat might have turned out not to have been the motion of molecules. There were other alternative theories of heat proposed, for example, the caloric theory of heat. If these theories of heat had been correct, then heat would not have been the motion of molecules, but instead, some substance suffusing the hot object, called "caloric." And it was a matter of course of science and not of any logical necessity that the one theory turned out to be correct and the other theory turned out to be incorrect.

So, here again, we have, apparently, another plain example of a contingent identity statement. This has been supposed to be a very important example because of its connection with the mind-body problem. There have been many philosophers who have wanted to be materialists, and to be materialists in a particular form, which is known today as "the identity theory." According to this theory, a certain mental state, such as a person's being in pain, is identical with a certain state of his brain (or, perhaps, of his entire body, according to some theorists), at any rate, a certain material or neural state of his brain or body. And so, according to this theory, my being in pain at this instant, if I were, would be identical with my body's being or my brain's being in a certain state. Others have objected that this cannot be because, after all, we can imagine my pain existing even if the state of the body did not. We can perhaps imagine my not being embodied at all and still being in pain, or, conversely, we could imagine my body existing and being in the very same state even if there were no pain. In fact, conceivably, it could be in this state even though there were no mind 'back of it', so to speak, at all. The usual reply has been to concede that all of these things might have been the case, but to argue that these are irrelevant to the question of the identity of the mental state and the physical state. This identity, it is said, is just another contingent scientific identification, similar to the identification of heat with molecular motion, or water with H_2O. Just as we can imagine heat without any molecular motion, so we can imagine a mental state without any corresponding brain state. But, just as the first fact is not damaging to the identification of heat and the motion of molecules, so the second fact is not at all damaging to the identification of a mental state with the corresponding brain state. And so, many recent philosophers have held it to be very important for our theoretical understanding of the mind-body problem that there can be contingent identity statements of this form.

To state finally what *I* think, as opposed to what seems to be the case, or what others think, I think that in both cases, the case of names and the case of the theoretical identifications, the identity statements are necessary and not contingent. That is to say, they are necessary if true; of course, false identity statements are not necessary. How can one possibly defend such a view? Perhaps I lack a complete answer to this question, even though I am convinced that the view is true. But to begin an answer, let me make some distinctions that I want to use. The first is between a *rigid* and a *nonrigid designator*. What do these terms mean? As an example of a nonrigid designator, I can give an expression such as 'the inventor of bifocals'. Let us suppose it was Benjamin Franklin who invented bifocals, and so the expression, 'the inventor of bifocals', designates or refers to a certain man, namely, Benjamin Franklin. However, we can easily imagine that the world could have been different, that under different circumstances someone else would have come upon this invention before Benjamin Franklin did, and in that case, he would have been the inventor of bifocals. So, in this sense, the expression 'the inventor of bifocals' is nonrigid: Under certain circumstances one man would have been the inventor of bifocals; under other circumstances, another man would have. In contrast, consider the expression 'the square root of 25'. Independently of the empirical facts, we can give an arithmetical proof that the square root of 25 is in fact the number 5, and because we have proved this mathematically, what we have proved is necessary. If we think of numbers as entities at all, and let us suppose, at least for the purpose of this lecture, that we do, then the expression 'the square root of 25' necessarily designates a certain number, namely 5. Such an expression I call 'a *rigid* designator'. Some philosophers think that anyone who even uses the notions of rigid or nonrigid designator has already shown that he has fallen into a certain confusion or has not paid attention to certain facts. What do I mean by 'rigid designator'? I mean a term that designates the same object in all possible worlds. To get rid of one confusion which certainly is not mine, I do not use "might have designated a different object" to refer to the fact that language might have been used differently. For example, the expression 'the inventor of bifocals' might have been used by inhabitants of this planet always to refer to the man who corrupted Hadleyburg. This would have been the case, if, first, the people on this planet had not spoken English, but some other language, which phonetically overlapped with English; and if, second, in that language the expression 'the inventor of bifocals' meant the 'man who corrupted Hadleyburg'. Then it would refer, of course, in their language, to whoever in fact corrupted Hadleyburg in this counterfactual situation. That is not what I mean. What I mean by saying that a description might have referred to something different, I mean that in *our* language as *we* use it in describing a counterfactual situation, there might have been a different object satisfying the descriptive conditions *we* give for reference. So, for example, we use the phrase 'the inventor of bifocals', when we are talking about another possible world or a counterfactual situation, to refer to whoever in that counterfactual situation would have invented bifocals, not to the person whom people *in* that counterfactual situation would have called 'the inventor of bifocals'. *They* might have spoken a different language which phonetically overlapped with English in which 'the inventor of bifocals' is used in some other way. I am *not* concerned with that question here. For that matter, they might have been deaf and dumb, or there might have been no people at all. (There still could have been an inventor of bifocals even if there were no people – God, or Satan, will do.)

Second, in talking about the notion of a rigid designator, I do not mean to imply that the object referred to has to exist in all possible worlds, that is, that it has to necessarily exist. Some things, perhaps mathematical entities such as the positive integers, if they exist at all, necessarily exist. Some people have held that God both exists and necessarily exists; others, that He contingently exists; others, that He contingently fails to exist; and others, that He necessarily fails to exist:[8] all four options have been tried. But at any rate, when I use the notion of rigid designator, I do not imply that the object referred to necessarily exists. All I mean is that in any possible world where the object in question does exist, in any situation where the object *would* exist, we use the designator in question to designate that object. In a situation where the object does not exist, then we should say that the designator has no referent and that the object in question so designated does not exist.

As I said, many philosophers would find the very notion of rigid designator objectionable *per se*. And the objection that people make may be stated as follows: Look, you're talking about situations which are counterfactual, that is to say, you're talking about other possible worlds. Now these worlds are completely disjoint, after all, from the actual world which is not just another possible world; it is the actual world. So, before you talk about, let us say, such an object as Richard Nixon in another possible world at all, you have to say which object in this other possible world would *be* Richard Nixon. Let us talk about a situation in which, as *you* would say, Richard Nixon would have been a member of SDS. Certainly the member of SDS you are talking about is someone very different in many of his properties from Nixon. Before we even can say whether this man would have been Richard Nixon or not, we have to set up criteria of identity across possible worlds. Here are these other possible worlds. There are all kinds of objects in them with different properties from those of any actual object. Some of them resemble Nixon in some ways, some of them resemble Nixon in other ways. Well, which of these objects is Nixon? One has to give a criterion of identity. And this shows how the very notion of rigid designator runs in a circle. Suppose we designate a certain number as the number of planets. Then, if that is our favorite way, so to speak, of designating this number, then in any other possible worlds we will have to identify whatever number is the number of planets with the number 9, which in the actual world is the number of planets. So, it is argued by various philosophers, for example, implicitly by Quine, and explicitly by many others in his wake, we cannot really ask whether a designator is rigid or nonrigid because we first need a criterion of identity across possible worlds. An extreme view has even been held that, since possible worlds are so disjoint from our own, we cannot really say that any object in them is the same as an object existing now but only that there are some objects which resemble things in the actual world, more or less. We, therefore, should not really speak of what would have been true of Nixon in another possible world but, only of what 'counterparts' (the term which David Lewis uses[9]) of Nixon there would have been. Some people in other possible worlds have dogs whom they call 'Checkers'. Others favor the ABM but do not have any dog called Checkers. There are various people who resemble Nixon more or less, but none of them can really be said to be Nixon; they are only *counterparts* of Nixon, and you choose which one is the best counterpart by noting which resembles Nixon the most closely, according to your favorite criteria. Such views are widespread, both among the defenders of quantified modal logic and among its detractors.

All of this talk seems to me to have taken the metaphor of possible worlds much too seriously in some way. It is as if a 'possible world' were like a foreign country, or distant planet way out there. It is as if we see dimly through a telescope various actors on this distant planet. Actually David Lewis' view seems the most reasonable if one takes this picture literally. No one far away on another planet can be strictly identical with someone here. But, even if we have some marvellous methods of transportation to take one and the same person from planet to planet, we really need some epistemological criteria of identity to be able to say whether someone on this distant planet is the same person as someone here.

All of this seems to me to be a totally misguided way of looking at things. What it amounts to is the view that counterfactual situations have to be described purely qualitatively. So, we cannot say, for example, "If Nixon had only given a sufficient bribe to Senator X, he would have gotten Carswell through" because that refers to certain people, Nixon and Carswell, and talks about what things would be true of them in a counterfactual situation. We must say instead "If a man who has a hairline like such and such, and holds such and such political opinions had given a bribe to a man who was a senator and had such and such other qualities, then a man who was a judge in the South and had many other qualities resembling Carswell would have been confirmed." In other words, we must describe counterfactual situations purely qualitatively and then ask the question,

"Given that the situation contains people or things with such and such qualities, which of these people is (or is counterpart of) Nixon, which is Carswell, and so on?" This seems to me to be wrong. Who is to prevent us from saying "Nixon might have gotten Carswell through had he done certain things?" We are speaking of *Nixon* and asking what, in certain counterfactual situations, would have been true of *him*. We can say that if Nixon had done such and such, he would have lost the election to Humphrey. Those I am opposing would argue, "Yes, but how do you find out if the man you are talking about is in fact Nixon?" It would indeed be very hard to find out, if you were looking at the whole situation through a telescope, but that is not what we are doing here. Possible worlds are not something to which an epistemological question like this applies. And if the phrase 'possible worlds' is what makes anyone think some such question applies, he should just *drop* this phrase and use some other expression, say 'counterfactual situation,' which might be less misleading. If we say "If Nixon had bribed such and such a Senator, Nixon would have gotten Carswell through," what is given in the very description of that situation is that it is a situation in which we are speaking of Nixon, and of Carswell, and of such and such a Senator. And there seems to be no less objection to *stipulating* that we are speaking of certain *people* than there can be objection to stipulating that we are speaking of certain *qualities*. Advocates of the other view take speaking of certain qualities as unobjectionable. They do not say, "How do we know that this quality (in another possible world) is that of redness?" But they do find speaking of certain *people* objectionable. But I see no more reason to object in the one case than in the other. I think it really comes from the idea of possible worlds as existing out there, but very far off, viewable only through a special telescope. Even more objectionable is the view of David Lewis. According to Lewis, when we say "Under certain circumstances Nixon would have gotten Carswell through," we really mean "Some man, other than Nixon but closely resembling him, would have gotten some judge, other than Carswell but closely resembling him, through." Maybe that is so, that some man closely resembling Nixon could have gotten some man closely resembling Carswell through. But *that* would not comfort either Nixon or Carswell, nor would it make Nixon kick himself and say "*I* should have done such and such to get Carswell through." The question is whether under certain circumstances Nixon *himself* could have gotten *Carswell* through. And I think the objection is simply based on a misguided picture.

Instead, we can perfectly well talk about rigid and nonrigid designators. Moreover, we have a simple, intuitive test for them. We can say, for example, that the number or planets might have been a different number from the number it in fact is. For example, there might have been only seven planets. We can say that the inventor of bifocals might have been someone other than the man who *in fact* invented bifocals.[10] We cannot say, though, that the square root of 81 might have been a different number from the number it in fact is, for that number just has to be 9. If we apply this intuitive test to proper names, such as for example 'Richard Nixon', they would seem intuitively to come out to be rigid designators. First, when we talk even about the counterfactual situation in which we suppose Nixon to have done different things, we assume we are still talking about Nixon himself. We say, "If Nixon had bribed a certain Senator, he would have gotten Carswell through," and we assume that by 'Nixon' and 'Carswell' we are still referring to the very same people as in the actual world. And it seems that we cannot say "Nixon might have been a different man from the man he in fact was," unless, of course, we mean it metaphorically: He might have been a different *sort* of person (if you believe in free will and that people are not inherently corrupt). You might think the statement true in that sense, but Nixon could not have been in the other literal sense a different person from the person he, in fact, is, even though the thirty-seventh President of the United States might have been Humphrey. So the phrase the "thirty-seventh President" is non-rigid, but 'Nixon', it would seem, is rigid.

Let me make another distinction before I go back to the question of identity statements. This distinction is very fundamental and also hard to see through. In recent discussion, many philosophers who have debated the meaningfulness of various categories of truths, have regarded them as identical. Some of those who identify them are vociferous defenders of them, and others, such as Quine, say they are all identically meaningless. But usually they're not distinguished. These are categories such as 'analytic', 'necessary', 'a priori', and sometimes even 'certain'. I will not talk about all of these but only about the notions of a prioricity and necessity. Very often these are held to be synonyms. (Many philosophers probably should not be described as holding them to be synonyms; they simply *use* them interchangeably.) I wish to distinguish them. What do we mean by calling a statement *necessary*? We simply mean that the statement in question, first, is true, and, second, that it could not have been otherwise. When we say that something is *contingently* true, we mean that, though it is in fact the case, it could have been the case that things would have been otherwise. If we wish to assign this distinction to a branch of philosophy, we should assign it to metaphysics. To the contrary, there is the notion of an *a priori truth*. An a priori truth is to be one which can be *known* to be true independently of all experience. Notice that this does not in and of itself say anything about all possible worlds, unless this is put into the definition. All that it says is that it can be known to be true of the actual world, independently of all experience. It may, by some philosophical argument, follow from our knowing, independently of experience, that something is true of the actual world, that it has to be known to be true also of all possible worlds. But if this is to be established, it requires some philosophical argument to establish it. Now, *this* notion, if we were to assign it to a branch of philosophy, belongs, not to metaphysics, but to epistemology. It has to do with the way we can know certain things to be in fact true. Now, it may be the case, of course, that anything which is necessary is something which *can* be known a priori. (Notice, by the way, the notion a priori truth as thus defined has in it *another* modality: it can be known independently of all experience. It is a little complicated because there is a double modality here.) I will not have time to explore these notions in full detail here but one thing we can see from the outset is that these two notions are by no means trivially the same. If they are coextensive, it takes some philosophical argument to establish it. As stated, they belong to different domains of philosophy. One of them has something to do with *knowledge*, of what can be known in certain ways about the *actual* world. The other one has to do with *metaphysics*, how the world *could* have been; given that it is the way it is, could it have been otherwise, in certain ways? Now I hold, as a matter of fact, that neither class of statements is contained in the other. But, all we need to talk about here is this: Is everything that is necessary knowable a priori or known a priori? Consider the following example: the Goldbach conjecture. This says that every even number is the sum of two primes. It is a mathematical statement and if it is true at all, it has to be necessary. Certainly, one could not say that though in fact every even number is the sum of two primes, there could have been some extra number which was even and not the sum of two primes. What would that mean? On the other hand, the answer to the question whether every even number *is* in fact the sum of two primes is unknown, and we have no method at present for deciding. So we certainly do not know, a priori or even a posteriori, that every even number is the sum of two primes. (Well, perhaps we have some evidence in that no counterexample has been found.) But we certainly do not know a priori anyway, that every even number is, in fact the sum of two primes. But, of course, the definition just says "*can* be known independently of experience," and someone might say that if it is true, we *could* know it independently of experience. It is hard to see exactly what this claim means. It might be so. One thing it might mean is that if it were true we could *prove* it. This claim is certainly wrong if it is generally applied to mathematical statements and we have to work within some fixed system. This is what Gödel proved. And even if we mean an 'intuitive proof in general' it might just be the case (at least, this view is as clear and as probable as the contrary) that though the statement is true, there is just no way the human mind could ever prove it. Of course, one way an *infinite* mind might be able to prove it is by looking through each natural number one by one and checking. In this sense, of course, it can, perhaps, be known a priori, but only by an infinite mind, and then this gets into other complicated questions. I do not want to discuss questions about the conceivablilty of performing an infinite number of acts like looking through each number one by one. A vast philosophical literature has been written on this: Some have declared it is logically impossible; others that it is logically possible; and some do not know. The main point is that it is not trivial that just because such a statement is necessary it can be known a priori. Some considerable clarification is required before we decide that it can be so known. And so this shows that even if everything necessary is a priori in some sense, it should not be taken as a trivial matter of definition. It is a substantive philosophical thesis which requires some work.

Another example that one might give relates to the problem of essentialism. Here is a lectern. A question which has often been raised in philosophy is: What are its essential properties? What properties, aside from trivial ones like self-identity, are such that this object has to have them if it exists at all,[11] are such that if an object did not have it, it would not be this object?[12] For example, being made of wood, and not of ice, might be an essential property of this lectern. Let us just take the weaker statement that it is not made of ice. That will establish it as strongly as we need it, perhaps as dramatically. Supposing this lectern is in fact made of wood, could this very lectern have been made from the very beginning of its existence from ice, say frozen from water in the Thames? One has a considerable feeling that it could *not*, though in fact one certainly could have made a lectern of water from the Thames, frozen it into ice by some process, and put it right there in place of this thing. If one had done so, one would have made, of course, a *different* object. It would not have been *this very lectern*, and so one would not have a case in which this very lectern here was made of ice, or was made from water from the Thames. The question of whether it could afterward, say in a minute from now, turn into ice is something else. So, it would seem, if an example like this is correct – and this is what advocates of essentialism have held – that this lectern could not have been made of ice, that is in any counterfactual situation of which we would say that this lectern existed at all, we would have to say also that it was not made from water from the Thames frozen into ice. Some have rejected, of course, any such notion of essential property as meaningless. Usually, it is because (and I think this is what Quine, for example, would say) they have held that it depends on the notion of identity across possible worlds, and that this is itself meaningless. Since I have rejected this view already, I will not deal with it again. We can talk about *this very object*, and whether it could have had certain properties which it does not in fact have. For example, it could have been in another room from the room it in fact is in, even at this very time, but it could not have been made from the very beginning from water frozen into ice.

If the essentialist view is correct, it can only be correct if we sharply distinguish between the notions of a posteriori and a priori truth on the one hand, and contingent and necessary truth on the other hand, for although the statement that this table, if it exists at all, was not made of ice, is necessary, it certainly is not something that we know a priori. What we know is that first, lecterns usually are not made of ice, they are usually made of wood. This looks like wood. It does not feel cold and it probably would if it were made of ice. Therefore, I conclude, probably this is not made of ice. Here my entire judgment is a posteriori. I could find out that an ingenious trick has been played upon me and that, in fact, this lectern is made of ice; but what I am saying is, given that it is in fact not made of ice, in fact is made of wood, one cannot imagine that under certain circumstances it could have been made of ice. So we have to say that though we cannot know a priori whether this table was made of ice or not, given that it is not made of ice, it is *necessarily* not made of ice. In other words, if P is the statement that the lectern is not made of ice, one knows by a priori philosophical analysis, some conditional of the form "if P, then necessarily P." If the table is not made of ice, it is necessarily not made of ice. On the other hand, then, we know by empirical investigation that P, the antecedent of the conditional, is true – that this table is not made of ice. We can conclude by modus ponens:

$$P \supset \Box\, P$$
$$P$$
$$\text{--------}$$
$$\Box\, P$$

The conclusion – '$\Box\ P$' – is that it is necessary that the table not be made of ice, and this conclusion is known a posteriori, since one of the premises on which it is based is a posteriori. So, the notion of essential properties can be maintained only by distinguishing between the notions of a priori and necessary truth, and I do maintain it.

Let us return to the question of identities. Concerning the statement 'Hesperus is Phosphorus' or the statement 'Cicero is Tully', one can find all of these out by empirical investigations, and we might turn out to be wrong in our empirical beliefs. So, it is usually argued, such statements must therefore be contingent. Some have embraced the other side of the coin and have held "Because of this argument about necessity, identity statements between names have to be knowable a priori, so, only a very special category of names, possibly, really works as names; the other things are bogus names, disguised descriptions, or something of the sort. However, a certain very narrow class of statements of identity are known a priori, and these are the ones which contain the genuine names." If one accepts the distinctions that I have made, one need not jump to either conclusion. One can hold that certain statements of identity between names, though often known a posteriori, and maybe not knowable a priori, are in fact necessary, if true. So, we have some room to hold this. But, of course, to have some room to hold it does not mean that we should hold it. So let us see what the evidence is. First, recall the remark that I made that proper names seem to be rigid designators, as when we use the name 'Nixon' to talk about a certain man, even in counterfactual situations. If we say, "If Nixon had not written the letter to Saxbe, maybe he would have gotten Carswell through," we are in this statement talking about Nixon, Saxbe, and Carswell, the very same men as in the actual world, and what would have happened to them under certain counterfactual circumstances. If names are rigid designators, then there can be no question about identities being necessary, because 'a' and 'b' will be rigid designators of a certain man or thing x. Then even in every possible world, a and b will both refer to this same object x, and to no other, and so there will be no situation in which a might not have been b. That would have to be a situation in which the object which we are also now calling 'x' would not have been identical with itself. Then one could not possibly have a situation in which Cicero would not have been Tully or Hesperus would not have been Phosphorus.[13]

Aside from the identification of necessity with a priority, what has made people feel the other way? There are two things which have made people feel the other way.[14] Some people tend to regard the identity statements as metalinguistic statements, to identify the statement "Hesperus is Phosphorus" with the metalinguistic statement, "'Hesperus' and 'Phosphorus' are names of the same heavenly body." And that, of course, might have been false. We might have used the terms 'Hesperus' and 'Phosphorus' as names of *two* different heavenly bodies. But, of course, this has nothing to do with the necessity of identity. In the same sense "2+2 = 4" might have been false. The phrases "2+2" and "4" might have been used to refer to two different numbers. One can imagine a language, for example, in which "+", "2", and "=" were used in the standard way, but "4" was used as the name of, say, the square root of minus 1, as we should call it, "*i*." Then "2+2 = 4" would be false, for 2 plus 2 is not equal to the square root of minus 1. But this is not what we want. We do not want just to say that a certain statement which we in fact use to express something true could have expressed something false. We want to use the statement in *our* way and see if it could have been false. Let us do this. What is the idea people have? They say, "Look, Hesperus might not have been Phosphorus. Here a certain planet was seen in the morning, and it was seen in the evening; and it just turned out later on as a matter of empirical fact that they were one and the same planet. If things had turned out otherwise, they would have been two different planets, or two different heavenly bodies, so how can you say that such a statement is necessary?"

Now there are two things that such people can mean. First, they can mean that we do not know a priori whether Hesperus is Phosphorus. This I have already conceded. Second, they may mean that they can actually imagine circumstances that they would call circumstances in which Hesperus would not have been Phosphorus. Let us think what would be such a circumstance, using these terms here as *names* of a planet. For example, it could have been the case that Venus did indeed rise in the morning in exactly the position in which we saw it, but that on the other hand, in the position which is in fact occupied by Venus in the evening, Venus was not there, and Mars took its place. This is all counterfactual because in fact Venus is there. Now one can also imagine that in this counterfactual other possible world, the earth would have been inhabited by people and that they should have used the names 'Phosphorus' for Venus in the morning and 'Hesperus' for Mars in the evening. Now, this is all very good, but would it be a situation in which Hesperus was not Phosphorus? Of course, it is a situation in which people would have been able to *say*, truly, "Hesperus is not Phosphorus"; but we are supposed to describe it in our language. Well, how could it actually happen that Venus would not be in that position in the evening? For example, let us say that there is some comet that comes around every evening and yanks things over a little bit. (That would be a very simple scientific way of imagining it: not really too simple – that is very hard to imagine actually.) It just happens to come around every evening, and things get yanked over a little bit. Mars gets yanked over to the very position where Venus is, then the comet yanks things back to their normal position in the morning. Thinking of this planet which we now call 'Phosphorus', what should we say? Well, we can say that the comet passes it and yanks Phosphorus over so that it is not in the position normally occupied by Phosphorus in the evening. If we do say this, and really use 'Phosphorus' as the name of a planet, then we have to say that, under such circumstances, Phosphorus in the evening would not be in the position where we, in fact, saw it; or alternatively, Hesperus in the evening would not be in the position in which we, in fact, saw it. We might say that under such circumstances, we would not have called Hesperus 'Hesperus' because Hesperus would have been in a different position. But that still would not make Phosphorus different from Hesperus; but what would then be the case instead is that Hesperus would have been in a different position from the position it in fact is and, perhaps, not in such a position that people would have called it 'Hesperus'. But that would not be a situation in which Phosphorus would not have been Hesperus.

Let us take another example which may be clearer. Suppose someone uses 'Tully' to refer to the Roman orator who denounced Cataline and uses the name 'Cicero' to refer to the man whose works he had to study in third-year Latin in high school. Of course, he may not know in advance that the very same man who denounced Cataline wrote these works, and that is a contingent statement. But the fact that this statement in contingent should not make us think that the statement that Cicero is Tully, if it is true, and it is in fact true, is contingent. Suppose, for example, that Cicero actually did denounce Cataline, but thought that this political achievement was so great that he should not bother writing any literary works. Would we say that these would be circumstances under which he would not have been Cicero? It seems to me that the answer is no, that instead we would say that, under such circumstances, Cicero would not have written any literary works. It is not a necessary property of Cicero – the way the shadow follows the man – that he should have written certain works; we can easily imagine a situation in which Shakespeare would not have written the works of Shakespeare, or one in which Cicero would not have written the works of Cicero. What may be the case is that we *fix the reference* of the term 'Cicero' by use of some descriptive phrase, such as 'the author of these works'. But once we have this reference fixed, we then use the name 'Cicero' *rigidly* to designate the man who in fact we have identified by his authorship of these works. We do not use it to designate whoever would have written these works in place of Cicero, if someone else wrote them. It might have been the case that the man who wrote these works was not the man who denounced Cataline. Cassius might have written these works. But we would not then say that Cicero would have been Cassius, unless we were speaking in a very loose and metaphorical way. We would say that Cicero, whom we may have identified and come to know by his works, would not have written them, and that someone else, say Cassius, would have written them in his place.

Such examples are not grounds for thinking that identity statements are contingent. To take them as such grounds is to misconstrue the relation between a *name* and a *description used to fix its reference*, to take them to be *synonyms*. Even if we fix the reference of such a name as 'Cicero' as the man who wrote such and such works, in speaking of counterfactual situations, when we speak of Cicero, we do not then speak of whoever in such counterfactual situations would have written such and such works, but rather of Cicero, whom we have identified by the contingent property that he is the man who in fact, that is, in the actual world, wrote certain works.[15]

I hope this is reasonably clear in a brief compass. Now, actually I have been presupposing something I do not really believe to be, in general, true. Let us suppose that we do fix the reference of a name by a description. Even if we do so, we do not then make the name *synonymous* with the description, but instead we use the name *rigidly* to refer to the object so named, even in talking about counterfactual situations where the thing named would not satisfy the description in question. Now, this is what I think in fact is true for those cases of naming where the reference is fixed by description. But, in fact, I also think, contrary to most recent theorists, that the reference of names is rarely or almost never fixed by means of description. And by this I do not just mean what Searle says: "It's not a single description, but rather a cluster, a family of properties which fixes the reference." I mean that properties in this sense are not used *at all*. But I do not have the time to go into this here. So, let us suppose that at least one half of prevailing views about naming is true, that the reference is fixed by descriptions. Even were that true, the name would not be synonymous with the description, but would be used to *name* an object which we pick out by the contingent fact that it satisfies a certain description. And so, even though we can imagine a case where the man who wrote these works would not have been the man who denounced Cataline, we should not say that that would be a case in which Cicero would not have been Tully. We should say that it is a case in which Cicero did not write these works, but rather that Cassius did. And the identity of Cicero and Tully still holds.

Let me turn to the case of heat and the motion of molecules. Here surely is a case that is contingent identity! Recent philosophy has emphasized this again and again. So, if it is a case of contingent identity, then let us imagine under what circumstances it would be false. Now, concerning this statement I hold that the circumstances philosophers apparently have in mind as circumstances under which it would have been false are not in fact such circumstances. First, of course, it is argued that "Heat is the motion of molecules" is an a posteriori judgment; scientific investigation might have turned out otherwise. As I said before, this shows nothing against the view that it is necessary – at least if I am right. But here, surely, people had very specific circumstances in mind under which, so they thought, the judgment that heat is the motion of molecules would have been false. What were these circumstances? One can distill them out of the fact that we found out empirically that heat is the motion of molecules. How was this? What did we find out first when we found out that heat is the motion of molecules? There is a certain external phenomenon which we can sense by the sense of touch, and it produces a sensation which we call "the sensation of heat." We then discover that the external phenomenon which produces this sensation, which we sense, by means of our sense of touch, is in fact that of molecular agitation in the thing that we touch, a very high degree of molecular agitation. So, it might be thought, to imagine a situation in which heat would not have been the motion of molecules, we need only imagine a situation in which we could have had the very same sensation and it would have been produced by something other than the motion of molecules. Similarly, if we wanted to imagine a situation in which light was not a stream of photons, we could imagine a situation in which we were sensitive to something else in exactly the same way, producing what we call visual experiences, though not through a stream of photons. To make the case stronger, or to look at another side of the coin, we could also consider a situation in which we are concerned with the motion of molecules but in which such motion does not give us the sensation of heat. And it might also have happened that we, or, at least, the creatures inhabiting this planet, might have been so constituted that, let us say, an increase in the motion of molecules did not give us this sensation but that, on the contrary, a slowing down of the molecules did give us the very same sensation. This would be a situation, so it might be thought, in which heat would not be the motion of molecules, or, more precisely, in which temperature would not be mean molecular kinetic energy.

But I think it would not be so. Let us think about the situation again. First, let us think about it in the actual world. Imagine right now the world invaded by a number of Martians, who do indeed get the very sensation that we call "the sensation of heat" when they feel some ice which has slow molecular motion, and who do not get a sensation of heat – in fact, maybe just the reverse – when they put their hand near a fire which causes a lot of molecular agitation. Would we say, "Ah, this casts some doubt on heat being the motion of molecules, because there are these other people who don't get the same sensation"? Obviously not, and no one would think so. We would say instead that the Martians somehow feel the very sensation we get when we feel heat when they feel cold and that they do not get a sensation of heat when they feel heat. But now let us think of a counterfactual situation.[16] Suppose the earth had from the very beginning been inhabited by such creatures. First, imagine it inhabited by no creatures at all: then there is no one to feel any sensations of heat. But we would not say that under such circumstances it would necessarily be the case that heat did not exist; we would say that heat might have existed, for example, if there were fires that heated up the air.

Let us suppose the laws of physics were not very different: Fires do heat up the air. Then there would have been heat even though there were no creatures around to feel it. Now let us suppose evolution takes place, and life is created, and there are some creatures around. But they are not like us, they are more like the Martians. Now would we say that heat has suddenly turned to cold, because of the way the creatures of this planet sense it? No, I think we should describe this situation as a situation in which, though the creatures on this planet got our sensation of heat, they did not get it when they were exposed to heat. They got it when they were exposed to cold. And that is something we can surely well imagine. We can imagine it just as we can imagine our planet being invaded by creatures of this sort. Think of it in two steps. First there is a stage where there are no creatures at all, and one can certainly imagine the planet still having both heat and cold, though no one is around to sense it. Then the planet comes through an evolutionary process to be peopled with beings of different neural structure from ourselves. Then these creatures could be such that they were insensitive to heat; they did not feel it in the way we do; but on the other hand, they felt cold in much the same way that we feel heat. But still, heat would be heat, and cold would be cold. And particularly, then, this goes in no way against saying that in this counterfactual situation heat would still *be* the molecular motion, *be* that which is produced by fires, and so on, just as it would have been if there had been no creatures on the planet at all. Similarly, we could imagine that the planet was inhabited by creatures who got visual sensation when there were sound waves in the air. We should not therefore say, "Under such circumstances, sound would have been light." Instead we should say, "The planet was inhabited by creatures who were in some sense visually sensitive to sound, and maybe even visually sensitive to light." If this is correct, it can still be and will still be a necessary truth that heat is the motion of molecules and that light is a stream of photons.

To state the view succinctly: we use both the terms 'heat' and 'the motion of molecules' as rigid designators for a certain external phenomenon. Since heat is in fact the motion of molecules, and the designators are rigid, by the argument I have given here, it is going to be *necessary* that heat is the motion of molecules. What gives us the illusion of contingency is the fact we have identified the heat by the contingent fact that there happen to be creatures on this planet – (namely, ourselves) who are sensitive to it in a certain way, that is, who are sensitive to the motion of molecules or to heat – these are one and the same thing. And this is contingent. So we use the description, 'that which causes such and such sensations, or that which we sense in such and such a way', to identify heat. But in using this fact we use a contingent property of heat, just as we use the contingent property of Cicero as having written such and such works to identify him. We then use the terms 'heat' in the one case and 'Cicero' in the other *rigidly* to designate the objects for which they stand. And of course the term 'the motion of molecules' is rigid; it always stands for the motion of molecules, never for any other phenomenon. So, as Bishop Butler said, "everything is what it is and not another thing." Therefore, "Heat is the motion of molecules" will be necessary, not contingent, and one only has the *illusion* of contingency in the way one could have the illusion of contingency in thinking that this table might have been made of ice. We might think one could imagine it, but if we try, we can see on reflection that what we are really imagining is just there being another lectern in this very position here which was in fact made of ice. The fact that we may identify this lectern by being the object we see and touch in such and such a position is something else.

Now how does this relate to the problem of mind and body? It is usually held that this is a contingent identity statement just like "Heat is the motion of molecules." That cannot be. It cannot be a contingent identity statement just like "Heat is the motion of molecules" because, if I am right, "Heat is the motion of molecules" is not a contingent identity statement. Let us look at this statement. For example, "My being in pain at such and such a time is my being in such and such a brain state at such and such a time," or, "Pain in general is such and such a neural (brain) state."

This is held to be contingent on the following grounds. First, we can imagine the brain state existing though there is no pain at all. It is only a scientific fact that whenever we are in a certain brain state we have a pain. Second, one might imagine a creature being in pain, but not being in any specified brain state at all, maybe not having a brain at all. People even think, at least prima facie, though they may be wrong, that they can imagine totally disembodied creatures, at any rate certainly not creatures with bodies anything like our own. So it seems that we can imagine definite circumstances under which this relationship would have been false. Now, if these circumstances are circumstances, notice that we cannot deal with them simply by saying that this is just an illusion, something we can apparently imagine, but in fact cannot in the way we thought erroneously that we could imagine a situation in which heat was not the motion of molecules. Because although we can say that we pick out heat contingently by the contingent property that it affects us in such and such a way, we cannot similarly say that we pick out pain contingently by the fact that it affects us in such and such a way. On such a picture there would be the brain state, and we pick it out by the contingent fact that it affects us as pain. Now that might be true of the brain state, but it cannot be true of the pain. The experience itself has to be *this experience*, and I cannot say that it is a contingent property of the pain I now have that it is a pain.[17] In fact, it would seem that both the terms, 'my pain' and 'my being in such and such a brain state' are, first of all, both rigid designators. That is, whenever anything is such and such a pain, it is essentially that very object, namely, such and such a pain, and wherever anything is such and such a brain state, it is essentially that very object, namely, such and such a brain state. So both of these are rigid designators. One cannot say this pain might have been something else, some other state. These are both rigid designators.

Second, the way we would think of picking them out – namely, the pain by its being an experience of a certain sort, and the brain state by its being the state of a certain material object, being of such and such molecular configuration – both of these pick out their objects essentially and not accidentally, that is, they pick them out by essential properties. Whenever the molecules are in this configuration, we do have such and such a brain state. Whenever you feel *this*, you do have a pain. So it seems that the identity theorist is in some trouble, for, since we have two rigid designators, the identity statement in question is necessary. Because they pick out their objects essentially, we cannot say the case where you seem to imagine the identity statement is false is really an illusion like the illusion one gets in the case of heat and molecular motion, because that illusion depended on the fact that we pick out heat by a certain contingent property. So there is very little room to manoeuvre; perhaps none.[18] The identity theorist, who holds that pain is the brain state, also has to hold that it necessarily is the brain state. He therefore cannot concede, but has to deny, that there would have been situations under which one would have had pain but not the corresponding brain state. Now usually in arguments on the identity theory, this is very far from being denied. In fact, it is conceded from the outset by the materialist as well as by his opponent. He says, "Of course, it *could* have been the case that we had pains without the brain states. It is a contingent identity." But that cannot be. He has to hold that we are under some illusion in thinking that we can imagine that there could have been pains without brain states. And the only model I can think of for what the illusion might be, or at least the model given by the analogy the materialists themselves suggest, namely, heat and molecular motion, simply does not work in this case. So the materialist is up against a very stiff challenge. He has to show that these things we think we can see to be possible are in fact not possible. He has to show that these things which we can imagine are not in fact things we can imagine. And that requires some very different philosophical argument from the sort which has been given in the case of heat and molecular motion. And it would have to be a deeper and subtler argument than I can fathom and subtler than has ever appeared in any materialist literature that I have read. So the conclusion of this investigation would be that the analytical tools we are using go against the identity thesis and so go against the general thesis that mental states are just physical states.[19]

The next topic would be my own solution to the mind-body problem, but that I do not have.

NOTES

1. This paper was presented orally, without a written text, to the New York University lecture series on identity which makes up this volume. The lecture was taped, and the present paper represents a transcription of these tapes, edited only slightly with no attempt to change the style of the original. If the reader imagines the sentences of this paper as being delivered, extemporaneously, with proper pauses and emphases, this may facilitate his comprehension. Nevertheless, there may still be passages which are hard to follow, and the time allotted necessitated a condensed presentation of the argument. (A longer version of some of these views, still rather compressed and still representing a transcript of oral remarks, will appear elsewhere). Occasionally, reservations, amplifications, and gratifications of my remarks had to be repressed, especially in the discussion of theoretical identification and the mind-body problem. The footnotes, which were added to the original, would have become even more unwieldy if this had not been done.

2. R.J. Butler, ed., *Analytical Philosophy, Second Series*, Basil Blackwell, Oxford, 1965, p.41.

3. The second occurrence of the description has small scope.

4. In Russell's theory, $F(?xGx)$ follows from $(x)Fx$ and $(\exists!x)Gx$, provided that the description in $F(?xGx)$ has the entire context for its scope (in Russell's 1905 terminology, has a 'primary occurrence'). Only then is $F(?xGx)$ 'about' the denotation of '$?xGx$'. Applying this rule to (4), we get the results indicated in the text. Notice that, in the ambiguous form $\Box(?xGx=?xHx)$, if one or both of the descriptions has 'primary occurrences' the formula does not assert the necessity of $?xGx=?xHx$; if both have secondary occurrences, it does. Thus in a language without explicit scope indicators, descriptions must be construed with the smallest possible scope – only then will $\sim A$ be the negation of A, $\Box A$ the necessitation of A, and the like.

5. An earlier distinction with the same purpose was, of course, the medieval one of *de dicto-de re*. That Russell's distinction of scope eliminates modal paradoxes has been pointed out by many logicians, especially Smullyan.

   So as to avoid misunderstanding, let me emphasize that I am of course not asserting that Russell's notion of scope solves Quine's problem of 'essentialism'; what it does show, especially in conjunction with modern model-theoretic approaches to modal logic, is that quantified modal logic need not deny the truth of all instances of $(x)(y)(x=y \bullet \supset \bullet Fx \supset Fy)$, nor of all instances of '$(x)(Gx \supset Ga)$' (where 'a' is to be replaced by a nonvacuous definite description whose scope is all of 'Ga'), in order to avoid making it a necessary truth that one and the same man invented bifocals and headed the original Postal Department. Russell's contextual definition of descriptions need not be adopted in order to ensure these results; but other logical theories, Fregean or other, which take descriptions as primitive must somehow express the same logical facts. Frege showed that a simple, non-iterated context containing a definite description with small scope, which cannot be interpreted as being 'about' the denotation of the description, can be interpreted as about its 'sense'. Some logicians have been interested in the question of the conditions under which, in an intensional context, a description with small scope is equivalent to the same one with large scope. One of the virtues of a Russellian treatment of descriptions in modal logic is that the answer (roughly that the description be a 'rigid designator' in the sense of this lecture) then often follows from the other postulates for quantified modal logic; no special postulates are needed, as in Hintikka's treatment. Even if descriptions are taken as primitive, special postulations of when scope is irrelevant can often be deduced from more basic axioms.

6. "Modalities and Intensional Languages," *Boston Studies in the Philosophy of Science*, Vol. 1, Humanities Press, New York, 1963, pp. 71 ff. See also the "Comments" by Quine and the ensuing discussion.

7. It should. See her remark on p. 115, *op. cit.*, in the discussion following the papers.

8. If there is no deity, and especially if the nonexistence of a deity is *necessary*, it is dubious that we can use "He" to refer to a deity. The use in the text must be taken to be non-literal.

9. David K. Lewis, "Counterpart Theory and Quantified Modal Logic," *Journal of Philosophy* 65 (1968), pp. 113 ff.

10. Some philosophers think that definite descriptions, in English, are ambiguous, that sometimes 'the inventor of bifocals' rigidly designates the man who in fact invented bifocals. I am tentatively inclined to reject this view, construed as a thesis about English (as opposed to a possible hypothetical language), but I will not argue the question here.

What I do wish to note is that, contrary to some opinions, this alleged ambiguity cannot replace the Russellian notion of the scope of a description. Consider the sentence, "The number of planets might have been necessarily even." This sentence plainly can be read so as to express a truth; had there been eight planets, the number of planets would have been necessarily even. Yet without scope distinctions, both a 'referential' (rigid) and a non-rigid reading of the description will make the statement false. (Since the number of planets is nine, the rigid reading amounts to the falsity that nine might have been necessarily even.)

The 'rigid' reading is equivalent to the Russellian primary occurrence; the non-rigid, to innermost scope – some, following Donnellan, perhaps loosely, have called this reading the 'attributive' use. The possibility of intermediate scopes is then ignored. In the present instance, the intended reading of $\Diamond\Box$ (the number of planets is even) makes the scope of the description $\Box$ (the number of planets is even), neither the largest nor the smallest possible.

11. This definition is the usual formulation of the notion of essential property, but an exception must be made for existence itself; on the definition given, existence would be trivially essential. We should regard existence as essential to an object only if the object necessarily exists. Perhaps there are other recherché properties, involving existence, for which the definition is similarly objectionable. (I thank Michael Slote for this observation.)

12. The two clauses of the sentence footnoted give the equivalent definitions of the notion of essential property, since $\Box((\exists x)(x=a) \supset Fa)$ is equivalent to $\Box(x)(\sim Fx \supset x \neq a)$. The second formulation, however, has served as a powerful seducer in favor of theories of 'identification across possible worlds'. For it suggests that we consider 'an object b in another possible world' and test whether it is identifiable with a by asking whether it lacks any of the essential properties of a. Let me therefore emphasize that, although an essential property is (trivially) a property without which an object cannot be a, it by no means follows that the essential, purely qualitative properties of a jointly form a sufficient condition for being a, nor that any purely qualitative conditions are sufficient for an object to be a. Further, even if necessary and sufficient qualitative conditions for an object to be Nixon may exist, there would still be little justification for the demand for a purely qualitative description of all counterfactual situations. We can ask whether Nixon might have been a Democrat without engaging in these subtleties.

13. I thus agree with Quine, that "Hesperus is Phosphorus" is (or can be) an empirical discovery; with Marcus, that it is necessary. Both Quine and Marcus, according to the present standpoint, err in identifying the epistemological and the metaphysical issues.

14. The two confusions alleged, especially the second, are both related to the confusion of the metaphysical question of the necessity of "Hesperus is Phosphorus" with the epistemological question of its a prioricity. For if Hesperus is identified by its position in the sky in the evening, and Phosphorus by its position in the morning, an investigator may well know, in advance of empirical research, that Hesperus is Phosphorus if and only if one and the same body occupies position x in the evening and position y in the morning. The a priori material equivalence of the two statements, however, does not imply their strict (necessary) equivalence. (The same remarks apply to the case of heat and molecular motion below.) Similar remarks apply to some extent to the relationship between "Hesperus is Phosphorus" and "'Hesperus' and 'Phosphorus' name the same thing." A confusion that also operates is, of course, the confusion between what *we* would say of a counterfactual situation and how people *in* that situation would have described it; this confusion, too, is probably related to the confusion between a prioricity and necessity.

15. If someone protests, regarding the lectern, that it *could* after all have *turned out* to have been made of ice, and therefore could have been made of ice, I would reply that what he really means is that a *lectern* could have looked just like this one, and have been placed in the same position as this one, and yet have been made of ice. In short, I could have been in the *same epistemological situation* in relation to *a lectern made of ice* as I actually am in relation to *this* lectern. In the main text, I have argued that the same reply should be given to protests that Hesperus could have turned out be other than Phosphorus, or Cicero other than Tully. Here, then, the notion of 'counterpart' comes into its own. For it is not this table, but an epistemic 'counterpart', which was hewn from ice; not Hesperus-Phosphorus-Venus, but two distinct counterparts thereof, in two of the roles Venus actually plays (that of Evening Star and Morning Star), which are different. Precisely because of this fact, it is not *this table* which could have been made of ice. Statements about the modal properties of

this table never refer to counterparts. However, if someone confuses the epistemo-logical and the metaphysical problems, he will be well on the way to the counter-part theory Lewis and others have advocated.

16. Isn't the situation I just described also counterfactual? At least it may well be, if such Martians never in fact invade. Strictly speaking, the distinction I wish to draw compares how we *would* speak in a (possibly counterfactual) situation, *if* it obtained, and how we *do* speak *of* a counterfactual situation, knowing that it does not obtain – i.e., the distinction between the language we would have used in a situation and the language we *do* use to describe it. (Consider the description: "Suppose we all spoke German." This description is in English.) The former case can be made vivid by imagining the counterfactual situation to be actual.

17. The most popular identity theories advocated today explicitly fail to satisfy this simple requirement. For these theories usually hold that a mental state is a brain state, and that what makes the brain state into a mental state is its 'causal role', the fact that it tends to produce certain behavior (as intentions produce actions, or pain, pain behavior) and to be produced by certain stimuli (e.g. pain, by pinpricks). If the relations between the brain state and its causes and effects are regarded as contin-gent, then *being such-and-such-a-mental* state is a contingent property of the brain state. Let X be a pain. The causal-role identity theorist holds (1) that X is a brain state, (2) that the fact that X is a pain is to be analyzed (roughly) as the fact that X is produced by certain stimuli and produces certain behavior. The fact mentioned in (2) is, of course, regarded as contingent; the brain state X might well exist and not tend to produce the appropriate behavior in the absence of other conditions. Thus (1) and (2) assert that a certain pain X might have existed, yet not have been a pain. This seems to me self-evidently absurd. Imagine any pain: is it possible that *it itself* could have existed, yet not have been a pain?

If $x = y$, then x and y share all properties, including modal properties. If x is a pain and y the corresponding brain state, then *being a pain* is an essential prop-erty of x, and *being a brain state* is an essential property of y. If the correspondence relation is, in fact, identity, then it must be *necessary* of y that it corresponds to a pain, and *necessary* of x that it correspond to a brain state, indeed, to this particular brain state, y. Both assertions seem false; it *seems* clearly possible that x should have existed without the corresponding brain state; or that the brain state should have existed without being felt as a pain. Identity theorists cannot, contrary to their almost universal present practice, accept these intuitions; they must deny them, and explain them away. This is none too easy a thing to do.

18. A brief restatement of the argument may be helpful here. If "pain" and "C-fiber stimulation" are rigid designators of phenomena, one who identifies them must regard the identity as necessary. How can this necessity be reconciled with the apparent fact that C-fiber stimulation might have turned out not to be correlated with pain at all? We might try to reply by analogy to the case of heat and molecular motion; the latter identity, too, is necessary, yet someone may believe that, before scientific investigation showed otherwise, molecular motion might have turned out not to be heat. The reply is, of course, that what really is possible is that people (or

some rational sentient beings) could have been in the *same epistemic situation* as we actually are, and identify *a phenomenon* in the same way we identify heat, namely, by feeling it by the sensation we call "the sensation of heat," without the phenomenon being molecular motion. Further, the beings might not have been sensitive to molecular motion (i.e., to heat) by any neural mechanism whatsoever. It is impossible to explain the apparent possibility of C-fiber stimulations not having been pain in the same way. Here, too, we would have to suppose that we could have been in the same epistemological situation, and identify something in the same way we identify pain, without its corresponding C-fiber stimulation. But the way we identify pain is by feeling it, and if a C-fiber stimulation could have occurred without our feeling any pain, then the C-fiber stimulation would have occurred without there *being* any pain, contrary to the necessity of the identity. The trouble is that although 'heat' is a rigid designator, heat is picked out by the contingent property of its being felt in a certain way; pain, on the other hand, is picked out by an essential (indeed necessary and sufficient) property. For a sensation to be *felt* as pain is for it to *be* pain.

19. All arguments against the identity theory which rely on the necessity of identity, or on the notion of essential property, are, of course, inspired by Descartes' argument for his dualism. The earlier arguments which superficially were rebutted by the analogies of heat and molecular motion, and the bifocals inventor who was also Postmaster General, had such an inspiration; and so does my argument here. R. Albritton and M. Slote have informed me that they independently have attempted to give essentialist arguments against the identity theory, and probably others have done so as well.

The simplest Cartesian argument can perhaps be restated as follows: Let 'A' be a *name* (rigid designator) of Descartes' body. Then Descartes argues that since he could exist even if A did not, $\Diamond$ (Descartes $\neq$ A), hence, Descartes $\neq$ A. Those who have accused him of a modal fallacy have forgotten that 'A' is rigid. His argument is valid, and his conclusion is correct, provided its (perhaps dubitable) premise is accepted. On the other hand, provided that Descartes is regarded as having ceased to exist upon his death, "Descartes $\neq$ A" can be established without the use of a modal argument; for if so, no doubt A survived Descartes when A was a corpse. Thus A had a property (existing at a certain time) which Descartes did not. The same argument can establish that a statue is not the hunk of stone, or the congery of molecules, of which it is composed. Mere non-identity, then, may be a weak conclusion. (See D. Wiggins, *Philosophical Review*, Vol. 77 (1968), pp. 90 ff.) The Cartesian modal argument, however, surely can be deployed to maintain relevant stronger conclusions as well.

II

Mental States and Linguistic Content (The Knowledge Perspective)

Meanings and Ideas

MEANING

H. Paul Grice

Consider the following sentences:

> Those spots mean (meant) measles.
> Those spots didn't mean anything to me, but to the doctor they meant measles.
> The recent budget means that we shall have a hard year.

(1) I cannot say, "Those spots meant measles, but he hadn't got measles," and I cannot say, "The recent budget means that we shall have a hard year, but we shan't have." That is to say, in cases like the above, x meant that p and x means that p entail p.

(2) I cannot argue from "Those spots mean (meant) measles" to any conclusion about "what is (was) meant by those spots"; for example, I am not entitled to say, "What was meant by those spots was that he had measles." Equally I cannot draw from the statement about the recent budget the conclusion "What is meant by the recent budget is that we shall have a hard year."

(3) I cannot argue from "Those spots meant measles" to any conclusion to the effect that somebody or other meant by those spots so-and-so. *Mutatis mutandis*, the same is true of the sentence about the recent budget.

(4) For none of the above examples can a restatement be found in which the verb "mean" is followed by a sentence or phrase in inverted commas. Thus "Those spots meant measles" cannot be reformulated as "Those spots meant 'measles'" or "Those spots meant 'he has measles.'"

(5) On the other hand, for all these examples an approximate restatement can be found beginning with the phrase "The fact that ..."; for example, "The fact that he had those spots meant that he had measles" and

"The fact that the recent budget was as it was means that we shall have a hard year."

Now contrast the above sentences with the following:

Those three rings on the bell (of the bus) mean that the "bus is full."

That remark, "Smith couldn't get on without his trouble and strife," meant that Smith found his wife indispensable.

(1) I can use the first of these and go on to say, "But it isn't in fact full – the conductor has made a mistake"; and I can use the second and go on, "But in fact Smith deserted her seven years ago." That is to say, here x *means that p* and x *meant that p* do not entail p.

(2) I can argue from the first to some statement about "what is (was) meant" by the rings on the bell and from the second to some statement about "what is (was) meant" by the quoted remark.

(3) I can argue from the first sentence to the conclusion that somebody (viz., the conductor) meant, or at any rate should have meant, by the rings that the bus is full, and I can argue analogously for the second sentence.

(4) The first sentence can be restated in a form in which the verb "mean" is followed by a phrase in inverted commas, that is, "Those three rings on the bell mean 'the bus is full.'" So also can the second sentence.

(5) Such a sentence as "The fact that the bell has been rung three times means that the bus is full" is not a restatement of the meaning of the first sentence. Both may be true, but they do not have, even approximately, the same meaning.

When the expressions "means," "means something," "means that" are used in the kind of way in which they are used in the first set of sentences, I shall speak of the sense, or senses, in which they are used, as the *natural* sense, or senses, of the expressions in question. When the expressions are used in the kind of way in which they are used in the second set of sentences, I shall speak of the sense, or senses, in which they are used, as the *nonnatural* sense, or senses, of the expressions in question. I shall use the abbreviation "means$_{NN}$" to distinguish the nonnatural sense or senses.

I propose, for convenience, also to include under the head of natural senses of "mean" such senses of "mean" as may be exemplified in sentences of the pattern "A means (meant) *to do* so-and-so (by x)," where A is a human agent. By contrast, as the previous examples show, I include under the head of nonnatural senses of "mean" any senses of "mean" found in sentences of the patterns "A means (meant) something by x" or "A means (meant) by x that ..." (This is overrigid; but it will serve as an indication.)

I do not want to maintain that *all* our uses of "mean" fall easily, obviously, and tidily into one of the two groups I have distinguished; but I think that in most cases we should be at least fairly strongly inclined to assimilate a use of "mean" to one group rather than to the other. The question which now arises is this: "What more can be said about the distinction between the cases where we should say that the word is applied in a natural sense and the cases where we should say that the word is applied in a nonnatural sense?" Asking this question will not of course prohibit us from trying to give an explanation of "meaning$_{NN}$" in terms of one or another natural sense of "mean."

This question about the distinction between natural and nonnatural meaning is, I think, what people are getting at when they display an interest in a distinction between "natural" and "conventional" signs. But I think my formulation is better. For some things which can mean$_{NN}$ something are not signs (e.g., words are not), and some are not conventional in any ordinary sense (e.g., certain gestures); while some things which mean naturally are not signs of what they mean (the recent budget example).

I want first to consider briefly, and reject, what I might term a causal type of answer to the question, "What is meaning$_{NN}$?" We might try to say, for instance, more or less with C.L. Stevenson,[1] that for *x* to mean$_{NN}$ something, *x* must have (roughly) a tendency to produce in an audience some attitude (cognitive or otherwise) and a tendency, in the case of a speaker, to *be* produced *by* that attitude, these tendencies being dependent on "an elaborate process of conditioning attending the use of the sign in communication."[2] This clearly will not do.

(1) Let us consider a case where an utterance, if it qualifies at all as meaning$_{NN}$ something, will be of a descriptive or informative kind and the relevant attitude, therefore, will be a cognitive one, for example, a belief. (I use "utterance" as a neutral word to apply to any candidate for meaning$_{NN}$; it has a convenient act-object ambiguity.) It is no doubt the case that many people have a tendency to put on a tail coat when they think they are about to go to a dance, and it is also no doubt the case that many people, on seeing someone put on a tail coat, would conclude that the person in question was about to go to a dance. Does this satisfy us that putting on a tail coat means$_{NN}$ that one is about to go to a dance (or indeed means$_{NN}$ anything at all)? Obviously not. It is no help to refer to the qualifying phrase "dependent on an elaborate process of conditioning...." For if all this means is that the response to the sight of a tail coat being put on is in some way learned or acquired, it will not exclude the present case from being one of meaning$_{NN}$. But if we have to take seriously the second part of the qualifying phrase ("attending the use of the sign in communication"), then the account of meaning$_{NN}$ is obviously circular. We might just as well say, "X has meaning$_{NN}$ if it is used in communication," which, though true, is not helpful.

(2) If this is not enough, there is a difficulty – really the same difficulty, I think – which Stevenson recognizes: how we are to avoid saying, for example, that "Jones is tall" is part of what is meant by "Jones is an athlete," since to tell someone that Jones is an athlete would tend to make him believe that Jones is tall. Stevenson here resorts to invoking linguistic rules, namely, a permissive rule of language that "athletes may be nontall." This amounts to saying that we are not prohibited by rule from speaking of "nontall athletes." But why are we not prohibited? Not because it is not bad grammar, or is not impolite, and so on, but presumably because it is not meaningless (or, if this is too strong, does not in any way violate the rules of meaning for the expressions concerned). But this seems to involve us in another circle. Moreover, one wants to ask why, if it is legitimate to appeal here to rules to distinguish what is meant from what is suggested, this appeal was not made earlier, in the case of groans, for example, to deal with which Stevenson originally introduced the qualifying phrase about dependence on conditioning.

A further deficiency in a causal theory of the type just expounded seems to be that, even if we accept it as it stands, we are furnished with an analysis only of statements about the *standard* meaning, or the meaning in general, of a "sign." No provision is made for dealing with statements about what a particular speaker or writer means by a sign on a particular occasion (which may well diverge from the standard meaning of the sign); nor is it obvious how the theory could be adapted to make such provision. One might even go further in criticism and maintain that the causal theory ignores the fact that the meaning (in general) of a sign needs to be explained in terms of what users of the sign do (or should) mean by it on particular occasions; and so the latter notion, which is unexplained by the causal theory, is in fact the fundamental one. I am sympathetic to this more radical criticism, though I am aware that the point is controversial.

I do not propose to consider any further theories of the "causal-tendency" type. I suspect no such theory could avoid difficulties analogous to those I have outlined without utterly losing its claim to rank as a theory of this type.

I will now try a different and, I hope, more promising line. If we can elucidate the meaning of

> "x meant$_{NN}$ something (on a particular occasion)"
> and
> "x meant$_{NN}$ that so-and-so (on a particular occasion)"

and of

> "A meant$_{NN}$ something by x (on a particular occasion)"
> and
> "A meant$_{NN}$ by x that so-and-so (on a particular occasion),"

this might reasonably be expected to help us with

"x means$_{NN}$ (timeless) something (that so-and-so),"
"A means$_{NN}$ (timeless) by x something (that so-and-so),"

and with the explication of "means the same as," "understands," "entails," and so on. Let us for the moment pretend that we have to deal only with utterances which might be informative or descriptive.

A first shot would be to suggest that "x meant$_{NN}$ something" would be true if x was intended by its utterer to induce a belief in some "audience" and that to say what the belief was would be to say what x meant$_{NN}$. This will not do. I might leave B's handkerchief near the scene of a murder in order to induce the detective to believe that B was the murderer; but we should not want to say that the handkerchief (or my leaving it there) meant$_{NN}$ anything or that I had meant$_{NN}$ by leaving it that B was the murderer. Clearly we must at least add that, for x to have meant$_{NN}$ anything, not merely must it have been "uttered" with the intention of inducing a certain belief but also the utterer must have intended an "audience" to recognize the intention behind the utterance.

This, though perhaps better, is not good enough. Consider the following cases:

(1) Herod presents Salome with the head of St. John the Baptist on a charger.
(2) Feeling faint, a child lets its mother see how pale it is (hoping that she may draw her own conclusion and help).
(3) I leave the china my daughter has broken lying around for my wife to see.

Here we seem to have cases which satisfy the conditions so far given for meaning$_{NN}$. For example, Herod intended to make Salome believe that John the Baptist was dead and no doubt also intended Salome to recognize that he intended her to believe that St. John the Baptist was dead. Similarly for the other cases. Yet I certainly do not think that we should want to say that we have here cases of meaning$_{NN}$.

What we want to find is the difference between, for example, "deliberately and openly letting someone know" and "telling" and between "getting someone to think" and "telling."

The way out is perhaps as follows. Compare the following two cases:

(1) I show Mr. X a photograph of Mr. Y displaying undue familiarity to Mrs. X.
(2) I draw a picture of Mr. Y behaving in this manner and show it to Mr. X.

I find that I want to deny that in (1) the photograph (or my showing it to Mr. X) meant$_{NN}$ anything at all; while I want to assert that in (2) the picture (or my drawing and showing it) meant$_{NN}$ something (that Mr. Y had been unduly unfamiliar), or at least that I had meant$_{NN}$ by it that Mr. Y had been unduly familiar. What is the difference between the two cases? Surely that in case (1) Mr. X's recognition of my intention to make him believe that there is something between Mr. Y and Mrs. X is (more or less) irrelevant to the production of this effect by the photograph. Mr. X would be led by the photograph at least to suspect Mrs. X even if instead of showing it to him I had left it in his room by accident; and I (the photograph shower) would not be unaware of this. But it will make a difference to the effect of my picture on Mr. X whether or not he takes me to be intending to inform him (make him believe something) about Mrs. X, and not to be just doodling or trying to produce a work of art.

But now we seem to be landed in a further difficulty if we accept this account. For consider now, say, frowning. If I frown spontaneously, in the ordinary course of events, someone looking at me may well treat the frown as a natural sign of displeasure. But if I frown deliberately (to convey my displeasure), an onlooker may be expected, provided he recognizes my intention, *still* to conclude that I am displeased. Ought we not then to say, since it could not be expected to make any difference to the onlooker's reaction whether he regards my frown as spontaneous or as intended to be informative, that my frown (deliberate) does *not* mean$_{NN}$ anything? I think this difficulty can be met; for though in general a deliberate frown may have the same effect (as regards inducing belief in my displeasure) as a spontaneous frown, it can be expected to have the same effect only *provided* the audience takes it as intended to convey displeasure. That is, if we take away the recognition of intention, leaving the other circumstances (including the recognition of the frown as deliberate), the belief-producing tendency of the frown must be regarded as being impaired or destroyed.

Perhaps we may sum up what is necessary for A to mean something by x as follows. A must intend to induce by x a belief in an audience, and he must also intend his utterance to be recognized as so intended. But these intentions are not independent; the recognition is intended by A to play its part in inducing the belief, and if it does not do so something will have gone wrong with the fulfillment of A's intentions. Moreover, A's intending that the recognition should play this part implies, I think, that he assumes that there is some chance that it will in fact play this part, that he does not regard it as a foregone conclusion that the belief will be induced in the audience whether or not the intention behind the utterance is recognized. Shortly, perhaps, we may say that "A meant$_{NN}$ something by x" is roughly equivalent to "A uttered x with the intention of inducing a belief by means of the recognition of this intention." (This seems to involve a reflexive paradox, but it does not really do so.)

Now perhaps it is time to drop the pretense that we have to deal only with "informative" cases. Let us start with some examples of imperatives or quasi-imperatives. I have a very avaricious man in my room, and I want him to go; so I throw a pound note out of the window. Is there here any utterance with a meaning$_{NN}$? No, because in behaving as I did, I did not intend his recognition of my purpose to be in any way effective in getting him to go. This is parallel to the photograph case. If on the other hand I had pointed to the door or given him a little push, then my behavior might well be held to constitute a meaningful$_{NN}$ utterance, just because the recognition of my intention would be intended by me to be effective in speeding his departure. Another pair of cases would be (1) a policeman who stops a car by standing in its way and (2) a policeman who stops a car by waving.

Or, to turn briefly to another type of case, if as an examiner I fail a man, I may well cause him distress or indignation or humiliation; and if I am vindictive, I may intend this effect and even intend him to recognize my intention. But I should not be inclined to say that my failing him meant$_{NN}$ anything. On the other hand, if I cut someone in the street I do feel inclined to assimilate this to the cases of meaning$_{NN}$, and this inclination seems to me dependent on the fact that I could not reasonably expect him to be distressed (indignant, humiliated) unless he recognized my intention to affect him in this way. (Cf., if my college stopped my salary altogether I should accuse them of ruining me; if they cut it by 2/6^d I might accuse them of insulting me; with some intermediate amounts I might not know quite what to say.)

Perhaps then we may make the following generalizations:

(1) "A meant$_{NN}$ something by x" is (roughly) equivalent to "A intended the utterance of x to produce some effect in an audience by means of the recognition of this intention"; and we may add to that to ask what A meant is to ask for a specification of the intended effect (though, of course, it may not always be possible to get a straight answer involving a "that" clause, for example, "a belief that....").

(2) "x meant something" is (roughly) equivalent to "Somebody meant$_{NN}$ something by x." Here again there will be cases where this will not quite work. I feel inclined to say that (as regards traffic lights) the change to red meant$_{NN}$ that the traffic was to stop; but it would be very unnatural to say, "Somebody (e.g., the corporation) meant$_{NN}$ by the red-light change that the traffic was to stop." Nevertheless, there seems to be some sort of reference to somebody's intentions.

(3) "x means$_{NN}$ (timeless) that so-and-so" might as a first shot be equated with some statement or disjunction of statements about what "people" (vague) intend (with qualifications about "recognition") to effect by x. I shall have a word to say about this.

Will any kind of intended effect do, or may there be cases where any effect is intended (with the required qualifications) and yet we should not want to talk of meaning$_{NN}$? Suppose I discovered some person so constituted that, when I told him that whenever I grunted in a special way I wanted him to blush or to incur some physical malady, thereafter whenever he recognized the grunt (and with it my intention), he did blush or incur the malady. Should we then want to say that the grunt meant$_{NN}$ something? I do not think so. This points to the fact that for x to have meaning$_{NN}$, the intended effect must be something which in some sense is within the control of the audience, or that in some sense of "reason" the recognition of the intention behind x is for the audience a reason and not merely a cause. It might look as if there is a sort of pun here ("reason for believing" and "reason for doing"), but I do not think this is serious. For though no doubt from one point of view questions about reasons for believing are questions about evidence and so quite different from questions about reasons for doing, nevertheless to recognize an utterer's intention in uttering x (descriptive utterance), to have a reason for believing that so-and-so, is at least quite like "having a motive for" accepting so-and-so. Decisions "that" seem to involve decisions "to" (and this is why we can "refuse to believe" and also be "compelled to believe"). (The "cutting" case needs slightly different treatment, for one cannot in any straightforward sense "decide" to be offended; but one can refuse to be offended.) It looks then as if the intended effect must be something within the control of the audience, or at least the sort of thing which is within its control.

One point before passing to an objection or two. I think it follows that from what I have said about the connection between meaning$_{NN}$ and recognition of intention that (insofar as I am right) only what I may call the primary intention of an utterer is relevant to the meaning$_{NN}$ of an utterance. For if I utter x, intending (with the aid of the recognition of this intention) to induce an effect E, and intend this effect E to lead to a further effect F, then insofar as the occurrence of F is thought to be dependent solely on E, I cannot regard F as in the least dependent on recognition of my intention to include E. That is, if (say) I intend to get a man to do something by giving him some information, it cannot be regarded as relevant to the meaning$_{NN}$ of my utterance to describe what I intend him to do.

Now some question may be raised about my use, fairly free, of such words as "intention" and "recognition." I must disclaim any intention of peopling all our talking life with armies of complicated psychological occurrences. I do not hope to solve any philosophical puzzles about intending, but I do want briefly to argue that no special difficulties are raised by my use of the word "intention" in connection with meaning. First, there will be cases where an utterance is accompanied or preceded by a conscious "plan" or explicit formulation of intention (e.g., I declare how I am going to use x, or ask myself how to "get something across"). The presence of such an explicit "plan" obviously counts fairly heavily in favor of the utterer's intention (meaning) being as "planned"; though it is not, I think, conclusive; for example, a speaker who has declared an intention to use a familiar expression in an unfamiliar way may slip into the familiar use. Similarly in nonlinguistic cases: if we are asking about an agent's intention, a previous expression counts heavily; nevertheless, a man might plan to throw a letter in the dustbin and yet take it to the post; when lifting his hand he might "come to" and say *either* "I didn't intend to do this at all" or "I suppose I must have been intending to put it in."

Explicitly formulated linguistic (or quasi-linguistic) intentions are no doubt comparatively rare. In their absence we would seem to rely on very much the same kinds of criteria as we do in the case of nonlinguistic intentions where there is a general usage. An utterer is held to intend to convey what is normally conveyed (or normally intended to be conveyed), and we require a good reason for accepting that a particular use diverges from the general usage (e.g., he never knew or had forgotten the general usage). Similarly in nonlinguistic cases: we are presumed to intend the normal consequences of our actions.

Again, in cases where there is doubt, say, about which of two or more things an utterer intends to convey, we tend to refer to the context (linguistic or otherwise) of the utterance and ask which of the alternatives would be relevant to other things he is saying or doing, or which intention in a particular situation would fit in with some purpose he obviously has (e.g., a man who calls for a "pump" at a fire would not want a bicycle pump). Nonlinguistic parallels are obvious: context is a criterion in settling the question of why a man who has just put a cigarette in his mouth has put his hand in his pocket; relevance to an obvious end is a criterion in settling why a man is running away from a bull.

In certain linguistic cases we ask the utterer afterward about his intention, and in a few of these cases (the very difficult ones, like a philosopher asked to explain the meaning of an unclear passage in one of his works), the answer is not based on what he remembers but is more like a decision, a decision about how what he said is to be taken. I cannot find a nonlinguistic parallel here; but the case is so special as not to seem to contribute a vital difference.

All this is very obvious; but surely to show that the criteria for judging linguistic intentions are very like the criteria for judging nonlinguistic intentions is to show that linguistic intentions are very like nonlinguistic intentions.

NOTES

1. *Ethics and Language* (New Haven: 1944), ch. 3.

2. *Ibid.*, p. 57.

PROPOSITIONAL ATTITUDES

Jerry A. Fodor

Some philosophers (Dewey, for example, and maybe Austin) hold that philosophy is what you do to a problem until it's clear enough to solve it by doing science. Others (Ryle, for example, and maybe Wittgenstein) hold that if a philosophical problem succumbs to empirical methods, that shows it wasn't *really* philosophical to begin with. Either way, the facts seem clear enough: questions first mooted by philosophers are sometimes coopted by people who do experiments. This seems to be happening now to the question "What are propositional attitudes?" and cognitive psychology is the science of note.

One way to elucidate this situation is to examine theories that cognitive psychologists endorse, with an eye to explicating the account of propositional attitudes that the theories presuppose. That was my strategy in Fodor (1975). In this paper, however, I'll take another tack. I want to outline a number of a priori conditions which, on my view, a theory of propositional attitudes (PAs) ought to meet. I'll argue that, considered together, these conditions pretty clearly demand a treatment of PAs as relations between organisms and internal representations; precisely the view that the psychologists have independently arrived at. I'll thus be arguing that we have good reasons to endorse the psychologists' theory even aside from the empirical exigencies that drove them to it. I take it that this convergence between what's plausible a priori and what's demanded ex post facto is itself a reason for believing that the theory is probably true.

Three preliminary remarks: first, I'm not taking "a priori" all that seriously. Some of the points I'll be making are, I suppose, strictly conceptual, but others are merely self-evident. What I've got is a set of glaring facts about propositional attitudes. I don't doubt that we might rationally adopt an account of the attitudes which contravenes some or maybe even all of them. But the independent evidence for such an account would have to be extremely persuasive or I, for one, would get the jitters. Second, practically everything I'll say about the attitudes has been said previously in the philosophical literature. All I've done is bring the stuff together. I do think, however, that the various constraints that I'll discuss illuminate one another; it is only when one attempts to satisfy them all at once that one sees how univocal their demands are. Finally, though I intend what I say to apply, mutatis mutandis, to PAs at large, I shall run the discussion pretty much exclusively on beliefs and wants. These seem to be the root cases for a systematic cognitive psychology; thus learning and perception are presumably to be treated as varieties of the fixation of belief, and the theory of action is presumably continuous with the theory of utility.[1] Here, then, are my conditions, with comments.

I. Propositional attitudes should be analyzed as relations. In particular, the verb in a sentence like "John believes it's raining" expresses a relation between John and something else, and a token of that sentence is true if John stands in the belief-relation to that thing.[2] Equivalently, for these purposes, "it's raining" is a term in "John believes it's raining."[3] I have three arguments for imposing condition I, all of them inconclusive.

(I-a) It's intuitively plausible. "Believes" looks like a two-place relation, and it would be nice if our theory of belief permitted us to save the appearances.

No doubt, appearances sometimes deceive. The "s" in "Mary's sake" looks as though it's expressing a relation (of possession) between Mary and a sake; but it doesn't, or so we're told. In fact, "Mary's sake" doesn't look *very* relational, since *x's sake* would surely qualify as an idiom even if we had no ontological scruples to placate. There's something syntactically wrong with: "Mary's sake is Fer than Bill's," "Mary has a (little) sake," etc. For that matter, there's something syntactically wrong with "a sake" *tout court*. Yet we'd expect all such expressions to be well formed if "Mary's sake" contained a true possessive. "Mary's sake" doesn't bear comparison with "Mary's lamb."

Still, there are some cases of *non*-idiomatic expressions which appear to be relational but which, upon reflection, maybe aren't. "Mary's voice" goes through the transformations even if "Mary's sake" does not (Dennett, 1969). Yet there aren't, perhaps, such *things* as voices; and, if there aren't, "Mary's voice" can't refer in virtue of a relation between Mary and one of them.[4] I think it is fair to view the "surface" grammar as ontologically misleading in *these* cases, but only because we know how to translate into more parsimonious forms. "Mary has a good voice (bad voice; little voice; better voice than Bill's)" goes over, pretty much without residue, into "Mary sings well (badly, weakly, less well than Bill)." If, however, we were *un*able to provide (or, anyhow, to envision providing) the relevant translations, what right would we have to view such expressions as onto-logically promiscuous? "Bill believes it's raining" is not an idiom, and there is, so far as anybody knows, no way of translating sentences nominally about beliefs into sentences of reduced ontological load. (Behaviorists used to think such translations might be forthcoming, but they were wrong.) We must, then, either take the apparent ontological commitments seriously or admit to playing fast and loose.

(I-b) Existential Generalization applies to the syntactic objects of verbs of propositional attitude; from "John believes it's raining" we can infer "John believes something" and "there is something that John believes" (viz., that it's raining). EG may not be *criterial* for ontological commitment, but it is surely a straw in the wind.[5]

(I-c) The only known alternative to the view that verbs of propo-sitional attitude express relations is that they are (semantically) "fused" with their objects, and that view would seem to be hopeless.[6]

The fusion story is the proposal that sentences like "John believes it's raining" ought really to be spelled "John believes-it's-raining"; that the logical form of such sentences acknowledges a referring expression ("John") and a one-place predicate with no internal structure ("believes-it's-rain-ing"). "John believes it's raining" is thus an atomic sentence, similar *au fond* to "John is purple."

Talk about counter-intuitive! Moreover:

1. There are infinitely many (semantically distinct) sentences of the form *a believes complement*. If all such sentences are atomic, how is English learned? (Davidson, 1965).

2. Different propositional attitudes are often "focused" on the same content; for example, one can both fear and believe that it will rain on Tuesday. But on the fusion view, "John fears that it will rain on Tuesday" has nothing in common with "John believes that it will rain on Tuesday" save only the reference to John. In particular, it's an *accident* that the form of words "it will rain on Tuesday" occurs in both.

3. Similarly, different beliefs can be related in such ways as the fol-lowing: John thinks Sam is nice; Mary thinks Sam is nasty. Under ordinary English representation these beliefs overlap at the "Sam" position, so the notation sustains the intuition that John and Mary disagree about Sam. But, if the fusion view is correct, "John thinks Sam is nice" and "Mary thinks Sam is nasty" have no more in common at the level of canonical notation than, say, "John eats" and "Mary swims." Talk about imperspicuous! In respect of saving the intuitions, the recommended reconstruction does *worse* than the undisciplined orthography that we started with.[7] (For that matter, there's nothing in "believes-that-S" to suggest that it's about believ-ing. Here, too, "believes that S" does much better.)

4. It could hardly be an accident that the declarative sentences of English constitute the (syntactic) objects of verbs like "believe." Whereas,

on the fusion view it's *precisely* an accident; the complement of "believes" in "John believes it's raining" bears no more relation to the sentence "It's raining" than, say, the word "dog" bears to the first syllable of "dogmatic."

5. On the fusion view, it's a sheer accident that if "John believes it's raining" is true, then what John believes is true if "it's raining" is true. But this, surely, is one accident too many. Surely the identity between the truth conditions on John's belief when he believes Fa, and those on the corresponding sentence "a is F" must be what connects the theory of sentence interpretation with the theory of PAs (and what explains our using "it's raining," and not some other form of words, to specify *which* belief John has when he believes it's raining).

It's the mark of a bad theory that it makes the data look fortuitous. I conclude that the fusion story is not to be taken very seriously; that neither the philosophy of language nor the philosophy of mind is advanced by proliferating hyphens. But the fusion story is (de facto) the only alternative to the view that "believe" expresses a relation. Hence, first blush, we had better assume that "believe" *does* express a relation and try to find an account of propositional attitudes which comports with that assumption.

II. A theory of PAs should explain the parallelism between verbs of PA and verbs of saying ("Vendler's Condition").

Rather generally, the things we can be said to *believe* (want, hope, regret, etc.) are the very things that we can be said to *say* (assert, state, etc.). So John can either believe or assert that it's about to blow; he can either hope that or inquire whether somebody has reefed the main; he can either doubt or demand that the crew should douse the Jenny. Moreover, as Vendler (1972) has shown, there are interesting consequences of classifying verbs of PA (on the one hand) and verbs of saying (on the other) by reference to the syntax of their object complements. It turns out that the taxonomies thus engendered are isomorphic down to surprisingly fine levels of grain. Now, of course, this *could* be just an accident, as could the semantic and syntactic parallelisms between the complements of verbs of PA and free standing declaratives (see above). Certainly, it's a substantial inference from the syntactic similarities that Vendler observes to the conclusion he draws: that the object of assertion is identical with the object of belief. Suffice it for now to make the less ambitious point: we should prefer a theory that explains the facts to one that merely shrugs its shoulders; viz., a theory that satisfies Vendler's condition to a theory that does not.

III. A theory of propositional attitudes should account for their opacity ("Frege's condition").

Thus far, I have stressed logico-syntactic analogies between the complements of belief clauses and the corresponding free-standing declaratives. However, it has been customary in the philosophical literature since Frege to stress one of their striking *dis*analogies: the former are, in general, opaque to inferential operations to which the latter are, in general, transparent. Since this aspect of the behavior of sentences that ascribe propositional attitudes has so dominated the philosophical discussion, I shall make the point quite briefly here. Sentences containing verbs of PA are not, normally, truth functions of their complements. Moreover, contexts subordinated to verbs of PA are normally themselves non-truth functional, and EG and substitution of identicals may apply at syntactic positions in a freestanding declarative while failing at syntactically comparable positions in belief sentences. A theory of PAs should explain why all this is so.

It should be acknowledged that, however gross the inadequacies of the fusion view, it does at least provide an account of propositional attitudes which meets Frege's condition. If S doesn't so much as occur in "John believes S," it's hardly surprising that the one should fail to be a truth function of the other; similarly, if "Mary" doesn't occur in "Bill believes that John bit Mary," it's hardly surprising that the sentence doesn't behave the way it would if "Mary" occurred referentially. The methodological moral is, perhaps, that Frege's condition under-constrains a theory of PAs; ideally, an acceptable account of opacity should follow from a theory that is independently plausible.

IV. The objects of propositional attitudes have logical form ("Aristotle's condition").

Mental states (including, especially, token havings of propositional attitudes) interact causally. Such interactions constitute the mental processes that eventuate (inter alia) in the behaviors of organisms. Now, it is crucial to the whole program of explaining behavior by reference to mental states that the propositional attitudes belonging to these chains are typically *non*-arbitrarily related in respect to their content (taking the "content" of a propositional attitude, informally, to be whatever it is that the complement of the corresponding PA-ascribing sentence expresses).

This is not an a priori claim, though perhaps it is a transcendental one. For though one can imagine the occurrence of causal chains of mental states which are not otherwise related (as, e.g., a thought that two is a prime number, causing a desire for tea, causing an intention to recite the alphabet backwards, causing an expectation of rain) and though such sequences doubtless actually occur (in dreams, say, and in madness), still if *all* our mental life were like this, it's hard to see what point ascriptions of contents to mental states would have. Even phenomenology presupposes some correspondence between the content of our beliefs and the content of our beliefs about our beliefs; else there would be no coherent introspections for phenomenologists to report.

The paradigm situation – the grist for the cognitivist's mill – is the one where propositional attitudes interact causally and do so *in virtue of* their content. And the paradigm of this paradigm is the practical syllogism. Since it is part of my point that the details matter not at all, I shall take liberties with Aristotle's text.

John believes that it will rain if he washes his car. John wants it to rain. So John acts in a manner intended to be a car-washing.

I take it that this might be a true, if informal, etiology of John's "car-washing behavior"; the car washing is an effect of the intention to carwash, and the intention to car-wash is an effect of the causal interaction between John's beliefs and his utilities. Moreover, the etiological account might be counterfactual-supporting in at least the following sense: John wouldn't have car-washed had the content of his beliefs, utilities, and intentions been other than they were. Or, if he did, he would have done so unintentionally, or for different reasons, or with other ends in view. To say that John's mental states interact causally *in virtue of* their content is, in part, to say that such counterfactuals hold.

If there are true, contingent counterfactuals which relate mental state *tokens* in virtue of their contents, that is presumably because there are true, contingent generalizations which relate mental state *types* in virtue of their contents. So, still following Aristotle at a distance, we can schematize etiologies like the one above to get the underlying generalization: if x believes that A is an action x can perform; and if x believes that a performance of A is sufficient to bring it about that Q; and if x wants it to be the case that Q; then x acts in a fashion intended be a performance of A.

I am not, for present purposes, interested in whether this is a plausible decision theory, still less in whether it is the decision theory that Aristotle thought plausible. What interests me here is rather: (a) that any decision theory we can now contemplate will surely look rather like this one, in that (b) it will entail generalizations about the causal relations among content-related beliefs, utilities, and intentions; and (c) such generalizations will be specified by reference to the form of the propositional attitudes which instantiate them. (This remains true even if, as some philosophers suppose, an adequate decision theory is irremediably in need of ceteris paribus clauses to flesh out its generalizations. See, for example, Grice, 1975.) So, in particular, we can't state the theory-relevant generalization that is instantiated by the relations among John's mental states unless we allow reference to beliefs of the form *if X then Y*; desires of the form *that Y*; intentions of the form *that X should come about*; and so forth. Viewed one way (material mode), the recurrent schematic letters require identities of content among propositional attitudes. Viewed the other way (linguistically), they require formal identities among the complements of the PA-ascribing sentences which instantiate the generalizations of the theory that explains John's behavior. Either way, the form of the generalization deter-

mines how the theory relates to the events that it subsumes. There is nothing remarkable about this, of course, except that form is here being ascribed
inside the scope of verbs of PA.

To summarize: our common-sense psychological generalizations
relate mental states in virtue of their content, and canonical representation
does what it can to reconstruct such content relations as relations of form.
"Aristotle's condition" requires that our theory of propositional attitudes
should rationalize this process by construing verbs of PA in a way that permits reference to the form of their objects. To do this is to legitimize the presuppositions of common-sense psychology and, for that matter, of real (viz.
cognitive) psychology as well. (See Fodor, 1975).

In fact, we can state (and satisfy) Aristotle's condition in a still
stronger version. Let anything be a *belief sentence* if it is of the form *a believes
that S*. Define the *correspondent* of such a sentence as the formula that consists of S standing alone (i.e. the sentence #S#).[8] We remarked above that
there is the following relation between the truth conditions on the belief
that a belief sentence ascribes and the truth conditions on the correspondent of the belief sentence: the belief is true if the correspondent is. This is,
presumably, at least part of what is involved in viewing the correspondent
of a belief sentence as *expressing* the ascribed belief.

It should not be surprising, therefore, to find that our intuitions
about the form of the belief ascribed by a given belief sentence are determined by the logical form of its correspondent. So, intuitively, John's belief
that Mary and Bill are leaving is a conjunctive belief (cf. the logical form of
"Mary and Bill are leaving"); John's belief that Alfred is a white swan is a
singulary belief (cf. the logical form of "Alfred is a white swan"); and so on.
It is, of course, essential that we understand "belief" *opaquely* in such examples; otherwise, the belief that P will have the logical form of any sentence
equivalent to P. But this is as it should be: it is in virtue of its *opaque* content that John's belief that P plays its systematic role in John's mental life –
e.g., in the determination of his actions and in the causation of his other
mental states. Hence it is the opaque construal that operates in such patterns of explanation as the practical syllogism and its spiritual heirs [see
ch. 9 of my *Representations*].

We are now in position to state Aristotle's condition in its
strongest (and final) version. A theory of propositional attitudes should
legitimize the ascription of form to the objects of propositional attitudes. In
particular, it should explain why the form of a belief is identical to the logical form of the correspondent of a sentence which (opaquely) ascribes that
belief.[9]

I digress: One may feel inclined to argue that the satisfaction of
Aristotle's condition is incompatible with the satisfaction of Frege's condition; that the opacity of belief sentences shows the futility of assigning logical form to their objects. The argument might go as follows. Sentences

have logical form in virtue of their behavior under logical transformations; the logical form of a sentence is that aspect of its structure in virtue of which it provides a domain for such transformations. But Frege shows us that the objects of verbs of propositional attitude are inferentially inert. Hence, it's a sort of charade to speak of the logical form of the objects of PAs; what's the force of saying that a sentence has the form P & Q if one must also say that simplification of conjunction does not apply?

Perhaps some such argument supplies the motive force of fusion theories. It is, in any event, misled. In particular, it muddles the distinction between what's entailed by what's believed, and what's entailed by believing what's believed. Less cryptically: if John believes that P & Q, then what John believes entails that P and what John believes entails that Q. This is surely incontestable; P & Q is what John believes, and P & Q entails P, Q. Full stop. It would thus be highly ill-advised to put Frege's condition as "P & Q is semantically inert when embedded in the context 'John believes ...'"; for this makes it sound as though P & Q sometimes doesn't entail P, viz. when it's in the scope of "believes." (A parallel bad argument: P & Q sometimes doesn't entail P, viz. when it's in the scope of the operator "not.") What falls under Frege's condition, then, is not the sentence that expresses what John believes (viz. P & Q) but the sentence that expresses John's believing what he believes (viz. the sentence "John believes that P & Q"). Note that the inertia of this latter sentence isn't an exception to simplification of conjunction, since simplification of conjunction isn't defined for sentences of the form *a believes that P & Q*; only for sentences of the form *P & Q*.

"Still," one might say, "if the form of words 'P & Q' is logically inert when embedded in the form of words 'John believes ...', what's the *point* of talking about the logical form of beliefs?" This isn't an argument, of course, but it's a fair question. Answers: (a) because we may want to satisfy Aristotle's condition (e.g., in order to be in a position to state the practical syllogism); (b) because we may want to compare beliefs in respect of their form (John's belief that (x) Fx → Gx is a generalization of Mary's belief that a is F and G; Sam's belief that P is incompatible with Bill's belief that not-P; etc.); (c) because we may wish to speak of the consequences of a belief, even while cheerfully admitting that the consequences of a belief may not themselves be objects of belief (viz. believed in). Indeed, we need the notion of the consequences of a belief if only in order to say that belief isn't closed under the consequence relation.

I cease to digress.

V. A theory of propositional attitudes should mesh with empirical accounts of mental processes.

We want a theory of PAs to say what (token) propositional attitudes *are*, or, at least, what the facts are in virtue of which PA ascriptions are true. It seems to me self-evident that no such theory could be acceptable unless it lent itself to explanations of the data – gross and commonsensical or subtle and experimental – about mental states and processes. This is not, of course, to require that a theory of PAs legitimize our *current* empirical psychology; only that it comport with some psychology or other that is independently warranted. I hear this as analogous to: the theory that water is H_2O couldn't be acceptable unless, taken together with appropriate empirical premises, it leads to explanations of the macro-and micro-properties of water. Hence, I hear it as undeniable.

I think, in fact, that the requirement that a theory of propositional attitudes should be empirically plausible can be made to do quite a lot of work – much more work than philosophers have usually realized. I'll return to this presently, when we have some theories in hand.

Those, then, are the conditions that I want a theory of propositional attitudes to meet. I shall argue that, taken together, they strongly suggest that propositional attitudes are relations between organisms and formulae in an internal language; between organisms and internal sentences, as it were. It's convenient, however, to give the arguments in two steps; first, to show that conditions I-V comport nicely with the view that the objects of PAs are sentences, and then to show that these sentences are plausibly internal.

I begin by anticipating a charge of false advertising. The arguments to be reviewed are explicitly non-demonstrative. All I claim for the internal language theory is that it works (a) surprisingly well, and (b) better than any of the available alternatives. The clincher comes at the end: even if we didn't need internal sentences for purposes of I-V, we'd need them to do our psychology. Another non-demonstrative argument, no doubt, but one I find terrifically persuasive.

Carnap's theory

Carnap suggested, in *Meaning and Necessity* (1947), that PAs might be construed as relations between people and sentences they are disposed to utter; e.g., between people and sentences of English. What Carnap had primarily in mind was coping with the opacity problem, but it's striking and instructive that his proposal does pretty well with *all* the conditions I've enumerated. Consider:

I. If propositional attitudes are relations to sentences, then they are relations *tout court*. Moreover, assume that the relations ascribed by a sentence of the form *a believes* … holds between the individual denoted by "a" and the correspondent of the complement clause. It is then immediately clear why the belief ascribed to *a* is true if the correspondent is; the correspondent is the *object* of the belief (i.e., the correspondent is what's believed-true) if Carnap's story is right.

II. Vendler's condition is presumably satisfiable, though how the details go will depend on how we construe the objects of verbs of saying. A natural move for a neo-Carnapian to make would be to take "John said that P" to be true in virtue of some relation between John and a token of the type P. Since, on this account, saying that P and believing that P involve relations to tokens of the very same sentence, it's hardly surprising that formulae which express the object of the *says-that* relation turn out to be logico-syntactically similar to formulae which express the object of the *believes-that* relation.

III. Frege's condition is satisfied; the opacity of belief is construed as a special case of the opacity of quotation. To put it slightly differently; "John said 'Bill bit Mary'" expresses a relation between John and a (quoted) sentence, so we're unsurprised by the fact that John may bear *that* relation to *that* sentence, while not bearing it to some arbitrarily similar but distinct sentence, e.g., to the sentence "somebody bit Mary" or to the sentence "Bill bit somebody," etc. But ditto, *mutatis mutandis*, if "John believes Bill bit Mary" *also* expresses a relation between John and a quoted sentence.

IV. Aristotle's condition is satisfied in the strong form. The logical form of the object of a belief sentence is inherited from the logical form of the correspondent of the belief sentence. Of course it is, since on the Carnap view, the correspondent of the belief sentence *is* the object of the belief.

V. Whether you think that Carnap's theory can claim empirical plausibility depends on what you take the empirical facts about propositional attitudes to be and how ingenious you are in exploiting the theory to provide explanations of the facts. Here's one example of how such an explanation might go.

It's plausible to claim that there is a fairly general parallelism between the complexity of beliefs and the complexity of the sentences that express them. So, for example, I take it that "the Second Punic War was fought under conditions which neither of the combatants could have desired or foreseen" is a more complex sentence than, e.g., "it's raining"; and, correspondingly, I take it that the thought that the Second Punic War was fought under conditions which neither of the combatants could have desired or foreseen is a more complicated thought than the thought that it's raining. Carnap's theory provides for this parallelism,[10] since, according to the theory, what makes a belief ascription true is a relation between an organism and the correspondent of the belief-ascribing sentence. To hold the belief that the Second Punic War ..., etc. is thus to be related to a more complex sentence than the one you are related to when you hold the belief that it's raining, and it's quite plausible that being disposed to utter a complex sentence should be a more complex state than being disposed to utter a simple sentence, ceteris paribus.

Some people need to count noses before they will admit to having one. In which case, see the discussion of "codability" in Brown and Lenneberg (1954) and Brown (1976). What the experiments showed is that the relative complexity of the descriptions which subjects supply for color chips predicts the relative difficulty that the subjects have in identifying the chips in a recognition-recall task. Brown and Lenneberg explain the finding along strictly (though inadvertently) Carnapian lines: complex descriptions correspond to complex memories because it's the description which the subject (opaquely) remembers when he (transparently) remembers the color of the chip.

We can now begin to see *one* of the ways in which condition V is supposed to work. A theory of propositional attitudes specifies a construal of the objects of the attitudes. It tells for such a theory if it can be shown to mesh with an independently plausible story about the "cost accounting" for mental processes. A cost accounting function is just a (partial) ordering of mental states by their relative complexity. Such an ordering is, in turn, responsive to a variety of types of empirical data, both intuitive and experimental. Roughly, one has a "mesh" between an empirically warranted cost accounting and a theory of the objects of PAs when one can predict the relative complexity of a mental state (or process) from the relative complexity of whatever the theory assigns as its object (or domain). (So, if Carnap is right, then the relative complexity of beliefs should be predictable from the relative linguistic complexity of the correspondents of belief-ascribing sentences.)

There's a good deal more to be said about all this than I have space for here. Again, roughly: to require that the complexity of the putative objects of PAs predict the cost accounting for the attitudes is to impose empirical constraints on the *notation* of (canonical) belief-ascribing sentences. So, for example, we would clearly get different predictions about the relative complexity of beliefs if we take the object of a PA to be the correspondent of the belief ascribing sentence than if we take it to be, e.g., the correspondent transformed into disjunctive form. The fact that there are empirical consequences of the notation we use to specify the objects of PAs is, of course, part and parcel of the fact that we are construing the attitude ascriptions *opaquely*; it is precisely under opaque construal that we distinguish (e.g.,) the mental state of believing that P & Q from the mental state of believing that neither not-P nor not-Q.

In short, Carnap's theory fares rather well with conditions I-V; there's more to be said in its favor than one might gather from the muted enthusiasm which philosophers have generally accorded it. Nevertheless, I think the philosophical consensus is warranted; Carnap's theory won't do. Here are some of the reasons.

1. Carnap has a theory about the objects of the propositional attitudes (viz., they're sentences) and a theory about the character of the relation to those objects in virtue of which one has a belief, desire, etc. Now, the latter theory is blatantly behavioristic; on Carnap's view, to believe that so-and-so is to be disposed (under presumably specifiable conditions) to utter tokens of the correspondent of the belief-ascribing sentence. But, patently, beliefs aren't behavioral dispositions; a fortiori, they aren't dispositions to utter. Hence, something's wrong with at least part of Carnap's account of the attitudes.

I put this objection first because it's the easiest to meet. So far as I can see, nothing prevents Carnap from keeping his account of the *objects* of belief while scuttling the behavioristic analysis of the belief relation. This would leave him wanting an answer to such questions as: what relation to the sentence "it's raining" is such that you believe that it's raining if you and the sentence are in that relation? In particular, he'd want some answer other than the behavioristic: "It's the relation of being disposed to utter tokens of that sentence when ..."

The natural solution would be for Carnap to turn functionalist; to hold that to believe it's raining is to have a token of "it's raining" play a certain role in the causation of your behavior and of your (other) mental states, said role eventually to be specified in the course of the detailed working out of empirical psychology ... etc., etc. This is, perhaps, not much of a story, but it's fashionable, I know of nothing better, and it does have the virtue of explaining why propositional attitudes are opaque: You wouldn't expect to be able to infer from "tokens of the sentences S_1 have the causal role R" to "tokens of the sentences S_2 have the causal role of R" on the basis of any logical relation between S_1 and S_2 (except, of course, identity). More generally, so far as I can see, a functionalist account of the way quoted sentences figure in the having of PAs will serve as well as a disposition-to-utter account in coping with all of conditions I-V. From now on, I'll take this emendation for granted.

2. The natural way to read the Carnap theory is to take type identity of the correspondents of belief-ascribing sentences as necessary and sufficient for type identity of the ascribed beliefs; and it's at least arguable that this cuts the PAs too thin. So, for example, one might plausibly hold that "John believes Mary bit Bill" and "John believes Bill was bitten by Mary" ascribe the same belief (see note 9). In effect, this is the sinister side of the strategy of inheriting the opacity of belief from the opacity of quotation. The strategy fails whenever the identity conditions on beliefs are *different* from the identity conditions on sentences.

A way to cope would be to allow that the objects of beliefs are, in effect, *translation sets* of sentences; something like this seems to be the impetus for Carnap's doctrine of intentional isomorphism. In any event, the problems in this area are well-known. It may well be, for example, that the right way to characterize a translation relation for sentences is by referring to the communicative intentions of speaker/hearers of whatever language the sentences belong to. (S_1 translates S_2 if the two sentences are both standardly used with the same communicative intentions.) But, of course, we can't both identify translations by reference to intentions and individuate propositional attitudes (including, n.b., intentions) by reference to translations. This problem holds quite independent of epistemological worries about the facticity of ascriptions of propositional attitudes, the determinacy or otherwise of translations, etc., which suggests that it may be serious.

3. You can believe that it's raining even if you don't speak English. This is a variant of the thickness of slice problem just mentioned; it again suggests that the appropriate objects of belief are translation sets and raises the specters that haunt that treatment.

4. You can, surely, believe that it's raining even if you don't speak any language at all. To say this is to say that at least *some* human cognitive psychology generalizes to infra-human organisms; if it didn't, we would find the behavior of animals *utterly* bewildering, which, in fact, we don't.

Of course, relations are cheap; there must be *some* relation which a dog bears to "it's raining" iff the dog believes that it's raining; albeit, perhaps, some not very interesting relation. So, why not choose *it* as the relation in virtue of which the belief-ascription holds of the dog? The problem is condition V. It would simply be a miracle if there were a relation between dogs and tokens of "it's raining" such that any of the empirical facts about the propositional attitudinizing of dogs proved explicable in terms of that relation. (We can't, for example, choose any functional/causal relation because the behavior of dogs is surely not in any way caused by tokens of English sentences.) To put it generally if crudely, satisfying condition V depends on assuming that whatever the theory takes to be the object of a PA plays an appropriate role in the mental processes of the organism to which the attitude is ascribed. But English sentences play no role in the mental life of dogs. (Excepting, perhaps, such sentences as "Down, Rover!" which, in any event, don't play the kind of role envisaged.)

5. We argued that the truth conditions on beliefs are inherited from the truth conditions on the correspondents of belief-ascribing sentences, but this won't work if, for example, there are inexpressible beliefs. This problem is especially serious for behaviorist (or functionalist) accounts of the belief relation; to believe that P can't be a question of being disposed to utter (or of having one's behavior caused by) tokens of the sentence P if, as a matter of fact, there is no such sentence. Yet it is the appeal to quoted sentences which does the work in such theories: which allows them to satisfy I-V.

6. We remarked that there's a rough correspondence between the complexity of thoughts and the complexity of the sentences which express them, and that the (neo-) Carnapian theory provides for this; more generally, that the view that the objects of PAs are natural-language sentences might mesh reasonably well with an empirically defensible cost accounting for mental states and processes. Unfortunately this argument cuts both ways if we assume – as seems entirely plausible – that the correspondence is no better than partial. Whenever it fails, there's prima facie evidence *against* the theory that sentences are the objects of propositional attitudes.

In fact, we can do rather better than appealing to intuitions here. For example: we noted above that the "codability" (viz., mean simplicity of descriptions in English) of colors predicts their recallability in a population of English speakers, and that this comports with the view that what one remembers when one remembers a color is (at least sometimes) its description – i.e., with the view that descriptions are the objects of (at least some) propositional attitudes. It thus comes as a shock to find that codability *in English* also predicts recall for a monolingual Dani subject population. We can't explain this by assuming a correlation between codability-in-English and codability-in-Dani (i.e., by assuming that the colors that English speakers find easy to describe are the ones that Dani-speakers also find easy to describe), since, as it turns out, Dani has no vocabulary *at all* for chromatic variation; all such variation is *infinitely* uncodable in Dani. This comes close to being the paradox dreaded above: how could *English* sentences be the objects of the propositional attitudes of the Dani? And, if they are not, how could a property defined over English sentences mesh with a theory of cost accounting for the mental processes of the Dani? It looks as though either (a) some propositional attitudes are *not* relations to sentences, or (b) if they are – if English sentences are somehow the objects of Dani PAs – then sentences which constitute the objects of PAs need play no functional/causal role in the having of the attitudes. (For discussion of the cross-cultural results on codability, see Brown (1976). For details of the original studies, see Heider (1972) and Berlin and Kay (1969).)

7. If (token) sentences of a natural language are the objects of propositional attitudes, how are (first) languages learned? On any theory of language learning we can now imagine, that process must involve the collection of data, and the decision about which of the hypotheses the data best confirm. That is, it must involve such mental states and processes as beliefs, expectations and perceptual integrations. It's important to realize that *no* account of language learning which does not thus involve propositional attitudes and mental processes has ever been proposed by anyone, barring only behaviorists. And behaviorist accounts of language learning are, surely, not tenable. So, on pain of circularity, there must be *some* propositional attitudes which are not functional/causal relations to natural lan-

guage sentences. I see no way out of this which isn't a worse option than rejecting the Carnap theory.

So, the situation looks discouraging. On the one hand, we have a number of plausible arguments in favor of accepting the Carnap story (viz., I-V) and, on the other, we have a number of equally plausible arguments in favor of not (viz. 1-7). Never mind; for, at second blush, it seems we needn't accept the whole Carnap theory to satisfy I-V and we needn't reject the whole Carnap theory to avoid 1-7. Roughly, all that I-V require is the part of the story that says that the objects of PAs are *sentences* (hence have logical forms, truth conditions, etc.). Whereas what causes the trouble with 1-7 is only that part of the story which says that they are *natural language* sentences (hence raising problems about non-verbal organisms, first language learning, etc.) The recommended solution is thus to take the objects of PAs to be sentences of a *non*-natural language; in effect, formulae in an Internal Representational System.

The first point is to establish that this proposal does what it is supposed to: copes with I-V without running afoul of 1-7. In fact, I propose to do less than that, since, so far as I can see, the details would be extremely complicated. Suffice it here to indicate the general strategy.

Conditions I and III are relatively easy to meet. I demands that propositional attitudes be relations, and so they are if they are relations to internal representations. III demands a construal of opacity. Carnap met this demand by reducing the opacity of belief to the opacity of quotation, and so do we: the only difference is that, whereas for Carnap, "John believes it's raining" relates John to a sentence of English, for us it relates John to an internal formula.

Conditions II and IV stress logico/syntactic parallelism between the complements and the correspondents of belief-ascribing sentences; such relations are epitomized by the identity between the truth conditions on "it's raining" and those on what is believed when it's believed that it's raining. (Neo-) Carnap explained these symmetries by taking the correspondents of belief ascriptions to be the objects of beliefs. The present alternative is spiritually similar but one step less direct: we assume that the correspondent of a belief-ascriber inherits its logico-semantic properties from the same internal formula which functions as the object of the belief ascribed.

There are three pieces in play: there are (a) *belief-ascribers* (like "John believes it's raining"); (b) *complements* of belief ascribers (like "it's raining" in "John believes it's raining"); and (c) *correspondents* of belief ascribers (like "it's raining" standing free). The idea is to get all three to converge (though of course, by different routes) on the same internal formula (call it "F (it's raining)"),[11] thereby providing the groundwork for explaining the analogies that II and IV express.

To get this to work out right would be to supply detailed instructions for connecting the theory of PAs with the theory of sentence interpretation, and I have misplaced mine. But the general idea is apparent. Belief-ascribers are true in virtue of functional/causal (call them "belief making") relations between organisms and tokens of internal formulae. Thus, in particular, "John believes it's raining" is true in virtue of a belief-making relation between John and a token of F (it's raining). It is , of course, the complement of a belief-ascriber that determines *which* internal formula is involved in its truth conditions; in effect "it's raining" in "John believes it's raining" functions as an index which picks out F (it's raining) and not, for example, F (elephants have wings), as the internal formula that John is related to iff "John believes it's raining" is true.

So, viewed along one vector, the complement of a belief-ascriber connects it with an internal formula. But, viewed along another vector, the complement of a belief-ascriber connects it to its correspondent: if the correspondent of "John believes it's raining" is "it's raining," that is because the form of words "it's raining" constitutes its complement. And now we can close the circle, since, of course, F (it's raining) is *also* semantically connected with the correspondent of "John believes it's raining" viz., by the principle that "it's raining" is the sentence that English speakers use when they are in the belief-making relation to a token of F (it's raining) and wish to use a sentence of English to say what it is that they believe.

There are various ways of thinking about the relation between internal formulae and the correspondents of belief-ascribers. One is to think of the conventions of a natural language as functioning to establish a pairing of its verbal forms with the internal formulae that mediate the propositional attitudes of its users; in particular, as pairing the internal objects of beliefs with the form of words that speaker/hearers use to express their beliefs. This is a natural way to view the situation if you think of a natural language as a system of conventional vehicles for the expression of thoughts (a view to which I know of no serious objections). So in the present case, the conventions of English pair: "it's raining" with F (it's raining) (viz., with the object of the belief that it's raining); "elephants have wings" with F (elephants have wings) (viz., with the object of the belief that elephants have wings); and, generally, the object of each belief with the correspondent of some belief-ascribing sentence.[12]

Another option is to assume that F (it's raining) is distinguished by the fact that its tokens play a causal/functional role (not only as the object of the belief that it's raining, but also) in the production of linguistically regular utterances of "it's raining." Indeed, this option would plausibly be exercised in tandem with the one mentioned just above, since it would be reasonable to construe "linguistically regular" utterances as the ones that are produced in light of the speaker's knowledge of the linguistic conventions.

The basic idea, in any event, would be to implicate F (it's raining) as the object of the communicative intentions that utterances of "it's raining" standardly function to express; hence, as among the mental causes of such utterances. I take it that, given this relation, it ought to be possible to work out detailed tactics for the satisfaction of conditions II and IV, but this is the bit I propose to leave to the ingenuity of the reader. What I want to emphasize here is the way the linguistic structure of the complement of a belief-ascriber connects it with free declaratives (in one direction) and with internal formulae (in the other). Contrary to the fusion story, it's no accident that "it's raining" occurs in "John believes it's raining." Rather, the availability of natural languages for saying *both* what one believes *and* that one believes it turns on the exploitation of this elegant symmetry.

What about condition V? I shall consider this in conjunction with 2-7, since what's noteworthy about the latter is that they all register *empirical* complaints against the Carnap account. For example, 3, 4 and 6 would be without force if only everybody (viz., every subject of true propositional attitude ascriptions) talked English. 2 and 5 depend upon the empirical likelihood that English sentences fail to correspond one to one to objects of propositional attitudes. 7 would be met if only English were innate. Indeed, I suppose an ultra hard-line Neo-Carnapian might consider saving the bacon by claiming that – appearances to the contrary nonwithstanding – English *is* innate, universal, just rich enough, etc. My point is that this is the right *kind* of move to make; all we have against it is its palpable untruth.

Whereas, it's part of the charm of the internal language story that, since practically nothing is known about the details of cognitive processes, we can make the corresponding assumptions about the internal representational system risking no more than gross implausibility at the very worst.

So, let's assume – what we don't, at any event, *know* to be false – that the internal language is innate, that it's formulae correspond one to one with the contents of propositional attitudes (e.g., that "John bit Mary" and "Mary was bitten by John" correspond to the same "internal sentences"), and that it is as universal as human psychology; viz., that to the extent that an organism shares our mental processes, it also shares our system of internal representations. On these assumptions, everything works. It's no longer paradoxical, for example, that codability *in English* predicts the relative complexity of the mental processes of the Dani; for, by assumption, it's not *really* the complexity of English sentences that predicts *our* cost accounting; we wouldn't expect *that* correspondence to be better than partial (see objection 6). What really predicts our cost accounting is the relative complexity of the internal representations that we use English sentences to express. And, again by assumption, the underlying system of internal representations is common to the Dani and to us. If you don't like this assumption, try and find some other hypothesis that accounts for the facts about the Dani.

Notice that to say that we can have our empirical assumptions isn't to say that we can have them for free. They carry a body of empirical commitments which, if untenable, will defeat the internal representation view. Imagine, for example, that cost accounting for English speakers proves utterly unrelated to cost accounting for (e.g.,) speakers of Latvian. (Imagine, in effect, that the Whorf-Sapir hypothesis turns out to be more or less true.) It's then hard to see how the system of internal representations could be universal. But if it's not universal, it's presumably not innate. And if it's not innate, it's not available to mediate the learning of first languages. And if it's not available to mediate the learning of first languages, we lose our means of coping with objection 7. There are plenty of ways in which we could find out that the theory's wrong if, in fact, it is.

Where we've got to is this: the general characteristics of propositional attitudes appear to demand sentence-like entities to be their objects. And broadly empirical conditions appear to preclude identifying these entities with sentences of *natural* languages – hence internal representations and private languages. How bad is it to have got here? I now want to argue that the present conclusion is independently required because it is presupposed by the best – indeed the only – psychology that we've got. Not just, as one philosopher has rather irresponsibly remarked, that "some psychologists like to talk that way," but that the best accounts of mental processes we have are quite unintelligible unless something like the internal representation story is true.

The long way of making this point is via a detailed discussion of such theories, but I've done that elsewhere and enough is enough. Suffice it here to consider a single example – which is, however, prototypical. I claim again that the details don't matter, that one could make the same points by considering phenomena drawn from any area of cognitive psychology that is sufficiently well worked out to warrant talk of a theory *in situ*.

So, consider a fragment of contemporary (psycho) linguistics; consider the explanation of the ambiguity of a sentence like "they are flying planes" (hereinafter, frequently, S). The conventional story goes as follows: the sentence is ambiguous because there are two ways of grouping the word sequence into phrases, two ways of "bracketing" it. One bracketing, corresponding to the reading of the sentence which answers "what are those things?", goes: (they) (are) (flying planes) – viz., the sentence is copular, the main verb is "are," and "flying" is an adjectival modifier of "planes." Whereas, on the other bracketing – corresponding to the reading on which the sentence answers "What are those guys doing?" – the bracketing goes: (they) (are flying) (planes) – viz. The sentence is transitive, the main verb is "flying," and "are" belongs to the auxiliary. I assume without argument that something like this is, or at least contributes to, the explanation of the ambiguity of S. The evidence for such treatments is overwhelming, and there is, literally, no alternative theory in the field.

But what could it mean to speak of S as "having" two bracketings? I continue to tread the well-worn path: S has two bracketings in that there exists a function (call it G-proper) from (as it might be) the word "sentence" onto precisely those bracketed word strings which constitute the sentences of English. And both "(they) (are) (flying planes)" and "(they) (are flying) (planes)" are in the range of that function. (Moreover, no other bracketing of that word sequence is in the range of G-proper ... etc.)

Now, the trouble with this explanation, as it stands, is that it is either enthymemic or silly. For one wants to ask, how *could* the mere, as it were Platonic, existence of G-proper account for the facts about the ambiguity of English sentences? Or, to put it another way, sure there is, Platonically, a function under which S gets two bracketings. But there is also, Platonically, a function G¹ under which it gets sixteen; and a function G" under which it gets seven; and a function G‴ under which it gets none. Since G¹, G", and G‴ are all, qua functions, just as good as G-proper, how could the mere *existence* of the latter explain the linguistic properties of S; (You may feel inclined to say: "Ah, but G-proper is the (or perhaps is *the*) grammar of English, and that distinguishes it from G¹, G", and the rest." But this explanation takes one nowhere, since it invites the question why does the grammar of English play a special role in the explanation of English sentences? Or, to put the same question minutely differently: call G¹ the schmamar of English. We now want to know how come it's the bracketing assigned by English grammar and not the bracketing assigned by English schmamar, which predicts the ambiguity of "they are flying planes"?)

So far as I can see, there's only one way such questions can conceivably be answered – viz., by holding that G-proper (not only exists but) specifies the very system of (internal (what else?)) representations that English speaker/hearers use to parse the sentences of their language. But, then, if we accept this, we are willy-nilly involved in talking of at least *some* mental processes (processes of understanding and producing sentences) as involving at least some relations to at least some internal representations. And, if we have to have internal representations anyhow, why not take them to be the objects of propositional attitudes, thereby placating I-V? I say "if we accept this"; but really we have no choice. For the account is well evidenced, not demonstrably incoherent, and, again, it's the only one in the field. A working science is ipso facto in philosophical good repute.

So, by a series of non-demonstrative arguments: there are internal representations and propositional attitudes are relations that we bear to them. It remains to discuss two closely related objections.

Objection 1: Why not take the object of propositional attitudes to be *propositions*?

This suggestion has, no doubt, a ring of etymological plausibility; in fact, for all I know, it may be right. The mistake is in supposing it somehow conflicts with the present proposal.

I am taking seriously the idea that the system of internal representations constitutes a (computational) language. Qua language, it presumably has a syntax and a semantics; specifying the language involves saying
what the properties are in virtue of which its formulae are well-formed, and
what relations(s) obtain between the formulae and things in the (non-lin-
guistic) world. I have no idea what an adequate semantics for a system of
internal representations would look like; suffice it that, if propositions come
in at all, they come in here. In particular, nothing stops us from specifying
a semantics for the IRS by saying (inter alia) that some of its formulae
express propositions. If we do say this, then we can make sense of the notion
that propositional attitudes are relations to propositions – viz., they are
mediated relations to propositions, with internal representations doing the
mediating.

This is, quite generally, the way that representational theories of
the mind work. So, in classical versions, thinking of John (construed
opaquely) is a relation to an "idea" – viz., to an internal representation of
John. But this is quite compatible with its also being (transparently) con-
struable as a relation *to John*. In particular, when Smith is thinking of John,
he (normally) stands in relation to John and does so *in virtue* of his standing in relation to an idea of John. Similarly, mutatis mutandis, if thinking
that it will rain is standing in relation to a proposition, then, on the present
account, you stand in that relation in virtue of your (functional/causal) relation to an internal formula which expresses the proposition. No doubt, the
"expressing" bit is obscure; but that's a problem about propositions, not a
problem about internal representations.

"Ah, but if you are going to allow propositions as the *mediate*
objects of propositional attitudes, why bother with internal representations
as their immediate objects? Why not just say: 'propositional attitudes are
relations to propositions. Punkt!'" There's a small reason and a big reason.
The small reason is that propositions don't have the right properties for our
purposes. In particular, one anticipates problems of cost-accounting.
Condition V, it will be remembered, permits us to choose among theories of
PAs in virtue of the lexico-syntactic form of the entities they assign as
objects of the attitudes. Now, the problem with propositions is that they are
the sorts of things which don't, in the relevant respects, *have* forms.
Propositions neutralize the lexico-syntactic differences between various
ways of saying the same thing. That's what they're *for*. I say that this is a
small problem, but it looms prodigious if you hanker after a theory of the
object of PAs which claims empirical repute. After all, it's not just cost-
accounting that is supposed to be determined by formal aspects of the
objects of PAs; it's *all* the mental processes and properties that cognitive psychology explains. That's what it *means* to speak of a *computational* psychology. Computational principles are ones that apply in virtue of the form of
entities in their domain.

But my main reason for not saying "propositional attitudes are relations to propositions. Punkt." is that I don't understand it. I don't see how an organism can stand in an (interesting epistemic) relation to a proposition except by standing in a (causal/functional) relation to some token of a formula that expresses the proposition. I am aware that there is a philosophical tradition to the contrary. Plato says (I think) that there is a special intellectual faculty (theoria) wherewith one peers at abstract objects. Frege says that one *apprehends* (what I'm calling) propositions, but I can find no doctrine about what apprehension comes to beyond the remark (in "The Thought") that it's not sense perception because its objects are abstract and it's not introspection because its objects aren't mental. (He also says that grasping a thought isn't much like grasping a hammer. To be sure.) As for me, I want a *mechanism* for the relation between organisms and propositions, and the only one I can think of is mediation by internal representations.[13]

Objection 2: Surely it's *conceivable* that propositional attitudes are *not* relations to internal representations.

I think it is; the theory that propositional attitudes are relations to internal representations is a piece of empirical psychology, not an analysis. For there might have been angels, or behaviorism might have been true, and then the internal representation story would have been false. The moral is, I think, that we ought to give up asking for analyses; psychology is all the philosophy of mind that we are likely to get.

But, moreover, it may be *empirically* possible that there should be creatures that have the same propositional attitudes we do (e.g., the same beliefs) but *not* the same system of internal representations; creatures that, as it were, share our epistemic states but not our psychology. Suppose, for example, it turns out that Martians, or porpoises, believe what we do but have a very different sort of cost accounting. We might then want to say that there are translation relations among systems of internal representation (viz., that formally distinct representations can express the same proposition). Presumably *which* proposition an internal representation expresses – what content it has – would be complexly determined by its functional role in the organism's mental life, including, especially, the way it is connected to stimulations and responses. Functional identity of internal representations would then be criterial for their intertranslatability. Whether we can actually make sense of this sort of view remains to be seen; we can barely think about the question prior to the elaboration of theories about how representational systems are semantically interpreted; and as things now stand, we haven't got semantic theories for natural languages, to say nothing of languages of thought. Perhaps it goes without saying that it's no objection to a doctrine that it *may* run us into incoherencies. Or, rather, if it is an objection, there's an adequate reply: "Yes, but also it may not."

I'll end on the note just sounded. Contemporary cognitive psychology is, in effect, a revival of the representational theory of the mind. The favored treatment of PAs arises in this context. So, in particular, the mind is conceived of as an organ whose function is the manipulation of representations and these, in turn, provide the domain of mental processes and the (immediate) objects of mental state. That's what it is to see the mind as something like a computer. (Or rather, to put the horse back in front of the cart, that's what it is to see a computer as something like the mind. We give sense to the analogy by treating selected states of the machine as formulae and by specifying which semantic interpretations the formulae are to bear. It is in the context of such specifications that we speak of machine processes as computations and of machine states as intensional.)

If the representational theory of the mind is true, then we know what propositional attitudes are. But the net total of philosophical problems is surely not decreased thereby. We must now face what has always been *the* problem for representational theories to solve: what relates internal representations to the world? What is it for a system of internal representations to be semantically interpreted? I take it that this problem is now the main content of the philosophy of mind.[14]

NOTES

1. I shall have nothing at all to say about knowing, discovering, recognizing, or any other "factive" attitudes. The justification for this restriction is worth discussing, but not here....

2. I haven't space to discuss here the idea that "John believes" should be construed as an operator on "it's raining." Suffice it (a) that it's going to be hard to square that account with such observations as I-b below; and (b) that it seems quite implausible for such sentences as "John believes what Mary said" (and what Mary said might *be* that it's raining). In general, the objects of propositional-attitude verbs exhibit syntax of object-noun phrases, which is just what the operator account would not predict.

3. I assume that this is approximately correct: given a sentence of syntactic form $(NP_1 (V (NP_2)))$, V expresses a relation if NP_1 and NP_2 refer. So, for present purposes, the question whether "believes" expresses a relation in "John believes it's raining" comes down to the question whether there are such things as objects of belief. I shan't, therefore, bother to distinguish among these various ways of putting the question in the discussion which follows.

4. Of course, it might refer in virtue of a relation between Mary and something other than a voice. "John is taller than the average man" isn't true in virtue of a relation between John and the average man ("the average man" doesn't refer). But the sentence is relational for all that. It's for this sort of reason that such principles as the one announced in note 3 hold only to a first approximation.

5. Note that verbs of propositional attitude are transparent, in this sense, only when their objects are *complements*; one can't infer "there is something Ponce de Leon sought" from "Ponce de Leon sought the Fountain of Youth." It may, however, be worth translating "seek" to "try to find" to save the generalization. This would give us: "Ponce de Leon tried to find the Fountain of Youth," which does, I suppose entail that there is something that Ponce de Leon tried (viz., tried to do; viz., to find the Fountain of Youth).

Also, to say that EG applies *to* the complement of verbs of PA is, of course, not to say that it applies *in* the complement of verbs of PA. "John wants to marry Marie of Rumania" implies that there is something that John wants (viz., to marry Marie of Rumania); it notoriously does *not* imply that there is someone whom John wants to marry (see III below).

6. Fusion has been contemplated as a remedy for untransparency in several philosophical contexts; see Goodman (1968); Dennett (1969); Nagel (1965). Note "contemplated," not "embraced."

7. 3 is not a point about EG. On the fusion view, there's no representation of the fact that "the belief that Sam is nice" is about Sam even when "belief" and "about" are both construed *opaquely*.

8. Defining "correspondent" gets complicated where verbs of PA take *transformed* sentences as their objects, but the technicalities needn't concern us here. Suffice it that we want the correspondent of "John wants to leave" to be "John leaves," the correspondent of "John objects to Mary and Bill being elected" to be "Mary and Bill are elected," etc.

9. I am assuming that two sentences with correspondents of *different* logico-syntactic form cannot assign the same (opaque) belief, and someone might wish to challenge this; consider "John believes that Mary bit Bill" and "John believes that Bill was bitten by Mary." This sort of objection is serious and will be accomodated later on.

10. In speaking of Carnap's theory, I don't wish to imply that Carnap would endorse the uses to which I'm putting it; quite the contrary, I should imagine.

11. Where F might be thought of as a function from (e.g., English) sentences onto internal formulae.

12. Assuming as we may, but now needn't, do that all beliefs are expressible in English. It is, of course, a consequence of the present view that all the beliefs we can entertain are expressible in the internal code.

13. The notion that the apprehension of propositions is mediated by linguistic objects is not entirely foreign even to the Platonistic tradition. Church says: "... the preference of (say) seeing over *understanding* as a method of observation seems to me capricious. For just as an opaque body may be seen, so a concept may be understood or grasped ... in both cases the observation is not direct but through intermediaries ... linguistic expressions in the case of the concept" (1951). See also the discussion in Dummett (1973, pp. 156-57).

14. All of the following helped: Professors Ned Block, Noam Chomsky, Dan Dennett, Hartrey Field, Janet Dean Fodor, Keith Lehrer, and Brian Loar. Many thanks.

REFERENCES

Berlin, B. and Kay, P. (1969). *Basic Color Terms*, Berkeley, University of California Press.

Brown, R. (1976). "Reference – in Memorial Tribute to Eric Lenneberg," *Cognition*, 4: 125-153.

Brown, R. and Lenneberg, E. (1954). "A Study in Language and Cognition," *Journal of Abnormal and Social Psychology*, 49: 454-462.

Carnap, R. (1947). *Meaning and Necessity*, Chicago, Phoenix Books, University of Chicago Press.

Church, A. (1951). "The Need for Abstract Entities in Semantic Analysis," in *Contributions to the Analysis and Synthesis of Knowledge*, Proceedings of the American Academy of Arts and Sciences, 80: 100-112.

Davidson, D. (1965). "Theories of Meaning and Learnable Language," in *Logic, Methodology and Philosophy of Science*, Y. Bar-Hillel, Amsterdam.

Dennett, D. (1969). *Content and Consciousness*, New York and London, Routledge and Kegan Paul.

Dummett, M. (1973). *Frege: Philosophy of Language*, London, Duckworth and Company.

Fodor, J.A. (1975). *The Language of Thought*, New York, Thomas Y. Crowell, Company, paperback version, Harvard University Press, 1979.

Goodman, N. (1968). *Languages of Art*, New York, Bobbs-Merrill.

Grice, H.P. (1975). "Method in Philosophical Psychology," *Proceedings and Addresses of the American Philosophical Association*, 48: 23-53.

Heider, E. (1972). "Universals in Color Naming and Memory," *Journal of Experimental Psychology*, 93: 10-20.

Nagel, T. (1965). "Physicalism," *Philosophical Review*, 74: 339-356.

Vendler, Z. (1972). *Res Cogitans*, Ithaca, N.Y., Cornell University Press.

THREE KINDS OF INTENTIONAL PSYCHOLOGY

Daniel C. Dennett

Folk Psychology as a Source of Theory

Suppose you and I both believe that cats eat fish. Exactly what feature must we share for this to be true of us? More generally, recalling Socrates's favorite style of question, what must be in common between things truly ascribed an *intentional* predicate – such as "wants to visit China" or "expects noodles for supper"? As Socrates points out, in the *Meno* and else-where, such questions are ambiguous or vague in their intent. One can be asking on the one hand for something rather like a definition, or on the other hand for something rather like a theory. (Socrates of course preferred the former sort of answer.) What do all magnets have in common? First answer: they all attract iron. Second answer: they all have such-and-such a microphysical property (a property that explains their capacity to attract iron). In one sense people knew what magnets were – they were things that attracted iron – long before science told them what magnets were. A child learns what the word "magnet" means not, typically, by learning an explic-it definition, but by learning the "folk physics" of magnets, in which the ordinary term "magnet" is embedded or implicitly defined as a theoretical term.

Sometimes terms are embedded in more powerful theories, and sometimes they are embedded by explicit definition. What do all chemical elements with the same valence have in common? First answer: they are dis-posed to combine with other elements in the same integral ratios. Second answer: they all have such-and-such a microphysical property (a property which explains their capacity so to combine). The theory of valences in chemistry was well in hand before its microphysical explanation was known. In one sense chemists knew what valences were before physicists told them.

So what appears in Plato to be a contrast between giving a definition and giving a theory can be viewed as just a special case of the contrast between giving one theoretical answer and giving another, more "reductive" theoretical answer. Fodor (1975) draws the same contrast between "conceptual" and "causal" answers to such questions and argues that Ryle (1949) champions conceptual answers at the expense of causal answers, wrongly supposing them to be in conflict. There is justice in Fodor's charge against Ryle, for there are certainly many passages in which Ryle seems to propose his conceptual answers as a bulwark against the possibility of *any* causal, scientific, psychological answers, but there is a better view of Ryle's (or perhaps at best a view he ought to have held) that deserves rehabilitation. Ryle's "logical behaviorism" is composed of his steadfastly conceptual answers to the Socratic questions about matters mental. If Ryle thought these answers ruled out psychology, ruled out causal (or reductive) answers to the Socratic questions, he was wrong, but if he thought only that the conceptual answers to the questions were not to be given by a microreductive psychology, he was on firmer ground. It is one thing to give a causal explanation of some phenomenon and quite another to cite the cause of a phenomenon in the analysis of the concept of it.

Some concepts have what might be called an essential causal element (see Fodor 1975, p. 7, n6). For instance, the concept of a genuine Winston Churchill *autograph* has it that how the trail of ink was in fact caused is essential to its status as an autograph. Photocopies, forgeries, inadvertently indistinguishable signatures – but perhaps not carbon copies – are ruled out. These considerations are part of the *conceptual* answer to the Socratic question about autographs.

Now some, including Fodor, have held that such concepts as the concept of intelligent action also have an essential causal element; behavior that appeared to be intelligent might be shown not to be by being shown to have the wrong sort of cause. Against such positions Ryle can argue that even if it is true that every instance of intelligent behavior is caused (and hence has a causal explanation), exactly *how* it is caused is inessential to its being intelligent – something that could be true even if all intelligent behavior exhibited in fact some common pattern of causation. That is, Ryle can plausibly claim that no account in causal terms could capture the class of intelligent actions except *per accidens*. In aid of such a position – for which there is much to be said in spite of the current infatuation with causal theories – Ryle can make claims of the sort Fodor disparages ("it's not the mental activity that makes the clowning clever because what makes the clowning clever is such facts as that it took place out where the children can see it") without committing the error of supposing causal and conceptual answers are incompatible.[1]

Ryle's logical behaviorism was in fact tainted by a groundless anti-scientific bias, but it need not have been. Note that the introduction of the concept of valence in chemistry was a bit of *logical chemical behaviorism*: to have valence *n* was "by definition" to be disposed to behave in such-and-such ways under such-and-such conditions, *however* that disposition to behave might someday be explained by physics. In this particular instance the relation between the chemical theory and the physical theory is now well charted and understood – even if in the throes of ideology people sometimes misdescribe it – and the explanation of those dispositional combinatorial properties by physics is a prime example of the sort of success in science that inspires reductionist doctrines. Chemistry has been shown to reduce, in some sense, to physics, and this is clearly a Good Thing, the sort of thing we should try for more of.

Such progress invites the prospect of a parallel development in psychology. First we will answer the question "What do all believers-that-*p* have in common?" the first way, the "conceptual" way, and then see if we can go on to "reduce" the theory that emerges in our first answer to something else – neurophysiology most likely. Many theorists seem to take it for granted that some such reduction is both possible and desirable, and perhaps even inevitable, even while recent critics of reductionism, such as Putnam and Fodor, have warned us of the excesses of "classical" reductionist creeds. No one today hopes to conduct the psychology of the future in the vocabulary of the neurophysiologist, let alone that of the physicist, and principled ways of relaxing the classical "rules" of reduction have been proposed. The issue, then, is *what kind* of theoretical bonds can we expect – or ought we to hope – to find uniting psychological claims about beliefs, desires, and so forth with the claims of neurophysiologists, biologists, and other physical scientists?

Since the terms "belief" and "desire" and their kin are parts of ordinary language, like "magnet," rather than technical terms like "valence," we must first look to "folk psychology" to see what kind of things we are being asked to explain. What do we learn beliefs are when we learn how to use the words "believe" and "belief"? The first point to make is that we do not really learn what beliefs are when we learn how to use these words.[2] Certainly no one *tells us* what beliefs are, or if someone does, or if we happen to speculate on the topic on our own, the answer we come to, wise or foolish, will figure only weakly in our habits of thought about what people believe. We learn to *use* folk psychology as a vernacular social technology, a craft; but we don't learn it self-consciously as a theory – we learn no metatheory with the theory – and in this regard our knowledge of folk psychology is like our knowledge of the grammar of our native tongue. This fact does not make our knowledge of folk psychology entirely unlike human knowledge of explicit academic theories, however; one could probably be a good practicing chemist and yet find it embarrassingly difficult to produce a satisfactory textbook definition of a metal or an ion.

There are no introductory textbooks of folk psychology (although Ryle's *The Concept of Mind* might be pressed into service), but many explorations of the field have been undertaken by ordinary language philosophers (under slightly different intentions) and more recently by more theoretically minded philosophers of mind, and from all this work an account of folk psychology – part truism and the rest controversy – can be gleaned. What are beliefs? Very roughly, folk psychology has it that *beliefs* are information-bearing states of people that arise from perceptions and that, together with appropriately related *desires*, lead to intelligent *action*. That much is relatively uncontroversial, but does folk psychology also have it that nonhuman animals have beliefs? If so, what is the role of language in belief? Are beliefs constructed of parts? If so, what are the parts? Ideas? Concepts? Words? Pictures? Are beliefs like speech acts or maps or instruction manuals or sentences? Is it implicit in folk psychology that beliefs enter into causal relations, or that they don't? How do decisions and intentions intervene between belief-desire complexes and actions? Are beliefs introspectible, and if so, what authority do the believer's pronouncements have?

All these questions deserve answers, but one must bear in mind that there are different reasons for being interested in the details of folk psychology. One reason is that it exists as a phenomenon, like a religion or a language or a dress code, to be studied with the techniques and attitudes of anthropology. It may be a myth, but it is a myth we live in, so it is an "important" phenomenon in nature. A different reason is that it seems to be a true theory, by and large, and hence is a candidate – like the folk physics of magnets and unlike the folk science of astrology – for incorporation into science. These different reasons generate different but overlapping investigations. The anthropological question should include in its account of folk psychology whatever folk actually include in their theory, however misguided, incoherent, gratuitous some of it may be. (When the anthropologist marks part of the catalogue of folk theory as false, he may speak of *false consciousness* or *ideology*, but the role of such false theory *qua* anthropological phenomenon is not thereby diminished.) The proto-scientific quest, on the other hand, as an attempt to prepare folk theory for subsequent incorporation into, or reduction to, the rest of science, should be critical and should eliminate all that is false or ill founded, however well entrenched in popular doctrine. (Thales thought that lodestones had souls, we are told. Even if most people agreed, this would be something to eliminate from the folk physics of magnets prior to "reduction.") One way of distinguishing the good from the bad, the essential from the gratuitous, in folk theory is to see what must be included in the theory to account for whatever predictive or explanatory success it seems to have in ordinary use. In this way we can criticize as we analyze, and it is even open to us in the end to discard folk psychology if it turns out to be a bad theory, and with it the presumed theoretical entities named therein. If we discard folk psychology as a theory, we would have to replace it with another theory, which, while it did violence to many ordinary intuitions, would explain the predictive power of the residual folk craft.

We use folk psychology all the time, to explain and predict each other's behavior; we attribute beliefs and desires to each other with confidence – and quite unselfconsciously – and spend a substantial portion of our waking lives formulating the world – not excluding ourselves – in these terms. Folk psychology is about as pervasive a part of our second nature as is our folk physics of middle-sized objects. How good is folk psychology? If we concentrate on its weaknesses we will notice that we often are unable to make sense of particular bits of human behavior (our own included) in terms of belief and desire, even in retrospect; we often cannot predict accurately or reliably what a person will do or when; we often can find no resources within the theory for settling disagreements about particular attributions of belief or desire. If we concentrate on its strengths we find first that there are large areas in which it is extraordinarily reliable in its predictive power. Every time we venture out on a highway, for example, we stake our lives on the reliability of our general expectations about the perceptual beliefs, normal desires, and decision proclivities of the other motorists. Second, we find that it is a theory of great generative power and efficiency. For instance, watching a film with a highly original and unstereotypical plot, we see the hero smile at the villain and we all swiftly and effortlessly arrive at the same complex theoretical diagnosis: "Aha!" we conclude (but perhaps not consciously), "he wants her to think he doesn't know she intends to defraud his brother!" Third, we find that even small children pick up facility with the theory at a time when they have a very limited experience of human activity from which to induce a theory. Fourth, we find that we all use folk psychology knowing next to nothing about what actually happens inside people's skulls. "Use your head," we are told, and we know some people are brainier than others, but our capacity to use folk psychology is quite unaffected by ignorance about brain processes – or even by large-scale misinformation about brain processes.

As many philosophers have observed, a feature of folk psychology that sets it apart from both folk physics and the academic physical sciences is that explanations of actions citing beliefs and desires normally not only describe the provenance of the actions, but at the same time defend them as reasonable under the circumstances. They are reason-giving explanations, which make an ineliminable allusion to the rationality of the agent. Primarily for this reason, but also because of the pattern of strengths and weaknesses just described, I suggest that folk psychology might best be viewed as a rationalistic calculus of interpretation and prediction – an idealizing, abstract, instrumentalistic interpretation method that has evolved because it works and works because we have evolved. We approach each other as *intentional systems* (Dennett 1971), that is, as entities whose behavior can be predicted by the method of attributing beliefs, desires, and rational acumen according to the following rough and ready principles:

(1) A system's beliefs are those it *ought to have*, given its perceptual capacities, its epistemic needs, and its biography. Thus, in general, its beliefs are both true and relevant to its life, and when false beliefs are attributed, special stories must be told to explain how the error resulted from the presence of features in the environment that are deceptive relative to the perceptual capacities of the system.

(2) A system's desires are those it *ought to have*, given its biological needs and the most practicable means of satisfying them. Thus intentional systems desire survival and procreation, and hence desire food, security, health, sex, wealth, power, influence, and so forth, and also whatever local arrangements tend (in their eyes – given their beliefs) to further these ends in appropriate measure. Again, "abnormal" desires are attributable if special stories can be told.

(3) A system's behavior will consist of those acts that *it would be rational* for an agent with those beliefs and desires to perform.

In (1) and (2) "ought to have" means "would have if it were ideally ensconced in its environmental niche." Thus all dangers and vicissitudes in its environment it will *recognize as such* (i.e., *believe* to be dangers) and all the benefits – relative to its needs, of course – it will *desire*. When a fact about its surroundings is particularly relevant to its current projects (which themselves will be the projects such a being ought to have in order to get ahead in its world), it will *know* that fact and act accordingly. And so forth and so on. This gives us the notion of an ideal epistemic and conative operator or agent, relativized to a set of needs for survival and procreation and to the environment(s) in which its ancestors have evolved and to which it is adapted. But this notion is still too crude and overstated. For instance, a being may come to have an epistemic need that its perceptual apparatus cannot provide for (suddenly all the green food is poisonous, but alas it is colorblind), hence the relativity to perceptual capacities. Moreover, it may or may not have had the occasion to learn from experience about something, so its beliefs are also relative to its biography in this way: it will have learned what it ought to have learned, viz., what it had been given evidence for in a form compatible with its cognitive apparatus – providing the evidence was "relevant" to its project then.

But this is still too crude, for evolution does not give us a best of all possible worlds, but only a passable jury-rig, so we should look for design shortcuts that in specifiably abnormal circumstances yield false perceptual beliefs, etc. (We are not immune to illusions – which we would be if our perceptual systems were *perfect*.) To offset the design shortcuts we should also expect design bonuses: circumstances in which the "cheap" way for nature to design a cognitive system has the side benefit of giving good, reliable results even outside the environment in which the system evolved. Our eyes are well adapted for giving us true beliefs on Mars as well as on Earth, because the cheap solution for our Earth-evolving eyes happens to be a more general solution (cf. Sober 1981).

I propose that we can continue the mode of thinking just illustrated *all the way in* – not just for eye design, but for deliberation design and belief design and strategy-concocter design. In using this optimistic set of assumptions (nature has built us to do things right; look for systems to believe the truth and love the good), we impute no occult powers to epistemic needs, perceptual capacities, and biography but only the powers common sense already imputes to evolution and learning.

In short, we treat each other as if we were rational agents, and this myth – for surely we are not all that rational – works very well because we are *pretty* rational. This single assumption, in combination with home truths about our needs, capacities and typical circumstances, generates both an intentional interpretation of us as believers and desirers and actual predictions of behavior in great profusion. I am claiming, then, that folk psychology can best be viewed as a sort of logical behaviorism: *what it means* to say that someone believes that *p*, is that that person is disposed to behave in certain ways under certain conditions. What ways under what conditions? The ways it would be rational to behave, given the person's other beliefs and desires. The answer looks in danger of being circular, but consider: an account of what it is for an element to have a particular valence will similarly make ineliminable reference to the valences of other elements. What one is given with valence talk is a whole system of interlocking attributions, which is saved from vacuity by yielding independently testable predictions.

I have just described in outline a method of predicting and explaining the behavior of people and other intelligent creatures. Let me distinguish two questions about it: is it something we could do, and is it something we in fact do? I think the answer to the first is obviously yes, which is not to say the method will always yield good results. That much one can ascertain by reflection and thought experiment. Moreover, one can recognize that the method is familiar. Although we don't usually use the method self-consciously, we do use it self-consciously on those occasion when we are perplexed by a person's behavior, and then it often yields satisfactory results. Moreover, the ease and naturalness with which we resort to this self-conscious and deliberate form of problem-solving provide some support for the claim that what we are doing on those occasions is not switching methods but simply becoming self-conscious and explicit about what we ordinarily accomplish tacitly or unconsciously.

No other view of folk psychology, I think, can explain the fact that we do so well predicting each other's behavior on such slender and peripheral evidence; treating each other as intentional systems works (to the extent that it does) because we really are well designed by evolution and hence we *approximate* to the ideal version of ourselves exploited to yield the predictions. But not only does evolution not guarantee that we will always do what is rational; it guarantees that we won't. If we are designed by evolution, then we are almost certainly nothing more than a bag of tricks, patched together by a *satisficing* Nature – Herbert Simon's term (1957) – and no better than our ancestors had to be to get by. Moreover, the demands of nature and the demands of a logic course are not the same. Sometimes – even *normally* in certain circumstances – it pays to jump to conclusions swiftly (and even to forget that you've done so), so by most philosophical measures of rationality (logical consistency, refraining from invalid inference) there has probably been some positive evolutionary pressure in favor of "irrational" methods.[3]

How rational are we? Recent research in social and cognitive psychology (e.g., Tversky and Kahneman 1974; Nisbett and Ross 1978) suggests we are only minimally rational, appallingly ready to leap to conclusions or be swayed by logically irrelevant features of situations, but this jaundiced view is an illusion engendered by the fact that these psychologists are deliberately trying to produce situations that provoke irrational responses – inducing pathology in a system by putting strain on it – and succeeding, being good psychologists. No one would hire a psychologist to prove that people will choose a paid vacation to a week in jail if offered an informed choice. At least not in the better psychology departments. A more optimistic impression of our rationality is engendered by a review of the difficulties encountered in artificial intelligence research. Even the most sophisticated AI programs stumble blindly into misinterpretations and misunderstandings that even small children reliably evade without a second thought (see, e.g., Schank 1976; Schank and Ableson 1977). From this vantage point we seem marvellously rational.

However rational we are, it is the myth of our rational agenthood that structures and organizes our attributions of belief and desire to others and that regulates our own deliberations and investigations. We aspire to rationality, and without the myth of our rationality the concepts of belief and desire would be uprooted. Folk psychology, then, is *idealized* in that it produces its predictions and explanations by calculating in a normative system; it predicts what we will believe, desire, and do, by determining what we ought to believe, desire, and do.[4]

Folk psychology is *abstract* in that the beliefs and desires it attributes are not – or need not be – presumed to be intervening distinguishable states of an internal behavior-causing system. (The point will be enlarged upon later.) The role of the concept of belief is like the role of the concept of a center of gravity, and the calculations that yield the predictions are more like the calculations one performs with a parallelogram of forces than like the calculations one performs with a blueprint of internal levers and cogs.

Folk psychology is thus *instrumentalistic* in a way the most ardent realist should permit: people really do have beliefs and desires, on my version of folk psychology, just the way they really have centers of gravity and the earth has an Equator.[5] Reichenbach distinguished between two sorts of referents for theoretical terms: *illata* – posited theoretical entities – and *abstracta* – calculation-bound entities or logical constructs.[6] Beliefs and desires of folk psychology (but not all mental events and states) are *abstracta*.

This view of folk psychology emerges more clearly when contrasted to a diametrically opposed view, each of whose tenets has been held by some philosopher, and at least most of which have been espoused by Fodor:

> Beliefs and desires, just like pains, thoughts, sensations and other episodes, are taken by folk psychology to be real, intervening, internal states or events, in causal interaction, subsumed under covering laws of causal stripe. Folk psychology is not an idealized, rationalistic calculus but a naturalistic, empirical, descriptive theory, imputing causal regularities discovered by extensive induction over experience. To suppose two people share a belief is to suppose them to be ultimately in some structurally similar internal condition, e.g. for them to have the same words of Mentalese written in the functionally relevant places in their brains.

I want to deflect this head-on collision of analyses by taking two steps. First, I am prepared to grant a measure of the claims made by the opposition. Of course we don't all sit in the dark in our studies like mad Leibnizians rationalistically excogitating behavioral predictions from pure, idealized concepts of our neighbors, nor do we derive all our readiness to attribute desires from a careful generation of them from the ultimate goal of survival. We may observe that some folks seem to desire cigarettes, or pain, or notoriety (we observe this by hearing them tell us, seeing what they choose, etc.) and without any conviction that these people, given their circumstances, ought to have these desires, we attribute them anyway. So rationalistic generation of attributions is augmented and even corrected on occasion by empirical generalizations about belief and desire that guide our attributions and are learned more or less inductively. For instance, small children believe in Santa Claus, people are inclined to believe the more self-serving of two interpretations of an event in which they are involved (unless they are depressed), and people can be made to want things they don't need by making them believe that glamorous people like those things. And so forth in familiar profusion. This folklore does not consist in *laws* – even probabilistic laws – but some of it is being turned into science of a sort, for example theories of "hot cognition" and cognitive dissonance. I grant the existence of all this naturalistic generalization, and its role in the normal calculations of folk psychologists – that is, all of us. People do rely on their own parochial group of neighbors when framing intentional interpretations. That is why people have so much difficulty understanding foreigners – their behavior, to say nothing of their languages. They impute more of their own beliefs and desires, and those of their neighbors, than they would if they followed my principles of attribution slavishly. Of course this is a perfectly reasonable shortcut for people to take, even when it often leads to bad results. We are in this matter, as in most, satisficers, not optimizers, when it comes to information gathering and theory construction. I would insist, however, that all this empirically obtained lore is laid over a fundamental generative and normative framework that has the features I have described.

My second step away from the conflict I have set up is to recall that the issue is not what folk psychology as found in the field truly is, but what it is at its best, what deserves to be taken seriously and incorporated into science. It is not particularly to the point to argue against me that folk psychology is *in fact* committed to beliefs and desires as distinguishable, causally interacting *illata*; what must be shown is that it ought to be. The latter claim I will deal with in due course. The former claim I *could* concede without embarrassment to my overall project, but I do not concede it, for it seems to me that the evidence is quite strong that our ordinary notion of belief has next to nothing of the concrete in it. Jacques shoots his uncle dead in Trafalgar Square and is apprehended on the spot by Sherlock; Tom reads about it in the *Guardian* and Boris learns of it in *Pravda*. Now Jacques, Sherlock, Tom, and Boris have had remarkably different experiences – to say nothing of their earlier biographies and future prospects – but there is one thing they share: they all believe that a Frenchman has committed murder in Trafalgar Square. They did not all say this, not even "to themselves"; *that proposition* did not, we can suppose, "occur to" any of them, and even if it had, it would have had entirely different import for Jacques, Sherlock, Tom, and Boris. Yet they all believe that a Frenchman committed murder in Trafalgar Square. This is a shared property that is visible, as it were, only from one very limited point of view – the point of view of folk psychology. Ordinary folk psychologists have no difficulty imputing such useful but elusive commonalities to people. If they then insist that in doing so they are postulating a similarly structured object in each head, this is a gratuitous bit of misplaced concreteness, a regrettable lapse in ideology.

But in any case there is no doubt that folk psychology is a mixed bag, like folk productions generally, and there is no reason in the end not to grant that it is much more complex, variegated (and in danger of incoherence) than my sketch has made it out to be. The *ordinary* notion of belief no doubt does place beliefs somewhere midway between being *illata* and being *abstracta*. What this suggests to me is that the concept of belief found in ordinary understanding, that is, in folk psychology, is unappealing as a scientific concept. I am reminded of Anaxagoras's strange precursor to atomism: the theory of seeds. There is a portion of everything in everything, he is reputed to have claimed. Every object consists of an infinity of seeds, of all possible varieties. How do you make bread out of flour, yeast, and water? Flour contains bread seeds in abundance (but flour seeds predominate – that's what makes it flour) and so do yeast and water, and when these ingredients are mixed together, the bread seeds form a new majority, so bread is what you get. Bread nourishes by containing flesh and blood and bone seeds in addition to its majority of bread seeds. Not good theoretical entities, these seeds, for as a sort of bastardized cross between properties and proper parts they have a penchant for generating vicious regresses, and their identity conditions are problematic to say the least.

Beliefs are rather like that. There seems no comfortable way of avoiding the claim that we have an infinity of beliefs, and common intuition does not give us a stable answer to such puzzles as whether the belief that 3 is greater than 2 is none other than the belief that 2 is less than 3. The obvious response to the challenge of an infinity of beliefs with slippery identity conditions is to suppose these beliefs are not all "stored separately"; many – in fact most if we are really talking about infinity – will be stored *implicitly* in virtue of the *explicit* storage of a few (or a few million) – the core beliefs (see Dennett 1975; also Fodor 1975 and Field 1978). The core beliefs will be "stored separately," and they look like promising *illata* in contrast to the virtual or implicit beliefs which look like paradigmatic *abstracta*. But although this might turn out to be the way our brains are organized, I suspect things will be more complicated than this: there is no reason to suppose the core *elements*, the concrete, salient, separately stored representation tokens (and there must be some such elements in any complex information processing system), will explicitly represent (or *be*) a subset of our *beliefs* at all. That is, if you were to sit down and write out a list of a thousand or so of your paradigmatic beliefs, *all* of them could turn out to be virtual, only implicitly stored or represented, and what was explicitly stored would be information (e.g. about memory addresses, procedures for problem-solving, or recognition, etc.) that was entirely unfamiliar. It would be folly to prejudge this empirical issue by insisting that our core representations of information (whichever they turn out to be) are beliefs *par excellence*, for when the facts are in, our intuitions may instead support the contrary view: the least controversial self-attributions of belief may pick out beliefs that from the vantage point of developed cognitive theory are invariably virtual.[7]

In such an eventuality what could we say about the causal roles we assign ordinarily to beliefs (e.g. "Her belief that John knew her secret caused her to blush")? We could say that whatever the core elements were in virtue of which she virtually believed that John knew her secret, they, the core elements, played a direct causal role (somehow) in triggering the blushing response. We would be wise, as this example shows, not to tamper with our *ordinary* catalogue of beliefs (virtual though they might all turn out to be), for these are predictable, readily understandable, manipulable regularities in psychological phenomena in spite of their apparent neutrality with regard to the explicit/implicit (or core/virtual) distinction. What Jacques, Sherlock, Boris, and Tom have in common is probably only a virtual belief "derived" from largely different explicit stores of information in each of them, but virtual or not, it is their sharing of *this* belief that would explain (or permit us to predict) in some imagined circumstances their all taking the same action when given the same new information. ("And now for one million dollars, Tom [Jacques, Sherlock, Boris], answer our jackpot question correctly: has a French citizen ever committed a major crime in London?")

At the same time we want to cling to the equally ordinary notion that beliefs can cause not only actions, but blushes, verbal slips, heart attacks, and the like. Much of the debate over whether or not intentional explanations are causal explanations can be bypassed by noting how the core elements, *whatever they may be*, can be cited as playing the causal role, while belief remains virtual. "Had Tom not believed that p and wanted that q, he would not have done A." Is this a causal explanation? It is tantamount to this: Tom was in some one of an indefinitely large number of structurally different states of type B that have in common just that each one of them licenses attribution of belief that p and desire that q in virtue of its normal relations with many other states of Tom, and this state, whichever one it was, was causally sufficient, given the "background conditions" of course, to initiate the intention to perform A, and thereupon A was performed, and had he not been in one of those indefinitely many type B states, he would not have done A. One can call this a causal explanation because it talks about causes, but it is surely as unspecific and unhelpful as a causal explanation can get. It commits itself to there being some causal explanation or other falling within a broad area (i.e., the intentional interpretation is held to be supervenient on Tom's bodily condition), but its true informativeness and utility in actual prediction lie, not surprisingly, in its assertion that Tom, however his body is currently structured, has a particular set of these elusive intentional properties, beliefs, and desires.

The ordinary notion of belief is pulled in two directions. If we want to have good theoretical entities, good *illata*, or good logical constructs, good *abstracta*, we will have to jettison some of the ordinary freight of the concepts of belief and desire. So I propose a divorce. Since we seem to have both notions wedded in folk psychology, let's split them apart and create two new theories: one strictly abstract, idealizing, holistic, instrumentalistic – pure intentional system theory – and the other a concrete, microtheoretical science of the actual realization of those intentional systems – what I will call sub-personal cognitive psychology. By exploring their differences and interrelations, we should be able to tell whether any plausible "reductions" are in the offing.

Intentional System Theory as a Competence Theory

The first new theory, intentional system theory, is envisaged as a close kin of, and overlapping with, such already existing disciplines as decision theory and game theory, which are similarly abstract, normative, and couched in intentional language. It borrows the ordinary terms "belief" and "desire" but gives them a technical meaning within the theory. It is a sort of holistic logical behaviorism because it deals with the prediction and explanation from belief-desire profiles of the actions of whole systems (either alone in environments or in interaction with other intentional systems), but it treats the individual realizations of the systems as black boxes. The *subject* of all the intentional attributions is the whole system (the person, the animal, or even the corporation or nation [see Dennett 1976]) rather than any of its parts, and individual beliefs and desires are not attributable in isolation, independently of other belief and desire attributions. The latter point distinguishes intentional system theory most clearly from Ryle's logical behaviorism, which took on the impossible burden of characterizing individual beliefs (and other mental states) as particular individual dispositions to outward behavior.

The theory deals with the "production" of new beliefs and desires from old, via an interaction among old beliefs and desires, features in the environment, and the systems actions; and this creates the illusion that the theory contains naturalistic descriptions of internal processing in the systems the theory is about, when in fact the processing is all in the manipulation of the theory and consists in updating the intentional characterization of the whole system according to the rules of attribution. An analogous illusion of process would befall a naive student who, when confronted with a parallelogram of forces, supposed that it pictured a mechanical linkage of rods and pivots of some kind instead of being simply a graphic way of representing and plotting the effect of several simultaneously acting forces.

Richard Jeffrey (1970), in developing his concept of probability kinematics, has usefully drawn attention to an analogy with the distinction in physics between kinematics and dynamics. In kinematics,

> you talk about the propagation of motions through a system in terms of such constraints as rigidity and manner of linkage. It is the physics of position and time, in terms of which you can talk about velocity and acceleration, but not about force and mass. When you talk about forces – causes of accelerations – you are in the realm of dynamics. (p. 172)

Kinematics provides a simplified and idealized level of abstraction appropriate for many purposes – for example, for the *initial* design development of a gearbox – but when one must deal with more concrete details of systems – when the gearbox designer must worry about friction, bending, energetic efficiency, and the like – one must switch to dynamics for more detailed and reliable predictions, at the cost of increased complexity and diminished generality. Similarly, one can approach the study of belief (and desire and so forth) at a highly abstract level, ignoring problems of realization and simply setting out what the normative demands on the design of a believer are. For instance, one can ask such questions as "What must a system's epistemic capabilities and propensities be for it to survive in environment A?" (cf. Campbell 1973, 1977) or "What must this system already know in order for it to be able to learn B?" or "What intentions must this system have in order to mean something by saying something?"

Intentional system theory deals just with the performance specifications of believers while remaining silent on how the systems are to be implemented. In fact this neutrality with regard to implementation is the most useful feature of intentional characterizations. Consider, for instance, the role of intentional characterizations in evolutionary biology. If we are to explain the evolution of complex behavioral capabilities or cognitive talents by natural selection, we must note that it is the intentionally characterized capacity (e.g., the capacity to acquire a belief, a desire, to perform an intentional action) that has survival value, however it happens to be realized as a result of mutation. If a particularly noxious insect makes its appearance in an environment, the birds and bats with a survival advantage will be those that come to believe this insect is not good to eat. In view of the vast differences in neural structure, genetic background, and perceptual capacity between birds and bats, it is highly unlikely that this useful trait they may come to share has a common description at any level more concrete or less abstract than intentional system theory. It is not only that the intentional predicate is a projectible predicate in evolutionary theory; since it is more general than its species-specific counterpart predicates (which characterize the successful mutation just in birds, or just in bats), it is preferable. So from the point of view of evolutionary biology, we would not want to "reduce" all intentional characterizations even if we knew in particular instances what the physiological implementation was.

This level of generality is essential if we want a theory to have anything meaningful and defensible to say about such topics as intelligence in general (as opposed, say, to just human or even terrestrial or natural intelligence) or such grand topics as meaning or reference or representation. Suppose, to pursue a familiar philosophical theme, we are invaded by Martians, and the question arises: do they have beliefs and desires? Are they that much *like us*? According to intentional system theory, if these Martians are smart enough to get here, then they most certainly have beliefs and desires – in the technical sense proprietary to the theory – no matter what their internal structure, and no matter how our folk-psychological intuitions rebel at the thought.

This principled blindness of intentional system theory to internal structure seems to invite the retort: but there has to be *some* explanation of the *success* of intentional prediction of the behavior of systems (e.g., Fodor 1985, p. 79). It isn't just magic. It isn't a mere coincidence that one can generate all these *abstracta*, manipulate them via some version of practical reasoning, and come up with an action prediction that has a good chance of being true. There must be some way in which the internal processes of the system mirror the complexities of the intentional interpretation, or its success would be a miracle.

Of course. This is all quite true and important. Nothing without a great deal of structural and processing complexity could conceivably realize an intentional system of any interest, and the complexity of the realization will surely bear a striking resemblance to the complexity of the instrumentalistic interpretation. Similarly, the success of valence theory in chemistry is no coincidence, and people were entirely right to expect that deep microphysical similarities would be discovered between elements with the same valence and that the structural similarities found would explain the dispositional similarities. But since people and animals are unlike atoms and molecules not only in being the products of a complex evolutionary history, but also in being the products of their individual learning histories, there is no reason to suppose that individual (human) believers that p – like individual (carbon) atoms with valence 4 – regulate their dispositions with *exactly* the same machinery. Discovering the constraints on design and implementation variation, and demonstrating how particular species and individuals in fact succeed in realizing intentional systems, is the job for the third theory: subpersonal cognitive psychology.

Sub-personal Cognitive Psychology as a Performance Theory

The task of sub-personal cognitive psychology is to explain something that at first glance seems utterly mysterious and inexplicable. The brain, as intentional system theory and evolutionary biology show us, is a *semantic engine*; its task is to discover what its multifarious inputs *mean*, to discriminate them by their significance and "act accordingly."[8] That's what brains *are for*. But the brain, as physiology or plain common sense shows us, is just a *syntactic engine*; all it can do is discriminate its inputs by their structural, temporal, and physical features and let its entirely mechanical activities be governed by these "syntactic" features of its inputs. That's all brains *can do*. Now how does the brain manage to get semantics from syntax? How could any entity (how could a genius or an angel or God) get the semantics of a system from nothing but its syntax? It couldn't. The syntax of a system doesn't determine its semantics. By what alchemy, then, does the brain extract semantically reliable results from syntactically driven operations? It cannot be designed to do an impossible task, but it could be designed to *approximate* the impossible task, to *mimic* the behavior of the impossible object (the semantic engine) by capitalizing on close (close enough) fortuitous correspondences between structural regularities – of the environment and of its own internal states and operations – and semantic types.

The basic idea is familiar. An animal needs to know when it has satisfied the goal of finding and ingesting food, but it settles for a friction-in-the-throat-followed-by-stretched-stomach detector, a mechanical switch turned on by a relatively simple mechanical condition that normally co-occurs with the satisfaction of the animals "real" goal. It's not fancy and can easily be exploited to trick the animal into either eating when it shouldn't or leaving off eating when it shouldn't, but it does well enough by the animal in its normal environment. Or suppose I am monitoring telegraph transmissions and have been asked to intercept all *death threats* (but only death threats in English – to make it "easy"). I'd like to build a machine to save me the trouble of interpreting semantically every message sent, but how could this be done? No machine could be designed to do the job perfectly, for that would require defining the semantic category *death threat in English* as some tremendously complex feature of strings of alphabetic symbols, and there is utterly no reason to suppose this could be done in a principled way. (If somehow by brute-force inspection and subsequent enumeration we could list all and only the English death threats of, say, less than a thousand characters, we could easily enough build a filter to detect them, but we are looking for a principled, projectible, extendable method.) A really crude device could be made to discriminate all messages containing the symbol strings

... I will kill you ...
or
... you ... die ... unless ...
or
... (for some finite disjunction of likely patterns to be found in English death threats).

This device would have some utility, and further refinements could screen the material that passed this first filter, and so on. An unpromising beginning for constructing a sentence understander, but if you want to get semantics out of syntax (whether the syntax of messages in a natural language or the syntax of afferent neuron impulses), variations on this basic strategy are your only hope.[9] You must put together a bag of tricks and hope nature will be kind enough to let your device get by. Of course some tricks are elegant and appeal to deep principles of organization, but in the end all one can hope to produce (all natural selection can have produced) are systems that *seem* to discriminate meanings by actually discriminating things (tokens of no doubt wildly disjunctive types) that co-vary reliably with meanings.[10] Evolution has designed our brains not only to do this but to evolve and follow strategies of self-improvement in this activity during their individual lifetimes (see Dennett 1974).

It is the task of sub-personal cognitive psychology to propose and test models of such activity – of pattern recognition or stimulus generalization, concept learning, expectation, learning, goal-directed behavior, problem-solving – that not only produce a simulacrum of genuine content-sensitivity, but that do this in ways demonstrably like the way people's brains do it, exhibiting the same powers and the same vulnerabilities to deception, overload, and confusion. It is here that we will find our good theoretical entities, our useful *illata*, and while some of them may well resemble the familiar entities of folk psychology – beliefs, desires, judgments, decisions – many will certainly not (see, e.g., the sub-doxastic states proposed by Stich 1978). The only similarity we can be sure of discovering in the *illata* of sub-personal cognitive psychology is the intentionality of their labels (see *Brainstorms*, pp. 23-38). They will be characterized as events with content, bearing information, signaling this and ordering that.

In order to give the *illata* these labels, in order to maintain any intentional interpretation of their operation at all, the theorist must always keep glancing outside the system, to see what normally produces the configuration he is describing, what effects the system's responses normally have on the environment, and what benefit normally accrues to the whole system from this activity. In other words the cognitive psychologist cannot ignore the fact that it is the realization of an intentional system he is studying on pain of abandoning semantic interpretation and hence psychology.

On the other hand, progress in sub-personal cognitive psychology will blur the boundaries between it and intentional system theory, knitting them together much as chemistry and physics have been knit together.

The alternative of ignoring the external world and its relation to the internal machinery (what Putnam has called psychology in the narrow sense, or methodological solipsism, and Gunderson has lampooned as black world glass box perspectivalism) is not really psychology at all, but just at best abstract neurophysiology – pure internal syntax with no hope of a semantic interpretation.

Black Box Behaviorism   Black World Glass Box Perspectivalism

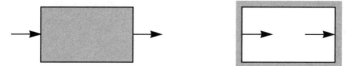

Psychology "reduced" to neurophysiology in this fashion would not be psychology, for it would not be able to provide an explanation of the regularities it is psychology's particular job to explain: the reliability with which "intelligent" organisms can cope with their environments and thus prolong their lives. Psychology can, and should, work toward an account of the physiological foundations of psychological processes, not by eliminating psychological or intentional characterizations of those processes, but by exhibiting how the brain implements the intentionally characterized performance specifications of sub-personal theories.

Friedman, discussing the current perplexity in cognitive psychology, suggests that the problem

> is the direction of reduction. Contemporary psychology tries to explain *individual* cognitive activity independently from *social* cognitive activity, and then tries to give a *micro* reduction of social cognitive activity – that is, the use of a public language – in terms of a prior theory of individual cognitive activity. The opposing suggestion is that we first look for a theory of social activity, and then try to give a *macro* reduction of individual cognitive activity – the activity of applying concepts, making judgments, and so forth – in terms of our prior social theory. (1981, pp. 15-16.)

With the idea of macro-reduction in psychology I largely agree, except that Friedman's identification of the macro level as explicitly social is only part of the story. The cognitive capacities of non-language-using animals (and Robinson Crusoes, if there are any) must also be accounted for, and not just in terms of an analogy with the practices of us language users. The macro level *up* to which we should relate microprocesses in the brain in order to understand them as psychological is more broadly the level of organism-environment interaction, development, and evolution. That level includes social interaction as a particularly important part (see Burge 1979), but still a proper part.

There is no way to capture the semantic properties of things (word tokens, diagrams, nerve impulses, brain states) by a micro-reduction. Semantic properties are not just relational but, you might say, super-relational, for the relation a particular vehicle of content, or token, must bear in order to have content is not just a relation it bears to other similar things (e.g., other tokens, or parts of tokens, or sets of tokens, or causes of tokens) but a relation between the token and the whole life – and counterfactual life[11] – of the organism it "serves" and that organism's requirements for survival and its evolutionary ancestry.

The Prospects of Reduction

Of our three psychologies – folk psychology, intentional system theory, and sub-personal cognitive psychology – what then might reduce to what? Certainly the one-step micro-reduction of folk psychology to physiology alluded to in the slogans of the early identity theorists will never be found – and should never be missed, even by staunch friends of materialism and scientific unity. A prospect worth exploring, though, is that folk psychology (more precisely, the part of folk psychology worth caring about) reduces – conceptually – to intentional system theory. What this would amount to can best be brought out by contrasting this proposed conceptual reduction with more familiar alternatives: "type-type identity theory" and "Turing machine functionalism." According to type-type identity theory, for every mentalistic term or predicate "M," there is some predicate "P" *expressible in the vocabulary of the physical sciences* such that a creature is M if and only if it is P. In symbols:

$$(1) \qquad (x)\,(Mx \equiv Px)$$

This is reductionism with a vengeance, taking on the burden of replacing, in principle, all mentalistic predicates with co-extensive predicates composed truth-functionally from the predicates of physics. It is now widely agreed to be hopelessly too strong a demand. Believing that cats eat fish is, intuitively, a *functional* state that might be variously implemented physically, so there is no reason to suppose the commonality referred to on the left-hand side of (1) can be reliably picked out by any predicate, however complex, of physics. What is needed to express the predicate on the right-hand side is, it seems, a physically neutral language for speaking of functions and functional states, and the obvious candidates are the languages used to describe automata – for instance, Turing machine language.

The Turing machine functionalist then proposes

(2) (x) $(Mx \equiv x$ realizes some Turing machine k in logical state A)

In other words, for two things both to believe that cats eat fish they need not be physically similar in any specifiable way, but they must both be in a "functional" condition specifiable in principle in the most general functional language; they must share a Turing machine description according to which they are both in some particular logical state. This is still a reductionist doctrine, for it proposes to identify each mental type with a functional type picked out in the language of automata theory. But this is still too strong, for there is no more reason to suppose Jacques, Sherlock, Boris, and Tom "have the same program" in *any* relaxed and abstract sense, considering the differences in their nature and nurture, than that their brains have some crucially identical physico-chemical feature. We must weaken the requirements for the right-hand side of our formula still further.

Consider

(3) (x) $(x$ believes that $p \equiv x$ can be predictively attributed the belief that $p)$

This appears to be blatantly circular and uninformative, with the language on the right simply mirroring the language on the left. But all we need to make an informative answer of this formula is a systematic way of making the attributions alluded to on the right-hand side. Consider the parallel case of Turing machines. What do two different realizations or embodiments of a Turing machine have in common when they are in the same logical state? Just this: there is a system of description such that according to it both are described as being realizations of some particular Turing machine, and according to this description, which is predictive of the operation of both entities, both are in the same state of that Turing machine's machine table. One doesn't *reduce* Turing machine talk to some more fundamental idiom; one *legitimizes* Turing machine talk by providing it with rules of attributions and exhibiting its predictive powers. If we can similarly legitimize "mentalistic" talk, we will have no need of a reduction, and that is the point of the concept of an intentional system. Intentional systems are supposed to play a role in the legitimization of mentalistic predicates parallel to the role played by the abstract notion of a Turing machine in setting down rules for the interpretation of artifacts as computational automata. I fear my concept is woefully informal and unsystematic compared with Turing's, but then the domain it attempts to systematize – our everyday attributions in mentalistic or intentional language – is itself something of a mess, at least compared with the clearly defined field of recursive function theory, the domain of Turing machines.

The analogy between the theoretical roles of Turing machines and intentional systems is more than superficial. Consider that warhorse in the philosophy of mind, Brentano's Thesis that intentionality is the mark of the mental: all mental phenomena exhibit intentionality and no physical phenomena exhibit intentionality. This has been traditionally taken to be an *irreducibility* thesis: the mental, in virtue of its intentionality, cannot be reduced to the physical. But given the concept of an intentional system, we can construe the first half of Brentano's Thesis – all mental phenomena are intentional – as a *reductionist* thesis of sorts, parallel to Church's Thesis in the foundations of mathematics.

According to Church's Thesis, every "effective" procedure in mathematics is recursive, that is, Turing-computable. Church's Thesis is not provable, since it hinges on the intuitive and informal notion of an effective procedure, but it is generally accepted, and it provides a very useful reduction of a fuzzy-but-useful mathematical notion to a crisply defined notion of apparently equal scope and greater power. Analogously, the claim that every mental phenomenon alluded to in folk psychology is *intentional-system-characterizable* would, if true, provide a reduction of the mental as ordinarily understood – a domain whose boundaries are at best fixed by mutual acknowledgement and shared intuition – to a clearly defined domain of entities whose principles of organization are familiar, relatively formal and systematic, and entirely general.[12]

This reduction claim, like Church's Thesis, cannot be proven but could be made compelling by piecemeal progress on particular (and particularly difficult) cases – a project I set myself elsewhere (in *Brainstorms*). The final reductive task would be to show not how the terms of intentional system theory are eliminable in favor of physiological terms via sub-personal cognitive psychology, but almost the reverse: to show how a system described in physiological terms could warrant an interpretation as a realized intentional system.

NOTES

1. This paragraph corrects a misrepresentation of both Fodor's and Ryle's positions in my critical notice of Fodor's book in *Mind* (1977) reprinted in *Brainstorms*, pp. 90-108.

2. I think it is just worth noting that philosophers' use of "believe" as the standard and general ordinary language term is a considerable distortion. We seldom talk about what people *believe*; we talk about what they *think* and what they *know*.

3. While in general true beliefs have to be more useful than false beliefs (and hence a system ought to have true beliefs), in special circumstances it may be better to have a few false beliefs. For instance it might be better for beast B to have some false beliefs about whom B can beat up and whom B can't. Ranking B's likely antagonists from ferocious to pushover, we certainly want B to believe it can't beat up all the ferocious ones and can beat up all the obvious pushovers, but it is better (because it "costs less" in discrimination tasks and protects against random perturbations such as bad days and lucky blows) for B to extend "I can't beat up *x*" to cover even some beasts it can in fact beat up. *Erring on the side of prudence* is a well-recognized good strategy, and so Nature can be expected to have valued it on occasions when it came up. An alternative strategy in this instance would be to abide by the rule: avoid conflict with penumbral cases. But one might have to "pay more" to implement that strategy than to implement the strategy designed to produce, and rely on, some false beliefs. [On false beliefs, see my paper "True Believers".]

4. It tests its predictions in two ways: action predictions it tests directly by looking to see what the agent does; belief and desire predictions are tested indirectly by employing the predicted attibutions in further predictions of eventual action. As usual, the Duhemian thesis holds: belief and desire attributions are under-determined by the available data.

5. Michael Friedman's "Theoretical Explanation" (1981) provides an excellent analysis of the role of instrumentalistic thinking within realistic science. Scheffler (1963) provides a useful distinction between *instrumentalism* and *fictionalism*. In his terms I am characterizing folk psychology as instrumentalistic, not fictionalistic.

6. "Our observations of concrete things confer a certain probability on the existence of *illata*-nothing more.... Second, there are inferences to *abstracta*. These inferences are ... equivalences, not probability inferences. Consequently, the existence of abstracta is reducible to the existence of concreta. There is, therefore, no problem of their objective existence; their status depends on a convention." (Reichenbach 1938, pp. 211-12).

7. See Field 1978, p. 55, n. 12 on "minor concessions" to such instrumentalistic treatments of belief.

8. More accurately if less picturesquely, the brain's task is to come to produce internal mediating responses that reliably vary in concert with variation in the actual environmental significance (the natural and nonnatural meanings, in Grice's (1957) sense) of their distal causes and independently of meaning-irrelevant variations in their proximal causes, and moreover to respond to its own mediating responses in ways that systematically tend to improve the creature's prospects in its environment if the mediating responses are varying as they ought to vary.

9. One might think that while in principle one cannot derive the semantics of a system from nothing but its syntax, in practice one might be able to cheat a little and exploit syntactic features that don't imply a semantical interpretation but strongly suggest one. For instance, faced with the task of deciphering isolated documents in an entirely unknown and alien language, one might note that while the symbol that looks like a duck doesn't have to mean "duck," there is a good chance that it does, especially if the symbol that looks like a wolf seems to be eating the symbol that looks like a duck, and not vice versa. Call this *hoping for hieroglyphics* and note the form it has taken in psychological theories from Locke to the present: we will be able to tell which mental representations are which (which idea is the idea of *dog* and which of *cat*) because the former will look like a dog and the latter like a cat. This is all very well as a crutch for us observers on the outside, trying to assign content to the events in some brain, but it is of no use to the brain ... because brains don't know what dogs look like! Or better, this cannot be the brain's fundamental method of eking semantic classes out of raw syntax, for any brain (or brain part) that could be said – in an extended sense – to know what dogs look like would be a brain (or brain part) that had already solved its problem, that was already (a simulacrum of) a semantic engine. But this is still misleading, for brains in any event do not *assign* content to their own events in the way observers might: brains *fix* the content of their internal events in the act of reacting as they do. There are good reasons for positing *mental images* of one sort or another in cognitive theories (see "Two Approaches to Mental Images" in *Brainstorms*, pp. 174-89) but hoping for hieroglyphics isn't one of them, though I suspect it is covertly influential.

10. I take this point to be closely related to Davidson's reasons for claiming there can be no psycho-physical laws, but I am unsure that Davidson wants to draw the same conclusions from it that I do. See Davidson 1970.

11. What I mean is this: counterfactuals enter because content is in part a matter of the *normal* or *designed* role of a vehicle whether or not it ever gets to play that role. Cf. Sober 1981 and Millikan 1984.

12. Ned Block (1978) presents arguments supposed to show how the various possible functionalist theories of mind all slide into the sins of "chauvinism" (improperly excluding Martians from the class of possible mind-havers) or "liberalism" (improperly including various contraptions, human puppets, and so forth among the mind-havers). My view embraces the broadest liberalism, gladly paying the price of a few recalcitrant intuitions for the generality gained.

REFERENCES

Block, N. (1978). "Troubles with Functionalism," in C.W. Savage (ed.) *Perception and Cognition: Issues in the Foundations of Psychology*, Minneapolis, University of Minnesota Press. (Reprinted in Block 1980, vol. 1.)

Burge, T. (1979). "Individualism and the Mental," *Midwest Studies in Philosophy*, IV: 73-121.

Campbell, D.T. (1973). "Evolutionary Epistemology," in Paul Schilpp (ed.) *The Philosophy of Karl Popper*, La Salle, IL, Open Court Press.

Campbell, D.T. (1977). "Descriptive Epistemology: Psychological Sociological, and Evolutionary," William James Lectures, Harvard University.

Davidson, D. (1970). "Mental Events," in L. Foster and J. Swanson (eds.) *Experience and Theory*, Amherst, University of Massachusetts Press.

Dennett, D.C. (1971). "Intentional Systems," *Journal of Philosophy*, 8: 87-106. (Reprinted in Dennett 1978.)

Dennett, D.C. (1974). "Comment on Wilfrid Sellars," *Synthese*, 27: 439-44.

Dennett, D.C. (1975). "Brain Writing and Mind Reading," in K. Gunderson (ed.) *Language, Mind, and Meaning*, Minnesota Studies in Philosophy of Science, VII, Minneapolis, University of Minnesota Press.

Dennett, D.C. (1976). "Conditions of Personhood," in A. Rorty (ed.) *The Identities of Persons*, Berkeley, University of California Press. (Reprinted in Dennett 1978.)

Dennett, D.C. (1978). *Brainstorms*. Cambridge MA: The MIT Press.

Field, H. (1978). "Mental Representation," *Erkenntnis*, 13: 9-61.

Fodor, J. (1975). *The Language of Thought*, Hassocks, Sussex, Harvester Press; Scranton, PA: Crowell.

Fodor, J. (1985). "Fodor's Guide to Mental Representation," *Mind*, XCIV: 76-100.

Friedman, M. (1981). "Theoretical Explanation," in R. Healy (ed.) *Reduction, Time and Reality*, Cambridge, Cambridge University Press, 2-31.

Grice, H.P. (1957). "Meaning," *Philosophical Review*, 66: 377-88.

Jeffrey, R. (1970). "Dracula Meets Wolfman: Acceptance vs. Partial Belief," in M. Swain (ed.) *Induction, Acceptance and Rational Belief*, Dordrecht, Reidel.

Millikan, R. (1984). *Language, Thought and Other Biological Categories*, Cambridge, MA, The MIT Press/A Bradford Book.

Nisbett, R.E. and Ross, L.D. (1980). *Human Inference: Strategy and Shortcomings*, Englewood Cliffs, Prentice Hall.

Reichenbach, H. (1938). *Experience and Prediction*, Chicago, University of Chicago Press.

Ryle, G. (1949). *The Concept of Mind*, London, Hutchinson.

Schank, R.C. (1976). *Research Report* No. 84, Yale University Department of Computer Science.

Schank, R. and Abelson, R. (1977). *Scripts, Plans, Goals and Understanding*, Hillside, NJ: Erlbaum.

Scheffler, I. (1963). *The Anatomy of Inquiry*, New York, Knopf.

Simon, H. (1957). *Models of Man*, New York, Wiley.

Sober, E. (1981). "The Evolution of Rationality," *Synthese*, 46: 95-120.

Stich, S. (1978). "Beliefs and Sub-Doxastic States," *Philosophy of Science*, 45: 499-518.

Tversky, A. and Kahneman, D. (1974). "Judgement Under Uncertainty: Heuristics and Biases," *Science*, 185: 499-518.

Skeptical Worries

TWO DOGMAS OF EMPIRICISM

W.V. Quine

Modern empiricism has been conditioned in large part by two dogmas. One is a belief in some fundamental cleavage between truths which are *analytic*, or grounded in meanings independently of matters of fact, and truths which are *synthetic*, or grounded in fact. The other dogma is *reductionism*: the belief that each meaningful statement is equivalent to some logical construct upon terms which refer to immediate experience. Both dogmas, I shall argue, are ill-founded. One effect of abandoning them is, as we shall see, a blurring of the supposed boundary between speculative metaphysics and natural science. Another effect is a shift toward pragmatism.

1. Background for Analyticity

Kant's cleavage between analytic and synthetic truths was foreshadowed in Hume's distinction between relations of ideas and matters of fact, and in Leibniz's distinction between truths of reason and truths of fact. Leibniz spoke of the truths of reason as true in all possible worlds. Picturesqueness aside, this is to say that the truths of reason are those which could not possibly be false. In the same vein we hear analytic statements defined as statements whose denials are self-contradictory. But this definition has small explanatory value; for the notion of self-contradictoriness, in the quite broad sense needed for this definition of analyticity, stands in exactly the same need of clarification as does the notion of analyticity itself. The two notions are the two sides of a single dubious coin.

Kant conceived of an analytic statement as one that attributes to its subject no more than is already conceptually contained in the subject. This formulation has two shortcomings: it limits itself to statements of subject-predicate form, and it appeals to a notion of containment which is left at a metaphorical level. But Kant's intent, evident more from the use he makes of the notion of analyticity than from his definition of it, can be restated thus: a statement is analytic when it is true by virtue of meanings and independently of fact. Pursuing this line, let us examine the concept of *meaning* which is presupposed.

Meaning, let us remember, is not to be identified with naming. Frege's example of "Evening Star" and "Morning Star," and Russell's of "Scott" and "the author of *Waverley*," illustrate that terms can name the same thing but differ in meaning. The distinction between meaning and naming is no less important at the level of abstract terms. The terms "9" and "the number of the planets" name one and the same abstract entity but presumably must be regarded as unlike in meaning; for astronomical observation was needed, and not mere reflection on meanings, to determine the sameness of the entity in question.

The above examples consist of singular terms, concrete and abstract. With general terms, or predicates, the situation is somewhat different but parallel. Whereas a singular term purports to name an entity, abstract or concrete, a general term does not; but a general term is *true of* an entity, or of each of many, or of none. The class of all entities of which a general term is true is called the *extension* of the term. Now paralleling the contrast between the meaning of a singular term and the entity named, we must distinguish equally between the meaning of a general term and its extension. The general terms "creature with a heart" and "creature with kidneys," for example, are perhaps alike in extension but unlike in meaning.

Confusion of meaning with extension, in the case of general terms, is less common than confusion of meaning with naming in the case of singular terms. It is indeed a commonplace in philosophy to oppose intension (or meaning) to extension, or, in a variant vocabulary, connotation to denotation.

The Aristotelian notion of essence was the forerunner, no doubt, of the modern notion of intension or meaning. For Aristotle it was essential in men to be rational, accidental to be two legged. But there is an important difference between this attitude and the doctrine of meaning. From the latter point of view it may indeed be conceded (if only for the sake of argument) that rationality is involved in the meaning of the word "man" while two-leggedness is not; but two-leggedness may at the same time be viewed as involved in the meaning of "biped" while rationality is not. Thus from the point of view of the doctrine of meaning it makes no sense to say of the actual individual, who is at once a man and a biped, that his rationality is essential and his two-leggedness accidental or vice versa. Things had essences, for Aristotle, but only linguistic forms have meanings. Meaning is what essence becomes when it is divorced from the object of reference and wedded to the word.

For the theory of meaning a conspicuous question is the nature of its objects: what sort of things are meanings? A felt need for meant entities may derive from an earlier failure to appreciate that meaning and reference are distinct. Once the theory of meaning is sharply separated from the theory of reference, it is a short step to recognizing as the primary business of the theory of meaning simply the synonymy of linguistic forms and the analyticity of statements; meanings themselves, as obscure intermediary entities, may well be abandoned.

The problem of analyticity then confronts us anew. Statements which are analytic by general philosophical acclaim are not, indeed, far to seek. They fall into two classes. Those of the first class, which may be called *logically true*, are typified by:

(1) No unmarried man is married.

The relevant feature of this example is that it not merely is true as it stands, but remains true under any and all reinterpretations of "man" and "married." If we suppose a prior inventory of *logical* particles, comprising "no," "un-," "not," "if," "then," "and," etc., then in general a logical truth is a statement which is true and remains true under all reinterpretations of its components other than the logical particles.

But there is also a second class of analytic statements, typified by:

(2) No bachelor is married.

The characteristic of such a statement is that it can be turned into a logical truth by putting synonyms for synonyms; thus (2) can be turned into (1) by putting "unmarried man" for its synonym "bachelor." We still lack a proper characterization of this second class of analytic statements, and therewith of analyticity generally, inasmuch as we have had in the above description to lean on a notion of "synonymy" which is no less in need of clarification than analyticity itself.

In recent years Carnap has tended to explain analyticity by appeal to what he calls state-descriptions.[1] A state-description is any exhaustive assignment of truth values to the atomic, or noncompound, statements of the language. All other statements of the language are, Carnap assumes, built up of their component clauses by means of the familiar logical devices, in such a way that the truth value of any complex statement is fixed for each state-description by specifiable logical laws. A statement is then explained as analytic when it comes out true under every state description. This account is an adaptation of Leibniz's "true in all possible worlds." But note that this version of analyticity serves its purpose only if the atomic statements of the language are, unlike "John is a bachelor" and "John is married," mutually independent. Otherwise there would be a state-description which assigned truth to "John is a bachelor" and to "John is married," and consequently "No bachelors are married" would turn out synthetic rather than analytic under the proposed criterion. Thus the criterion of analyticity in terms of state-descriptions serves only for languages devoid of extralogical synonym-pairs, such as "bachelor" and "unmarried man" – synonym-pairs of the type which give rise to the "second class" of analytic statements. The criterion in terms of state-descriptions is a reconstruction at best of logical truth, not of analyticity.

I do not mean to suggest that Carnap is under any illusions on this point. His simplified model language with its state-descriptions is aimed primarily not at the general problem of analyticity but at another purpose, the clarification of probability and induction. Our problem, however, is analyticity; and here the major difficulty lies not in the first class of analytic statements, the logical truths, but rather in the second class, which depends on the notion of synonymy.

2. Definition

There are those who find it soothing to say that the analytic statements of the second class reduce to those of the first class, the logical truths, by *definition*; "bachelor," for example, is *defined* as "unmarried man." But how do we find that "bachelor" is defined as "unmarried man"? Who defined it thus, and when? Are we to appeal to the nearest dictionary, and accept the lexicographer's formulation as law? Clearly this would be to put the cart before the horse. The lexicographer is an empirical scientist, whose business is the recording of antecedent facts; and if he glosses "bachelor" as "unmarried man" it is because of his belief that there is a relation of synonymy between those forms, implicit in general or preferred usage prior to his own work. The notion of synonymy presupposed here has still to be clarified, presumably in terms relating to linguistic behavior. Certainly the "definition" which is the lexicographer's report of an observed synonymy cannot be taken as the ground of the synonymy.

Definition is not, indeed, an activity exclusively of philologists. Philosophers and scientists frequently have occasion to "define" a recondite term by paraphrasing it into terms of a more familiar vocabulary. But ordinarily such a definition, like the philologist's, is pure lexicography, affirming a relation of synonymy antecedent to the exposition in hand.

Just what it means to affirm synonymy, just what the interconnections may be which are necessary and sufficient in order that two linguistic forms be properly describable as synonymous, is far from clear; but, whatever these interconnections may be, ordinarily they are grounded in usage. Definitions reporting selected instances of synonymy come then as reports upon usage.

There is also, however, a variant type of definitional activity which does not limit itself to the reporting of pre-existing synonymies. I have in mind what Carnap calls *explication* – an activity to which philosophers are given, and scientists also in their more philosophical moments. In explication the purpose is not merely to paraphrase the definiendum into an outright synonym, but actually to improve upon the definiendum by refining or supplementing its meaning. But even explication, though not merely reporting a pre-existing synonymy between definiendum and definiens, does rest nevertheless on *other* pre-existing synonymies. The matter may be viewed as follows. Any word worth explicating has some contexts which, as wholes, are clear and precise enough to be useful; and the purpose of explication is to preserve the usage of these favored contexts while sharpening the usage of other contexts. In order that a given definition be suitable for purposes of explication, therefore, what is required is not that the definiendum in its antecedent usage be synonymous with the definiens, but just that each of these favored contexts of the definiendum, taken as a whole in its antecedent usage, be synonymous with the corresponding context of the definiens.

Two alternative definientia may be equally appropriate for the purposes of a given task of explication and yet not be synonymous with each other; for they may serve interchangeably within the favored contexts but diverge elsewhere. By cleaving to one of these definientia rather than the other, a definition of explicative kind generates, by fiat, a relation of synonymy between definiendum and definiens which did not hold before. But such a definition still owes its explicative function, as seen, to pre-existing synonymies.

There does, however, remain still an extreme sort of definition which does not hark back to prior synonymies at all: namely, the explicitly conventional introduction of novel notations for purposes of sheer abbreviation. Here the definiendum becomes synonymous with the definiens simply because it has been created expressly for the purpose of being synonymous with the definiens. Here we have a really transparent case of synonymy created by definition; would that all species of synonymy were as intelligible. For the rest, definition rests on synonymy rather than explaining it.

The word "definition" has come to have a dangerously reassuring sound, owing no doubt to its frequent occurrence in logical and mathematical writings. We shall do well to digress now into a brief appraisal of the role of definition in formal work.

In logical and mathematical systems either of two mutually antagonistic types of economy may be striven for, and each has its peculiar practical utility. On the one hand we may seek economy of practical expression – ease and brevity in the statement of multifarious relations. This sort of economy calls usually for distinctive concise notations for a wealth of concepts. Second, however, and oppositely, we may seek economy in grammar and vocabulary; we may try to find a minimum of basic concepts such that, once a distinctive notation has been appropriated to each of them, it becomes possible to express any desired further concept by mere combination and iteration of our basic notations. This second sort of economy is impractical in one way, since a poverty in basic idioms tends to a necessary lengthening of discourse. But it is practical in another way: it greatly simplifies theoretical discourse *about* the language, through minimizing the terms and the forms of construction wherein the language consists.

Both sorts of economy, though prima facie incompatible, are valuable in their separate ways. The custom has consequently arisen of combining both sorts of economy by forging in effect two languages, the one a part of the other. The inclusive language, though redundant in grammar and vocabulary, is economical in message lengths, while the part, called primitive notation, is economical in grammar and vocabulary. Whole and part are correlated by rules of translation whereby each idiom not in primitive notation is equated to some complex built up of primitive notation. These rules of translation are the so-called *definitions* which appear in formalized systems. They are best viewed not as adjuncts to one language but as correlations between two languages, the one a part of the other.

But these correlations are not arbitrary. They are supposed to show how the primitive notations can accomplish all purposes, save brevity and convenience, of the redundant language. Hence the definiendum and its definiens may be expected, in each case, to be related in one or another of the three ways lately noted. The definiens may be a faithful paraphrase of the definiendum into the narrower notation, preserving a direct synonymy[2] as of antecedent usage; or the definiens may, in the spirit of explication, improve upon the antecedent usage of the definiendum; or finally, the definiendum may be a newly created notation, newly endowed with meaning here and now.

In formal and informal work alike, thus, we find that definition – except in the extreme case of the explicitly conventional introduction of new notations – hinges on prior relations of synonymy. Recognizing then that the notion of definition does not hold the key to synonymy and analyticity, let us look further into synonymy and say no more of definition.

3. Interchangeability

A natural suggestion, deserving close examination, is that the synonymy of two linguistic forms consists simply in their interchangeability in all contexts without change of truth value – interchangeability, in Leibniz's phrase, *salva veritate*.[3] Note that synonyms so conceived need not even be free from vagueness, as long as the vaguenesses match.

But it is not quite true that the synonyms "bachelor" and "unmarried man" are everywhere interchangeable *salva veritate*. Truths which become false under substitution of "unmarried man" for "bachelor" are easily constructed with the help of "bachelor of arts "or "bachelor's buttons"; also with the help of quotation, thus:

"Bachelor" has less than ten letters.

Such counterinstances can, however, perhaps be set aside by treating the phrases "bachelor of arts" and "bachelor's buttons" and the quotation "bachelor" each as a single indivisible word and then stipulating that the interchangeability *salva veritate* which is to be the touchstone of synonymy is not supposed to apply to fragmentary occurrences inside of a word. This account of synonymy, supposing it acceptable on other counts, has indeed the drawback of appealing to a prior conception of "word" which can be counted on to present difficulties of formulation in its turn. Nevertheless some progress might be claimed in having reduced the problem of synonymy to a problem of wordhood. Let us pursue this line a bit, taking "word" for granted.

The question remains whether interchangeability *salva veritate* (apart from occurrences within words) is a strong enough condition for synonymy, or whether, on the contrary, some heteronymous expressions might be thus interchangeable. Now let us be clear that we are not concerned here with synonymy in the sense of complete identity in psychological associations or poetic quality; indeed no two expressions are synonymous in such a sense. We are concerned only with what may be called *cognitive* synonymy. Just what this is cannot be said without successfully finishing the present study; but we know something about it from the need which arose for it in connection with analyticity in §1. The sort of synonymy needed there was merely such that any analytic statement could be turned into a logical truth by putting synonyms for synonyms. Turning the tables and assuming analyticity, indeed, we could explain cognitive synonymy of terms as follows (keeping to the familiar example): to say that "bachelor" and "unmarried man" are cognitively synonymous is to say no more nor less than that the statement:

(3) All and only bachelors are unmarried men

is analytic.[4]

What we need is an account of cognitive synonymy not presupposing analyticity – if we are to explain analyticity conversely with help of cognitive synonymy as undertaken in §1. And indeed such an independent account of cognitive synonymy is at present up for consideration, namely, interchangeability *salva veritate* everywhere except within words. The question before us, to resume the thread at last, is whether such interchangeability is a sufficient condition for cognitive synonymy. We can quickly assure ourselves that it is, by examples of the following sort. The statement:

(4) Necessarily all and only bachelors are bachelors

is evidently true, even supposing "necessarily" so narrowly construed as to be truly applicable only to analytic statements. Then, if "bachelor" and "unmarried man" are interchangeable *salva veritate*, the result:

(5) Necessarily all and only bachelors are unmarried men

of putting "unmarried man" for an occurrence of "bachelor" in (4) must, like (4), be true. But to say that (5) is true is to say that (3) is analytic, and hence that "bachelor" and "unmarried man" are cognitively synonymous.

Let us see what there is about the above argument that gives it its air of hocus-pocus. The condition of interchangeability *salve veritate* varies in its force with variations in the richness of the language at hand. The above argument supposes we are working with a language rich enough to contain the adverb "necessarily," this adverb being so construed as to yield truth when and only when applied to an analytic statement. But can we condone a language which contains such an adverb? Does the adverb really make sense? To suppose that it does is to suppose that we have already made satisfactory sense of "analytic." Then what are we so hard at work on right now?

Our argument is not flatly circular, but something like it. It has the form, figuratively speaking, of a closed curve in space.

Interchangeability *salve veritate* is meaningless until relativized to a language whose extent is specified in relevant respects. Suppose now we consider a language containing just the following materials. There is an indefinitely large stock of one-place predicates (for example, "F" where "Fx" means that x is a man) and many-place predicates (for example, "G" where "Gxy" means that x loves y), mostly having to do with extralogical subject matter. The rest of the language is logical. The atomic sentences consist each of a predicate followed by one or more variables "x," "y," etc.; and the complex sentences are built up of the atomic ones by truth functions ("not," "and," "or," etc.) and quantification. In effect such a language enjoys the benefits also of descriptions and indeed singular terms generally, these being contextually definable in known ways. Even abstract singular terms naming classes, classes of classes, etc., are contextually definable in case the assumed stock of predicates includes the two-place predicate of class membership. Such a language can be adequate to classical mathematics and indeed to scientific discourse generally, except in so far as the latter involves debatable devices such as contrary-to-fact conditionals or modal adverbs like "necessarily".[5] Now a language of this type is extensional, in this sense: any two predicates which agree extensionally (that is, are true of the same objects) are interchangeable *salva veritate*.[6]

In an extensional language, therefore, interchangeability *salva veritate* is no assurance of cognitive synonymy of the desired type. That "bachelor" and "unmarried man" are interchangeable *salva veritate* in an extensional language assures us of no more than that (3) is true. There is no assurance here that the extensional agreement of "bachelor" and "unmarried man" rests on meaning rather than merely on accidental matters of fact, as does the extensional agreement of "creature with a heart" and "creature with kidneys."

For most purposes extensional agreement is the nearest approximation to synonymy we need care about. But the fact remains that extensional agreement falls far short of cognitive synonymy of the type required for explaining analyticity in the manner of §1. The type of cognitive synonymy required there is such as to equate the synonymy of "bachelor" and "unmarried man" with the analyticity of (3), not merely with the truth of (3).

So we must recognize that interchangeability *salva veritate*, if construed in relation to an extensional language, is not a sufficient condition of cognitive synonymy in the sense needed for deriving analyticity in the manner of §1. If a language contains an intensional adverb "necessarily" in the sense lately noted, or other particles to the same effect, then interchangeability *salva veritate* in such a language does afford a sufficient condition of cognitive synonymy; but such a language is intelligible only in so far as the notion of analyticity is already understood in advance.

The effort to explain cognitive synonymy first, for the sake of deriving analyticity from it afterward as in §1, is perhaps the wrong approach. Instead we might try explaining analyticity somehow without appeal to cognitive synonymy. Afterward we could doubtless derive cognitive synonymy from analyticity satisfactorily enough if desired. We have seen that cognitive synonymy of "bachelor" and "unmarried man" can be explained as analyticity of (3). The same explanation works for any pair of one-place predicates, of course, and it can be extended in obvious fashion to many-place predicates. Other syntactical categories can also be accommodated in fairly parallel fashion. Singular terms may be said to be cognitively synonymous when the statement of identity formed by putting "=" between them is analytic. Statements may be said simply to be cognitively synonymous when their biconditional (the result of joining them by "if and only if") is analytic.[7] If we care to lump all categories into a single formulation, at the expense of assuming again the notion of "word" which was appealed to early in this section, we can describe any two linguistic forms as cognitively synonymous when the two forms are interchangeable (apart from occurrences within "words") *salva* (no longer *veritate* but) *analyticitate.* Certain technical questions arise, indeed, over cases of ambiguity or homonymy; let us not pause for them, however, for we are already digressing. Let us rather turn our backs on the problem of synonymy and address ourselves anew to that of analyticity.

4. Semantical Rules

Analyticity at first seemed most naturally definable by appeal to a realm of meanings. On refinement, the appeal to meanings gave way to an appeal to synonymy or definition. But definition turned out to be a will-o'-the-wisp, and synonymy turned out to be best understood only by dint of a prior appeal to analyticity itself. So we are back at the problem of analyticity.

I do not know whether the statement "Everything green is extended" is analytic. Now does my indecision over this example really betray an incomplete understanding, an incomplete grasp of the "meanings," of "green" and "extended"? I think not. The trouble is not with "green" or "extended," but with "analytic."

It is often hinted that the difficulty in separating analytic statements from synthetic ones in ordinary language is due to the vagueness of ordinary language and that the distinction is clear when we have a precise artificial language with explicit "semantical rules." This, however, as I shall now attempt to show, is a confusion.

The notion of analyticity about which we are worrying is a purported relation between statements and languages: a statement S is said to be *analytic for* a language L, and the problem is to make sense of this relation generally, that is, for variable "S" and "L." The gravity of this problem is not perceptibly less for artificial languages than for natural ones. The problem of making sense of the idiom "S is analytic for L," with variable "S" and "L," retains its stubbornness even if we limit the range of the variable "L" to artificial languages. Let me now try to make this point evident.

For artificial languages and semantical rules we look naturally to the writings of Carnap. His semantical rules take various forms, and to make my point I shall have to distinguish certain of the forms. Let us suppose, to begin with, an artificial language L_0 whose semantical rules have the form explicitly of a specification, by recursion or otherwise, of all the analytic statements of L_0. The rules tell us that such and such statements, and only those, are the analytic statements of L_0. Now here the difficulty is simply that the rules contain the word "analytic," which we do not understand! We understand what expressions the rules attribute analyticity to, but we do not understand what the rules attribute to those expressions. In short, before we can understand a rule which begins "A statement S is analytic for language L_0 if and only if ...," we must understand the general relative term "analytic for"; we must understand "S is analytic for L" where "S" and "L" are variables.

Alternatively we may, indeed, view the so-called rule as a conventional definition of a new simple symbol "analytic-for-L_0," which might better be written untendentiously as "K" so as not to seem to throw light on the interesting word "analytic." Obviously any number of classes K, M, N, etc. of statements of L_0 can be specified for various purposes or for no purpose; what does it mean to say that K, as against M, N, etc., is the class of the "analytic" statements of L_0?

By saying what statements are analytic for L_0 we explain "analytic-for-L_0" but not "analytic," not "analytic for." We do not begin to explain the idiom "S is analytic for L" with variable "S" and "L," even if we are content to limit the range of "L" to the realm of artificial languages.

Actually we do know enough about the intended significance of "analytic" to know that analytic statements are supposed to be true. Let us then turn to a second form of semantical rule, which says not that such and such statements are analytic but simply that such and such statements are included among the truths. Such a rule is not subject to the criticism of containing the un-understood word "analytic"; and we may grant for the sake of argument that there is no difficulty over the broader term "true." A semantical rule of this second type, a rule of truth, is not supposed to specify all the truths of the language; it merely stipulates, recursively or otherwise, a certain multitude of statements which, along with others unspecified, are to count as true. Such a rule may be conceded to be quite clear. Derivatively, afterward, analyticity can be demarcated thus: a statement is analytic if it is (not merely true but) true according to the semantical rule.

Still there is really no progress. Instead of appealing to an unexplained word "analytic," we are now appealing to an unexplained phrase "semantical rule." Not every true statement which says that the statements of some class are true can count as a semantical rule – otherwise *all* truths would be "analytic" in the sense of being true according to semantical rules. Semantical rules are distinguishable, apparently, only by the fact of appearing on a page under the heading "Semantical Rules"; and this heading is itself then meaningless.

We can say indeed that a statement is analytic-for-L_0 if and only if it is true according to such and such specifically appended "semantical rules," but then we find ourselves back at essentially the same case which was originally discussed: "S is analytic-for-L_0 if and only if...." Once we seek to explain "S is analytic for L" generally for variable "L" (even allowing limitation of "L" to artificial languages), the explanation "true according to the semantical rules of L" is unavailing; for the relative term "semantical rule of" is as much in need of clarification, at least, as "analytic for."

It may be instructive to compare the notion of semantical rule with that of postulate. Relative to a given set of postulates, it is easy to say what a postulate is: it is a member of the set. Relative to a given set of semantical rules, it is equally easy to say what a semantical rule is. But given simply a notation, mathematical or otherwise, and indeed as thoroughly understood a notation as you please in point of the translations or truth conditions of its statements, who can say which of its true statements rank as postulates? Obviously the question is meaningless – as meaningless as asking which points in Ohio are starting points. Any finite (or effectively specifiable infinite) selection of statements (preferably true ones, perhaps) is as much a set of postulates as any other. The word "postulate" is significant only relative to an act of inquiry; we apply the word to a set of statements just in so far as we happen, for the year or the moment, to be thinking of those statements in relation to the statements which can be reached from them by some set of transformations to which we have seen fit to direct our attention. Now the notion of semantical rule is as sensible and meaningful as that of postulate, if conceived in a similarly relative spirit – relative, this time, to one or another particular enterprise of schooling unconversant persons in sufficient conditions for truth of statements of some natural or artificial language L. But from this point of view no one signalization of a subclass of the truths of L is intrinsically more a semantical rule than another; and, if "analytic" means "true by semantical rules," no one truth of L is analytic to the exclusion of another.[8]

It might conceivably be protested that an artificial language L (unlike a natural one) is a language in the ordinary sense *plus* a set of explicit semantical rules – the whole constituting, let us say, an ordered pair; and that the semantical rules of L then are specifiable simply as the second component of the pair L. But, by the same token and more simply, we might construe an artificial language L outright as an ordered pair whose second component is the class of its analytic statements; and then the analytic statements of L become specifiable simply as the statements in the second component of L. Or better still, we might just stop tugging at our bootstraps altogether.

Not all the explanations of analyticity known to Carnap and his readers have been covered explicitly in the above considerations, but the extension to other forms is not hard to see. Just one additional factor should be mentioned which sometimes enters: sometimes the semantical rules are in effect rules of translation into ordinary language, in which case the analytic statements of the artificial language are in effect recognized as such from the analyticity of their specified translations in ordinary language. Here certainly there can be no thought of an illumination of the problem of analyticity from the side of the artificial language.

From the point of view of the problem of analyticity the notion of an artificial language with semantical rules is a *feu follet par excellence*. Semantical rules determining the analytic statements of an artificial language are of interest only in so far as we already understand the notion of analyticity; they are of no help in gaining this understanding.

Appeal to hypothetical languages of an artificially simple kind could conceivably be useful in clarifying analyticity, if the mental or behavioral or cultural factors relevant to analyticity – whatever they may be – were somehow sketched into the simplified model. But a model which takes analyticity merely as an irreducible character is unlikely to throw light on the problem of explicating analyticity.

It is obvious that truth in general depends on both language and extralinguistic fact. The statement "Brutus killed Caesar" would be false if the world had been different in certain ways, but it would also be false if the word "killed" happened rather to have the sense of "begat." Thus one is tempted to suppose in general that the truth of a statement is somehow analyzable into a linguistic component and a factual component. Given this supposition, it next seems reasonable that in some statements the factual component should be null; and these are the analytic statements. But, for all its a priori reasonableness, a boundary between analytic and synthetic statements simply has not been drawn. That there is such a distinction to be drawn at all is an unempirical dogma of empiricists, a metaphysical article of faith.

5. The Verification Theory and Reductionism

In the course of these somber reflections we have taken a dim view first of the notion of meaning, then of the notion of cognitive synonymy, and finally of the notion of analyticity. But what, it may be asked, of the verification theory of meaning? This phrase has established itself so firmly as a catchword of empiricism that we should be very unscientific indeed not to look beneath it for a possible key to the problem of meaning and the associated problems.

The verification theory of meaning, which has been conspicuous in the literature from Peirce onward, is that the meaning of a statement is the method of empirically confirming or infirming it. An analytic statement is that limiting case which is confirmed no matter what.

As urged in §1, we can as well pass over the question of meanings as entities and move straight to sameness of meaning, or synonymy. Then what the verification theory says is that statements are synonymous if and only if they are alike in point of method of empirical confirmation or infirmation.

This is an account of cognitive synonymy not of linguistic forms generally, but of statements.[9] However, from the concept of synonymy of statements we could derive the concept of synonymy for other linguistic forms, by considerations somewhat similar to those at the end of §3. Assuming the notion of 'word,' indeed, we could explain any two forms as synonymous when the putting of the one form for an occurrence of the other in any statement (apart from occurrences within 'words') yields a synonymous statement. Finally, given the concept of synonymy thus for linguistic forms generally, we could define analyticity in terms of synonymy and logical truth as in §1. For that matter, we could define analyticity more simply in terms of just synonymy of statements together with logical truth; it is not necessary to appeal to synonymy of linguistic forms other than statements. For a statement may be described as analytic simply when it is synonymous with a logically true statement.

So, if the verification theory can be accepted as an adequate account of statement synonymy, the notion of analyticity is saved after all. However, let us reflect. Statement synonymy is said to be likeness of method of empirical confirmation or infirmation. Just what are these methods which are to be compared for likeness? What, in other words, is the nature of the relation between a statement and the experiences which contribute to or detract from its confirmation?

The most naïve view of the relation is that it is one of direct report. This is *radical reductionism*. Every meaningful statement is held to be translatable into a statement (true or false) about immediate experience. Radical reductionism, in one form or another, well antedates the verification theory of meaning explicitly so called. Thus Locke and Hume held that every idea must either originate directly in sense experience or else be compounded of ideas thus originating; and taking a hint from Tooke we might rephrase this doctrine in semantical jargon by saying that a term, to be significant at all, must be either a name of a sense datum or a compound of such names or an abbreviation of such a compound. So stated, the doctrine remains ambiguous as between sense data as sensory events and sense data as sensory qualities; and it remains vague as to the admissible ways of compounding. Moreover, the doctrine is unnecessarily and intolerably restrictive in the term-by-term critique which it imposes. More reasonably, and without yet exceeding the limits of what I have called radical reductionism, we may take full statements as our significant units – thus demanding that our statements as wholes be translatable into sense-datum language, but not that they be translatable term by term.

This emendation would unquestionably have been welcome to Locke and Hume and Tooke, but historically it had to await an important reorientation in semantics – the reorientation whereby the primary vehicle of meaning came to be seen no longer in the term but in the statement. This reorientation, explicit in Frege (1950: §60), underlies Russell's concept of incomplete symbols defined in use; also it is implicit in the verification theory of meaning, since the objects of verification are statements.

Radical reductionism, conceived now with statements as units, set itself the task of specifying a sense-datum language and showing how to translate the rest of significant discourse, statement by statement, into it. Carnap embarked on this project in the *Aufbau*.

The language which Carnap adopted as his starting point was not a sense-datum language in the narrowest conceivable sense, for it included also the notations of logic, up through higher set theory. In effect it included the whole language of pure mathematics. The ontology implicit in it (that is, the range of values of its variables) embraced not only sensory events but classes, classes of classes, and so on. Empiricists there are who would boggle at such prodigality. Carnap's starting point is very parsimonious, however, in its extralogical or sensory part. In a series of constructions in which he exploits the resources of modern logic with much ingenuity, Carnap succeeds in defining a wide array of important additional sensory concepts which, but for his constructions, one would not have dreamed were definable on so slender a basis. He was the first empiricist who, not content with asserting the reducibility of science to terms of immediate experience, took serious steps toward carrying out the reduction.

If Carnap's starting point is satisfactory, still his constructions were, as he himself stressed, only a fragment of the full program. The construction of even the simplest statements about the physical world was left in a sketchy state. Carnap's suggestions on this subject were, despite their sketchiness, very suggestive. He explained spatio-temporal point-instants as quadruples of real numbers and envisaged assignment of sense qualities to point-instants according to certain canons. Roughly summarized, the plan was that qualities should be assigned to point-instants in such a way as to achieve the laziest world compatible with our experience. The principle of least action was to be our guide in constructing a world from experience.

Carnap did not seem to recognize, however, that his treatment of physical objects fell short of reduction not merely through sketchiness, but in principle. Statements of the form "Quality q is at point-instant x; y; z; t" were, according to his canons, to be apportioned truth values in such a way as to maximize and minimize certain overall features, and with growth of experience the truth values were to be progressively revised in the same sprit. I think this is a good schematization (deliberately oversimplified, to be sure) of what science really does; but it provides no indication, not even the sketchiest, of how a statement of the form "Quality q is at x; y; z; t" could ever be translated into Carnap's initial language of sense data and logic. The connective "is at" remains an added undefined connective; the canons counsel us in its use but not in its elimination.

Carnap seems to have appreciated this point afterward; for in his later writings he abandoned all notion of the translatability of statements about the physical world into statements about immediate experience. Reductionism in its radical form has long since ceased to figure in Carnap's philosophy.

But the dogma of reductionism has, in a subtler and more tenuous form, continued to influence the thought of empiricists. The notion lingers that to each statement, or each synthetic statement, there is associated a unique range of possible sensory events such that the occurrence of any of them would add to the likelihood of truth of the statement, and that there is associated also another unique range of possible sensory events whose occurrence would detract from that likelihood. This notion is of course implicit in the verification theory of meaning.

The dogma of reductionism survives in the supposition that each statement, taken in isolation from its fellows, can admit of confirmation or infirmation at all. My countersuggestion, issuing essentially from Carnap's doctrine of the physical world in the *Aufbau*, is that our statements about the external world face the tribunal of sense experience not individually but only as a corporate body.[10]

The dogma of reductionism, even in its attenuated form, is intimately connected with the other dogma – that there is a cleavage between the analytic and the synthetic. We have found ourselves led, indeed, from the latter problem to the former through the verification theory of meaning. More directly, the one dogma clearly supports the other in this way: as long as it is taken to be significant in general to speak of the confirmation and infirmation of a statement, it seems significant to speak also of a limiting kind of statement which is vacuously confirmed, *ipso facto*, come what may; and such a statement is analytic.

The two dogmas are, indeed, at root identical. We lately reflected that in general the truth of statements does obviously depend both upon language and upon extralinguistic fact; and we noted that this obvious circumstance carries in its train, not logically but all too naturally, a feeling that the truth of a statement is somehow analyzable into a linguistic component and a factual component. The factual component must, if we are empiricists, boil down to a range of confirmatory experiences. In the extreme case where the linguistic component is all that matters, a true statement is analytic. But I hope we are now impressed with how stubbornly the distinction between analytic and synthetic has resisted any straight-forward drawing. I am impressed also, apart from prefabricated examples of black and white balls in an urn, with how baffling the problem has always been of arriving at any explicit theory of the empirical confirmation of a synthetic statement. My present suggestion is that it is nonsense, and the root of much nonsense, to speak of a linguistic component and a factual component in the truth of any individual statement. Taken collectively, science has its double dependence upon language and experience; but this duality is not significantly traceable into the statements of science taken one by one.

The idea of defining a symbol in use was, as remarked, an advance over the impossible term-by-term empiricism of Locke and Hume. The statement, rather than the term, came with Frege to be recognized as the unit accountable to an empiricist critique. But what I am now urging is that even in taking the statement as unit we have drawn our grid too finely. The unit of empirical significance is the whole of science.

6. Empiricism Without the Dogmas

The totality of our so-called knowledge or beliefs, from the most casual matters of geography and history to the profoundest laws of atomic physics or even of pure mathematics and logic, is a man-made fabric which impinges on experience only along the edges. Or, to change the figure, total science is like a field of force whose boundary conditions are experience. A conflict with experience at the periphery occasions readjustments in the interior of the field. Truth values have to be redistributed over some of our statements. Reevaluation of some statements entails reevaluation of others, because of their logical interconnections – the logical laws being in turn simply certain further statements of the system, certain further elements of the field. Having reevaluated one statement we must reevaluate some others, which may be statements logically connected with the first or may be the statements of logical connections themselves. But the total field is so underdetermined by its boundary conditions, experience, that there is much latitude of choice as to what statements to reevaluate in the light of any single contrary experience. No particular experiences are linked with any particular statements in the interior of the field, except indirectly through considerations of equilibrium affecting the field as a whole.

If this view is right, it is misleading to speak of the empirical content of an individual statement – especially if it is a statement at all remote from the experiential periphery of the field. Furthermore it becomes folly to seek a boundary between synthetic statements, which hold contingently on experience, and analytic statements, which hold come what may. Any statement can be held true come what may, if we make drastic enough adjustments elsewhere in the system. Even a statement very close to the periphery can be held true in the face of recalcitrant experience by pleading hallucination or by amending certain statements of the kind called logical laws. Conversely, by the same token, no statement is immune to revision. Revision even of the logical law of the excluded middle has been proposed as a means of simplifying quantum mechanics; and what difference is there in principle between such a shift and the shift whereby Kepler superseded Ptolemy, or Einstein Newton, or Darwin Aristotle?

For vividness I have been speaking in terms of varying distances from a sensory periphery. Let me try now to clarify this notion without metaphor. Certain statements, though about physical objects and not sense experience, seem peculiarly germane to sense experience – and in a selective way: some statements to some experiences, others to others. Such statements, especially germane to particular experiences, I picture as near the periphery. But in this relation of "germaneness" I envisage nothing more than a loose association reflecting the relative likelihood, in practice, of our choosing one statement rather than another for revision in the event or recalcitrant experience. For example, we can imagine recalcitrant experiences to which we would surely be inclined to accommodate our system by reevaluating just the statement that there are brick houses on Elm Street, together with related statements on the same topic. We can imagine other recalcitrant experiences to which we would be inclined to accommodate our system by reevaluating just the statement that there are no centaurs, along with kindred statements. A recalcitrant experience can, I have urged, be accommodated by any of various alternative reevaluations in various alternative quarters of the total system; but, in the cases which we are now imagining, our natural tendency to disturb the total system as little as possible would lead us to focus our revisions upon these specific statements concerning brick houses or centaurs. These statements are felt, therefore, to have a sharper empirical reference than highly theoretical statements of physics or logic or ontology. The latter statements may be thought of as relatively centrally located within the total network, meaning merely that little preferential connection with any particular sense data obtrudes itself.

As an empiricist I continue to think of the conceptual scheme of science as a tool, ultimately, for predicting future experience in the light of past experience. Physical objects are conceptually imported into the situation as convenient intermediaries – not by definition in terms of experience, but simply as irreducible posits comparable, epistemologically, to the gods of Homer. For my part I do, qua lay physicist, believe in physical objects and not in Homer's gods; and I consider it a scientific error to believe otherwise. But in point of epistemological footing the physical objects and the gods differ only in degree and not in kind. Both sorts of entities enter our conception only as cultural posits. The myth of physical objects is epistemologically superior to most in that it has proved more efficacious than other myths as a device for working a manageable structure into the flux of experience.

Positing does not stop with macroscopic physical objects. Objects
at the atomic level are posited to make the laws of macroscopic objects, and
ultimately the laws of experience, simpler and more manageable; and we
need not expect or demand full definition of atomic and subatomic entities
in terms of macroscopic ones, any more than definition of macroscopic
things in terms of sense data. Science is a continuation of common sense,
and it continues the common-sense expedient of swelling ontology to simplify theory.

Physical objects, small and large, are not the only posits. Forces are
another example; and indeed we are told nowadays that the boundary
between energy and matter is obsolete. Moreover, the abstract entities
which are the substance of mathematics – ultimately classes and classes of
classes and so on up – are another posit in the same spirit. Epistemologically
these are myths on the same footing with physical objects and gods, neither
better nor worse except for differences in the degree to which they expedite
our dealings with sense experiences.

The overall algebra of rational and irrational numbers is underdetermined by the algebra of rational numbers, but is smoother and more convenient; and it includes the algebra of rational numbers as a jagged or ger-
rymandered part. Total science, mathematical and natural and human, is
similarly but more extremely underdetermined by experience. The edge of
the system must be kept squared with experience; the rest, with all its elaborate myths or fictions, has as its objective the simplicity of laws.

Ontological questions, under this view, are on a par with questions
of natural science.[11] Consider the question whether to countenance classes
as entities. This, as I have argued elsewhere, is the question whether to
quantify with respect to variables which take classes as values. Now Carnap
(1950b) has maintained that this is a question not of matters of fact but of
choosing a convenient language form, a convenient conceptual scheme or
framework for science. With this I agree, but only on the proviso that the
same be conceded regarding scientific hypotheses generally. Carnap (1950b:
32) has recognized that he is able to preserve a double standard for ontological questions and scientific hypotheses only by assuming an absolute distinction between the analytic and the synthetic; and I need not say again
that this is a distinction which I reject.[12]

The issue over there being classes seems more a question of convenient conceptual scheme; the issue over there being centaurs, or brick houses on Elm Street, seems more a question of fact. But I have been urging that
this difference is only one of degree, and that it turns upon our vaguely pragmatic inclination to adjust one strand of the fabric of science rather than
another in accommodating some particular recalcitrant experience.
Conservatism figures in such choices, and so does the quest for simplicity.

Carnap, Lewis, and others take a pragmatic stand on the question of choosing between language forms, scientific frameworks; but their pragmatism leaves off at the imagined boundary between the analytic and the synthetic. In repudiating such a boundary I espouse a more thorough pragmatism. Each man is given a scientific heritage plus a continuing barrage of sensory stimulation; and the considerations which guide him in warping his scientific heritage to fit his continuing sensory promptings are, where rational, pragmatic.

NOTES

1. Carnap (1947: 9ff), (1950a: 70ff).

2. According to an important variant sense of "definition," the relation preserved may be the weaker relation of mere agreement in reference. But definition in this sense is better ignored in the present connection, being irrelevant to the question of synonymy.

3. Cf. Lewis (1918: 373).

4. This is cognitive synonymy in a primary, broad sense. Carnap (1947: 56ff) and Lewis (1946: 83ff) have suggested how, once this notion is at hand, a narrower sense of cognitive synonymy which is preferable for some purposes can in turn be derived. But this special ramification of concept-building lies aside from the present purposes and must not be confused with the broad sort of cognitive synonymy here concerned.

5. On such devices see also Quine (1961).

6. This is the substance of Quine (1951), *121.

7. The "if and only if" itself is intended in the truth functional sense. See Carnap (1947: 14).

8. The foregoing paragraph was not part of the present essay as originally published. It was prompted by Martin.

9. The doctrine can indeed be formulated with terms rather than statements as the units. Thus Lewis describes the meaning of a term as "a *criterion in mind*, by reference to which one is able to apply or refuse to apply the expression in question in the case of presented, or imagined, things or situations" (1946: 133). — For an instructive account of the vicissitudes of the verification theory of meaning, centered however on the question of meaningfulness rather than synonymy and analyticity, see Hempel.

10. This doctrine was well argued by Duhem, pp. 303-328. Or see Lowinger, pp. 132-140.

11. "L'ontologie fait corps avec la science elle-même et ne peut en être separée." Meyerson, p. 439.

12. For an effective expression of further misgivings over this distinction, see White.

REFERENCES

Carnap, R. (1947). *Meaning and Necessity*, Chicago, University of Chicago Press.
Carnap, R. (1950a). *Logical Foundations of Probability*, Chicago, University of Chicago Press.
Carnap, R. (1950b). "Empiricism, Semantics, and Ontology," *Revue Internationale de Philosophie*, IV: 20-40.
Duhem, P. (1906). *La Théorie physique son objet et sa structure*, Paris.
Frege, G. (1950). *Foundations of Arithmetic*, New York Philosophical Library.
Hempel, C.G. (1950). "Problems and Changes in the Empiricist Criterion of Meaning," in *Revue Internationale de Philosophie*, IV: 41-63.
Lewis, C.I. (1918). *A survey of Symbolic Logic*, Berkely.
Lewis, C.I. (1946). *An Analysis of Knowledge and Valuation*, La Salle Il, Open Court Publishing Co.
Lowinger, A. (1941). *The Methodology of Pierre Duhem*, New York, Columbia University Press.
Martin, R.M. (1952). "On 'Analytic'," *Philosophical Studies*, III: 42-47.
Meyerson, É. (1908). *Identité et realité*, Paris.
Quine, W.V. (1961). *From A Logical Point of View*, New York, Harper & Row.
Quine, W.V. (1951). *Mathematical Logic*, Cambridge, Harvard University of Press.
White, M. (1950). "The Analytic and the Synthetic: An Untenable Dualism," in Sidney Hook (ed.) *John Dewey Philosopher of Science and Freedom*, New York, The Dial Press, Inc.

SELECTIONS FROM PHILOSOPHICAL INVESTIGATIONS

Ludwig Wittgenstein

143. Let us now examine the following kind of language-game: when A gives an order B has to write down series of signs according to a certain formation rule.

The first of these series is meant to be that of the natural numbers in decimal notation. – How does he get to understand this notation? – First of all series of numbers will be written down for him and he will be required to copy them. (Do not balk at the expression "series of numbers"; it is not being used wrongly here.) And here already there is a normal and an abnormal learner's reaction. – At first perhaps we guide his hand in writing out the series 0 to 9; but then the *possibility of getting him to understand* will depend on his going on to write it down independently. – And here we can imagine, e.g., that he does copy the figures independently, but not in the right order: he writes sometimes one sometimes another at random. And then communications stop at *that* point. – Or again, he makes '*mistakes*' in the order. – The difference between this and the first case will of course be one of frequency. – Or he makes a *systematic* mistake; for example, he copies every other number, or he copies the series 0, 1, 2, 3, 4, 5, ... like this: 1, 0, 3, 2, 5, 4,... Here we shall almost be tempted to say that he has understood *wrong*.

Notice, however, that there is no sharp distinction between a random mistake and a systematic one. That is, between what you are inclined to call "random" and what "systematic."

Perhaps it is possible to wean him from the systematic mistake (as from a bad habit). Or perhaps one accepts his way of copying and tries to teach him ours as an offshoot, a variant of his. – And here too our pupil's capacity to learn may come to an end.

144. What do I mean when I say "the pupil's capacity to learn *may* come to an end here"? Do I say this from my own experience? Of course not. (Even if I have had such experience.) Then what am I doing with that proposition? Well, I should like you to say: "Yes, it's true, you can imagine that too, that might happen too!" – But was I trying to draw someone's attention to the fact that he is capable of imagining that? – I wanted to put that picture before him, and his *acceptance* of the picture consists in his now being inclined to regard a given case differently: that is, to compare it with *this* rather than *that* set of pictures. I have changed his *way of looking at things*. (Indian mathematicians: "Look at this.")

145. Suppose the pupil now writes the series 0 to 9 to our satisfaction. – And this will only be the case when he is often successful, not if he does it right once in a hundred attempts. Now I continue the series and draw his attention to the recurrence of the first series in the units; and then to its recurrence in the tens. (Which only means that I use particular emphases, underline figures, write them one under another in such-and-such ways, and similar things.) – And now at some point he continues the series independently – or he does not. – But why do you say that? so much is obvious! – Of course; I only wished to say: the effect of any further *explanation* depends on his *reaction*.

Now, however, let us suppose that after some efforts on the teacher's part he continues the series correctly, that is, as we do it. So now we can say he has mastered the system. – But how far need he continue the series for us to have the right to say that? Clearly you cannot state a limit here.

146. Suppose I now ask: "Has he understood the system when he continues the series to the hundredth place?" Or – if I should not speak of "understanding" in connection with our primitive language-game: Has he got the system, if he continues the series correctly so far? – Perhaps you will say here: to have got the system (or, again, to understand it) can't consist in continuing the series up to *this* or *that* number: *that* is only applying one's understanding. The understanding itself is a state which is the *source* of the correct use.

What is one really thinking of here? Isn't one thinking of the derivation of a series from its algebraic formula? Or at least of something analogous? – But this is where we were before. The point is, we can think of more than *one* application of an algebraic formula; and every type of application can in turn be formulated algebraically; but naturally this does not get us any further. – The application is still a criterion of understanding.

147. "But how can it be? When *I* say I understand the rule of a series, I am surely not saying so because I have *found out* that up to now I have applied the algebraic formula in such-and-such a way! In my own case in all events I surely know that I mean such-and-such a series; it doesn't matter how far I have actually developed it." –

Your idea, then, is that you know the application of the rule of the series quite apart from remembering actual applications to particular numbers. And you will perhaps say: "Of course! For the series is infinite and the bit of it that I can have developed finite."

148. But what does this knowledge consist in? Let me ask: *When* do you know that application? Always? Day and night? Or only when you are actually thinking of the rule? Do you know it, that is, in the same way as you know the alphabet and the multiplication table? Or is what you call "knowledge" a state of consciousness or a process – say a thought of something, or the like?

149. If one says that knowing the ABC is a state of the mind one is thinking of a state of a mental apparatus (perhaps of the brain) by means of which we explain the *manifestations* of that knowledge. Such a state is called a disposition. But there are objections to speaking of a state of the mind here, inasmuch as there ought to be two different criteria for such a state: a knowledge of the construction of the apparatus, quite apart from what it does. (Nothing would be more confusing here than to use the words "conscious" and "unconscious" for the contrast between states of consciousness and dispositions. For this pair of terms covers up a grammatical difference.)

150. The grammar of the word "knows" is evidently closely related to that of "can", "is able to". But also closely related to that of "understands". ('Mastery' of a technique.)[a,b]

151. But there is also *this* use of the word "to know": we say "Now I know!" – and similarly "Now I can do it!" and "Now I understand!"

Let us imagine the following example: A writes series of numbers down. B watches him and tries to find a law for the sequence of numbers. If he succeeds he exclaims: "Now I can go on!" – So this capacity, this understanding, is something that makes its appearance in a moment. So let us try and see what it is that makes its appearance here. – A has written down the numbers 1, 5, 11, 19, 29; at this point B says he knows how to go on. What happened here? Various things may have happened; for example, while A was slowly putting one number after another, B was occupied with trying various algebraic formulae on the numbers which had been written down. After A had written the number 19 B tried the formula $a_n = n^2 + n - 1$; and the next number confirmed his hypothesis.

Or again, B does not think of formulae. He watches A writing his numbers down with a certain feeling of tension, and all sorts of vague thoughts go through his head. Finally he asks himself: "What is the series of differences?" He finds the series 4, 6, 8, 10 and says: Now I can go on.

Or he watches and says "Yes, I know *that* series" – and continues it, just as he would have done if A had written down the series 1, 3, 5, 7, 9. – Or he says nothing at all and simply continues the series. Perhaps he had what may be called the sensation "that's easy!". (Such a sensation is for example, that of a light quick intake of breath, as when one is slightly startled.)

152. But are the processes which I have described here *understanding?*

"B understands the principle of the series" surely doesn't mean simply: the formula "$a_n = ...$" occurs to B. For it is perfectly imaginable that the formula should occur to him and that he should nevertheless not understand. "He understands" must have more in it than: the formula occurs to him. And equally, more than any of those more or less characteristic *accompaniments* or manifestations of understanding.

153. We are trying to get hold of the mental process of understanding which seems to be hidden behind those coarser and therefore more readily visible accompaniments. But we do not succeed; or, rather, it does not get as far as a real attempt. For even supposing I had found something that happened in all those cases of understanding, – why should *it* be the understanding? And how can the process of understanding have been hidden, when I said "Now I understand" *because* I understood?! And if I say it is hidden – then how do I know what I have to look for? I am in a muddle.

154. But wait – if "Now I understand the principle" does not mean the same as "The formula ... occurs to me" (or "I say the formula", "I write it down", etc.) – does it follow from this that I employ the sentence "Now I understand...." or "Now I can go on" as a description of a process occurring behind or side by side with that of saying the formula?

If there has to be anything "behind the utterance of the formula" it is *particular circumstances*, which justify me in saying I can go on – when the formula occurs to me.

Try not to think of understanding as a 'mental process' at all. – For *that* is the expression which confuses you. But ask yourself: in what sort of case, in what kind of circumstances, do we say, "Now I know how to go on," when, that is, the formula *has* occurred to me? –

In the sense in which there are processes (including mental processes) which are characteristic of understanding, understanding is not a mental process.

(A pain's growing more and less; the hearing of a tune or a sentence: these are mental processes.) ...

185. Let us return to our example (143). Now – judged by the usual criteria – the pupil has mastered the series of natural numbers. Next we teach him to write down other series of cardinal numbers and get him to the point of writing down series of the form

0, n, 2n, 3n, etc.

at an order of the form "+n"; so at the order "+1 " he writes down the series of natural numbers. – Let us suppose we have done exercises and given him tests up to 1000.

Now we get the pupil to continue a series (say +2) beyond 1000 – and he writes 1000, 1004, 1008, 1012.

We say to him: "Look what you've done!" – He doesn't understand. We say: "You were meant to add *two*: look how you began the series!" – He answers "Yes, isn't it right? I thought that was how I was *meant* to do it." – Or suppose he pointed to the series and said: "But I went on in the same way." – It would now be no use to say: "But can't you see ...?" – and repeat the old examples and explanations. – In such a case we might say, perhaps: It comes natural to this person to understand our order with our explanations as we should understand the order: "Add 2 up to 1000, 4 up to 2000, 6 up to 3000 and so on."

Such a case would present similarities with one in which a person naturally reacted to the gesture of pointing with the hand by looking in the direction of the line from finger-tip to wrist, not from wrist to finger-tip.

186. "What you are saying, then, comes to this: a new insight – intuition – is needed at every step to carry out the order '+n' correctly." – To carry it out correctly! How is it decided what is the right step to take at any particular stage? – "The right step is the one that accords with the order – as it was *meant*." – So when you gave the order +2 you meant that he was to write 1002 after 1000 – and did you also mean that he should write 1868 after 1866, and 100036 after 100034, and so on – an infinite number of such propositions? – "No: what I meant was, that he should write the next but one number after *every* number that he wrote; and from this all those propositions follow in turn." – But that is just what is in question: what, at any stage, does follow from that sentence. Or, again, what, at any stage we are to call "being in accord" with that sentence (and with the *mean*-ing you then put into the sentence – whatever that may have consisted in). It would almost be more correct to say, not that an intuition was needed at every stage, but that a new decision was needed at every stage.

187. "But I already knew, at the time when I gave the order, that he ought to write 1002 after 1000." – Certainly; and you can also say you *meant* it then; only you should not let yourself be misled by the grammar of the words "know" and "mean". For you don't want to say that you thought of the step from 1000 to 1002 at that time – and even if you did think of this step, still you did not think of other ones. When you said "I already knew at the time ..." that meant something like: "If I had then been asked what number should be written after 1000, I should have replied '1002'."

And that I don't doubt. This assumption is rather of the same kind as: "If he had fallen into the water then, I should have jumped in after him." – Now, what was wrong with your idea?

188. Here I should first of all like to say: your idea was that that act of meaning the order had in its own way already traversed all those steps: that when you meant it your mind as it were flew ahead and took all the steps before you physically arrived at this or that one.

Thus you were inclined to use such expressions as: "The steps are *really* already taken, even before I take them in writing or orally or in thought." And it seemed as if they were in some *unique* way predetermined, anticipated – as only the act of meaning can anticipate reality.

189. "But *are* the steps then *not* determined by the algebraic formula?" – The question contains a mistake.

We use the expression: "The steps are determined by the formula ...". *How* is it used? – We may perhaps refer to the fact that people are brought by their education (training) so to use the formula $y = x^2$, that they all work out the same value for y when they substitute the same number for x. Or we may say: "These people are so trained that they all take the same step at the same point when they receive the order 'add 3'." We might express this by saying: for these people the order "add 3" completely determines every step from one number to the next. (In contrast with other people who do not know what they are to do on receiving this order, or who react to it with perfect certainty, but each one in a different way.)

On the other hand we can contrast different kinds of formula, and the different kinds of use (different kinds of training) appropriate to them. Then we *call* formulae of a particular kind (with the appropriate methods of use) "formulae which determine a number y for a given value of x", and formulae of another kind, ones which "do not determine the number y for a given value of x". ($y = x^2$ would be of the first kind, $y \neq x^2$ of the second.) The proposition "The formula ... determines a number y" will then be a statement about the form of the formula – and now we must distinguish such a proposition as "The formula which I have written down determines y", or "Here is a formula which determines y", from one of the following kind: "The formula $y = x^2$ determines the number y for a given value of x". The question "Is the formula written down there one that determines y?" will then mean the same as "Is what is there a formula of this kind or that?" – but it is not clear off-hand what we are to make of the question "Is $y = x^2$ a formula which determines y for a given value of x?" One might address this question to a pupil in order to test whether he understands the use of the word "to determine"; or it might be a mathematical problem to prove in a particular system that x has only one square.

190. It may now be said: "The way the formula is meant determines which steps are to be taken." What is the criterion for the way the formula is meant? It is, for example, the kind of way we always use it, the

way we are taught to use it.

We say, for instance, to someone who uses a sign unknown to us: "If by '$x!2$' you mean x^2, then you get *this* value for y, if you mean $2x$, *that* one." – Now ask yourself, how does one *mean* the one thing or the other by "$x!2$"?

That will be how meaning it can determine the steps in advance.

191. "It is as if we could grasp the whole use of the word in a flash." Like *what* e.g.? – Can't the use – in a certain sense – be grasped in a flash? And in *what* sense can it not? – The point is, that it is as if we could 'grasp it in a flash' in yet another and much more direct sense than that. – But have you a model for this? No. It is just that this expression suggests itself to us. As the result of the crossing of different pictures....

195. "But I don't mean that what I do now (in grasping a sense) determines the future use *causally* and as a matter of experience, but that in a *queer* way, the use itself is in some sense present." – But of course it is, 'in *some* sense'! Really the only thing wrong with what you say is the expression "in a queer way". The rest is all right; and the sentence only seems queer when one imagines a different language-game for it from the one in which we actually use it. (Someone once told me that as a child he had been surprised that a tailor could 'sew a dress' – he thought this meant that a dress was produced by sewing alone, by sewing one thread on to another.)

196. In our failure to understand the use of a word we take it as the expression of a queer *process*. (As we think of time as a queer medium, of the mind as a queer kind of being.)

197. "It's as if we could grasp the whole use of a word in a flash." – And that is just what we say we do. That is to say: we sometimes describe what we do in these words. But there is nothing astonishing, nothing queer, about what happens. It becomes queer when we are led to think that the future development must in some way already be present in the act of grasping the use and yet isn't present. – For we say that there isn't any doubt that we understand the word, and on the other hand its meaning lies in its use. There is no doubt that I now want to play chess, but chess is the game it is in virtue of all its rules (and so on). Don't I know, then, which game I want to play until I *have* played it? or are all the rules contained in my act of intending? Is it experience that tells me that this sort of game is the usual consequence of such an act of intending? so is it impossible for me to be certain what I am intending to do? And if that is nonsense – what kind of super-strong connexion exists between the act of intending and the thing intended? – Where is the connexion effected between the sense of the expression "Let's play a game of chess" and all the rules of the game? – Well, in the list of rules of the game, in the teaching of it, in the day-to-day practice of playing.

198. But how can a rule shew me what I have to do at *this* point? Whatever I do is, on some interpretation, "in accord with the rule." – That is not what we ought to say, but rather: any interpretation still hangs in the air along with what it interprets, and cannot give it any support. Interpretations by themselves do not determine meaning.

"Then can whatever I do be brought into accord with the rule?" – Let me ask this: what has the expression of a rule – say a sign-post – got to do with my actions? What sort of connexion is there here? Well, perhaps this one: I have been trained to react to this sign in a particular way, and now I do so react to it.

But that is only to give a causal connexion; to tell how it has come about that we now go by the sign-post; not what this going-by-the-sign really consists in. On the contrary; I have further indicated that a person goes by a sign-post only in so far as there exists a regular use of sign-posts, a custom.

199. Is what we call "obeying a rule" something that it would be possible for only *one* man to do, and to do only *once* in his life? – This is of course a note on the grammar of the expression "to obey a rule."

It is not possible that there should have been only one occasion on which someone obeyed a rule. It is not possible that there should have been only one occasion on which a report was made, an order given or understood; and so on. – To obey a rule, to make a report, to give an order, to play a game of chess, are *customs* (uses, institutions).

To understand a sentence means to understand a language. To understand a language means to be master of a technique.

200. It is, of course, imaginable that two people belonging to a tribe unacquainted with games should sit at a chess-board and go through the moves of a game of chess; and even with all the appropriate mental accompaniments. And if *we* were to see it we should say they were playing chess. But now imagine a game of chess translated according to certain rules into a series of actions which we do not ordinarily associate with a *game* – say into yells and stamping of feet. And now suppose those two people to yell and stamp instead of playing the form of chess that we are used to; and this in such a way that their procedure is translatable by suitable rules into a game of chess. Should we still be inclined to say they were playing a game? What right would one have to say so?

201. This was our paradox: no course of action could be determined by a rule, because every course of action can be made out to accord with the rule. The answer was: if everything can be made out to accord with the rule, then it can also be made out to conflict with it. And so there would be neither accord nor conflict here.

It can be seen that there is a misunderstanding here from the mere fact that in the course of our argument we give one interpretation after another; as if each one contented us at least for a moment, until we thought of yet another standing behind it. What this shews is that there is a way of grasping a rule which is *not* an *interpretation*, but which is exhibited in what we call "obeying the rule" and "going against it" in actual cases.

Hence there is an inclination to say: every action according to the rule is an interpretation. But we ought to restrict the term "interpretation" to the substitution of one expression of the rule for another.

202. And hence also 'obeying a rule' is a practice. And to *think* one is obeying a rule is not to obey a rule. Hence it is not possible to obey a rule 'privately': otherwise thinking one was obeying a rule would be the same thing as obeying it....

217. "How am I able to obey a rule?" – if this is not a question about causes, then it is about the justification for my following the rule in the way I do.

If I have exhausted the justifications I have reached bedrock, and my spade is turned. Then I am inclined to say: "This is simply what I do."

(Remember that we sometimes demand definitions for the sake not of their content, but of their form. Our requirement is an architectural one; the definition a kind of ornamental coping that supports nothing.)

218. Whence comes the idea that the beginning of a series is a visible section of rails invisibly laid to infinity? Well, we might imagine rails instead of a rule. And infinitely long rails correspond to the unlimited application of a rule.

219. "All the steps are really already taken" means: I no longer have any choice. The rule, once stamped with a particular meaning, traces the lines along which it is to be followed through the whole of space. – But if something of this sort really were the case, how would it help?

No; my description only made sense if it was to be understood symbolically. – I should have said: *This is how it strikes me.*

When I obey a rule, I do not choose.

I obey the rule *blindly*....

243. A human being can encourage himself, give himself orders, obey, blame and punish himself; he can ask himself a question and answer it. We could even imagine human beings who spoke only in monologue; who accompanied their activities by talking to themselves. – An explorer who watched them and listened to their talk might succeed in translating their language into ours. (This would enable him to predict these people's actions correctly, for he also hears them making resolutions and decisions.)

But could we also imagine a language in which a person could write down or give vocal expression to his inner experiences – his feelings, moods, and the rest – for his private use? – Well, can't we do so in our ordinary language? – But that is not what I mean. The individual words of this language are to refer to what can only be known to the person speaking; to his immediate private sensations. So another person cannot understand the language.

244. How do words *refer* to sensations? – There doesn't seem to be any problem here; don't we talk about sensations every day, and give them names? But how is the connexion between the name and the thing named set up? This question is the same as: how does a human being learn the meaning of the names of sensations? – of the word "pain" for example. Here is one possibility: words are connected with the primitive, the natural, expressions of the sensation and used in their place. A child has hurt himself and he cries; and then adults talk to him and teach him exclamations and, later, sentences. They teach the child new pain-behaviour.

"So you are saying that the word 'pain' really means crying?" – On the contrary: the verbal expression of pain replaces crying and does not describe it.

245. For how can I go so far as to try to use language to get between pain and its expression?

246. In what sense are my sensations *private*? – Well, only I can know whether I am really in pain; another person can only surmise it. – In one way this is wrong, and in another nonsense. If we are using the word "to know" as it is normally used (and how else are we to use it?), then other people very often know when I am in pain. – Yes, but all the same not with the certainty with which I know it myself! – It can't be said of me at all (except perhaps as a joke) that I *know* I am in pain. What is it supposed to mean – except perhaps that I *am* in pain?

Other people cannot be said to learn of my sensations *only* from my behaviour – for I cannot be said to learn of them. I *have* them.

The truth is: it makes sense to say about other people that they doubt whether I am in pain; but not to say it about myself.

247. "Only you can know if you had that intention." One might tell someone this when one was explaining the meaning of the word "intention" to him. For then it means: *that* is how we use it.

(And here "know" means that the expression of uncertainty is senseless.)

248. The proposition "Sensations are private" is comparable to: "One plays patience by oneself."

249. Are we perhaps over-hasty in our assumption that the smile of an unweaned infant is not a pretence? – And on what experience is our assumption based?

(Lying is a language-game that needs to be learned like any other one.)

250. Why can't a dog simulate pain? Is he too honest? Could one teach a dog to simulate pain? Perhaps it is possible to teach him to howl on particular occasions as if he were in pain, even when he is not. But the surroundings which are necessary for this behaviour to be real simulation are missing.

251. What does it mean when we say: "I can't imagine the opposite of this" or "What would it be like, if it were otherwise?" – For example, when someone has said that my images are private, or that only I myself can know whether I am feeling pain, and similar things.

Of course, here "I can't imagine the opposite" doesn't mean: my powers of imagination are unequal to the task. These words are a defence against something whose form makes it look like an empirical proposition, but which is really a grammatical one.

But why do we say: " I can't imagine the opposite"? Why not: "I can't imagine the thing itself"?

Example: "Every rod has a length." That means something like: we call something (or *this*) "the length of a rod" – but nothing "the length of a sphere." Now can I imagine 'every rod having a length'? Well, I simply imagine a rod. Only this picture, in connexion with this proposition, has a quite different role from one used in connexion with the proposition "This table has the same length as the one over there." For here I understand what it means to have a picture of the opposite (nor need it be a mental picture).

But the picture attaching to the grammatical proposition could only shew, say, what is called "the length of a rod". And what should the opposite picture be?

((Remark about the negation of an a priori proposition.))

252. "This body has extension." To this we might reply: "Nonsense!" – but are inclined to reply "Of course!" – Why is this?

253. "Another person can't have my pains." – Which are *my* pains? What counts as a criterion of identity here? Consider what makes it possible in the case of physical objects to speak of "two exactly the same," for example, to say "This chair is not the one you saw here yesterday, but is exactly the same as it."

In so far as it makes *sense* to say that my pain is the same as his, it is also possible for us both to have the same pain. (And it would also be imaginable for two people to feel pain in the same – not just the corresponding – place. That might be the case with Siamese twins, for instance.)

I have seen a person in a discussion on this subject strike himself on the breast and say: "But surely another person can't have THIS pain!" – The answer to this is that one does not define a criterion of identity by emphatic stressing of the word "this". Rather, what the emphasis does is to suggest the case in which we are conversant with such a criterion of identity, but have to be reminded of it.

254. The substitution of "identical" for "the same" (for instance) is another typical expedient in philosophy. As if we were talking

about shades of meaning and all that were in question were to find words to hit on the correct nuance. That is in question in philosophy only where we have to give a psychologically exact account of the temptation to use a particular kind of expression. What we 'are tempted to say' in such a case is, of course, not philosophy; but it is its raw material. Thus, for example, what a mathematician is inclined to say about the objectivity and reality of mathematical facts, is not a philosophy of mathematics, but something for philosophical *treatment*.

255. The philosopher's treatment of a question is like the treatment of an illness.

256. Now, what about the language which describes my inner experiences and which only I myself can understand? *How* do I use words to stand for my sensations? – As we ordinarily do? Then are my words for sensations tied up with my natural expressions of sensation? In that case my language is not a 'private' one. Someone else might understand it as well as I. – But suppose I didn't have any natural expression for the sensation, but only had the sensation? And now I simply *associate* names with sensations and use these names in descriptions . –

257. "What would it be like if human beings showed no outward signs of pain (did not groan, grimace, etc.)? Then it would be impossible to teach a child the use of the word 'tooth-ache'." – Well, let's assume the child is a genius and itself invents a name for the sensation! – But then, of course, he couldn't make himself understood when he used the word. – So does he understand the name, without being able to explain its meaning to anyone? – But what does it mean to say that he has 'named his pain'? – How has he done this naming of pain?! And whatever he did, what was its purpose? – When one says "He gave a name to his sensation" one forgets that a great deal of stage-setting in the language is presupposed if the mere act of naming is to make sense. And when we speak of someone's having given a name to pain, what is presupposed is the existence of the grammar of the word "pain"; it shews the post where the new word is stationed.

258. Let us imagine the following case. I want to keep a diary about the recurrence of a certain sensation. To this end I associate it with the sign "S" and write this sign in a calendar for every day on which I have the sensation. – I will remark first of all that a definition of the sign cannot be formulated. – But still I can give myself a kind of ostensive definition. – How? Can I point to the sensation? Not in the ordinary sense. But I speak, or write the sign down, and at the same time I concentrate my attention on the sensation – and so, as it were, point to it inwardly. – But what is this ceremony for? for that is all it seems to be! A definition surely serves to establish the meaning of a sign. – Well, that is done precisely by the concentrating of my attention; for in this way I impress on myself the connexion between the sign and the sensation. – But "I impress it on myself" can only mean: this process brings it about that I remember the connexion *right* in the future. But in the present case I have no criterion of correctness. One would like to say: whatever is going to seem right to me is right. And that only means that here we can't talk about 'right'.

259. Are the rules of the private language *impressions* of rules? – The balance on which impressions are weighed is not the *impression* of a balance.

260. "Well, I *believe* that this is the sensation S again." – Perhaps you *believe* that you believe it!

Then did the man who made the entry in the calendar make a note of *nothing whatever*? – Don't consider it a matter of course that a person is making a note of something when he makes a mark – say in a calendar. For a note has a function, and this "S" so far has none.

(One can talk to oneself. – If a person speaks when no one else is present, does that mean he is speaking to himself?)

261. What reason have we for calling "S" the sign for a *sensation*? For "sensation" is a word of our common language, not of one intelligible to me alone. So the use of this word stands in need of a justification which everybody understands. – And it would not help either to say that it need not be a *sensation*; that when he writes "S", he has *something* – and that is all that can be said. "Has" and "something" also belong to our common language. – So in the end when one is doing philosophy one gets to the point where one would like just to emit an inarticulate sound. – But such a sound is an expression only as it occurs in a particular language-game, which should now be described.

262. It might be said: if you have given yourself a private definition of a word, then you must inwardly *undertake* to use the word in such-and-such a way. And how do you undertake that? Is it to be assumed that you invent the technique of using the word; or that you found it ready-made?

263. "But I can (inwardly) undertake to call THIS 'pain' in the future." – "But is it certain that you have undertaken it? Are you sure that it was enough for this purpose to concentrate your attention on your feeling?" – A queer question. –

264. "Once you know *what* the word stands for, you understand it, you know its whole use."

265. Let us imagine a table (something like a dictionary) that exists only in our imagination. A dictionary can be used to justify the translation of a word X by a word Y. But are we also to call it a justification if such a table is to be looked up only in the imagination? – "Well, yes; then it is a subjective justification." – But justification consists in appealing to something independent. – "But surely I can appeal from one memory to another. For example, I don't know if I have remembered the time of depar-

ture of a train right and to check it I call to mind how a page of the time-table looked. Isn't it the same here?" – No; for this process has got to produce a memory which is actually *correct*. If the mental image of the time-table could not itself be *tested* for correctness, how could it confirm the correctness of the first memory? (As if someone were to buy several copies of the morning paper to assure himself that what it said was true.)

Looking up a table in the imagination is no more looking up a table than the image of the result of an imagined experiment is the result of an experiment.

266. I can look at the clock to see what time it is: but I can also look at the dial of a clock in order to *guess* what time it is; or for the same purpose move the hand of a clock till its position strikes me as right. So the look of a clock may serve to determine the time in more than one way. (Looking at the clock in imagination.)

267. Suppose I wanted to justify the choice of dimensions for a bridge which I imagine to be building, by making loading tests on the material of the bridge in my imagination. This would, of course, be to imagine what is called justifying the choice of dimensions for a bridge. But should we also call it justifying an imagined choice of dimensions?

268. Why can't my right hand give my left hand money? – My right hand can put it into my left hand. My right hand can write a deed of gift and my left hand a receipt. – But the further practical consequences would not be those of a gift. When the left hand has taken the money from the right, etc., we shall ask: "Well, and what of it?" And the same could be asked if a person had given himself a private definition of a word; I mean, if he has said the word to himself and at the same time has directed his attention to a sensation.

269. Let us remember that there are certain criteria in a man's behaviour for the fact that he does not understand a word: that it means nothing to him, that he can do nothing with it. And criteria for his 'thinking he understands', attaching some meaning to the word, but not the right one. And, lastly, criteria for his understanding the word right. In the second case one might speak of a subjective understanding. And sounds which no one else understands but which I '*appear to understand*' might be called a "private language".

270. Let us now imagine a use for the entry of the sign "S" in my diary. I discover that whenever I have a particular sensation a manometer shews that my blood-pressure rises. So I shall be able to say that my blood-pressure is rising without using any apparatus. This is a useful result. And now it seems quite indifferent whether I have recognized the sensation *right* or not. Let us suppose I regularly identify it wrong, it does not matter in the least. And that alone shews that the hypothesis that I make a mistake is mere show. (We as it were turned a knob which looked as if it could be used to turn on some part of the machine; but it was a mere ornament, not con-nected with the mechanism at all.)

And what is our reason for calling "S" the name of a sensation here? Perhaps the kind of way this sign is employed in this language-game. – And why a "particular sensation," that is, the same one every time? Well, aren't we supposing that we write "S" every time?

271. "Imagine a person whose memory could not retain *what* the word 'pain' meant – so that he constantly called different things by that name – but nevertheless used the word in a way fitting in with the usual symptoms and presuppositions of pain" – in short he uses it as we all do. Here I should like to say: a wheel that can be turned though nothing else moves with it, is not part of the mechanism.

272. The essential thing about private experience is really not that each person possesses his own exemplar, but that nobody knows whether other people also have *this* or something else. The assumption would thus be possible – though unverifiable – that one section of mankind had one sensation of red and another section another.

273. What am I to say about the word "red"? – that it means some-thing 'confronting us all' and that everyone should really have another word, besides this one, to mean his *own* sensation of red? Or is it like this: the word "red" means something known to everyone; and in addition, for each person, it means something known only to him? (Or perhaps rather: it *refers* to something known only to him.)

274. Of course, saying that the word "red" "refers to" instead of "means" something private does not help us in the least to grasp its func-tion; but it is the more psychologically apt expression for a particular expe-rience in doing philosophy. It is as if when I uttered the word I cast a side-long glance at the private sensation, as it were in order to say to myself: I know all right what I mean by it.

275. Look at the blue of the sky and say to yourself "How blue the sky is!" – When you do it spontaneously – without philosophical intentions – the idea never crosses your mind that this impression of colour belongs only to *you*. And you have no hesitation in exclaiming that to someone else. And if you point at anything as you say the words you point at the sky. I am saying: you have not the feeling of pointing-into-yourself, which often accompanies 'naming the sensation' when one is thinking about 'private language'. Nor do you think that really you ought not to point to the colour with your hand, but with your attention. (Consider what it means "to point to something with the attention".)

276. But don't we at least *mean* something quite definite when we look at a colour and name our colour-impression? It is as if we detached the colour-*impression* from the object, like a membrane. (This ought to arouse our suspicions.)

277. But how is it even possible for us to be tempted to think that we use a word to *mean* at one time the colour known to everyone – and at another the "visual impression" which I am getting *now*? How can there be so much as a temptation here? – I don't turn the same kind of attention on the colour in the two cases. When I mean the colour impression that (as I should like to say) belongs to me alone I immerse myself in the colour – rather like when I 'cannot get my fill of a colour'. Hence it is easier to produce this experience when one is looking at a bright colour, or at an impressive colour-scheme.

278. "I know how the colour green looks to *me*" – surely that makes sense! – Certainly: what use of the proposition are you thinking of?

279. Imagine someone saying: "But I know how tall I am!" and laying his hand on top of his head to prove it.

280. Someone paints a picture in order to shew how he imagines a theatre scene. And now I say: "This picture has a double function: it informs others, as pictures or words inform – but for the one who gives the information it is a representation (or piece of information?) of another kind: for him it is the picture of his image, as it can't be for anyone else. To him his private impression of the picture means what he has imagined, in a sense in which the picture cannot mean this to others." – And what right have I to speak in this second case of a representation or piece of information – if these words were rightly used in the *first* case?

281. "But doesn't what you say come to this: that there is no pain, for example, without *pain-behaviour*"? – It comes to this: only of a living human being and what resembles (behaves like) a living human being can one say: it has sensations; it sees; is blind; hears; is deaf; is conscious or unconscious.

282. "But in a fairy tale the pot too can see and hear!" (Certainly; but it *can* also talk.)

"But the fairy tale only invents what is not the case: it does not talk *nonsense*." – It is not as simple as that. Is it false or nonsensical to say that a pot talks? Have we a clear picture of the circumstances in which we should say of a pot that it talked? (Even a nonsense-poem is not nonsense in the same way as the babbling of a child.)

We do indeed say of an inanimate thing that it is in pain: when playing with dolls for example. But this use of the concept of pain is a secondary one. Imagine a case in which people ascribed pain *only* to inanimate things; pitied *only* dolls! (When children play at trains their game is connected with their knowledge of trains. It would nevertheless be possible for the children of a tribe unacquainted with trains to learn this game from others, and to play it without knowing that it was copied from anything. One might say that the game did not make the same *sense* to them as to us.)

283. What gives us *so much as the idea* that living beings, things, can feel?

Is it that my education has led me to it by drawing my attention to feelings in myself, and now I transfer the idea to objects outside myself? That I recognize that there is something there (in me) which I can call "pain" without getting into conflict with the way other people use this word? – I do not transfer my idea to stones, plants, etc.

Couldn't I imagine having frightful pains and turning to stone while they lasted? Well, how do I know, if I shut my eyes, whether I have not turned into a stone? And if that has happened, in what sense will *the stone* have the pains? In what sense will they be ascribable to the stone? And why need the pain have a bearer at all here?!!

And can one say of the stone that it has a soul and *that* is what has the pain? What has a soul, or pain, to do with a stone?

Only of what behaves like a human being can one say that it *has* pains.

For one has to say it of a body, or, if you like of a soul which some body *has*. And how can a body *have* a soul?

284. Look at a stone and imagine it having sensations. – One says to oneself: How could one so much as get the idea of ascribing a *sensation* to a *thing*? One might as well ascribe it to a number! – And now look at a wriggling fly and at once these difficulties vanish and pain seems able to get a foothold here, where before everything was, so to speak, too smooth for it.

And so, too, a corpse seems to us quite inaccessible to pain. – Our attitude to what is alive and to what is dead, is not the same. All our reactions are different. – If anyone says: "That cannot simply come from the fact that a living thing moves about in such-and-such a way and a dead one not," then I want to intimate to him that this is a case of the transition "from quantity to quality."

285. Think of the recognition of *facial expressions*. Or of the description of facial expressions – which does not consist in giving the measurements of the face! Think, too, how one can imitate a man's face without seeing one's own in a mirror.

286. But isn't it absurd to say of a *body* that it has pain? – And why does one feel an absurdity in that? In what sense is it true that my hand does not feel pain, but I in my hand?

What sort of issue is: Is it the *body* that feels pain? – How is it to be decided? What makes it plausible to say that it is *not* the body? – Well, something like this: if someone has a pain in his hand, then the hand does not say so (unless it writes it) and one does not comfort the hand, but the sufferer: one looks into his face.

287. How am I filled with pity *for this man*? How does it come out what the object of my pity is? (Pity, one may say, is a form of conviction that someone else is in pain.)

288. I turn to stone and my pain goes on. – Suppose I were in error and it was no longer *pain*? – But I can't be in error here; it means nothing to doubt whether I am in pain! – That means: if anyone said "I do not know if what I have got is a pain or something else," we should think something like, he does not know what the English word "pain" means; and we should explain it to him. – How? Perhaps by means of gestures, or by pricking him with a pin and saying: "See, that's what pain is!" This explanation, like any other, he might understand right, wrong, or not at all. And he will shew which he does by his use of the word, in this as in other cases.

If he now said, for example: "Oh, I know what 'pain' means; what I don't know is whether *this*, that I have now, is pain" – we should merely shake our heads and be forced to regard his words as a queer reaction which we have no idea what to do with. (It would be rather as if we heard some-one say seriously: "I distinctly remember that some time before I was born I believed....")

That expression of doubt has no place in the language-game; but if we cut out human behaviour, which is the expression of sensation, it looks as if I might *legitimately* begin to doubt afresh. My temptation to say that one might take a sensation for something other than what it is arises from this: if I assume the abrogation of the normal language-game with the expression of a sensation, I need a criterion of identity for the sensation; and then the possibility of error also exists.

289. "When I say 'I am in pain' I am at any rate justified *before myself*." – What does that mean? Does it mean: "If someone else could know what I am calling 'pain,' he would admit that I was using the word correctly"?

To use a word without a justification does not mean to use it without right.

290. What I do is not, of course, to identify my sensation by criteria: but to repeat an expression. But this is not the *end* of the language-game: it is the beginning.

But isn't the beginning the sensation – which I describe? – Perhaps this word "describe" tricks us here. I say "I describe my state of mind" and "I describe my room". You need to call to mind the differences between the language-games.

291. What we call "*descriptions*" are instruments for particular uses. Think of a machine-drawing, a cross-section, an elevation with measurements, which an engineer has before him. Thinking of a description as a word-picture of the facts has something misleading about it: one tends to think only of such pictures as hang on our walls: which seem simply to portray how a thing looks, what it is like. (These pictures are as it were idle.)

292. Don't always think that you read off what you say from the facts; that you portray these in words according to rules. For even so you would have to apply the rule in the particular case without guidance.

293. If I say of myself that it is only from my own case that I know what the word "pain" means – must I not say the same of other people too? And how can I generalize the one case so irresponsibly?

Now someone tells me that *he* knows what pain is only from his own case! – Suppose everyone had a box with something in it: we call it a "beetle". No one can look into anyone else's box, and everyone says he knows what a beetle is only by looking at *his* beetle. – Here it would be quite possible for everyone to have something different in his box. One might even imagine such a thing constantly changing – But suppose the word "beetle" had a use in these people's language? – If so it would not be used as the name of a thing. The thing in the box has no place in the language-game at all; not even as a *something*: for the box might even be empty. – No, one can 'divide through' by the thing in the box; it cancels out, whatever it is.

That is to say: if we construe the grammar of the expression of sensation on the model of 'object and designation' the object drops out of consideration as irrelevant.

294. If you say he sees a private picture before him, which he is describing, you have still made an assumption about what he has before him. And that means that you can describe it or do describe it more closely. If you admit that you haven't any notion what kind of thing it might be that he has before him – then what leads you into saying, in spite of that, that he has something before him? Isn't it as if I were to say of someone: "He *has* something. But I don't know whether it is money, or debts, or an empty till."

295. "I know ... only from my *own* case" – what kind of proposition is this meant to be at all? An experiential one? No. – A grammatical one?

Suppose everyone does say about himself that he knows what pain is only from his own pain. – Not that people really say that, or are even prepared to say it. But *if* everybody said it – it might be a kind of exclamation. And even if it gives no information, still it is a picture, and why should we not want to call up such a picture? Imagine an allegorical painting take the place of those words.

When we look into ourselves as we do philosophy, we often get to see just such a picture. A full-blown pictorial representation of our grammar. Not facts; but as it were illustrated turns of speech.

296. "Yes, but there is *something* there all the same accompanying my cry of pain. And it is on account of that that I utter it. And this something is what is important – and frightful." – Only whom are we informing of this? And on what occasion?

297. Of course, if water boils in a pot, steam comes out of the pot and also pictured steam comes out of the pictured pot. But what if one insisted on saying that there must also be something boiling in the picture of the pot?

298. The very fact that we should so much like to say: "*This* is the important thing" – while we point privately to the sensation – is enough to shew how much we are inclined to say something which gives no information.

299. Being unable – when we surrender ourselves to philosophical thought – to help saying such-and-such; being irresistibly inclined to say it – does not mean being forced into an *assumption*, or having an immediate perception or knowledge of a state of affairs.

300. It is – we should like to say – not merely the picture of the behaviour that plays a part in the language game with the words "he is in pain", but also the picture of the pain. Or, not merely the paradigm of the behaviour, but also that of the pain. – It is a misunderstanding to say "The picture of pain enters into the language-game with the word 'pain'." The image of pain is not a picture and *this* image is not replaceable in the language-game by anything that we should call a picture. – The image of pain certainly enters into the language game in a sense; only not as a picture.

301. An image is not a picture, but a picture can correspond to it.

302. If one has to imagine someone else's pain on the model of one's own, this is none too easy a thing to do: for I have to imagine pain which I *do not feel* on the model of the pain which I *do feel*. That is, what I have to do is not simply to make a transition in imagination from one place of pain to another. As, from pain in the hand to pain in the arm. For I am not to imagine that I feel pain in some region of his body. (Which would also be possible.)

Pain-behaviour can point to a painful place – but the subject of pain is the person who gives it expression.

303. "I can only *believe* that that someone else is in pain, but I *know* it if I am". – Yes: one can make the decision to say "I believe he is in pain" instead of "He is in pain." But that is all. – What looks like an explanation here, or like a statement about a mental process, is in truth an exchange of one expression for another which, while we are doing philosophy, seems the more appropriate one.

Just try – in a real case – to doubt someone else's fear or pain.

304. "But you will surely admit that there is a difference between pain-behaviour accompanied by pain and pain-behaviour without any pain?" – Admit it? What greater difference could there be? – "And yet you again and again reach the conclusion that the sensation itself is a *nothing*." – Not at all. It is not a *something*, but not a *nothing* either! The conclusion was only that a nothing would serve just as well as a something about which nothing could be said. We have only rejected the grammar which tries to force itself on us here.

The paradox disappears only if we make a radical break with the idea that language always functions in one way, always serves the same purpose: to convey thoughts – which may be about houses, pains, good and evil, or anything else you please.

305. "But you surely cannot deny that, for example, in remembering, an inner process takes place." – What gives the impression that we want to deny anything? When one says "Still, an inner process does take place here" – one wants to go on: "After all, you *see* it." And it is this inner process that one means by the word "remembering". – The impression that we wanted to deny something arises from our setting our faces against the picture of the 'inner process'. What we deny is that the picture of the inner process gives us the correct idea of the use of the word "to remember". We say that this picture with its ramifications stands in the way of our seeing the use of the word as it is.

306. Why should I deny that there is a mental process? But "There has just taken place in me the mental process of remembering ..." means nothing more than: "I have just remembered ...". To deny the mental process would mean to deny the remembering; to deny that anyone ever remembers anything.

307. "Are you not really a behaviourist in disguise? Aren't you at bottom really saying that everything except human behaviour is a fiction?" – If I do speak of a fiction, then it is of a *grammatical* fiction.

308. How does the philosophical problem about mental processes and states and about behaviourism arise? – The first step is the one that altogether escapes notice. We talk of processes and states and leave their nature undecided. Sometime perhaps we shall know more about them – we think. But that is just what commits us to a particular way of looking at the matter. For we have a definite concept of what it means to learn to know a process better. (The decisive movement in the conjuring trick has been made, and it was the very one that we thought quite innocent.) – And now the analogy which was to make us understand our thoughts falls to pieces. So we have to deny the yet uncomprehended process in the yet unexplored medium. And now it looks as if we had denied mental processes. And naturally we don't want to deny them.

309. What is your aim in philosophy? – To shew the fly the way out of the fly-bottle.

310. I tell someone I am in pain. His attitude to me will then be that of belief; disbelief; suspicion; and so on. Let us assume he says: "It's not so bad." – Doesn't that prove that he believes in something behind the outward expression of pain? – His attitude is a proof of his attitude. Imagine not merely the words "I am in pain" but also the answer "It's not so bad" replaced by instinctive noises and gestures.

311. "What difference could be greater?" – In the case of pain I believe that I can give myself a private exhibition of the difference. But I can give anyone an exhibition of the difference between a broken and an unbroken tooth. – But for the private exhibition you don't have to give yourself actual pain; it is enough to *imagine* it – for instance, you screw up your face a bit. And do you know that what you are giving yourself this exhibition of is pain and not, for example, a facial expression? And how do you know what you are to give yourself an exhibition of before you do it? This *private* exhibition is an illusion.

312. But again, *aren't* the cases of the tooth and the pain similar? For the visual sensation in the one corresponds to the sensation of pain in the other. I can exhibit the visual sensation to myself as little or as well as the sensation of pain.

Let us imagine the following: The surfaces of the things around us (stones, plants, etc.) have patches and regions which produce pain in our skin when we touch them. (Perhaps through the chemical composition of these surfaces. But we need not know that.) In this case we should speak of pain-patches on the leaf of a particular plant just as at present we speak of red patches. I am supposing that it is useful to us to notice these patches and their shapes; that we can infer important properties of the objects from them.

313. I can exhibit pain, as I exhibit red, and as I exhibit straight and crooked and trees and stones. – *That* is what we *call* "exhibiting".

314. It shews a fundamental misunderstanding, if I am inclined to study the headache I have now in order to get clear about the philosophical problem of sensation.

315. Could someone understand the word "pain", who had *never* felt pain? – Is experience to teach me whether this is so or not? – And if we say "A man could not imagine pain without having sometime felt it" – how do we know? How can it be decided whether it is true?...

NOTES

(a) "Understanding a word": a state. But a *mental* state? – Depression, excitement, pain, are called mental states. Carry out a grammatical investigation as follows: we say "He was depressed the whole day." "He was in great excitement the whole day." "He has been in continuous pain since yesterday." – We also say "Since yesterday I have understood this word." "Continuously," though? – To be sure, one can speak of an interruption of understanding. But in what cases? Compare: "When did your pains get less?" and "When did you stop understanding that word?"

(b) "Suppose it were asked: "*When* do you know how to play chess? All the time? or just while you are making a move? And the *whole* of chess during each move? – How queer that knowing how to play chess should take such a short time, and a game so much longer!

III

Language and Speakers (The Use Perspective)

Speech Acts

PERFORMATIVE UTTERANCES

John L. Austin

I

You are more than entitled not to know what the word "performative" means. It is a new word and an ugly word, and perhaps it does not mean anything very much. But at any rate there is one thing in its favor, it is not a profound word. I remember once when I had been talking on this subject that somebody afterwards said: "You know, I haven't the least idea what he means, unless it could be that he simply means what he says." Well, that is what I should like to mean.

Let us consider first how this affair arises. We have not got to go very far back in the history of philosophy to find philosophers assuming more or less as a matter of course that the sole business, the sole interesting business, of any utterance – that is, of anything we say – is to be true or at least false. Of course they had always known that there are other kinds of things which we say – things like imperatives, the expressions of wishes, and exclamations – some of which had even been classified by grammarians, though it wasn't perhaps too easy to tell always which was which. But still philosophers have assumed that the only things that they are interested in are utterances which report facts or which describe situations truly or falsely. In recent times this kind of approach has been questioned – in two stages, I think. First of all people began to say: "Well, if these things are true or false it ought to be possible to decide which they are, and if we can't decide which they are they aren't any good but are, in short, nonsense." And this new approach did a great deal of good; a great many things which probably are nonsense were found to be such. It is not the case, I think, that all kinds of nonsense have been adequately classified yet, and perhaps some things have been dismissed as nonsense which really are not; but still this movement, the verification movement, was, in its way, excellent.

However, we then come to the second stage. After all, we set some limits to the amount of nonsense that we talk, or at least the amount of nonsense that we are prepared to admit we talk; and so people began to ask whether after all some of those things which, treated as statements, were in danger of being dismissed as nonsense did after all really set out to be statements at all. Mightn't they perhaps be intended not to report facts but to influence people in this way or that, or to let off steam in this way or that? Or perhaps at any rate some elements in these utterances performed such functions, or, for example, drew attention in some way (without actually reporting it) to some important feature of the circumstances in which the utterance was being made. On these lines people have now adopted a new slogan, the slogan of the "different uses of language." The old approach, the old statemental approach, is sometimes called even a fallacy, the descriptive fallacy.

Certainly there are a great many uses of language. It's rather a pity that people are apt to invoke a new use of language whenever they feel so inclined, to help them out of this, that, or the other well-known philosophical tangle; we need more of a framework in which to discuss these uses of language; and also I think we should not despair too easily and talk, as people are apt to do, about the *infinite* uses of language. Philosophers will do this when they have listed as many, let us say, as seventeen; but even if there were something like ten thousand uses of language, surely we could list them all in time. This, after all, is no larger than the number of species of beetle that entomologists have taken the pains to list. But whatever the defects of either of these movements – the "verification" movement or the "use of language" movement – at any rate they have effected, nobody could deny, a great revolution in philosophy and, many would say, the most salutary in its history. (Not, if you come to think of it, a very immodest claim.)

Now it is one such sort of use of language that I want to examine here. I want to discuss a kind of utterance which looks like a statement and grammatically, I suppose, would be classed as a statement, which is not nonsensical, and yet is not true or false. These are not going to be utterances which contain curious verbs like "could" or "might," or curious words like "good," which many philosophers regard nowadays simply as danger signals. They will be perfectly straightforward utterances, with ordinary verbs in the first person singular present indicative active, and yet we shall see at once that they couldn't possibly be true or false. Furthermore, if a person makes an utterance of this sort we should say that he is *doing* something rather than merely *saying* something. This may sound a little odd, but the examples I shall give will in fact not be odd at all, and may even seem decidedly dull. Here are three or four. Suppose, for example, that in the course of a marriage ceremony I say, as people will, "I do" – (sc. take this woman to be my lawful wedded wife). Or again, suppose that I tread on your toe and say

"I apologize." Or again, suppose that I have the bottle of champagne in my hand and say "I name this ship the *Queen Elizabeth*." Or suppose I say "I bet you sixpence it will rain tomorrow." In all these cases it would be absurd to regard the thing that I say as a report of the performance of the action which is undoubtedly done – the action of betting, or christening, or apologizing. We should say rather that, in saying what I do, I actually perform that action. When I say "I name this ship the *Queen Elizabeth*" I do not describe the christening ceremony, I actually perform the christening; and when I say "I do" (sc. take this woman to be my lawful wedded wife), I am not reporting on a marriage, I am indulging in it.

Now these kinds of utterance are the ones that we call *performative* utterances. This is rather an ugly word, and a new word, but there seems to be no word already in existence to do the job. The nearest approach that I can think of is the word "operative," as used by lawyers. Lawyers when talking about legal instruments will distinguish between the preamble, which recites the circumstances in which a transaction is effected, and on the other hand the operative part – the part of it which actually performs the legal act which it is the purpose of the instrument to perform. So the word "operative" is very near to what we want. "I give and bequeath my watch to my brother" would be an operative clause and is a performative utterance. However, the word "operative" has other uses, and it seems preferable to have a word specially designed for the use we want.

Now at this point one might protest, perhaps even with some alarm, that I seem to be suggesting that marrying is simply saying a few words, that just saying a few words *is* marrying. Well, that certainly is not the case. The words have to be said in the appropriate circumstances, and this is a matter that will come up again later. But the one thing we must not suppose is that what is needed in addition to the saying of the words in such cases is the performance of some internal spiritual act, of which the words then are to be the report. It's very easy to slip into this view at least in difficult, portentous cases, though perhaps not so easy in simple cases like apologizing. In the case of promising – for example, "I promise to be there tomorrow" – it's very easy to think that the utterance is simply the outward and visible (that is, verbal) sign of the performance of some inward spiritual act of promising, and this view has certainly been expressed in many classic places. There is the case of Euripides' Hippolytus, who said "My tongue swore to, but my heart did not" – perhaps it should be "mind" or "spirit" rather than "heart," but at any rate some kind of backstage artiste. Now it is clear from this sort of example that, if we slip into thinking that such utterances are reports, true or false, of the performance of inward and spiritual acts, we open a loophole to perjurers and welshers and bigamists and so on, so that there are disadvantages in being excessively solemn in this way. It is better, perhaps, to stick to the old saying that our word is our bond.

However, although these utterances do not themselves report facts and are not themselves true or false, saying these things does very often *imply* that certain things are true and not false, in some sense at least of that rather woolly word "imply." For example, when I say "I do take this woman to be my lawful wedded wife," or some other formula in the marriage cere-mony, I do imply that I'm not already married, with wife living, sane, undi-vorced, and the rest of it. But still it is very important to realize that to imply that something or other is true, is not at all the same as saying something which is true itself.

These performative utterances are not true or false, then. But they do suffer from certain disabilities of their own. They can fail to come off in special ways, and that is what I want to consider next. The various ways in which a performative utterance may be unsatisfactory we call, for the sake of a name, the infelicities; and an infelicity arises – that is to say, the utter-ance is unhappy – if certain rules, transparently simple rules, are broken. I will mention some of these rules and then give examples of some infringe-ments.

First of all, it is obvious that the conventional procedure which by our utterance we are purporting to use must actually exist. In the examples given here this procedure will be a verbal one, a verbal procedure for mar-rying or giving or whatever it may be; but it should be borne in mind that there are many nonverbal procedures by which we can perform exactly the same acts as we perform by these verbal means. It's worth remembering too that a great many of the things we do are at least in part of this conventional kind. Philosophers at least are too apt to assume that an action is always in the last resort the making of a physical movement, whereas it's usually, at least in part, a matter of convention.

The first rule is, then, that the convention invoked must exist and be accepted. And the second rule, also a very obvious one, is that the cir-cumstances in which we purport to invoke this procedure must be appro-priate for its invocation. If this is not observed, then the act that we purport to perform would not come off – it will be, one might say, a misfire. This will also be the case if, for example, we do not carry through the procedure – whatever it may be – correctly and completely, without a flaw and without a hitch. If any of these rules are not observed, we say that the act which we purported to perform is void, without effect. If, for example, the purported act was an act of marrying, then we should say that we "went through a form" of marriage, but we did not actually succeed in marrying.

Here are some examples of this kind of misfire. Suppose that, liv-ing in a country like our own, we wish to divorce our wife. We may try standing her in front of us squarely in the room and saying, in a voice loud enough for all to hear, "I divorce you." Now this procedure is not accepted. We shall not thereby have succeeded in divorcing our wife, at least in this country and others like it. This is a case where the convention, we should say, does not exist or is not accepted. Again, suppose that, picking sides at a children's party, I say "I pick George." But George turns red in the face and says "Not playing." In that case I plainly, for some reason or another, have not picked George – whether because there is no convention that you can pick people who aren't playing, or because George in the circumstances is an inappropriate object for the procedure of picking. Or consider the case in which I say "I appoint you Consul," and it turns out that you have been appointed already – or perhaps it may even transpire that you are a horse; here again we have the infelicity of inappropriate circumstances, inappropriate objects, or what not. Examples of flaws and hitches are perhaps scarcely necessary – one party in the marriage ceremony says "I will," the other says "I won't"; I say "I bet sixpence," but nobody says "Done," nobody takes up the offer. In all these and other such cases, the act which we purport to perform, or set out to perform, is not achieved.

But there is another and a rather different way in which this kind of utterance may go wrong. A good many of these verbal procedures are designed for use by people who hold certain beliefs or have certain feelings or intentions. And if you use one of these formulae when you do not have the requisite thoughts or feelings or intentions then there is an abuse of the procedure, there is insincerity. Take, for example, the expression, "I congratulate you." This is designed for use by people who are glad that the person addressed has achieved a certain feat, believe that he was personally responsible for the success, and so on. If I say "I congratulate you" when I'm not pleased or when I don't believe that the credit was yours, then there is insincerity. Likewise if I say I promise to do something, without having the least intention of doing it or without believing it feasible. In these cases there is something wrong certainly, but it is not like a misfire. We should not say that I didn't in fact promise, but rather that I did promise but promised insincerely; I did congratulate you but the congratulations were hollow. And there may be an infelicity of a somewhat similar kind when the performative utterance commits the speaker to future conduct of a certain description and then in the future he does not in fact behave in the expected way. This is very obvious, of course, if I promise to do something and then break my promise, but there are many kinds of commitment of a rather less tangible form than that in the case of promising. For instance, I may say "I welcome you," bidding you welcome to my home or wherever it may be, but then I proceed to treat you as though you were exceedingly unwelcome. In this case the procedure of saying "I welcome you" has been abused in a way rather different from that of simple insincerity.

Now we might ask whether this list of infelicities is complete, whether the kinds of infelicity are mutually exclusive, and so forth. Well, it is not complete, and they are not mutually exclusive; they never are.

Suppose that you are just about to name the ship, you have been appointed to name it, and you are just about to bang the bottle against the stem; but at that very moment some low type comes up, snatches the bottle out of your hand, breaks it on the stem, shouts out "I name this ship the *Generalissimo Stalin*," and then for good measure kicks away the chocks. Well, we agree of course on several things. We agree that the ship certainly isn't now named the *Generalissimo Stalin*, and we agree that it's an infernal shame and so on and so forth. But we may not agree as to how we should classify the particular infelicity in this case. We might say that here is a case of a perfectly legitimate and agreed procedure which, however, has been invoked in the wrong circumstances, namely by the wrong person, this low type instead of the person appointed to do it. But on the other hand we might look at it differently and say that this is a case where the procedure has not as a whole been gone through correctly, because part of the procedure for naming a ship is that you should first of all get yourself appointed as the person to do the naming and that's what this fellow did not do. Thus the way we should classify infelicities in different cases will be perhaps rather a difficult matter, and may even in the last resort be a bit arbitrary. But of course lawyers, who have to deal very much with this kind of thing, have invented all kinds of technical terms and have made numerous rules about different kinds of cases, which enable them to classify fairly rapidly what in particular is wrong in any given case.

As for whether this list is complete, it certainly is not. One further way in which things may go wrong is, for example, through what in general may be called misunderstanding. You may not hear what I say, or you may understand me to refer to something different from what I intended to refer to, and so on. And apart from further additions which we might make to the list, there is the general overriding consideration that, as we are performing an act when we issue these performative utterances, we may of course be doing so under duress or in some other circumstances which make us not entirely responsible for doing what we are doing. That would certainly be an unhappiness of a kind – any kind of nonresponsibilty might be called an unhappiness; but of course it is a quite different kind of thing from what we have been talking about. And I might mention that, quite differently again, we could be issuing any of these utterances, as we can issue an utterance of any kind whatsoever, in the course, for example, of acting a play or making a joke or writing a poem – in which case of course it would not be seriously meant and we shall not be able to say that we seriously performed the act concerned. If the poet says "Go and catch a falling star" or whatever it may be, he doesn't seriously issue an order. Considerations of this kind apply to any utterance at all, not merely to performatives.

That, then, is perhaps enough to be going on with. We have discussed the performative utterance and its infelicities. That equips us, we may suppose, with two shining new tools to crack the crib of reality maybe. It also equips us – it always does – with two shining new skids under our metaphysical feet. The question is how we use them.

II

So far we have been going firmly ahead, feeling the firm ground of prejudice glide away beneath our feet which is always rather exhilarating, but what next? You will be waiting for the bit when we bog down, the bit where we take it all back, and sure enough that's going to come but it will take time. First of all let us ask a rather simple question. How can we be sure, how can we tell, whether any utterance is to be classed as a performative or not? Surely, we feel, we ought to be able to do that. And we should obviously very much like to be able to say that there is a grammatical criterion for this, some grammatical means of deciding whether an utterance is performative. All the examples I have given hitherto do in fact have the same grammatical form; they all of them begin with the verb in the first person singular present indicative active – not just any kind of verb of course, but still they all are in fact of that form. Furthermore, with these verbs that I have used there is a typical asymmetry between the use of this person and tense of the verb and the use of the same verb in other persons and other tenses, and this asymmetry is rather an important clue.

For example, when we say "I promise that ...," the case is very different from when we say "He promises that ...," or in the past tense "I promised that...." For when we say "I promise that ..." we do perform an act of promising – we give a promise. What we do *not* do is to report on somebody's performing an act of promising – in particular, we do not report on somebody's use of the expression "I promise." We actually do use it and do the promising. But if I say "He promises," or in the past tense "I promised," I precisely do report on an act of promising, that is to say an act of using this formula "I promise" – I report on a present act of promising by him, or on a past act of my own. There is thus a clear difference between our first person singular present indicative active, and other persons and tenses. This is brought out by the typical incident of little Willie whose uncle says he'll give him half-a-crown if he promises never to smoke till he's 55. Little Willie's anxious parent will say "Of course he promises, don't you, Willie?" giving him a nudge, and little Willie just doesn't vouchsafe. The point here is that he must do the promising himself by saying "I promise," and his parent is going too fast in saying he promises.

That, then, is a bit of a test for whether an utterance is perfomative or not, but it would not do to suppose that every performative utterance has to take this standard form. There is at least one other standard form, every bit as common as this one, where the verb is in the passive voice and in the second or third person, not in the first. The sort of case I mean is that of a notice inscribed "Passengers are warned to cross the line by the bridge only," or of a document reading "You are hereby authorized" to do so-and-so. These are undoubtedly performative, and in fact a signature is often required in order to show who it is that is doing the act of warning, or authorizing, or whatever it may be. Very typical of this kind of perfomative – especially liable to occur in written documents of course – is that the little word "hereby" either actually occurs or might naturally be inserted.

Unfortunately, however, we still can't possibly suggest that every utterance which is to be classed as a performative has to take one or another of these two, as we might call them, standard forms. After all it would be a very typical performative utterance to say "I order you to shut the door." This satisfies all the criteria. It is performing the act of ordering you to shut the door, and it is not true or false. But in the appropriate circumstances surely we could perform exactly the same act by simply saying "Shut the door," in the imperative. Or again, suppose that somebody sticks up a notice "This bull is dangerous," or simply "Dangerous bull," or simply "Bull." Does this necessarily differ from sticking up a notice, appropriately signed, saying "You are hereby warned that this bull is dangerous"? It seems that the simple notice "Bull" can do just the same job as the more elaborate formula. Of course the difference is that if we just stick up "Bull" it would not be quite clear that it is a warning; it might be there just for interest or information, like "Wallaby" on the cage at the zoo, or "Ancient Monument." No doubt we should know from the nature of the case that it was a warning, but it would not be explicit.

Well, in view of this breakdown of grammatical criteria, what we should like to suppose – and there is a good deal in this – is that any utterance which is performative could be reduced or expanded or analysed into one of these two standard forms beginning "I ..." so and so or beginning "You (or he) hereby ..." so and so. If there was any justification for this hope, as to some extent there is, then we might hope to make a list of all the verbs which can appear in these standard forms, and then we might classify the kinds of acts that can be performed by performative utterances. We might do this with the aid of a dictionary, using such a test as that already mentioned – whether there is the characteristic asymmetry between the first person singular present indicative active and the other persons and tenses – in order to decide whether a verb is to go into our list or not. Now if we make such a list of verbs we do in fact find that they fall into certain fairly well-marked classes. There is the class of cases where we deliver verdicts and make estimates and appraisals of various kinds. There is the class where we give undertakings, commit ourselves in various ways by saying something. There is the class where by saying something we exercise various rights and powers, such as appointing and voting and so on. And there are one or two other fairly well-marked classes.

Suppose this task accomplished. Then we could call these verbs in our list explicit performative verbs, and any utterance that was reduced to one or the other of our standard forms we could call an explicit performative utterance. "I order you to shut the door" would be an explicit performative utterance, whereas "Shut the door" would not – that is simply a 'primary' performative utterance or whatever we like to call it. In using the imperative we may be ordering you to shut the door, but it just isn't made clear whether we are ordering you or entreating you or imploring you or beseeching you or inciting you or tempting you, or one or another of many other subtly different acts which, in an unsophisticated primitive language, are very likely not yet discriminated. But we need not overestimate the unsophistication of primitive languages. There are a great many devices that can be used for making clear, even at the primitive level, what act it is we are performing when we say something – the tone of voice, cadence, gesture – and above all we can rely upon the nature of the circumstances, the context in which the utterance is issued. This very often makes it quite unmistakable whether it is an order that is being given or whether, say, I am simply urging you or entreating you. We may, for instance, say something like this: "Coming from him I was bound to take it as an order." Still, in spite of all these devices, there is an unfortunate amount of ambiguity and lack of discrimination in default of our explicit performative verbs. If I say something like "I shall be there," it may not be certain whether it is a promise, or an expression of intention, or perhaps even a forecast of my future behavior, of what is going to happen to me; and it may matter a good deal, at least in developed societies, precisely which of these things it is. And that is why the explicit performative verb is evolved – to make clear exactly which it is, how far it commits me and in what way, and so forth.

This is just one way in which language develops in tune with the society of which it is the language. The social habits of the society may considerably affect the question of which performative verbs are evolved and which, sometimes for rather irrelevant reasons, are not. For example, if I say "You are a poltroon," it might be that I am censuring you or it might be that I am insulting you. Now since apparently society approves of censuring or reprimanding, we have here evolved a formula "I reprimand you," or "I censure you," which enables us expeditiously to get this desirable business over. But on the other hand, since apparently we don't approve of insulting, we have not evolved a simple formula "I insult you," which might have done just as well.

By means of these explicit performative verbs and some other devices, then, we make explicit what precise act it is that we are performing when we issue our utterance. But here I would like to put in a word of warning. We must distinguish between the function of making explicit what act it is we are performing, and the quite different matter of *stating* what act it is we are performing. In issuing an explicit performative utterance we are not stating what act it is, we are showing or making explicit what act it is. We can draw a helpful parallel here with another case in which the act, the conventional act that we perform, is not a speech act but a physical performance. Suppose I appear before you one day and bow deeply from the waist. Well, this is ambiguous. I may be simply observing the local flora, tying my shoelace, something of that kind; on the other hand, conceivably I might be doing obeisance to you. Well, to clear up this ambiguity we have some device such as raising the hat, saying "Salaam," or something of that kind, to make it quite plain that the act being performed is the conventional one of doing obeisance rather than some other act. Now nobody would want to say that lifting your hat was stating that you were performing an act of obeisance; it certainly is not, but it does make it quite plain that you are. And so in the same way to say "I warn you that ..." or "I order you to ..." or "I promise that ..." is not to state that you are doing something, but makes it plain that you are – it does constitute your verbal performance, a performance of a particular kind.

So far we have been going along as though there was a quite clear difference between our performative utterances and what we have contrasted them with, statements or reports or descriptions. But now we begin to find that this distinction is not as clear as it might be. It's now that we begin to sink in a little. In the first place, of course, we may feel doubts as to how widely our performatives extend. If we think up some odd kinds of expression we use in odd cases, we might very well wonder whether or not they satisfy our rather vague criteria for being performative utterances. Suppose, for example, somebody says "Hurrah." Well, not true or false; he is performing the act of cheering. Does that make it a performative utterance in our sense or not? Or suppose he says "Damn"; he is performing the act of swearing, and it is not true or false. Does that make it performative? We feel that in a way it does and yet it's rather different. Again, consider cases of 'suiting the action to the words'; these too may make us wonder whether perhaps the utterance should be classed as performative. Or sometimes, if somebody says "I am sorry," we wonder whether this is just the same as "I apologize" – in which case of course we have said it's a performative utterance – or whether perhaps it's to be taken as a description, true or false, of the state of his feelings. If he had said "I feel perfectly awful about it," then we should think it must be meant to be a description of the state of his feelings. If he had said "I apologize," we should feel this was clearly a performative utterance, going through the ritual of apologizing. But if he says "I am sorry" there is an unfortunate hovering between the two. This phenomenon is quite common. We often find cases in which there is an obvious pure perfomative utterance and obvious other utterances connected with it which are not perfomative but descriptive, but on the other hand a good many in between where we're not quite sure which they are. On some occasions of course they are obviously used the one way, on some occasions the other way, but on some occasions they seem positively to revel in ambiguity.

Again, consider the case of the umpire when he says "Out" or "Over," or the jury's utterance when they say that they find the prisoner guilty. Of course, we say, these are cases of giving verdicts, performing the act of appraising and so forth, but still in a way they have some connection with the facts. They seem to have something like the duty to be true or false, and seem not to be so very remote from statements. If the umpire says "Over," this surely has at least something to do with six balls in fact having been delivered rather than seven, and so on. In fact in general we may remind ourselves that "I state that ..." does not look so very different from "I warn you that ..." or "I promise to...." It makes clear surely that the act that we are performing is an act of stating, and so functions just like 'I warn' or 'I order.' So isn't "I state that ..." a performative utterance? But then one may feel that utterances beginning "I state that ..." do have to be true or false, that they are statements.

Considerations of this sort, then, may well make us feel pretty unhappy. If we look back for a moment at our contrast between statements and performative utterances, we realize that we were taking statements very much on trust from, as we said, the traditional treatment. Statements, we had it, were to be true or false; performative utterances on the other hand were to be felicitous or infelicitous. They were the doing of something, whereas for all we said making statements was not doing something. Now this contrast surely, if we look back at it, is unsatisfactory. Of course statements are liable to be assessed in this matter of their correspondence or failure to correspond with the facts, that is, being true or false. But they are also liable to infelicity every bit as much as are performative utterances. In fact some troubles that have arisen in the study of statements recently can be shown to be simply troubles of infelicity. For example, it has been pointed out that there is something very odd about saying something like this: "The cat is on the mat but I don't believe it is." Now this is an outrageous thing to say, but it is not self-contradictory. There is no reason why the cat shouldn't be on the mat without my believing that it is. So how are we to classify what's wrong with this peculiar statement? If we remember now the doctrine of infelicity we shall see that the person who makes this remark about the cat is in much the same position as somebody who says something like this: "I promise that I shall be there, but I haven't the least intention of being there." Once again you can of course perfectly well promise to be there without having the least intention of being there, but there is something outrageous about saying it, about actually avowing the insincerity of the promise you give. In the same way there is insincerity in the case of the person who says "The cat is on the mat but I don't believe it is," and he is actually avowing that insincerity – which makes a peculiar kind of non-sense.

A second case that has come to light is the one about John's children – the case where somebody is supposed to say "All John's children are bald but John hasn't got any children." Or perhaps somebody says "All John's children are bald," when as a matter of fact – he doesn't say so – John has no children. Now those who study statements have worried about this; ought they to say that the statement "All John's children are bald" is mean-ingless in this case? Well, if it is, it is not a bit like a great many other more standard kinds of meaninglessness; and we see, if we look back at our list of infelicities, that what is going wrong here is much the same as what goes wrong in, say, the case of a contract for the sale of a piece of land when the piece of land referred to does not exist. Now what we say in the case of this sale of land, which of course would be effected by a performative utterance, is that the sale is void – void for lack of reference or ambiguity of reference; and so we can see that the statement about all John's children is likewise void for lack of reference. And if the man actually says that John has no children in the same breath as saying they're all bald, he is making the same kind of outrageous utterance as the man who says "The cat is on the mat and I don't believe it is," or the man who says "I promise to but I don't intend to."

In this way, then, ills that have been found to afflict statements can be precisely paralleled with ills that are characteristic of performative utter-ances. And after all when we state something or describe something or report something, we do perform an act which is every bit as much an act as an act of ordering or warning. There seems no good reason why stating should be given a specially unique position. Of course philosophers have been wont to talk as though you or I or anybody could just go round stating anything about anything and that would be perfectly in order, only there's just a little question: is it true or false? But besides the little question, is it true or false, there is surely the question: is it in order? Can you go round just making statements about anything? Suppose for example you say to me "I'm feeling pretty moldy this morning." Well, I say to you "You're not"; and you say "What the devil do you mean, I'm not?" I say "Oh nothing – I'm just stating you're not, is it true or false?" And you say "Wait a bit about whether it's true or false, the question is what did you mean by making statements about somebody else's feelings? I told you I'm feeling pretty moldy. You're just not in a position to say, to state that I'm not." This brings out that you can't just make statements about other people's feelings (though you can make guesses if you like); and there are very many things which, having no knowledge of, not being in a position to pronounce about, you just can't state. What we need to do for the case of stating, and by the same token describing and reporting, is to take them a bit off their pedestal, to realize that they are speech acts no less than all these other speech acts that we have been mentioning and talking about as performative.

Then let us look for a moment at our original contrast between the performative and the statement from the other side. In handling performatives we have been putting it all the time as though the only thing that a performative utterance had to do was to be felicitous, to come off, not to be a misfire, not to be an abuse. Yes, but that's not the end of the matter. At least in the case of many utterances which, on what we have said, we should have to class as performative – cases where we say "I warn you to...," "I advise you to ..." and so on – there will be other questions besides simply: was it in order, was it all right, as a piece of advice or a warning, did it come off? After that surely there will be the question: was it good or sound advice? Was it a justified warning? Or in the case, let us say, of a verdict or an estimate: was it a good estimate, or a sound verdict? And these are questions that can only be decided by considering how the content of the verdict or estimate is related in some way to fact, or to evidence available about the facts. This is to say that we do require to assess at least a great many performative utterances in a general dimension of correspondence with fact. It may still be said, of course, that this does not make them *very* like statements because still they are not true or false, and that's a little black and white speciality that distinguishes statements as a class apart. But actually – though it would take too long to go on about this – the more you think about truth and falsity the more you find that very few statements that we ever utter are just true or just false. Usually there is the question are they fair or are they not fair, are they adequate or not adequate, are they exaggerated or not exaggerated? Are they too rough, or are they perfectly precise, accurate, and so on? 'True' and 'false' are just general labels for a whole dimension of different appraisals which have something or other to do with the relation between what we say and the facts. If, then, we loosen up our ideas of truth and falsity we shall see that statements, when assessed in relation to the facts, are not so very different after all from pieces of advice, warnings, verdicts, and so on.

We see then that stating something is performing an act just as much as is giving an order or giving a warning; and we see, on the other hand, that, when we give an order or a warning or a piece of advice, there is a question about how this is related to fact which is not perhaps so very different from the kind of question that arises when we discuss how a statement is related to fact. Well, this seems to mean that in its original form our distinction between the perfomative and the statement is considerably weakened, and indeed breaks down. I will just make a suggestion as to how to handle this matter. We need to go very much farther back, to consider all the ways and senses in which saying anything at all is doing this or that – because of course it is always doing a good many different things. And one thing that emerges when we do do this is that, besides the question that has been very much studied in the past as to what a certain utterance *means*, there is a further question distinct from this as to what was the *force*, as we may call it, of the utterance. We may be quite clear what "Shut the door" means, but not yet at all clear on the further point as to whether as uttered at a certain time it was an order, an entreaty, or whatnot. What we need besides the old doctrine about meanings is a new doctrine about all the possible forces of utterances, towards the discovery of which our proposed list of explicit perfomative verbs would be a very great help; and then, going on from there, an investigation of the various terms of appraisal that we use in discussing speech-acts of this, that, or the other precise kind – orders, warnings, and the like.

The notions that we have considered then, are the performative, the infelicity, the explicit performative, and lastly, rather hurriedly, the notion of the forces of utterances. I dare say that all this seems a little unremunerative, a little complicated. Well, I suppose in some ways it is unremunerative, and I suppose it ought to be remunerative. At least, though, I think that if we pay attention to these matters we can clear up some mistakes in philosophy; and after all philosophy is used as a scapegoat, it parades mistakes which are really the mistakes of everybody. We might even clear up some mistakes in grammar, which perhaps is a little more respectable.

And is it complicated? Well, it is complicated a bit; but life and truth and things do tend to be complicated. It's not things, it's philosophers that are simple. You will have heard it said, I expect, that oversimplification is the occupational disease of philosophers, and in a way one might agree with that. But for a sneaking suspicion that it's their occupation.

WHAT IS A SPEECH ACT?

John R. Searle

I. Introduction

In a typical speech situation involving a speaker, a hearer, and an utterance by the speaker, there are many kinds of acts associated with the speaker's utterance. The speaker will characteristically have moved his jaw and tongue and made noises. In addition, he will characteristically have performed some acts within the class which includes informing or irritating or boring his hearers; he will further characteristically have performed acts within the class which includes referring to Kennedy or Khrushchev or the North Pole; and he will also have performed acts within the class which includes making statements, asking questions, issuing commands, giving reports, greeting, and warning. The members of this last class are what Austin[1] called illocutionary acts and it is with this class that I shall be concerned in this paper, so the paper might have been called "What is an Illocutionary Act?" I do not attempt to define the expression 'illocutionary act', although if my analysis of a particular illocutionary act succeeds it may provide the basis for a definition. Some of the English verbs and verb phrases associated with illocutionary acts are: state, assert, describe, warn, remark, comment, command, order, request, criticize, apologize, censure, approve, welcome, promise, express approval, and express regret. Austin claimed that there were over a thousand such expressions in English.

By way of introduction, perhaps I can say why I think it is of interest and importance in the philosophy of language to study speech acts, or, as they are sometimes called, language acts or linguistic acts. I think it is essential to any specimen of linguistic communication that it involve a linguistic act. It is not, as has generally been supposed, the symbol or word or sentence, or even the token of the symbol or word or sentence, which is the unit of linguistic communication, but rather it is the *production* of the token in the performance of the speech act that constitutes the basic unit of linguistic communication. To put this point more precisely, the production of the sentence token under certain conditions is the illocutionary act, and the illocutionary act is the minimal unit of linguistic communication.

I do not know how to *prove* that linguistic communication essentially involves acts but I can think of arguments with which one might attempt to convince someone who was sceptical. One argument would be to call the sceptic's attention to the fact that when he takes a noise or a mark on paper to be an instance of linguistic communication, as a message, one of the things that is involved in his so taking that noise or mark is that he should regard it as having been produced by a being with certain intentions. He cannot just regard it as a natural phenomenon, like a stone, a waterfall, or a tree. In order to regard it as an instance of linguistic communication one must suppose that its production is what I am calling a speech act. It is a logical presupposition, for example, of current attempts to decipher the Mayan hieroglyphs that we at least hypothesize that the marks we see on the stones were produced by beings more or less like ourselves and produced with certain kinds of intentions. If we were certain the marks were a consequence of, say, water erosion, then the question of deciphering them or even calling them hieroglyphs could not arise. To construe them under the category of linguistic communication necessarily involves construing their production as speech acts.

To perform illocutionary acts is to engage in a rule-governed form of behavior. I shall argue that such things as asking questions or making statements are rule-governed in ways quite similar to those in which getting a base hit in baseball or moving a knight in chess are rule-governed forms of acts. I intend therefore to explicate the notion of an illocutionary act by stating a set of necessary and sufficient conditions for the performance of a particular kind of illocutionary act, and extracting from it a set of semantical rules for the use of the expression (or syntactic device) which marks the utterance as an illocutionary act of that kind. If I am successful in stating the conditions and the corresponding rules for even one kind of illocutionary act, that will provide us with a pattern for analyzing other kinds of acts and consequently for explicating the notion in general. But in order to set the stage for actually stating conditions and extracting rules for performing an illocutionary act I have to discuss three other preliminary notions: *rules*, *propositions*, and *meaning*. I shall confine my discussion of these notions to those aspects which are essential to my main purposes in this paper, but, even so, what I wish to say concerning each of these notions, if it were to be at all complete, would require a paper for each; however, sometimes it may be worth sacrificing thoroughness for the sake of scope and I shall therefore be very brief.

II. Rules

In recent years there has been in the philosophy of language considerable discussion involving the notion of rules for the use of expressions. Some philosophers have even said that knowing the meaning of a word is simply a matter of knowing the rules for its use or employment. One disquieting feature of such discussions is that no philosopher, to my knowledge at least, has ever given anything like an adequate formulation of the rules for the use of even one expression. If meaning is a matter of rules of use, surely we ought to be able to state the rules for the use of expressions in a way which would explicate the meaning of those expressions. Certain other philosophers, dismayed perhaps by the failure of their colleagues to produce any rules, have denied the fashionable view that meaning is a matter of rules and have asserted that there are no semantical rules of the proposed kind at all. I am inclined to think that this scepticism is premature and stems from a failure to distinguish different sorts of rules, in a way which I shall now attempt to explain.

I distinguish between two sorts of rules: Some regulate antecedently existing forms of behavior; for example, the rules of etiquette regulate interpersonal relationships, but these relationships exist independently of the rules of etiquette. Some rules on the other hand do not merely regulate but create or define new forms of behavior. The rules of football, for example, do not merely regulate the game of football but as it were create the possibility of or define that activity. The activity of playing football is constituted by acting in accordance with these rules; football has no existence apart from these rules. I call the latter kind of rules constitutive rules and the former kind regulative rules. Regulative rules regulate a pre-existing activity, an activity whose existence is logically independent of the existence of the rules. Constitutive rules constitute (and also regulate) an activity the existence of which is logically dependent on the rules.[2]

Regulative rules characteristically take the form of or can be paraphrased as imperatives, e.g. "When cutting food hold the knife in the right hand," or "Officers are to wear ties at dinner." Some constitutive rules take quite a different form, e.g. a checkmate is made if the king is attacked in such a way that no move will leave it unattacked; a touchdown is scored when a player crosses the opponents' goal line in possession of the ball while a play is in progress. If our paradigms of rules are imperative regulative rules, such nonimperative constitutive rules are likely to strike us as extremely curious and hardly even as rules at all. Notice that they are almost tautological in character, for what the 'rule' seems to offer is a partial definition of 'checkmate' or 'touchdown'. But, of course, this quasi-tautological character is a necessary consequence of their being constitutive rules: the rules concerning touchdowns must define the notion of 'touchdown' in the same way that the rules concerning football define 'football'. That, for example, a touchdown can be scored in such and such ways and counts six points can appear sometimes as a rule, sometimes as an analytic truth; and that it can be construed as a tautology is a clue to the fact that the rule in question is a constitutive one. Regulative rules generally have the form "Do X" or "If Y do X." Some members of the set of constitutive rules have this form but some also have the form "X counts as Y."[3]

The failure to perceive this is of some importance in philosophy. Thus, e.g., some philosophers ask "How can a promise create an obligation?" A similar question would be "How can a touchdown create six points?" And as they stand both questions can only be answered by stating a rule of the form "X counts as Y."

I am inclined to think that both the failure of some philosophers to state rules for the use of expressions and the scepticism of other philosophers concerning the existence of any such rules stem at least in part from a failure to recognize the distinctions between constitutive and regulative rules. The model or paradigm of a rule which most philosophers have is that of a regulative rule, and if one looks in semantics for purely regulative rules one is not likely to find anything interesting from the point of view of logical analysis. There are no doubt social rules of the form "One ought not to utter obscenities at formal gatherings," but that hardly seems a rule of the sort that is crucial in explicating the semantics of a language. The hypothesis that lies behind the present paper is that the semantics of a language can be regarded as a series of systems of constitutive rules and that illocutionary acts are acts performed in accordance with these sets of constitutive rules. One of the aims of this paper is to formulate a set of constitutive rules for a certain kind of speech act. And if what I have said concerning constitutive rules is correct, we should not be surprised if not all these rules take the form of imperative rules. Indeed we shall see that the rules fall into several different categories, none of which is quite like the rules of etiquette. The effort to state the rules for an illocutionary act can also be regarded as a kind of test of the hypothesis that there are constitutive rules underlying speech acts. If we are unable to give any satisfactory rule formulations, our failure could be construed as partially disconfirming evidence against the hypothesis.

III. Propositions

Different illocutionary acts often have features in common with each other. Consider utterances of the following sentences:

(1) Will John leave the room?
(2) John will leave the room.
(3) John, leave the room!
(4) Would that John left the room.
(5) If John will leave the room, I will leave also.

Utterances of each of these on a given occasion would characteristically be performances of different illocutionary acts. The first would, characteristically, be a question, the second an assertion about the future, that is, a prediction, the third a request or order, the fourth an expression of a wish, and the fifth a hypothetical expression of intention. Yet in the performance of each the speaker would characteristically perform some subsidiary acts which are common to all five illocutionary acts. In the utterance of each the speaker *refers* to a particular person John and *predicates* the act of leaving the room of that person. In no case is that all he does, but in every case it is a part of what he does. I shall say, therefore, that in each of these cases, although the illocutionary acts are different, at least some of the nonillocutionary acts of reference and predication are the same.

The reference to some person John and predication of the same thing of him in each of these illocutionary acts inclines me to say that there is a common *content* in each of them. Something expressible by the clause "that John will leave the room" seems to be a common feature of all. We could, with not too much distortion, write each of these sentences in a way which would isolate this common feature: "I assert that John will leave the room," "I ask whether John will leave the room," etc.

For lack of a better word I propose to call this common content a proposition, and I shall describe this feature of these illocutionary acts by saying that in the utterance of each of (1)-(5) the speaker expresses the proposition that John will leave the room. Notice that I do not say that the sentence expresses the proposition; I do not know how sentences could perform acts of that kind. But I shall say that in the utterance of the sentence the speaker expresses a proposition. Notice also that I am distinguishing between a proposition and an assertion or statement of that proposition. The proposition that John will leave the room is expressed in the utterance of all of (1)-(5) but only in (2) is that proposition asserted. An assertion is an illocutionary act, but a proposition is not an act at all, although the act of expressing a proposition is a part of performing certain illocutionary acts.

I might summarize this by saying that I am distinguishing between the illocutionary act and the propositional content of an illocutionary act. Of course, not all illocutionary acts have a propositional content, for example, an utterance of "Hurrah!" or "Ouch!" does not. In one version or another this distinction is an old one and has been marked in different ways by authors as diverse as Frege, Sheffer, Lewis, Reichenbach and Hare, to mention only a few.

From a semantical point of view we can distinguish between the propositional indicator in the sentence and the indicator of illocutionary force. That is, for a large class of sentences used to perform illocutionary acts, we can say for the purpose of our analysis that the sentence has two (not necessarily separate) parts, the proposition indicating element and the function indicating device.[4] The function indicating device shows how the proposition is to be taken, or, to put it in another way, what illocutionary force the utterance is to have, that is, what illocutionary act the speaker is performing in the utterance of the sentence. Function indicating devices in English include word order, stress, intonation contour, punctuation, the mood of the verb, and finally a set of so-called performative verbs: I may indicate the kind of illocutionary act I am performing by beginning the sentence with "I apologize," "I warn," "I state," etc. Often in actual speech situations the context will make it clear what the illocutionary force of the utterance is, without its being necessary to invoke the appropriate function indicating device.

If this semantical distinction is of any real importance, it seems likely that it should have some syntactical analogue, and certain recent developments in transformational grammar tend to support the view that it does. In the underlying phrase marker of a sentence there is a distinction between those elements which correspond to the function indicating device and those which correspond to the propositional content.

The distinction between the function indicating device and the proposition indicating device will prove very useful to us in giving an analysis of an illocutionary act. Since the same proposition can be common to all sorts of illocutionary acts, we can separate our analysis of the proposition from our analysis of kinds of illocutionary acts. I think there are rules for expressing propositions, rules for such things as reference and predication, but those rules can be discussed independently of the rules for function indicating. In this paper I shall not attempt to discuss propositional rules but shall concentrate on rules for using certain kinds of function indicating devices.

IV. Meaning

Speech acts are characteristically performed in the utterance of sounds or the making of marks. What is the difference between *just* uttering sounds or making marks and performing a speech act? One difference is that the sounds or marks one makes in the performance of a speech act are characteristically said to *have meaning*, and a second related difference is that one is characteristically said to *mean something* by those sounds or marks. Characteristically when one speaks one means something by what one says, and what one says, the string of morphemes that one emits, is characteristically said to have a meaning. Here, incidentally, is another point at which our analogy between performing speech acts and playing games breaks down. The pieces in a game like chess are not characteristically said to have a meaning, and furthermore when one makes a move one is not characteristically said to mean anything by that move.

But what is it for one to mean something by what one says, and what is it for something to have a meaning? To answer the first of these questions I propose to borrow and revise some ideas of Paul Grice. In an article entitled "Meaning,"[5] Grice gives the following analysis of one sense of the notion of 'meaning'. To say that A meant something by x is to say that "A intended the utterance of x to produce some effect in an audience by means of the recognition of this intention." This seems to me a useful start on an analysis of meaning, first because it shows the close relationship between the notion of meaning and the notion of intention, and secondly because it captures something which is, I think, essential to speaking a language: In speaking a language I attempt to communicate things to my hearer by means of getting him to recognize my intention to communicate just those things. For example, characteristically, when I make an assertion, I attempt to communicate to and convince my hearer of the truth of a certain proposition; and the means I employ to do this are to utter certain sounds, which utterance I intend to produce in him the desired effect by means of his recognition of my intention to produce just that effect. I shall illustrate this with an example. I might on the one hand attempt to get you to believe that I am French by speaking French all the time, dressing in the French manner, showing wild enthusiasm for de Gaulle, and cultivating French acquaintances. But I might on the other hand attempt to get you to believe that I am French by simply telling you that I am French. Now, what is the difference between these two ways of my attempting to get you to believe that I am French? One crucial difference is that in the second case I attempt to get you to believe that I am French by getting you to recognize that it is my purported intention to get you to believe just that. That is one of the things involved in telling you that I am French. But of course if I try to get you to believe that I am French by putting on the act I described, then your recognition of my intention to produce in you the belief that I am French is not the means I am employing. Indeed in this case you would, I think, become rather suspicious if you recognized my intention.

However valuable this analysis of meaning is, it seems to me to be in certain respects defective. First of all, it fails to distinguish the different kinds of effects – perlocutionary versus illocutionary – that one may intend to produce in one's hearers, and it further fails to show the way in which these different kinds of effects are related to the notion of meaning. A second defect is that it fails to account for the extent to which meaning is a matter of rules or conventions. That is, this account of meaning does not show the connection between one's meaning something by what one says and what that which one says actually means in the language. In order to illustrate this point I now wish to present a counterexample to this analysis of meaning. The point of the counterexample will be to illustrate the connection between what a speaker means and what the words he utters mean.

Suppose that I am an American soldier in the Second World War and that I am captured by Italian troops. And suppose also that I wish to get these troops to believe that I am a German officer in order to get them to release me. What I would like to do is to tell them in German or Italian that I am a German officer. But let us suppose I don't know enough German or Italian to do that. So I, as it were, attempt to put on a show of telling them that I am a German officer by reciting those few bits of German that I know, trusting that they don't know enough German to see through my plan. Let us suppose I know only one line of German, which I remember from a poem I had to memorize in a high school German course. Therefore I, a captured American, address my Italian captors with the following sentence: "Kennst du das Land, wo die Zitronen blühen?" Now, let us describe the situation in Gricean terms. I intend to produce a certain effect in them, namely, the effect of believing that I am a German officer; and I intend to produce this effect by means of their recognition of my intention. I intend that they should think that what I am trying to tell them is that I am a German officer. But does it follow from this account that when I say "Kennst du das land ..." etc., what I mean is, "I am a German officer"? Not only does it not follow, but in this case it seems plainly false that when I utter the German sentence what I mean is "I am a German officer," or even "Ich bin ein deutscher Offizier," because what the words mean is, "Knowest thou the land where the lemon trees bloom?" Of course, I want my captors to be deceived into thinking that what I mean is "I am a German officer," but part of what is involved in the deception is getting them to think that that is what the words which I utter mean in German. At one point in the *Philosophical Investigations* Wittgenstein says "Say 'it's cold here' and mean 'it's warm here.'"[6] The reason we are unable to do this is that what we can mean is a function of what we are saying. Meaning is more than a matter of intention, it is also a matter of convention.

Grice's account can be amended to deal with counterexamples of this kind. We have here a case where I am trying to produce a certain effect by means of the recognition of my intention to produce that effect, but the device I use to produce this effect is one which is conventionally, by the rules governing the use of that device, used as a means of producing quite different illocutionary effects. We must therefore reformulate the Gricean account of meaning in such a way as to make it clear that one's meaning something when one says something is more than just contingently related to what the sentence means in the language one is speaking. In our analysis of illocutionary acts, we must capture both the intentional and the conventional aspects and especially the relationship between them. In the performance of an illocutionary act the speaker intends to produce a certain effect by means of getting the hearer to recognize his intention to produce that effect, and furthermore, if he is using words literally, he intends this recognition to be achieved in virtue of the fact that the rules for using the expressions he utters associate the expressions with the production of that effect. It is this *combination* of elements which we shall need to express in our analysis of the illocutionary act.

V. How to Promise

I shall now attempt to give an analysis of the illocutionary act of promising. In order to do this I shall ask what conditions are necessary and sufficient for the act of promising to have been performed in the utterance of a given sentence. I shall attempt to answer this question by stating these conditions as a set of propositions such that the conjunction of the members of the set entails the proposition that a speaker made a promise, and the proposition that the speaker made a promise entails this conjunction. Thus each condition will be a necessary condition for the performance of the act of promising, and taken collectively the set of conditions will be a sufficient condition for the act to have been performed.

　　If we get such a set of conditions we can extract from them a set of rules for the use of the function indicating device. The method here is analogous to discovering the rules of chess by asking oneself what are the necessary and sufficient conditions under which one can be said to have correctly moved a knight or castled or checkmated a player, etc. We are in the position of someone who has learned to play chess without ever having the rules formulated and who wants such a formulation. We learned how to play the game of illocutionary acts, but in general it was done without an explicit formulation of the rules, and the first step in getting such a formulation is to set out the conditions for the performance of a particular illocutionary act. Our inquiry will therefore serve a double philosophical purpose. By stating a set of conditions for the performance of a particular illocutionary act we shall have offered a partial explication of that notion and shall also have paved the way for the second step, the formulation of the rules.

　　I find the statement of the conditions very difficult to do, and I am not entirely satisfied with the list I am about to present. One reason for the difficulty is that the notion of a promise, like most notions in ordinary language, does not have absolutely strict rules. There are all sorts of odd, deviant, and borderline promises; and counterexamples, more or less bizarre, can be produced against my analysis. I am inclined to think we shall not be able to get a set of knockdown necessary and sufficient conditions that will exactly mirror the ordinary use of the word "promise." I am confining my discussion, therefore, to the center of the concept of promising and ignoring the fringe, borderline, and partially defective cases. I also confine my discussion to fullblown explicit promises and ignore promises made by elliptical turns of phrase, hints, metaphors, etc.

Another difficulty arises from my desire to state the conditions without certain forms of circularity. I want to give a list of conditions for the performance of a certain illocutionary act, which do not themselves mention the performance of any illocutionary acts. I need to satisfy this condition in order to offer an explication of the notion of an illocutionary act in general, otherwise I should simply be showing the relation between different illocutionary acts. However, although there will be no reference to illocutionary *acts*, certain illocutionary *concepts* will appear in the analysans as well as in the analysandum; and I think this form of circularity is unavoidable because of the nature of constitutive rules.

In the presentation of the conditions I shall first consider the case of a sincere promise and then show how to modify the conditions to allow for insincere promises. As our inquiry is semantical rather than syntactical, I shall simply assume the existence of grammatically well-formed sentences.

Given that a speaker S utters a sentence T in the presence of a hearer H, then, in the utterance of T, S sincerely (and nondefectively) promises that p to H if and only if:

(1) *Normal input and output conditions obtain.* I use the terms 'input' and 'output' to cover the large and indefinite range of conditions under which any kind of serious linguistic communication is possible. 'Output' covers the conditions for intelligible speaking and 'input' covers the conditions for understanding. Together they include such things as that the speaker and hearer both know how to speak the language; both are conscious of what they are doing; the speaker is not acting under duress or threats; they have no physical impediments to communication, such as deafness, aphasia, or laryngitis; they are not acting in a play or telling jokes, etc.

(2) *S expresses that p in the utterance of T.* This condition isolates the propositional content from the rest of the speech act and enables us to concentrate on the peculiarities of promising in the rest of the analysis.

(3) *In expressing that p, S predicates a future act A of S.* In the case of promising the function indicating device is an expression whose scope includes certain features of the proposition. In a promise an act must be predicated of the speaker and it cannot be a past act. I cannot promise to have done something, and I cannot promise that someone else will do something. (Although I can promise to see that he will do it.) The notion of an

act, as I am construing it for present purposes, includes refraining from acts, performing series of acts, and may also include states and conditions: I may promise not to do something, I may promise to do something repeatedly, and I may promise to be or remain in a certain state or condition. I call conditions (2) and (3) the *propositional content conditions.*

(4) *H would prefer S's doing A to his not doing A, and S believes H would prefer his doing A to his not doing A.* One crucial distinction between promises on the one hand and threats on the other is that a promise is a pledge to do something for you, not to you, but a threat is a pledge to do something to you, not for you. A promise is defective if the thing promised is something the promisee does not want done; and it is further defective if the promisor does not believe the promisee wants it done, since a nondefective promise must be intended as a promise and not as a threat or warning. I think both halves of this double condition are necessary in order to avoid fairly obvious counterexamples.

One can, however, think of apparent counterexamples to this condition as stated. Suppose I say to a lazy student "If you don't hand in your paper on time I promise you I will give you a failing grade in the course." Is this utterance a promise? I am inclined to think not; we would more naturally describe it as a warning or possibly even a threat. But why then is it possible to use the locution "I promise" in such a case? I think we use it here because "I promise" and "I hereby promise" are among the strongest function indicating devices for *commitment* provided by the English language. For that reason we often use these expressions in the performance of speech acts which are not strictly speaking promises but in which we wish to emphasize our commitment. To illustrate this, consider another apparent counterexample to the analysis along different lines. Sometimes, more commonly I think in the United States than in England, one hears people say "I promise" when making an emphatic assertion. Suppose, for example, I accuse you of having stolen the money. I say, "You stole that money, didn't you?" You reply "No, I didn't, I promise you I didn't." Did you make a promise in this case? I find it very unnatural to describe your utterance as a promise. This utterance would be more aptly described as an emphatic denial, and we can explain the occurrence of the function indicating device "I promise" as derivative from genuine promises and serving here as an expression adding emphasis to your denial.

In general the point stated in condition (4) is that if a purported promise is to be non-defective the thing promised must be something the hearer wants done, or considers to be in his interest, or would prefer being done to not being done, etc.; and the speaker must be aware of or believe or know, etc. that this is the case. I think a more elegant and exact formulation of this condition would require the introduction of technical terminology.

(5) *It is not obvious to both S and H that S will do A in the normal course of events.* This condition is an instance of a general condition on many different kinds of illocutionary acts to the effect that the act must have a point. For example, if I make a request to someone to do something which it is obvious that he is already doing or is about to do, then my request is pointless and to that extent defective. In an actual speech situation, listeners, knowing the rules for performing illocutionary acts, will assume that this condition is satisfied. Suppose, for example, that in the course of a public speech I say to a member of my audience "Look here, Smith, pay attention to what I am saying." In order to make sense of this utterance the audience will have to assume that Smith has not been paying attention or at any rate that it is not obvious that he has been paying attention, that the question of his paying attention has arisen in some way; because a condition for making a request is that it is not obvious that the hearer is doing or about to do the thing requested.

Similarly with promises. It is out of order for me to promise to do something that it is obvious I am going to do anyhow. If I do seem to be making such a promise, the only way my audience can make sense of my utterance is to assume that I believe that it is not obvious that I am going to do the thing promised. A happily married man who promises his wife he will not desert her in the next week is likely to provide more anxiety than comfort.

Parenthetically I think this condition is an instance of the sort of phenomenon stated in Zipf's law. I think there is operating in our language, as in most forms of human behavior, a principle of least effort, in this case a principle of maximum illocutionary ends with minimum phonetic effort; and I think condition (5) is an instance of it.

I call conditions such as (4) and (5) *preparatory conditions.* They are *sine quibus non* of happy promising, but they do not yet state the essential feature.

(6) *S intends to do A.* The most important distinction between sincere and insincere promises is that in the case of the sincere promise the speaker intends to do the act promised, in the case of the insincere promise he does not intend to do the act. Also in sincere promises the speaker believes it is possible for him to do the act (or to refrain from doing it), but I think the proposition that he intends to do it entails that he thinks it is possible to do (or refrain from doing) it, so I am not stating that as an extra condition. I call this condition the *sincerity condition.*

(7) *S intends that the utterance of T will place him under an obligation to do A.* The essential feature of a promise is that it is the undertaking of an obligation to perform a certain act. I think that this condition distinguishes promises (and other members of the same family such as vows) from other kinds of speech acts. Notice that in the statement of the condition we only

specify the speaker's intention; further conditions will make clear how that intention is realized. It is clear, however, that having this intention is a necessary condition of making a promise; for if a speaker can demonstrate that he did not have this intention in a given utterance, he can prove that the utterance was not a promise. We know, for example, that Mr. Pickwick did not promise to marry the woman because we know he did not have the appropriate intention.

I call this the *essential condition.*

(8) *S intends that the utterance of T will produce in H a belief that conditions (6) and (7) obtain by means of the recognition of the intention to produce that belief, and he intends this recognition to be achieved by means of the recognition of the sentence as one conventionally used to produce such beliefs.* This captures our amended Gricean analysis of what it is for the speaker to mean to make a promise. The speaker intends to produce a certain illocutionary effect by means of getting the hearer to recognize his intention to produce that effect, and he also intends this recognition to be achieved in virtue of the fact that the lexical and syntactical character of the item he utters conventionally associates it with producing that effect.

Strictly speaking this condition could be formulated as part of condition (1), but it is of enough philosophical interest to be worth stating separately. I find it troublesome for the following reason. If my original objection to Grice is really valid, then surely, one might say, all these iterated intentions are superfluous; all that is necessary is that the speaker should seriously utter a sentence. The production of all these effects is simply a consequence of the hearer's knowledge of what the sentence means, which in turn is a consequence of his knowledge of the language, which is assumed by the speaker at the outset. I think the correct reply to this objection is that condition (8) explicates what it is for the speaker to 'seriously' utter the sentence, i.e. to utter it and mean it, but I am not completely confident about either the force of the objection or of the reply.

(9) *The semantical rules of the dialect spoken by S and H are such that T is correctly and sincerely uttered if and only if conditions (1)-(8) obtain.* This condition is intended to make clear that the sentence uttered is one which by the semantical rules of the language is used to make a promise. Taken together with condition (8), it eliminates counterexamples like the captured soldier example considered earlier. Exactly what the formulation of the rules is, we shall soon see.

So far we have considered only the case of a sincere promise. But insincere promises are promises nonetheless, and we now need to show how to modify the conditions to allow for them. In making an insincere promise the speaker does not have all the intentions and beliefs he has when making a sincere promise. However, he purports to have them. Indeed it is because he purports to have intentions and beliefs which he does not have that we describe his act as insincere. So to allow for insincere promises we need only to revise our conditions to state that the speaker takes responsibility for having the beliefs and intentions rather than stating that he actually has them. A clue that the speaker does take such responsibility is the fact that he could not say without absurdity, e.g. "I promise to do A but I do not intend to do A." To say "I promise to do A" is to take responsibility for intending to do A, and this condition holds whether the utterance was sincere or insincere. To allow for the possibility of an insincere promise then we have only to revise condition (6) so that it states not that the speaker intends to do A, but that he takes responsibility for intending to do A, and to avoid the charge of circularity I shall phrase this as follows:

(6*) *S intends that the utterance of T will make him responsible for intending to do A.* Thus amended [and with 'sincerely' dropped from our analysandum and from condition (9)], our analysis is neutral on the question whether the promise was sincere or insincere.

VI. Rules for the Use of the Function Indicating Device

Our next task is to extract from our set of conditions a set of rules for the use of the function indicating device. Obviously not all of our conditions are equally relevant to this task. Condition (1) and conditions of the forms (8) and (9) apply generally to all kinds of normal illocutionary acts and are not peculiar to promising. Rules for the function indicating device for promising are to be found corresponding to conditions (2)-(7).

The semantical rules for the use of any function indicating device P for promising are:

Rule 1. P is to be uttered only in the context of a sentence (or larger stretch of discourse) the utterance of which predicates some future act A of the speaker S. I call this the *propositional content rule*. It is derived from the propositional content conditions (2) and (3).

Rule 2. P is to be uttered only if the hearer H would prefer S's doing A to his not doing A, and S believes H would prefer S's doing A to his not doing A.

Rule 3. P is to be uttered only if it is not obvious to both S and H that S will do A in the normal course of events. I call rules (2) and (3) *preparatory rules*. They are derived from the preparatory conditions (4) and (5).

Rule 4. P is to be uttered only if S intends to do A. I call this the *sincerity rule*. It is derived from the sincerity condition (6).

Rule 5. The utterance of P counts as the undertaking of an obligation to do A. I call this the *essential rule*.

These rules are ordered: Rules 2-5 apply only if rule 1 is satisfied, and rule 5 applies only if rules 2 and 3 are satisfied as well.

Notice that whereas rules 1-4 take the form of quasi-imperatives, i.e., they are of the form: utter P only if x, rule 5 is of the form: the utterance of P counts as Y. Thus rule 5 is of the kind peculiar to systems of constitutive rules which I discussed in section II.

Notice also that the rather tiresome analogy with games is holding up remarkably well. If we ask ourselves under what conditions a player could be said to move a knight correctly, we would find preparatory conditions, such as that it must be his turn to move, as well as the essential condition stating the actual positions the knight can move to. I think that there is even a sincerity rule for competitive games, the rule that each side tries to win. I suggest that the team which 'throws' the game is behaving in a way closely analogous to the speaker who lies or makes false promises. Of course, there usually are no propositional content rules for games, because games do not, by and large, represent states of affairs.

If this analysis is of any general interest beyond the case of promising then it would seem that these distinctions should carry over into other types of speech acts, and I think a little reflection will show that they do. Consider, e.g., giving an order. The preparatory conditions include that the speaker should be in a position of authority over the hearer, the sincerity condition is that the speaker wants the ordered act done, and the essential condition has to do with the fact that the utterance is an attempt to get the hearer to do it. For assertions, the preparatory conditions include the fact that the hearer must have some basis for supposing the asserted proposition is true, the sincerity condition is that he must believe it to be true, and the essential condition has to do with the fact that the utterance is an attempt to inform the hearer and convince him of its truth. Greetings are a much simpler kind of speech act, but even here some of the distinctions apply. In the utterance of "Hello" there is no propositional content and no sincerity condition. The preparatory condition is that the speaker must have just encountered the hearer, and the essential rule is that the utterance indicates courteous recognition of the hearer.

A proposal for further research then is to carry out a similar analysis of other types of speech acts. Not only would this give us an analysis of concepts interesting in themselves, but the comparison of different analyses would deepen our understanding of the whole subject and incidentally provide a basis for a more serious taxonomy than any of the usual facile categories such as evaluative versus descriptive, or cognitive versus emotive.

NOTES

1. Austin, J.L., *How To Do Things With Words* (Oxford: 1962).

2. This distinction occurs in J. Rawls, "Two Concepts of Rules", *Philosophical Review*, 1955, and J.R. Searle, "How to Derive 'Ought' from 'Is'", *Philosophical Review*, 1964.

3. The formulation "X counts as Y" was originally suggested to me by Max Black.

4. In the sentence "I promise that I will come" the function indicating device and the propositional element are separate. In the sentence "I promise to come," which means the same as the first and is derived from it by certain transformations, the two elements are not separate.

5. *Philosophical Review*, 1957.

6. *Philosophical Investigations* (Oxford: 1953), §510.

Speaker's Meaning
and Reference

LOGIC AND CONVERSATION

H. Paul Grice

It is a commonplace of philosophical logic that there are, or appear to be, divergences in meaning between, on the one hand, at least some of what I shall call the formal devices – ~, ∧, ∨ , ⊃, (x), (? x), (∃ x) (when these are given a standard two-valued interpretation) – and, on the other, what are taken to be their analogs or counterparts in natural language – such expressions as "not," "and," "or," "if," "all," "some" (or "at least one"), "the." Some logicians may at some time have wanted to claim that there are in fact no such divergences; but such claims, if made at all, have been somewhat rashly made, and those suspected of making them have been subjected to some pretty rough handling.

Those who concede that such divergences exist adhere, in the main, to one or the other of two rival groups, which for the purposes of this article I shall call the formalist and the informalist groups. An outline of a not uncharacteristic formalist position may be given as follows: Insofar as logicians are concerned with the formulation of very general patterns of valid inference, the formal devices possess a decisive advantage over their natural counterparts. For it will be possible to construct in terms of the formal devices a system of very general formulas, a considerable number of which can be regarded as, or are closely related to, patterns of inferences the expression of which involves some or all of the devices: Such a system may consist of a certain set of simple formulas that must be acceptable if the devices have the meaning that has been assigned to them, and an indefinite number of further formulas, many of them less obviously acceptable, each of which can be shown to be acceptable if the members of the original set are acceptable. We have, thus, a way of handling dubiously acceptable patterns of inference, and if, as is sometimes possible, we can apply a decision procedure, we have an even better way. Furthermore, from a philosophical point of view, the possession by the natural counterparts of those elements in their meaning, which they do not share with the corresponding formal devices, is to be regarded as an imperfection of natural languages; the elements in question are undesirable excrescences. For the presence of these elements has the result that the concepts within which they appear cannot be precisely/clearly defined, and that at least some statements involving them cannot, in some circumstances, be assigned a definite truth value; and the indefiniteness of these concepts is not only objectionable in itself but leaves open the way to metaphysics – we cannot be certain that none of these natural language expressions is metaphysically 'loaded'. For these reasons, the expressions, as used in natural speech, cannot be regarded as finally acceptable, and may turn out to be, finally, not fully intelligible. The proper course is to conceive and begin to construct an ideal language, incorporating the formal devices, the sentences of which will be clear, determinate in truth value, and certifiably free from metaphysical implications; the foundations of science will now be philosophically secure, since the statements of the scientist will be expressible (though not necessarily actually expressed) within this ideal language. (I do not wish to suggest that all formalists would accept the whole of this outline, but I think that all would accept at least some part of it.)

To this, an informalist might reply in the following vein. The philosophical demand for an ideal language rests on certain assumptions that should not be conceded; these are, that the primary yardstick by which to judge the adequacy of a language is its ability to serve the needs of science, that an expression cannot be guaranteed as fully intelligible unless an explication or analysis of its meaning has been provided, and that every explication or analysis must take the form of a precise definition that is the expression/assertion of a logical equivalence. Language serves many important purposes besides those of scientific inquiry; we can know perfectly well what an expression means (and so a fortiori that it is intelligible) without knowing its analysis, and the provision of an analysis may (and usually does) consist in the specification, as generalized as possible, of the conditions that count for or against the applicability of the expression being analyzed. Moreover, while it is no doubt true that the formal devices are especially amenable to systematic treatment by the logician, it remains the case that there are very many inferences and arguments, expressed in natural language and not in terms of these devices, that are nevertheless recognizably valid. So there must be a place for an unsimplified, and so more or less unsystematic, logic of the natural counterparts of these devices; this logic may be aided and guided by the simplified logic of the formal devices but cannot be supplanted by it; indeed, not only do the two logics differ, but sometimes they come into conflict; rules that hold for a formal device may not hold for its natural counterpart.

Now, on the general question of the place in philosophy of the reformation of natural language, I shall, in this article, have nothing to say. I shall confine myself to the dispute in its relation to the alleged divergences mentioned at the outset. I have, moreover, no intention of entering the fray on behalf of either contestant. I wish, rather, to maintain that the common assumption of the contestants that the divergences do in fact exist is (broadly speaking) a common mistake, and that the mistake arises from an inadequate attention to the nature and importance of the conditions governing conversation. I shall, therefore, proceed at once to inquire into the general conditions that, in one way or another, apply to conversation as such, irrespective of its subject matter.

Implicature

Suppose that A and B are talking about a mutual friend, C, who is now working in a bank. A asks B how C is getting on in his job, and B replies, "Oh quite well, I think; he likes his colleagues, and he hasn't been to prison yet." At this point, A might well inquire what B was implying, what he was suggesting, or even what he meant by saying that C had not yet been to prison. The answer might be any one of such things as that C is the sort of person likely to yield to the temptation provided by his occupation, that C's colleagues are really very unpleasant and treacherous people, and so forth. It might, of course, be quite unnecessary for A to make such an inquiry of B, the answer to it being, in the context, clear in advance. I think it is clear that whatever B implied, suggested, meant, etc., in this example, is distinct from what B said, which was simply that C had not been to prison yet. I wish to introduce, as terms of art, the verb "*implicate*" and the related nouns "implicature" (cf. implying) and "implicatum" (cf. what is implied). The point of this maneuver is to avoid having, on each occasion, to choose between this or that member of the family of verbs for which "implicate" is to do general duty. I shall, for the time being at least, have to assume to a considerable extent an intuitive understanding of the meaning of "say" in such contexts, and an ability to recognize particular verbs as members of the family with which "implicate" is associated. I can, however, make one or two remarks that may help to clarify the more problematic of these assumptions, namely, that connected with the meaning of the word "say."

In the sense in which I am using the word "say," I intend what someone has said to be closely related to the conventional meaning of the words (the sentence) he has uttered. Suppose someone to have uttered the sentence "He is in the grip of a vice." Given a knowledge of the English language, but no knowledge of the circumstances of the utterance, one would know something about what the speaker had said, on the assumption that he was speaking standard English, and speaking literally. One would know that he had said, about some particular male person or animal x, that at the time of the utterance (whatever that was), either (1) x was unable to rid himself of a certain kind of bad character trait or (2) some part of x's person was caught in a certain kind of tool or instrument (approximate account, of course). But for a full identification of what the speaker had said, one would need to know (a) the identity of x, (b) the time of utterance, and (c) the meaning, on the particular occasion of utterance, of the phrase "in the grip of a vice" [a decision between (1) and (2)]. This brief indication of my use of "say" leaves it open whether a man who says (today) "Harold Wilson is a great man" and another who says (also today) "The British Prime Minister is a great man" would, if each knew that the two singular terms had the same reference, have said the same thing. But whatever decision is made about this question, the apparatus that I am about to provide will be capable of accounting for any implicatures that might depend on the presence of one rather than another of these singular terms in the sentence uttered. Such implicatures would merely be related to different maxims.

In some cases the conventional meaning of the words used will determine what is implicated, besides helping to determine what is said. If I say (smugly), "He is an Englishman; he is, therefore, brave," I have certainly committed myself, by virtue of the meaning of my words, to its being the case that his being brave is a consequence of (follows from) his being an Englishman. But while I have said that he is an Englishman, and said that he is brave, I do not want to say that I have *said* (in the favored sense), that it follows from his being an Englishman that he is brave, though I have certainly indicated, and so implicated, that this is so. I do not want to say that my utterance of this sentence would be, *strictly speaking*, false should the consequence in question fail to hold. So *some* implicatures are conventional, unlike the one with which I introduced this discussion of implicature.

I wish to represent a certain subclass of nonconventional implicatures, which I shall call *conversational* implicatures, as being essentially connected with certain general features of discourse; so my next step is to try to say what these features are.

The following may provide a first approximation to a general principle. Our talk exchanges do not normally consist of a succession of disconnected remarks, and would not be rational if they did. They are characteristically, to some degree at least, cooperative efforts; and each participant recognizes in them, to some extent, a common purpose or set of purposes, or at least a mutually accepted direction. This purpose or direction may be fixed from the start (e.g., by initial proposal of a question for discussion), or it may evolve during the exchange; it may be fairly definite, or it may be so indefinite as to leave very considerable latitude to the participants (as in a casual conversation). But at each stage, *some* possible conversational moves would be excluded as conversationally unsuitable. We might then formulate a rough general principle which participants will be expected (ceteris paribus) to observe, namely: make your conversational contribution such as is required, at the stage at which it occurs, by the accepted purpose or direction of the talk exchange in which you are engaged. One might label this the *Cooperative Principle*.

On the assumption that some such general principle as this is acceptable, one may perhaps distinguish four categories under one or another of which will fall certain more specific maxims and submaxims, the following of which will, in general, yield results in accordance with the Cooperative Principle. Echoing Kant, I call these categories Quantity, Quality, Relation, and Manner. The category of *Quantity* relates to the quantity of information to be provided, and under it fall the following maxims: (1) Make your contribution as informative as is required (for the current purposes of the exchange). (2) Do not make your contribution more informative than is required. (The second maxim is disputable; it might be said that to be overinformative is not a transgression of the Cooperative Principle but merely a waste of time. However, it might be answered that such overinformativeness may be confusing in that it is liable to raise side issues; and there may also be an indirect effect, in that the hearers may be misled as a result of thinking that there is some particular *point* in the provision of the excess of information. However this may be, there is perhaps a different reason for doubt about the admission of this second maxim, namely, that its effect will be secured by a later maxim, which concerns relevance.)

Under the category of *Quality* falls a supermaxim – "Try to make your contribution one that is true" – and two more specific maxims:

1. Do not say what you believe to be false.
2. Do not say that for which you lack adequate evidence.

Under the category of *Relation* I place a single maxim, namely, "Be relevant." Though the maxim itself is terse, its formulation conceals a number of problems that exercise me a good deal: questions about what different kinds and focuses of relevance there may be, how these shift in the course of a talk exchange, how to allow for the fact that subjects of conversation are legitimately changed, and so on. I find the treatment of such questions exceedingly difficult, and I hope to revert to them in a later work.

Finally, under the category of *Manner*, which I understand as relating not (like the previous categories) to what is said but, rather, to *how* what is said is to be said, I include the supermaxim – "Be perspicuous" – and various maxims such as:

1. Avoid obscurity of expression.
2. Avoid ambiguity.
3. Be brief (avoid unnecessary prolixity).
4. Be orderly.

And one might need others.

It is obvious that the observance of some of these maxims is a matter of less urgency than is the observance of others; a man who has expressed himself with undue prolixity would, in general, be open to milder comment than would a man who has said something he believes to be false. Indeed, it might be felt that the importance of at least the first maxim of Quality is such that it should not be included in a scheme of the kind I am constructing; other maxims come into operation only on the assumption that this maxim of Quality is satisfied. While this may be correct, so far as the generation of implicatures is concerned it seems to play a role not totally different from the other maxims, and it will be convenient, for the present at least, to treat it as a member of the list of maxims.

There are, of course, all sorts of other maxims (aesthetic, social, or moral in character), such as "Be polite," that are also normally observed by participants in talk exchanges, and these may also generate nonconventional implicatures. The conversational maxims, however, and the conversational implicatures connected with them, are specially connected (I hope) with the particular purposes that talk (and so, talk exchange) is adapted to serve and is primarily employed to serve. I have stated my maxims as if this purpose were a maximally effective exchange of information; this specification is, of course, too narrow, and the scheme needs to be generalized to allow for such general purposes as influencing or directing the actions of others.

As one of my avowed aims is to see talking as a special case or variety of purposive, indeed rational, behavior, it may be worth noting that the specific expectations or presumptions connected with at least some of the foregoing maxims have their analogues in the sphere of transactions that are not talk exchanges. I list briefly one such analogue for each conversational category.

1. *Quantity*. If you are assisting me to mend a car, I expect your contribution to be neither more nor less than is required; if, for example, at a particular stage I need four screws, I expect you to hand me four, rather than two or six.

2. *Quality*. I expect your contributions to be genuine and not spurious. If I need sugar as an ingredient in the cake you are assisting me to make, I do not expect you to hand me salt; if I need a spoon, I do not expect a trick spoon made of rubber.

3. *Relation*. I expect a partner's contribution to be appropriate to immediate needs at each stage of the transaction; if I am mixing ingredients for a cake, I do not expect to be handed a good book, or even an oven cloth (though this might be an appropriate contribution at a later stage).

4. *Manner*. I expect a partner to make it clear what contribution he is making, and to execute his performance with reasonable dispatch.

These analogies are relevant to what I regard as a fundamental question about the Cooperative Principle and its attendant maxims, namely, what the basis is for the assumption which we seem to make, and on which (I hope) it will appear that a great range of implicatures depend, that talkers will in general (ceteris paribus and in the absence of indications to the contrary) proceed in the manner that these principles prescribe. A dull but, no doubt at a certain level, adequate answer is that it is just a well-recognized empirical fact that people *do* behave in these ways; they have learned to do so in childhood and not lost the habit of doing so; and, indeed, it would involve a good deal of effort to make a radical departure from the habit. It is much easier, for example, to tell the truth than to invent lies.

I am, however, enough of a rationalist to want to find a basis that underlies these facts, undeniable though they may be; I would like to be able to think of the standard type of conversational practice not merely as something that all or most do *in fact* follow but as something that it is *reasonable* for us to follow, that we *should not* abandon. For a time, I was attracted by the idea that observance of the Cooperative Principle and the maxims, in a talk exchange, could be thought of as a quasi-contractual matter, with parallels outside the realm of discourse. If you pass by when I am struggling with my stranded car, I no doubt have some degree of expectation that you will offer help, but once you join me in tinkering under the hood, my expectations become stronger and take more specific forms (in the absence of indications that you are merely an incompetent meddler); and talk exchanges seemed to me to exhibit, characteristically, certain features that jointly distinguish cooperative transactions:

1. The participants have some common immediate aim, like getting a car mended; their ultimate aims may, of course, be independent and even in conflict – each may want to get the car mended in order to drive off, leaving the other stranded. In characteristic talk exchanges, there is a common aim even if, as in an over-the-wall chat, it is a second-order one, namely, that each party should, for the time being, identify himself with the transitory conversational interests of the other.

2. The contributions of the participants should be dovetailed, mutually dependent.

3. There is some sort of understanding (which may be explicit but which is often tacit) that, other things being equal, the transaction should

continue in appropriate style unless both parties are agreeable that it should terminate. You do not just shove off or start doing something else.

But while some such quasi-contractual basis as this may apply to some cases, there are too many types of exchange, like quarreling and letter writing, that it fails to fit comfortably. In any case, one feels that the talker who is irrelevant or obscure has primarily let down not his audience but himself. So I would like to be able to show that observance of the Cooperative Principle and maxims is reasonable (rational) along the following lines: that any one who cares about the goals that are central to conversation/communication (e.g., giving and receiving information, influencing and being influenced by others) must be expected to have an interest, given suitable circumstances, in participating in talk exchanges that will be profitable only on the assumption that they are conducted in general accordance with the Cooperative Principle and the maxims. Whether any such conclusion can be reached, I am uncertain; in any case, I am fairly sure that I cannot reach it until I am a good deal clearer about the nature of relevance and of the circumstances in which it is required.

It is now time to show the connection between the Cooperative Principle and maxims, on the one hand, and conversational implicature on the other.

A participant in a talk exchange may fail to fulfill a maxim in various ways, which include the following:

1. He may quietly and unostentatiously *violate* a maxim; if so, in some cases he will be liable to mislead.

2. He may *opt out* from the operation both of the maxim and of the Cooperative Principle; he may say, indicate, or allow it to become plain that he is unwilling to cooperate in the way the maxim requires. He may say, for example, "I cannot say more; my lips are sealed."

3. He may be faced by a *clash*: He may be unable, for example, to fulfill the first maxim of Quantity (Be as informative as is required) without violating the second maxim of Quality (Have adequate evidence for what you say).

4. He may *flout* a maxim; that is, he may *blatantly* fail to fulfill it. On the assumption that the speaker is able to fulfill the maxim and to do so without violating another maxim (because of a clash), is not opting out, and is not, in view of the blatancy of his performance, trying to mislead, the hearer is faced with a minor problem: How can his saying what he did say be reconciled with the supposition that he is observing the overall Cooperative Principle? This situation is one that characteristically gives rise to a conversational implicature; and when a conversational implicature is generated in this way, I shall say that a maxim is being *exploited*.

I am now in a position to characterize the notion of conversation-al implicature. A man who, by (in, when) saying (or making as if to say) that *p* has implicated that *q*, may be said to have conversationally implicat-ed that *q*, *provided that* (1) he is to be presumed to be observing the conver-sational maxims, or at least the Cooperative Principle; (2) the supposition that he is aware that, or thinks that, *q* is required in order to make his say-ing or making as if to say *p* (or doing so in *those* terms) consistent with this presumption; and (3) the speaker thinks (and would expect the hearer to think that the speaker thinks) that it is within the competence of the hear-er to work out, or grasp intuitively, that the supposition mentioned in (2) *is* required. Apply this to my initial example, to B's remark that C has not yet been to prison. In a suitable setting A might reason as follows: "(1) B has apparently violated the maxim 'Be relevant' and so may be regarded as hav-ing flouted one of the maxims conjoining perspicuity, yet I have no reason to suppose that he is opting out from the operation of the CP; (2) given the circumstances, I can regard his irrelevance as only apparent if, and only if, I suppose him to think that C is potentially dishonest; (3) B knows that I am capable of working out step (2). So B implicates that C is potentially dishonest."

The presence of a conversational implicature must be capable of being worked out; for even if it can in fact be intuitively grasped, unless the intuition is replaceable by an argument, the implicature (if present at all) will not count as a *conversational* implicature; it will be a *conventional* impli-cature. To work out that a particular conversational implicature is present, the hearer will rely on the following data: (1) the conventional meaning of the words used, together with the identity of any references that may be involved; (2) the Cooperative Principle and its maxims; (3) the context, linguistic or otherwise, of the utterance; (4) other items of background knowledge; and (5) the fact (or supposed fact) that all relevant items falling under the previous headings are available to both participants and both par-ticipants know or assume this to be the case. A general pattern for the work-ing out of a conversational implicature might be given as follows: 'He has said that *p*; there is no reason to suppose that he is not observing the max-ims, or at least the Cooperative Principle; he could not be doing this unless he thought that *q*; he knows (and knows that I know that he knows) that I can see that the supposition that he thinks that *q is* required; he has done nothing to stop me thinking that *q*; he intends me to think, or is at least willing to allow me to think, that *q*; and so he has implicated that *q*.'

Examples

I shall now offer a number of examples, which I shall divide into three groups.

Group A.

Examples in which no maxim is violated, or at least in which it is not clear that any maxim is violated:
(1) A is standing by an obviously immobilized car and is approached by B, the following exchange takes place:

> A: I am out of petrol
> B: There is a garage round the corner.

(Gloss: B would be infringing the maxim "Be relevant" unless he thinks, or thinks it possible, that the garage is open, and has petrol to sell; so he implicates that the garage is, or at least may be open, etc.) In this example, unlike the case of the remark "He hasn't been to prison yet," the unstated connection between B's remark and A's remark is so obvious that, even if one interprets the supermaxim of Manner, "Be perspicuous," as applying not only to the expression of what is said but also to the connection of what is said with adjacent remarks, there seems to be no case for regarding that supermaxim as infringed in this example.
(2) The next example is perhaps a little less clear in this respect:

> A: Smith doesn't seem to have a girlfriend these days.
> B: He has been paying a lot of visits to New York lately.

B implicates that Smith has, or may have, a girlfriend in New York. (A gloss is unnecessary in view of that given for the previous example.)

In both examples, the speaker implicates that which he must be assumed to believe in order to preserve the assumption that he is observing the maxim of relation.

Group B.

An example in which a maxim is violated, but its violation is to be explained by the supposition of a clash with another maxim:
(3) A is planning with B an itinerary for a holiday in France. Both know that A wants to see his friend C, if to do so would not involve too great a prolongation of his journey:

A: Where does C live?
B: Somewhere in the South of France.

(Gloss: There is no reason to suppose that B is opting out; his answer is, as he well knows, less informative than is required to meet A's needs. This infringement of the first maxim of Quantity can be explained only by the supposition that B is aware that to be more informative would be to say something that infringed the maxim of Quality, "Don't say what you lack adequate evidence for," so B implicates that he does not know in which town C lives.)

Group C.

Examples that involve exploitation, that is, a procedure by which a maxim is flouted for the purpose of getting in a conversational implicature by means of something of the nature of a figure of speech:

In these examples, though some maxim is violated at the level of what is said, the hearer is entitled to assume that that maxim, or at least the overall Cooperative Principle, is observed at the level of what is implicated.
(1a) A flouting of the first maxim of Quantity.
A is writing a testimonial about a pupil who is a candidate for a philosophy job, and his letter reads as follows: "Dear Sir, Mr. X's command of English is excellent, and his attendance at tutorials has been regular. Yours, etc."
(Gloss: A cannot be opting out, since if he wished to be uncooperative, why write at all? He cannot be unable, through ignorance, to say more, since the man is his pupil; moreover, he knows that more information than this is wanted. He must, therefore, be wishing to impart information that he is reluctant to write down. This supposition is tenable only on the assumption that he thinks Mr. X is no good at philosophy. This, then, is what he is implicating.)
      Extreme examples of a flouting of the first maxim of Quantity are provided by utterances of patent tautologies like "Women are women" and "War is war." I would wish to maintain that at the level of what is said, in my favored sense, such remarks are totally noninfomative and so, at that level, cannot but infringe the first maxim of Quantity in any conversational context. They are, of course, informative at the level of what is implicated, and the hearer's identification of their informative content at this level is dependent on his ability to explain the speaker's selection of this *particular* patent tautology.
(1b) An infringement of the second maxim of Quantity, "Do not give more information than is required," on the assumption that the existence of such a maxim should be admitted. A wants to know whether *p*, and B volunteers

not only the information that p, but information to the effect that it is certain that p, and that the evidence for its being the case that p is so-and-so and such-and-such.

B's volubility may be undesigned, and if it is so regarded by A it may raise in A's mind a doubt as to whether B is as certain as he says he is ('Methinks the lady doth protest too much'). But if it is thought of as designed, it would be an oblique way of conveying that it is to some degree controversial whether or not p. It is, however, arguable that such an implicature could be explained by reference to the maxim of Relation without invoking an alleged second maxim of Quantity.

(2a) Examples in which the first maxim of Quality is flouted.

(i) Irony: X, with whom A has been on close terms until now, has betrayed a secret of A's to a business rival. A and his audience both know this. A says "X is a fine friend." (Gloss: It is perfectly obvious to A and his audience that what A has said or has made as if to say is something he does not believe, and the audience knows that A knows that this is obvious to the audience. So, unless A's utterance is entirely pointless, A must be trying to get across some other proposition than the one he purports to be putting forward. This must be some obviously related proposition; the most obviously related proposition is the contradictory of the one he purports to be putting forward.)

(ii) Metaphor: Examples like "You are the cream in my coffee" characteristically involve categorial falsity, so the contradictory of what the speaker has made as if to say will, strictly speaking, be a truism; so it cannot be *that* that such a speaker is trying to get across. The most likely supposition is that the speaker is attributing to his audience some feature or features in respect of which the audience resembles (more or less fancifully) the mentioned substance.

It is possible to combine metaphor and irony by imposing on the hearer two stages of interpretation. I say "You are the cream in my coffee," intending the hearer to reach first the metaphor interpretant "You are my pride and joy" and then the irony interpretant "You are my bane."

(iii) Meiosis: Of a man known to have broken up all the furniture, one says "He was a little intoxicated."

(iv) Hyperbole: Every nice girl loves a sailor.

(2b) Examples in which the second maxim of Quality, "Do not say that for which you lack adequate evidence," is flouted are perhaps not easy to find, but the following seems to be a specimen. I say of X's wife, "She is probably deceiving him this evening." In a suitable context, or with a suitable gesture or tone of voice, it may be clear that I have no adequate reason for supposing this to be the case. My partner, to preserve the assumption that the conversational game is still being played, assumes that I am getting at some related proposition for the acceptance of which I *do* have reasonable basis.

The related proposition might well be that she is given to deceiving her husband, or possibly that she is the sort of person who would not stop short of such conduct.

(3) Examples in which an implicature is achieved by real, as distinct from apparent, violation of the maxim of Relation are perhaps rare, but the following seems to be a good candidate. At a genteel tea party, A says "Mrs X is an old bag." There is a moment of appalled silence, and then B says "The weather has been quite delightful this summer, hasn't it?" B has blatantly refused to make what *he* says relevant to A's preceding remark. He thereby implicates that A's remark should not be discussed and, perhaps more specifically, that A has committed a social gaffe.

(4) Examples in which various maxims falling under the supermaxim "Be perspicuous" are flouted.

(i) Ambiguity. We must remember that we are concerned only with ambiguity that is deliberate, and that the speaker intends or expects to be recognized by his hearer. The problem the hearer has to solve is why a speaker should, when still playing the conversational game, go out of his way to choose an ambiguous utterance. There are two types of cases:

(a) Examples in which there is no difference, or no striking difference, between two interpretations of an utterance with respect to straightforwardness; neither interpretation is notably more sophisticated, less standard, more recondite or more far-fetched than the other. We might consider Blake's lines: "Never seek to tell thy love, Love that never told can be." To avoid the complications introduced by the presence of the imperative mood, I shall consider the related sentence, "I sought to tell my love, love that never told can be." There may be a double ambiguity here. "My love" may refer to either a state of emotion or an object of emotion, and "love that never told can be" may mean either "Love that cannot be told" or "love that if told cannot continue to exist." Partly because of the sophistication of the poet and partly because of internal evidence (that the ambiguity is kept up), there seems to be no alternative to supposing that the ambiguities are deliberate and that the poet is conveying both what he would be saying if one interpretation were intended rather than the other, and vice versa; though no doubt the poet is not explicitly *saying* any one of these things but only conveying or suggesting them (cf. "Since she [nature] pricked thee out of women's pleasure, mine be thy love, and thy love's use their treasure.")

(b) Examples in which one interpretation is notably less straightforward than another. Take the complex example of the British General who captured the town of Sind and sent back the message *Peccavi*. The ambiguity involved ("I have Sind"/"I have sinned") is phonemic, not morphemic; and the expression actually used is unambiguous, but since it is in a language foreign to speaker and hearer, translation is called for, and the ambiguity resides in the standard translation into native English.

Whether or not the straightforward interpretant ("I have sinned") is being conveyed, it seems that the nonstraightforward must be. There might be stylistic reasons for conveying by a sentence merely its non-straightforward interpretant, but it would be pointless, and perhaps also stylistically objectionable, to go to the trouble of finding an expression that nonstraightforwardly conveys that p, thus imposing on an audience the effort involved in finding this interpretant, if this interpretant were otiose so far as communication was concerned. Whether the straightforward interpretant is also being conveyed seems to depend on whether such a supposition would conflict with other conversational requirements, for example, would it be relevant, would it be something the speaker could be supposed to accept, and so on. If such requirements are not satisfied, then the straightforward interpretant is not being conveyed. If they are, it is. If the author of *Peccavi* could naturally be supposed to think that he had committed some kind of transgression, for example, had disobeyed his orders in capturing Sind, and if reference to such a transgression would be relevant to the presumed interests of the audience, then he would have been conveying both interpretants; otherwise he would be conveying only the nonstraightforward one.

(ii) Obscurity. How do I exploit, for the purposes of communication, a deliberate and overt violation of the requirement that I should avoid obscurity? Obviously, if the Cooperative Principle is to operate, I must intend my partner to understand what I am saying despite the obscurity I import into my utterance. Suppose that A and B are having a conversation in the presence of a third party, for example, a child, then A might be deliberately obscure, though not too obscure, in the hope that B would understand and the third party not. Furthermore, if A expects B to see that A is being deliberately obscure, it seems reasonable to suppose that, in making his conversational contribution in this way, A is implicating that the contents of his communication should not be imparted to the third party.

(iii) Failure to be brief or succinct. Compare the remarks:

(a) Miss X sang "Home sweet home."
(b) Miss X produced a series of sounds that corresponded closely with the score of "Home sweet home."

Suppose that a reviewer has chosen to utter (b) rather than (a). (Gloss: Why has he selected that rigmarole in place of the concise and nearly synonymous "sang"? Presumably, to indicate some striking difference between Miss X's performance and those to which the word "singing" is usually applied. The most obvious supposition is that Miss X's performance suffered from some hideous defect. The reviewer knows that this supposition is what is likely to spring to mind, so that is what he is implicating).

I have so far considered only cases of what I might call particular-ized conversational implicature – that is to say, cases in which an implica-ture is carried by saying that p on a particular occasion in virtue of special features of the context, cases in which there is no room for the idea that an implicature of this sort is *normally* carried by saying that p. But there are cases of generalized conversational implicature. Sometimes one can say that the use of a certain form of words in an utterance would normally (in the *absence* of special circumstances) carry such-and-such an implicature or type of implicature. Noncontroversial examples are perhaps hard to find, since it is all too easy to treat a generalized conversational implicature as if it were a conventional implicature. I offer an example that I hope may be fairly noncontroversial.

Anyone who uses a sentence of the form "X is meeting a woman this evening" would normally implicate that the person to be met was some-one other than X's wife, mother, sister, or perhaps even close platonic friend. Similarly, if I were to say "X went into a house yesterday and found a tortoise inside the front door," my hearer would normally be surprised if some time later I revealed that the house was X's own. I could produce sim-ilar linguistic phenomena involving the expressions "*a garden*," "*a car*," "*a college*," and so on. Sometimes, however, there would normally be no such implicature ("I have been sitting in a car all morning"), and sometimes a reverse implicature ("I broke a finger yesterday"). I am inclined to think that one would not lend a sympathetic ear to a philosopher who suggested that there are three senses of the form of expression "an X": one in which it means roughly 'something that satisfies the conditions defining the word X,' another in which it means approximately 'an X (in the first sense) that is only remotely related in a certain way to some person indicated by the con-text,' and yet another in which it means 'an X (in the first sense) that is closely related in a certain way to some person indicated by the context.' Would we not much prefer an account on the following lines (which, of course, may be incorrect in detail): When someone, by using the form of expression "an X," implicates that the X does not belong to or is not other-wise closely connected with some identifiable person, the implicature is pre-sent because the speaker has failed to be specific in a way in which he might have been expected to be specific, with the consequence that it is likely to be assumed that he is not in a position to be specific. This is a familiar impli-cature situation and is classifiable as a failure, for one reason or another, to fulfill the first maxim of Quantity. The only difficult question is why it should, in certain cases, be presumed, independently of information about particular contexts of utterance, that specification of the closeness or remoteness of the connection between a particular person or object and a further person who is mentioned or indicated by the utterance should be likely to be of interest. The answer must lie in the following region:

Transactions between a person and other persons or things closely connected with him are liable to be very different as regards their concomitants and
results from the same sort of transactions involving only remotely connected persons or things; the concomitants and results, for instance, of my finding a hole in my roof are likely to be very different from the concomitants
and results of my finding a hole in someone else's roof. Information, like
money, is often given without the giver's knowing to just what use the recip-
ient will want to put it. If someone to whom a transaction is mentioned
gives it further consideration, he is likely to find himself wanting the
answers to further questions that the speaker may not be able to identify in
advance; if the appropriate specification will be likely to enable the hearer
to answer a considerable variety of such questions for himself, then there is
a presumption that the speaker should include it in his remark; if not, then
there is no such presumption.

   Finally, we can now show that, conversational implicature being
what it is, it must possess certain features.

   1. Since, to assume the presence of a conversational implicature,
we have to assume that at least the Cooperative Principle is being observed,
and since it is possible to opt out of the observation of this principle, it follows that a generalized conversational implicature can be canceled in a particular case. It may be explicitly canceled, by the addition of a clause that
states or implies that the speaker has opted out, or it may be contextually
canceled, if the form of utterance that usually carries it is used in a context
that makes it clear that the speaker IS opting out.

   2. Insofar as the calculation that a particular conversational implicature is present requires, besides contextual and background information,
only a knowledge of what has been said (or of the conventional commitment of the utterance), and insofar as the manner of expression plays no
role in the calculation, it will not be possible to find another way of saying
the same thing, which simply lacks the implicature in question, except
where some special feature of the substituted version is itself relevant to the
determination of an implicature (in virtue of one of the maxims of
Manner). If we call this feature *nondetachability*, one may expect a generalized conversational implicature that is carried by a familiar, nonspecial locution to have a high degree of nondetachability.

   3. To speak approximately, since the calculation of the presence of
a conversational implicature presupposes an initial knowledge of the conventional force of the expression the utterance of which carries the implicature, a conversational implicatum will be a condition that is not included in the original specification of the expression's conventional force.
Though it may not be impossible for what starts life, so to speak, as a conversational implicature to become conventionalized, to suppose that this is
so in a given case would require special justification. So, initially at least,

conversational implicata are not part of the meaning of the expressions to the employment of which they attach.

    4. Since the truth of a conversational implicatum is not required by the truth of what is said (what is said may be true – what is implicated may be false), the implicature is not carried by what is said, but only by the saying of what is said, or by 'putting it that way.'

    5. Since, to calculate a conversational implicature is to calculate what has to be supposed in order to preserve the supposition that the Cooperative Principle is being observed, and since there may be various possible specific explanations, a list of which may be open, the conversational implicatum in such cases will be disjunction of such specific explanations; and if the list of these is open, the implicatum will have just the kind of indeterminacy that many actual implicata do in fact seem to possess.

ON REFERRING

Peter F. Strawson

We very commonly use expressions of certain kinds to mention or refer to some individual person or single object or particular event or place or process, in the course of doing what we should normally describe as making a statement about that person, object, place, event, or process. I shall call this way of using expressions the 'uniquely referring use'. The classes of expressions which are most commonly used in this way are: singular demonstrative pronouns ("this" and "that"); proper names e.g. ("Venice," "Napoleon," "John"); singular personal and impersonal pronouns ("he," "she," "I," "you," "it"); and phrases beginning with the definite article followed by a noun, qualified or unqualified, in the singular (e.g. "the table," "the old man," "the king of France"). Any expression of any of these classes can occur as the subject of what would traditionally be regarded as a singular subject-predicate sentence; and would, so occurring, exemplify the use I wish to discuss.

I do not want to say that expressions belonging to these classes never have any other use than the one I want to discuss. On the contrary, it is obvious that they do. It is obvious that anyone who uttered the sentence, "The whale is a mammal," would be using the expression "the whale" in a way quite different from the way it would be used by anyone who had occasion seriously to utter the sentence, "The whale struck the ship." In the first sentence one is obviously *not* mentioning, and in the second sentence one obviously *is* mentioning, a particular whale. Again if I said, "Napoleon was the greatest French soldier," I should be using the word "Napoleon" to mention a certain individual, but I should not be using the phrase, "the greatest French soldier," to mention an individual, but to say something about an individual I had already mentioned. It would be natural to say that in using this sentence I was talking *about* Napoleon and that what I was *saying* about him was that he was the greatest French soldier. But of course I *could* use the expression, "the greatest French soldier," to mention an individual; for example, by saying: "The greatest French soldier died in exile." So it is obvious that at least some expressions belonging to the classes I mentioned *can* have uses other than the use I am anxious to discuss. Another thing I do not want to say is that in any given sentence there is never more than one expression used in the way I propose to discuss. On the contrary, it is obvious that there may be more than one. For example, it would be natural to say that, in seriously using the sentence, "The whale struck the ship," I was saying something about both a certain whale and a certain ship, that I was using each of the expressions "the whale" and "the ship" to mention a particular object; or, in other words, that I was using each of these expressions in the uniquely referring way. In general, however, I shall confine my attention to cases where an expression used in this way occurs as the grammatical subject of a sentence.

I think it is true to say that Russell's theory of descriptions, which is concerned with the last of the four classes of expressions I mentioned above (i.e. with expressions of the form "the so-and-so"), is still widely accepted among logicians as giving a correct account of the use of such expressions in ordinary language. I want to show in the first place, that this theory, so regarded, embodies some fundamental mistakes.

What question or questions about phrases of the form "the so-and-so" was the theory of descriptions designed to answer? I think that at least one of the questions may be illustrated as follows. Suppose someone were now to utter the sentence, "The king of France is wise." No one would say that the sentence which had been uttered was meaningless. Everyone would agree that it was significant. But everyone knows that there is not at present a king of France. One of the questions the theory of descriptions was designed to answer was the question: How can such a sentence as "The king of France is wise" be significant even when there is nothing which answers to the description it contains, i.e., in this case, nothing which answers to the description "The king of France"? And one of the reasons why Russell thought it important to give a correct answer to this question was that he thought it important to show that another answer which might be given was wrong. The answer that he thought was wrong, and to which he was anxious to supply an alternative, might be exhibited as the conclusion of either of the following two fallacious arguments. Let us call the sentence "The king of France is wise" the sentence S. Then the first argument is as follows:

(1) The phrase, "the king of France," is the subject of the sentence S.
Therefore (2) if S is a significant sentence, S is a sentence *about* the king of France.

But (3) if there in no sense exists a king of France, the sentence is not about anything, and hence not about the king of France. Therefore (4) since S is significant, there must in some sense (in some world) exist (or subsist) the king of France.

And the second argument is as follows:

(1) If S is significant, it is either true or false.
(2) S is true if the king of France is wise and false if the king of France is not wise.
(3) But the statement that the king of France is wise and the statement that the king of France is not wise are alike true only if there is (in some sense, in some world) something which is the king of France.
Hence (4) since S is significant, there follows the same conclusion as before.

These are fairly obviously bad arguments, and, as we should expect, Russell rejects them. The postulation of a world of strange entities, to which the king of France belongs, offends, he says, against "that feeling for reality which ought to be preserved even in the most abstract studies." The fact that Russell rejects these arguments is, however, less interesting than the extent to which, in rejecting their conclusion, he concedes the more important of their principles. Let me refer to the phrase, "the king of France," as the phrase D. Then I think Russell's reasons for rejecting these two arguments can be summarized as follows. The mistake arises, he says, from thinking that D, which is certainly the *grammatical* subject of S, is also the *logical* subject of S. But D is not the logical subject of S. In fact S, although grammatically it has a singular subject and a predicate, is not logically a subject-predicate sentence at all. The proposition it expresses is a complex kind of *existential* proposition, part of which might be described as a "uniquely existential" proposition. To exhibit the logical form of the proposition, we should rewrite the sentence in a logically appropriate grammatical form, in such a way that the deceptive similarity of S to a sentence expressing a subject-predicate proposition would disappear, and we should be safeguarded against arguments such as the bad ones I outlined above. Before recalling the details of Russell's analysis of S, let us notice what his answer, as I have so far given it, seems to imply. His answer seems to imply that in the case of a sentence which is similar to S in that (1) it is grammatically of the subject-predicate form and (2) its grammatical subject does not refer to anything, then the only alternative to its being meaningless is that it should not really (i.e. logically) be of the subject-predicate form at all, but of some quite different form. And this in its turn seems to imply that if there are any sentences which are genuinely of the subject-predicate form, then the very fact of their being significant, having a meaning, guarantees that there *is* something referred to by the logical (and grammatical) subject. Moreover, Russell's answer seems to imply that there are such sentences. For if it is true that one may be misled by the grammatical similarity of S to other sentences into thinking that it is logically of the subject-predicate form, then surely there must be other sentences grammatically similar to S, which *are* of the subject-predicate form. To show not only that Russell's answer seems to imply these conclusions, but that he accepted at least the first two of them, it is enough to consider what he says about a class of expressions which he calls "logically proper names" and contrasts with expressions, like D, which he calls "definite descriptions." Of logically proper names Russell says or implies the following things:

> (1) That they and they alone can occur as subjects of sentences which are genuinely of the subject-predicate form.
> (2) That an expression intended to be a logically proper name is *meaningless* unless there is some single object for which it stands: for the *meaning* of such an expression just is the individual object which the expression designates. To be a name at all, therefore, it *must* designate something.

It is easy to see that if anyone believes these two propositions, then the only way for him to save the significance of the sentence S is to deny that it is a logically subject-predicate sentence. Generally, we may say that Russell recognizes only two ways in which sentences which seem, from their grammatical structure, to be about some particular person or individual object or event, can be significant:

> (1) The first is that their grammatical form should be misleading as to their logical form, and that they should be analyzable, like S, as a special kind of existential sentence.
> (2) The second is that their grammatical subject should be a logically proper name, of which the meaning is the individual thing it designates.

I think that Russell is unquestionably wrong in this, and that sentences which are significant, and which begin with an expression used in the uniquely referring way, fall into neither of these two classes. Expressions used in the uniquely referring way are never either logically proper names or descriptions, if what is meant by calling them "descriptions" is that they are to be analyzed in accordance with the model provided by Russell's theory of descriptions.

There are no logically proper names and there are no descriptions (in this sense).

Let us now consider the details of Russell's analysis. According to Russell, anyone who asserted S would be asserting that:

(1) There is a king of France
(2) There is not more than one king of France
(3) There is nothing which is king of France and is not wise

It is easy to see both how Russell arrived at this analysis, and how it enables him to answer the question with which we began, viz. the question: How can the sentence S be significant when there is no king of France? The way in which he arrived at the analysis was clearly by asking himself what would be the circumstances in which we would say that anyone who uttered the sentence S had made a true assertion. And it does seem pretty clear, and I have no wish to dispute, that the sentences (1)-(3) above do describe circumstances which are at least *necessary* conditions of anyone making a true assertion by uttering the sentence S. But, as I hope to show, to say this is not at all the same thing as to say that Russell has given a correct account of the use of the sentence S or even that he has given an account which, though incomplete, is correct as far as it goes; and is certainly not at all the same thing as to say that the model translation provided is a correct model for all (or for any) singular sentences beginning with a phrase of the form "the so-and-so."

It is also easy to see how this analysis enables Russell to answer the question of how the sentence S can be significant, even when there is no king of France. For, if this analysis is correct, anyone who utters the sentence S today would be jointly asserting three propositions, one of which (viz. that there is a king of France) would be false; and since the conjunction of three propositions, of which one is false, is itself false, the assertion as a whole would be significant, but false. So neither of the bad arguments for subsistent entities would apply to such an assertion.

II

As a step towards showing that Russell's solution of his problem is mistaken, and towards providing the correct solution, I want now to draw certain distinctions. For this purpose I shall, for the remainder of this section, refer to an expression which has a uniquely referring use as "an expression" for short; and to a sentence beginning with such an expression as "a sentence" for short. The distinctions I shall draw are rather rough and ready, and, no doubt, difficult cases could be produced which would call for their refinement. But I think they will serve my purpose. The distinctions are between:

(A1) a sentence
(A2) a use of a sentence
(A3) an utterance of a sentence

and, correspondingly, between:

(B1) an expression
(B2) a use of an expression
(B3) an utterance of an expression

Consider again the sentence, "The king of France is wise." It is easy to imagine that this sentence was uttered at various times from, say, the beginning of the seventeenth century onwards, during the reigns of each successive French monarch; and easy to imagine that it was also uttered during the subsequent periods in which France was not a monarchy. Notice that it was natural for me to speak of "the sentence" or "this sentence" being uttered at various times during this period; or, in other words, that it would be natural and correct to speak of one and the same sentence being uttered on all these various occasions. It is in the sense in which it would be correct to speak of *one and the same* sentence being uttered on all these various occasions that I want to use the expression (A1) "a sentence." There are, however, obvious differences between different *occasions of the use* of this sentence. For instance, if one man uttered it in the reign of Louis XIV and another man uttered it in the reign of Louis XV, it would be natural to say (to assume) that they were respectively talking about different people; and it might be held that the first man, in using the sentence, made a true assertion, while the second man, in using the same sentence, made a false assertion. If on the other hand two different men simultaneously uttered the sentence (e.g. if one wrote it and the other spoke it) during the reign of Louis XIV, it would be natural to say (assume) that they were both talking about the same person, and, in that case, in using the sentence, they *must* either both have made a true assertion or both have made a false assertion. And this illustrates what I mean by a *use* of a sentence. The two men who uttered the sentence, one in the reign of Louis XV and one in the reign of Louis XIV, each made a different use of the same sentence; whereas the two men who uttered the sentence simultaneously in the reign of Louis XIV, made the same use[1] of the same sentence. Obviously in the case of this sentence, and equally obviously in the case of many others, we cannot talk of *the sentence* being true or false, but only of its being used to make a true or false assertion or (if this is preferred) to express a true or a false proposition. And equally obviously we cannot talk of *the sentence* being *about* a particular person, for the same sentence may be used at different times to talk about quite different particular persons, but only of *a use* of the sentence to talk about a particular person. Finally it will make sufficiently clear what I mean by an utterance of a sentence if I say that the two men who simultaneously uttered the sentence in the reign of Louis XIV made two different utterances of the same sentence, though they made the same *use* of the sentence.

If we now consider not the whole sentence, "The king of France is wise," but that part of it which is the expression, "the king of France," it is obvious that we can make analogous, though not identical distinctions between (1) the expression, (2) a use of the expression, and (3) an utterance of the expression. The distinctions will not be identical; we obviously cannot correctly talk of the expression "the king of France" being used to express a true or false proposition, since in general only sentences can be used truly or falsely; and similarly it is only by using a sentence and not by using an expression alone, that you can talk about a particular person. Instead, we shall say in this case that you *use* the expression to *mention* or *refer* to a particular person in the course of using the sentence to talk about him. But obviously in this case, and a great many others, the *expression* (B1) cannot be said to mention, or refer to, anything, any more than the *sentence* can be said to be true or false. The same expression can have different mentioning-uses, as the same sentence can be used to make statements with different truth values. 'Mentioning', or 'referring', is not something an expression does; it is something that someone can use an expression to do. Mentioning, or referring to, something is a characteristic of *a use* of an expression, just as 'being about' something, and truth-or-falsity, are characteristics of *a use* of a sentence.

A very different example may help to make these distinctions clearer. Consider another case of an expression which has a uniquely referring use, viz. the expression "I"; and consider the sentence, "I am hot." Countless people may use this same sentence; but it is logically impossible for two different people to make *the same use* of this sentence: or, if this is preferred, to use it to express the same proposition. The expression "I" may correctly be used by (and only by) any one of innumerable people to refer to himself. To say this is to say something about the expression "I": it is, in a sense, to give its meaning. This is the sort of thing that can be said about *expressions*. But it makes no sense to say of the *expression* "I" that it refers to a particular person. This is the sort of thing that can be said only of a particular use of the expression.

Let me use "type" as an abbreviation for "sentence or expression." Then I am not saying that there are sentences and expressions (types), *and* uses of them, *and* utterances of them, as there are ships *and* shoes *and* sealing-wax. I am saying that we cannot say *the same things* about types, uses of types, and utterances of types. And the fact is that we do talk about types; and that confusion is apt to result from the failure to notice the differences between what we can say about these and what we can say only about the *uses* of types. We are apt to fancy we are talking about sentences and expressions when we are talking about the uses of sentences and expressions.

This is what Russell does. Generally, as against Russell, I shall say this. Meaning (in at least one important sense) is a function of the sentence or expression; mentioning and referring and truth or falsity, are functions of the use of the sentence or expression. To give the meaning of an expression (in the sense in which I am using the word) is to give *general directions* for its use to refer to or mention particular objects or persons; to give the meaning of a sentence is to give *general directions* for its use in making true or false assertions. It is not to talk about any particular occasion of the use of the sentence or expression. The meaning of an expression cannot be identified with the object it is used, on a particular occasion, to refer to. The meaning of a sentence cannot be identified with the assertion it is used, on a particular occasion, to make. For to talk about the meaning of an expression or sentence is not to talk about its use on a particular occasion, but about the rules, habits, conventions governing its correct use, on all occasions, to refer or to assert. So the question of whether a sentence or expression is *significant or not* has nothing whatever to do with the question of whether the sentence, *uttered on a particular occasion*, is, on that occasion, being used to make a true-or-false assertion or not, or of whether the expression is, on that occasion, being used to refer to, or mention, anything at all.

The source of Russell's mistake was that he thought that referring or mentioning, if it occurred at all, must be meaning. He did not distinguish (B1) from (B2); he confused expressions with their use in a particular context; and so confused meaning with mentioning, with referring. If I talk about my handkerchief, I can, perhaps, produce the object I am referring to out of my pocket. I cannot produce the meaning of the expression, "my handkerchief," out of my pocket. Because Russell confused meaning with mentioning, he thought that if there were any expressions having a uniquely referring use, which were what they seemed (i.e. logical subjects) and not something else in disguise, their meaning must *be* the particular object which they were used to refer to. Hence the troublesome mythology of the logically proper name. But if someone asks me the meaning of the expression "this" – once Russell's favorite candidate for this status – I do not hand him the object I have just used the expression to refer to, adding at the same time that the meaning of the word changes every time it is used. Nor do I hand him all the objects it ever has been, or might be, used to refer to. I explain and illustrate the conventions governing the use of the expression. This *is* giving the meaning of the expression. It is quite different from giving (in any sense of giving) the object to which it refers; for the expression itself does not refer to anything; though it can be used, on different occasions, to refer to innumerable things. Now as a matter of fact there is, in English, a sense of the word "mean" in which this word does approximate to "indicate, mention or refer to"; e.g. when somebody (unpleasantly) says, "I mean you"; or when I point and say, "That's the one I mean." But *the one I meant* is quite different from *the meaning of the expression* I used to talk of it. In this special sense of "mean," it is people who mean, not expressions.

People use expressions to refer to particular things. But the meaning of an expression is not the set of things or the single thing it may correctly be used to refer to: the meaning is the set of rules, habits, conventions for its use in referring.

It is the same with sentences: even more obviously so. Everyone knows that the sentence, "The table is covered with books" is significant, and everyone knows what it means. But if I ask, "What object is that sentence about?" I am asking an absurd question – a question which cannot be asked about the sentence, but only about some use of the sentence: and in this case the sentence has not been used to talk about something, it has only been taken as an example. In knowing what it means, you are knowing how it could correctly be used to talk about things: so knowing the meaning has nothing to do with knowing about any particular use of the sentence to talk about anything. Similarly, if I ask: "Is the sentence true or false?" I am asking an absurd question, which becomes no less absurd if I add, "It must be one or the other since it is significant." The question is absurd, because the *sentence* is neither true nor false any more than it is *about* some object. Of course the fact that it is significant is the same as the fact that it *can* correctly be used to talk about something and that, in so using it, someone will be making a true or false assertion. And I will add that it will be used to make a true or false assertion *only* if the person using it *is* talking about something. If, when he utters it, he is not talking about anything, then his use is not a genuine one, but a spurious or pseudo-use: he is not making either a true or a false assertion, though he may think he is. And this points the way to the correct answer to the puzzle to which the theory of descriptions gives a fatally incorrect answer. The important point is that the question of whether the sentence is significant or not is quite independent of the question that can be raised about a particular use of it, viz. the question whether it is a genuine or a spurious use, whether it is being used to talk about something, or in make-believe, or as an example in philosophy. The question whether the sentence is significant or not is the question whether there exist such language habits, conventions or rules that the sentence logically could be used to talk about something; and is hence quite independent of the question whether it is being so used on a particular occasion.

III

Consider again the sentence, "The king of France is wise," and the true and false things Russell says about it.

There are at least two true things which Russell would say about the sentence:

(1) The first is that it is significant; that if anyone were now to utter it, he would be uttering a significant sentence.

(2) The second is that anyone now uttering the sentence would be making a true assertion only if there in fact at present existed one and only one king of France, and if he were wise.

What are the false things which Russell would say about the sentence? They are:

(1) That anyone now uttering it would be making a true assertion or a false assertion.

(2) That part of what he would be asserting would be that there at present existed one and only one king of France.

I have already given some reasons for thinking that these two statements are incorrect. Now suppose someone were in fact to say to you with a perfectly serious air: "The king of France is wise." Would you say, "That's untrue"? I think it is quite certain that you would not. But suppose he went on to *ask* you whether you thought that what he had just said was true, or was false; whether you agreed or disagreed with what he had just said. I think you would be inclined, with some hesitation, to say that you did not do either; that the question of whether his statement was true or false simply *did not arise*, because there was no such person as the king of France.[2] You might, if he were obviously serious (had a dazed astray-in-the-centuries look), say something like: "I'm afraid you must be under a misapprehension. France is not a monarchy. There is no king of France." And this brings out the point that if a man seriously uttered the sentence, his uttering it would in some sense be *evidence* that he *believed* that there was a king of France. It would not be evidence for his believing this simply in the way in which a man's reaching for his raincoat is evidence for his believing that it is raining. But nor would it be evidence for his believing this in the way in which a man's saying, "It's raining," is evidence for his believing that it is raining. We might put it as follows. To say "The king of France is wise" is, in some sense of 'imply', to *imply* that there is a king of France. But this is a very special and odd sense of 'imply'. 'Implies' in this sense is certainly not equivalent to 'entails' (or 'logically implies'). And this comes out from the fact that when, in response to his statement, we say (as we should) "There is no king of France," we should certainly *not* say we were *contradicting* the statement that the king of France is wise. We are certainly not saying that it is false. We are, rather, giving a reason for saying that the question of whether it is true or false simply does not arise.

And this is where the distinction I drew earlier can help us. The sentence, "The king of France is wise," is certainly significant; but this does not mean that any particular use of it is true or false. We use it truly or false-ly when we use it to talk about someone; when, in using the expression, "The king of France," we are in fact mentioning someone. The fact that the sentence and the expression, respectively, are significant just is the fact that the sentence *could* be used, in certain circumstances, to say something true or false, that the expression *could* be used, in certain circumstances, to men-tion a particular person; and to know their meaning is to know what sort of circumstances these are. So when we utter the sentence without in fact mentioning anybody by the use of the phrase, "The king of France," the sen-tence does not cease to be significant: We simply *fail* to say anything true or false because we simply fail to mention anybody by this particular use of that perfectly significant phrase. It is, if you like, a spurious use of the sentence, and a spurious use of the expression; though we may (or may not) mistak-enly think it a genuine use.

And such spurious uses[3] are very familiar. Sophisticated romanc-ing, sophisticated fiction,[4] depend upon them. If I began, "The king of France is wise," and went on, "and he lives in a golden castle and has a hun-dred wives," and so on, a hearer would understand me perfectly well, with-out supposing *either* that I was talking about a particular person, *or* that I was making a false statement to the effect that there existed such a person as my words described. (It is worth adding that where the use of sentences and expressions is overtly fictional, the sense of the word "about" may change. As Moore said, it is perfectly natural and correct to say that some of the statements in *Pickwick Papers* are *about* Mr. Pickwick. But where the use of sentences and expressions is not overtly fictional, this use of "about" seems less correct; i.e. it would not *in general* be correct to say that a statement was about Mr. X or the so-and-so, unless there were such a person or thing. So it is where the romancing is in danger of being taken seriously that we might answer the question, "Who is he talking about?" with "He's not talking about anybody"; but, in saying this, we are not saying that what he is saying is either false or nonsense.)

Overtly fictional uses apart, however, I said just now that to use such an expression as "The king of France" at the beginning of a sentence was, in some sense of 'imply', to imply that there was a king of France. When a man uses such an expression, he does not *assert*, nor does what he says *entail*, a uniquely existential proposition. But one of the conventional functions of the definite article is to act as a *signal* that a unique reference is being made – a signal, not a disguised assertion. When we begin a sen-tence with "the such-and-such" the use of "the" shows, but does not state, that we are, or intended to be, referring to one particular individual of the species "such-and-such." *Which* particular individual is a matter to be deter-mined from context, time, place, and any other features of the situation of utterance. Now, whenever a man uses any expression, the presumption is that he thinks he is using it correctly: so when he uses the expression, "the such-and-such," in a uniquely referring way, the presumption is that he thinks both that there is *some* individual of that species, and that the context of use will sufficiently determine which one he has in mind. To use the word "the" in this way is then to imply (in the relevant sense of 'imply') that the existential conditions described by Russell are fulfilled. But to use "the" in this way is not to *state* that those conditions are fulfilled. If I begin a sentence with an expression of the form, "the so-and-so," and then am prevented from saying more, I have made no statement of any kind; but I may have succeeded in mentioning someone or something.

The uniquely existential assertion supposed by Russell to be part of any assertion in which a uniquely referring use is made of an expression of the form "the so-and-so" is, he observes, a compound of two assertions. To say that there is a ø is to say something compatible with there being several øs; to say there is not more than one ø is to say something compatible with there being none. To say there is one ø and one only is to compound these two assertions. I have so far been concerned mostly with the alleged assertion of existence and less with the alleged assertion of uniqueness. An example which throws the emphasis on the latter will serve to bring out more clearly the sense of 'implied' in which a uniquely existential assertion is implied, but not entailed, by the use of expressions in the uniquely referring way. Consider the sentence, "The table is covered with books." It is quite certain that in any normal use of this sentence, the expression "the table" would be used to make a unique reference, i.e. to refer to some one table. It is a quite strict use of the definite article, in the sense in which Russell talks on p. 30 of *Principia Mathematica*, of using the article "*strictly*, so as to imply uniqueness." On the same page Russell says that a phrase of the form "the so-and-so," used strictly, "will only have an application in the event of there being one so-and-so and no more." Now it is obviously quite false that the phrase "the table" in the sentence "the table is covered with books," used normally, will "only have an application in the event of there being one table and no more." It is indeed tautologically true that, in such a use, the phrase will have an application only in the event of there being one table and no more *which is being referred to*, and that it will be understood to have an application only in the event of there being one table and no more which it is understood as being used to refer to. To use the sentence is not to assert, but it is (in the special sense discussed) to imply, that there is only one thing which is *both* of the kind specified (i.e. a table) *and is being referred to* by the speaker. It is obviously not to assert this. To refer is not to say you are referring. To say there is *some table or other* to which you are referring is not the same as referring to a particular table. We should have no use for such phrases as "the individual I referred to" unless there were something which counted as referring. (It would make no sense to say you had pointed if there were nothing which counted as pointing.) So once more I draw the conclusion that referring to or mentioning a particular thing cannot be dissolved into any kind of assertion. To refer is not to assert, though you refer in order to go on to assert.

Let me now take an example of the uniquely referring use of an expression not of the form, "the so-and-so." Suppose I advance my hands, cautiously cupped, towards someone, saying, as I do so, "This is a fine red one." He, looking into my hands and seeing nothing there, may say: "What is? What are you talking about?" Or perhaps, "But there's nothing in your hands." Of course it would be absurd to say that, in saying "But you've got nothing in your hands," he was *denying* or *contradicting* what I said. So "this" is not a disguised description in Russell's sense. Nor is it a logically proper name. For one must know what the sentence means in order to react in that way to the utterance of it. It is precisely because the significance of the word "this" is independent of any particular reference it may be used to make, though not independent of the way it may be used to refer, that I can, as in this example, use it to *pretend* to be referring to something.

The general moral of all this is that communication is much less a matter of explicit or disguised assertion than logicians used to suppose. The particular application of this general moral in which I am interested is its application to the case of making a unique reference. It is a part of the significance of expressions of the kind I am discussing that they can be used, in an immense variety of contexts, to make unique references. It is no part of their significance to assert that they are being so used or that the conditions of their being so used are fulfilled. So the wholly important distinction we are required to draw is between

(1) using an expression to make a unique reference; and
(2) asserting that there is one and only one individual which has certain characteristics (e.g. is of a certain kind, or stands in a certain relation to the speaker, or both).

This is, in other words, the distinction between

(1) sentences containing an expression used to indicate or mention or refer to a particular person or thing; and
(2) uniquely existential sentences.

What Russell does is progressively to assimilate more and more sentences of class (1) to sentences of class (2), and consequently to involve himself in insuperable difficulties about logical subjects, and about values for individual variables generally: difficulties which have led him finally to the logically disastrous theory of names developed in the *Enquiry into Meaning and*

Truth and in *Human Knowledge*. That view of the meaning of logical-sub-ject-expressions which provides the whole incentive to the Theory of Descriptions at the same time precludes the possibility of Russell's ever find-ing any satisfactory substitutes for those expressions which, beginning with substantival phrases, he progressively degrades from the status of logical sub-jects.[5] It is not simply, as is sometimes said, the fascination of the relation between a name and its bearer, that is the root of the trouble. Not even names come up to the impossible standard set. It is rather the combination of two more radical misconceptions: first, the failure to grasp the impor-tance of the distinction (section II above) between what may be said of an expression and what may be said of a particular use of it; second, a failure to recognize the uniquely referring use of expressions for the harmless, neces-sary thing it is, distinct from, but complementary to, the predicative or ascriptive use of expressions. The expressions which can in fact occur as sin-gular logical subjects are expressions of the class I listed at the outset (demonstratives, substantival phrases, proper names, pronouns): to say this is to say that these expressions, together with context (in the widest sense), are what one uses to make unique references. The point of the conventions governing the uses of such expressions is, along with the situation of utter-ance, to secure uniqueness of reference. But to do this, enough is enough. We do not, and we cannot, while referring, attain the point of complete explicitness at which the referring function is no longer performed. The actual unique reference made, if any, is a matter of the particular use in the particular context; the significance of the expression used is the set of rules or conventions which permit such references to be made. Hence we can, using significant expressions, pretend to refer, in make-believe or in fiction, or mistakenly think we are referring when we are not referring to anything.[6]

This shows the need for distinguishing two kinds (among many others) of linguistic conventions or rules: rules for referring, and rules for attributing and ascribing; and for an investigation of the former. If we rec-ognize this distinction of use for what it is, we are on the way to solving a number of ancient logical and metaphysical puzzles.

My last two sections are concerned, but only in the barest outline, with these questions.

IV

One of the main purposes for which we use language is the purpose of stat-ing facts about things and persons and events. If we want to fulfill this pur-pose we must have some way of forestalling the question, "What (who, which one) are you talking about?" as well as the question, "What are you saying about it (him, her)?" The task of forestalling the first question is the referring (or identifying) task. The task of forestalling the second is the attributive (or descriptive or classificatory or ascriptive) task. In the conventional English sentence which is used to state, or to claim to state, a fact about an individual thing or person or event, the performance of these two tasks can be roughly and approximately assigned to separable expressions.[7] And in such a sentence, this assigning of expressions to their separate roles corresponds to the conventional grammatical classification of subject and predicate. There is nothing sacrosanct about the employment of separable expressions for these two tasks. Other methods could be, and are, employed. There is, for instance, the method of uttering a single word or attributive phrase in the conspicuous presence of the object referred to; or that analogous method exemplified by, e.g., the painting of the words "unsafe for lories" on a bridge, or the tying of a label reading "first prize" on a vegetable marrow. Or one can imagine an elaborate game in which one never used an expression in the uniquely referring way at all, but uttered only uniquely existential sentences, trying to enable the hearer to identify what was being talked of by means of an accumulation of relative clauses. (This description of the purposes of the game shows in what sense it would be a game: this is not the normal use we make of existential sentences.) Two points require emphasis. The first is that the necessity of performing these two tasks in order to state particular facts requires no transcendental explanation: To call attention to it is partly to elucidate the meaning of the phrase, "stating a fact." The second is that even this elucidation is made in terms derivative from the grammar of the conventional singular sentence; that even the overtly functional, linguistic distinction between the identifying and attributive roles that words may play in language is prompted by the fact that ordinary speech offers us separable expressions to which the different functions may be plausibly and approximately assigned. And this functional distinction has cast long philosophical shadows. The distinctions between particular and universal, between substance and quality, are such pseudo-material shadows, cast by the grammar of the conventional sentence, in which separable expressions play distinguishable roles.[8]

To use a separate expression to perform the first of these tasks is to use an expression in the uniquely referring way. I want now to say something in general about the conventions of use for expressions used in this way, and to contrast them with conventions of ascriptive use. I then proceed to the brief illustration of these general remarks and to some further applications of them.

What in general is required for making a unique reference is, obviously, some device, or devices, for showing both *that* a unique reference is intended and *what* unique reference it is; some device requiring and enabling the hearer or reader to identify what is being talked about. In securing this result, the context of utterance is of an importance which it is almost impossible to exaggerate; and by "context" I mean, at least, the time, the place, the situation, the identity of the speaker, the subjects which form the immediate focus of interest, and the personal histories of both the speaker and those he is addressing. Besides context, there is, of course, convention – linguistic convention. But, except in the case of genuine proper names, of which I shall have more to say later, the fulfillment of more or less precisely stateable contextual conditions is *conventionally* (or, in a wide sense of the word, *logically*) required for the correct referring use of expressions in a sense in which this is not true of correct ascriptive uses. The requirement for the correct application of an expression in its ascriptive use to a certain thing is simply that the thing should be of a certain kind, have certain characteristics. The requirement for the correct application of an expression in its referring use to a certain thing is something over and above any requirement derived from such ascriptive meaning as the expression may have; it is, namely, the requirement that the thing should be in a certain relation to the speaker and to the context of utterance. Let me call this the contextual requirement. Thus, for example, in the limiting case of the word "I" the contextual requirement is that the thing should be identical with the speaker; but in the case of most expressions which have a referring use this requirement cannot be so precisely specified. A further, and perfectly general, difference between conventions for referring and conventions for describing is one we have already encountered, viz. that the fulfillment of the conditions for a correct ascriptive use of an expression is a part of what is stated by such a use; but the fulfillment of the conditions for a correct referring use of an expression is never part of what is stated, though it is (in the relevant sense of 'implied') implied by such a use.

Conventions for referring have been neglected or misinterpreted by logicians. The reasons for this neglect are not hard to see, though they are hard to state briefly. Two of them are, roughly: (1) the preoccupation of most logicians with definitions; (2) the preoccupation of some logicians with formal systems.

(1) A definition, in the most familiar sense, is a specification of the conditions of the correct ascriptive or classificatory use of an expression. Definitions take no account of contextual requirements. So that in so far as the search for the meaning or the search for the analysis of an expression is conceived as the search for a definition, the neglect or misinterpretation of conventions other than ascriptive is inevitable. Perhaps it would be better to say (for I do not wish to legislate about "meaning" or "analysis") that logicians have failed to notice that problems of use are wider than problems of analysis and meaning.

(2) The influence of the preoccupation with mathematics and formal logic is most clearly seen (to take no more recent examples) in the cases of Leibniz and Russell. The constructor of calculuses, not concerned or

required to make factual statements, approaches applied logic with a prejudice. It is natural that he should assume that the types of convention with whose adequacy in one field he is familiar should be really adequate, if only one could see how, in a quite different field – that of statements of fact. Thus we have Leibniz striving desperately to make the uniqueness of unique references a matter of logic in the narrow sense, and Russell striving desperately to do the same thing, in a different way, both for the implication of uniqueness and for that of existence.

It should be clear that the distinction I am trying to draw is primarily one between different roles or parts that expressions may play in language, and not primarily one between different groups of expressions; for some expressions may appear in either role. Some of the kinds of words I shall speak of have predominantly, if not exclusively, a referring role. This is most obviously true of pronouns and ordinary proper names. Some can occur as wholes or parts of expressions which have a predominantly referring use and as wholes or parts of expressions which have a predominantly ascriptive or classificatory use. The obvious cases are common nouns; or common nouns preceded by adjectives, including participial adjectives; or, less obviously, adjectives or participial adjectives alone. Expressions capable of having a referring use also differ from one another in at least the three following, not mutually independent, ways.

(1) They differ in the extent to which the reference they are used to make is dependent on the context of their utterance. Words like "I" and "it" stand at one end of this scale – the end of maximum dependence – and phrases like "the author of *Waverley*" and "the eighteenth king of France" at the other.

(2) They differ in the degree of 'descriptive meaning' they possess: by 'descriptive meaning' I intend 'conventional limitation, in application, to things of a certain general kind, or possessing certain general characteristics'. At one end of this scale stand the proper names we most commonly use in ordinary discourse; men, dogs, and motor-bicycles may be called "Horace." The pure name has no descriptive meaning (except such as it may acquire *as a result of* some one of its uses as a name). A word like "he" has minimal descriptive meaning, but has some. Substantival phrases like "the round table" have the maximum descriptive meaning. An interesting intermediate position is occupied by 'impure' proper names like "The Round Table" – substantival phrases which have grown capital letters.

(3) Finally, they may be divided into the following two classes: (i) those of which the correct referring use is regulated by some *general* referring-cum-ascriptive conventions; (ii) those of which the correct referring use is regulated by no general conventions, either of the contextual or the ascriptive kind, but by conventions which are ad hoc for each particular use (though not for each particular utterance). To the first class belong both

pronouns (which have the least descriptive meaning) and substantival phrases (which have the most). To the second class belong, roughly speaking, the most familiar kind of proper names. Ignorance of a man's name is not ignorance of the language. This is why we do not speak of the meaning of proper names. (But it won't do to say they are meaningless.) Again an intermediate position is occupied by such phrases as "The Old Pretender." Only an old pretender may be so referred to; but to know which old pretender is not to know a general, but an ad hoc, convention.

In the case of phrases of the form "the so-and-so" used referringly, the use of "the" together with the position of the phrase in the sentence (i.e. at the beginning, or following a transitive verb or preposition) acts as a signal that a unique reference is being made; and the following noun, or noun and adjective, together with the context of utterance, shows *what* unique reference is being made. In general the functional difference between common nouns and adjectives is that the former are naturally and commonly used referringly, while the latter are not commonly, or so naturally, used in this way, except as qualifying nouns; though they can be, and are, so used alone. And of course this functional difference is not independent of the descriptive force peculiar to each word. In general we should expect the descriptive force of nouns to be such that they are more efficient tools for the job of showing what unique reference is intended when such a reference is signalized; and we should also expect the descriptive force of the words we naturally and commonly use to make unique references to mirror our interest in the salient, relatively permanent and behavioral characteristics of things. These two expectations are not independent of one another; and, if we look at the differences between the commoner sort of common nouns and the commoner sort of adjectives, we find them both fulfilled. These are differences of the kind that Locke quaintly reports, when he speaks of our ideas of substances being *collections* of simple ideas; when he says that "powers make up a great part of our ideas of substances"; and when he goes on to contrast the identity of real and nominal essence in the case of simple ideas with their lack of identity and the shiftingness of the nominal essence in the case of substances. 'Substance' itself is the troublesome tribute Locke pays to his dim awareness of the difference in predominant linguistic function that lingered even when the noun had been expanded into a more or less indefinite string of adjectives. Russell repeats Locke's mistake with a difference when, admitting the inference from syntax to reality to the extent of feeling that he can get rid of this metaphysical unknown only if he can purify language of the referring function altogether, he draws up his program for "abolishing particulars"; a programme, in fact, for abolishing the distinction of logical use which I am here at pains to emphasize.

The contextual requirement for the referring use of pronouns may be stated with the greatest precision in some cases (e.g. "I" and "you") and only with the greatest vagueness in others ("it" and "this"). I propose to say nothing further about pronouns, except to point to an additional symptom of the failure to recognize the uniquely referring use for what it is; the fact, namely, that certain logicians have actually sought to elucidate the nature of a variable by offering such *sentences* as "he is sick," "it is green," as examples of something in ordinary speech like a *sentential function*. Now of course it is true that the word "he" may be used on different occasions to refer to different people or different animals: so may the word "John" and the phrase "the cat." What deters such logicians from treating these two expressions as quasi-variables is, in the first case, the lingering superstition that a name is logically tied to a single individual, and, in the second case, the descriptive meaning of the word "cat." But "he," which has a wide range of applications and minimal descriptive force, only acquires a use as a referring word. It is this fact, together with the failure to accord to expressions, used referringly, the place in logic which belongs to them (the place held open for the mythical logically proper name), that accounts for the misleading attempt to elucidate the nature of the variable by reference to such words as "he," "she," "it."

Of ordinary proper names it is sometimes said that they are essentially words each of which is used to refer to just one individual. This is obviously false. Many ordinary personal names – names *par excellence* - are correctly used to refer to numbers of people. An ordinary personal name is, roughly, a word, used referringly, of which the use is *not* dictated by any descriptive meaning the word may have, and is *not* prescribed by any such general rule for use as a referring expression (or a part of a referring expression) as we find in the case of such words as "I," "this" and "the," but is governed by ad hoc conventions for each particular set of applications of the word to a given person. The important point is that the correctness of such applications does not follow from any *general* rule or convention for the use of the word as such. (The limit of absurdity and obvious circularity is reached in the attempt to treat names as disguised description in Russell's sense; for what is in the special sense implied, but not entailed, by my now referring to someone by name is simply the existence of someone, *now being referred to*, who is *conventionally referred to* by that name.) Even this feature of names, however, is only a symptom of the purpose for which they are employed. At present our choice of names is partly arbitrary, partly dependent on legal and social observances. It would be perfectly possible to have a thorough-going *system* of names, based e.g. on dates of birth, or on a minute classification of physiological and anatomical differences. But the success of any such system would depend entirely on the convenience of the resulting name-allotments for the purpose of making unique references; and this would depend on the multiplicity of the classifications used and the degree to which they cut haphazardly across normal social groupings. Given a sufficient degree of both, the selectivity supplied by context would do the rest; just as in the case with our present naming habits. Had we such a system, we could use name-words descriptively (as we do at present, to a limited extent and in a different way, with some famous names) as well as referringly. But it is by criteria derived from consideration of the requirements of the referring task that we should assess the adequacy of any system of naming. From the naming point of view, no kind of classification would be better or worse than any other simply because of the kind of classification – natal or anatomical – that it was.

I have already mentioned the class of quasi-names, of substantival phrases which grow capital letters, and of which such phrases as "the Glorious Revolution," "the Great War," "the Annunciation," "the Round Table" are examples. While the descriptive meaning of the words which follow the definite article is still relevant to their referring role, the capital letters are a sign of that extralogical selectivity in their referring use, which is characteristic of pure names. Such phrases are found in print or in writing when one member of some class of events or things is of quite outstanding interest in a certain society. These phrases are embryonic names. A phrase may, for obvious reasons, pass into, and out of, this class (e.g. "the Great War").

V

I want to conclude by considering, all too briefly, three further problems about referring uses.

(a) *Indefinite references*: Not all referring uses of singular expressions forestall the question "What (who, which one) are you talking about?" There are some which either invite this question, or disclaim the intention or ability to answer it. Examples are such sentence-beginnings as "A man told me that...," "Someone told me that...." The orthodox (Russellian) doctrine is that such sentences are existential, but not uniquely existential. This seems wrong in several ways. It is ludicrous to suggest that part of what is asserted is that the class of men or persons is not empty. Certainly this is *implied* in the by now familiar sense of implication; but the implication is also as much an implication of the *uniqueness* of the particular object of reference as when I begin a sentence with such a phrase as "the table." The difference between the use of the definite and indefinite articles is, very roughly, as follows. We use "the" either when a previous reference has been made, and when "the" signalizes that the same reference is being made; or when, in the absence of a previous indefinite reference, the context (including the hearer's assumed knowledge) is expected to enable the hearer to tell *what* reference is being made. We use "a" either when these conditions are not fulfilled, or when, although a definite reference *could* be made, we wish to keep dark the identity of the individual to whom, or to which, we are referring. This is the *arch* use of such a phrase as "a certain person" or "someone"; where it could be expanded, not into "someone, but you wouldn't (or I don't) know who" but into "someone, but I'm not telling you who."

(b) *Identification statements*: By this label I intend statements like the following:

(i*a*) That is the man who swam the channel twice on one day.
(ii*a*) Napoleon was the man who ordered the execution of the Duc d'Enghien.

The puzzle about these statements is that their grammatical predicates do not seem to be used in a straightforwardly ascriptive way as are the grammatical predicates of the statements:

(i*b*) That man swam the channel twice in one day.
(ii*b*) Napoleon ordered the execution of the Duc d'Enghien.

But if, in order to avoid blurring the difference between (i*a*) and (i*b*) and (ii*a*) and (ii*b*), one says that the phrases which form the grammatical complements of (i*a*) and (ii*a*) are being used referringly, one becomes puzzled about what is being said in these sentences. We seem then to be referring to the same person twice over and either saying nothing about him and thus making no statement, or identifying him with himself and thus producing a trivial identity.

The bogy of triviality can be dismissed. This only arises for those who think of the object referred to by the use of an expression as its meaning, and thus think of the subject and complement of these sentences as meaning the same because they could be used to refer to the same person.

I think the differences between sentences in the (*a*) group and sentences in the (*b*) group can best be understood by considering the differences between the circumstances in which you would say (i*a*) and the circumstances in which you would say (i*b*). You would say (i*a*) instead of (i*b*) if you knew or believed that your hearer knew or believed that *someone* had swum the channel twice in one day. You say (i*a*) when you take your hearer to be in the position of one who can ask: "Who swam the channel twice in one day?" (And in asking this, he is not saying that anyone did, though his asking it implies – in the relevant sense – that someone did.) Such sentences are like answers to such questions. They are better called 'identification-statements' than 'identities'. Sentence (i*a*) does not assert more or less than sentence (i*b*). It is just that you say (i*a*) to a man whom you take to know certain things that you take to be unknown to the man to whom you say (i*b*).

This is, in the barest essentials, the solution to Russell's puzzle about 'denoting phrases' joined by "is"; one of the puzzles which he claims for the theory of descriptions the merit of solving.

(c) *The logic of subjects and predicates*: Much of what I have said of the uniquely referring use of expressions can be extended, with suitable modifications, to the non-uniquely referring use of expressions; i.e. to some uses of expressions consisting of "the," "all the," "all," "some," "some of the," etc. followed by a noun, qualified or unqualified, in the *plural*; to some uses of "they," "them," "those," "these"; and to conjunctions of names. Expressions of the first kind have a special interest. Roughly speaking, orthodox modern criticism, inspired by mathematical logic, of such traditional doctrines as that of the Square of Opposition and of some of the forms of the syllogism traditionally recognized as valid, rests on the familiar failure to recognize the special sense in which existential assertions may be implied by the referring use of expressions. The universal propositions of the fourfold schedule, it is said, must *either* be given a negatively existential interpretation (e.g., for A, "there are no Xs which are not Ys") *or* they must be interpreted as conjunctions of negatively and positively existential statements of, negatively and positively existential statements of, e.g., the form (for A) "there are no Xs which are not Ys, and there are Xs." The I and O forms are normally given a positively existential interpretation. It is then seen that, whichever of the above alternatives is selected, some of the traditional laws have to be abandoned. The dilemma, however, is a bogus one. If we interpret the propositions of the schedule as neither positively, nor negatively, nor positively *and* negatively, existential, but as sentences such that *the question of whether they are being used to make true or false assertions does not arise except when the existential condition is fulfilled for the subject term*, then all the traditional laws hold good together. And this interpretation is far closer to the most common uses of expressions beginning with "all" and "some" than is any Russellian alternative. For these expressions are most commonly used in the referring way. A literal-minded and childless man asked whether all his children are asleep will certainly not answer "Yes" on the ground that he has none; but nor will he answer "No" on this ground. Since he has no children, the question does not arise. To say this is not to say that I may not use the sentence, "All my children are asleep," with the intention of letting someone know that I have children, or of deceiving him into thinking that I have. Nor is it any weakening of my thesis to concede that singular phrases of the form "the so-and-so" may sometimes be used with a similar purpose. Neither Aristotelian nor Russellian rules give the exact logic of any expression of ordinary language; for ordinary language has no exact logic.

NOTES

1. This usage of "use" is, of course, different from (*a*) the current usage in which "use" (of a particular word, phrase, sentence) = (roughly) "rules for using" = (roughly) "meaning"; and from (*b*) my own usage in the phrase "uniquely referring use of expressions" in which "use" = (roughly) "way of using."

2. Since this article was written, there has appeared a clear statement of this point by Mr Geach in *Analysis* 10 (4): 84-88. [Note added in 1968.]

3. The choice of the word "spurious" now seems to me unfortunate, at least for some nonstandard uses. I should now prefer to call some of these "secondary" uses. [Note added in 1956.]

4. The unsophisticated kind begins: "Once upon a time there was...."

5. And this in spite of the danger-signal of that phrase, "*misleading* grammatical form."

6. This sentence now seems to me objectionable in a number of ways, notably because of an unexplicitly restrictive use of the word 'refer'. It could be more exactly phrased as follows: "Hence we can, using significant expressions, refer in secondary ways, as in make-believe or in fiction, or mistakenly think we are referring to something in the primary way when we are not, in that way, referring to anything." [Note added in 1956.]

7. I neglect relational sentences; for these require, not a modification in the principle of what I say, but a complication of the detail.

8. What is said or implied in the last two sentences of this paragraph no longer seems to me true, unless considerably qualified. [Note added in 1956.]

REFERENCE AND DEFINITE DESCRIPTIONS

Keith Donnellan

Definite descriptions, I shall argue, have two possible functions. They are used to refer to what a speaker wishes to talk about, but they are also used quite differently. Moreover, a definite description occurring in one and the same sentence may, on different occasions of its use, function in either way. The failure to deal with this duality of function obscures the genuine referring use of definite descriptions. The best-known theories of definite descriptions, those of Russell and Strawson, I shall suggest, are both guilty of this. Before discussing this distinction in use, I will mention some features of these theories to which it is especially relevant.

On Russell's view a definite description may denote an entity: "if 'C' is a denoting phrase [as definite descriptions are by definition], it may happen that there is one entity x (there cannot be more than one) for which the proposition 'x is identical with C' is true.... We may then say that the entity x is the denotation of the phrase 'C.'"[1] In using a definite description, then, a speaker may use an expression which denotes some entity, but this is the only relationship between that entity and the use of the definite description recognized by Russell. I shall argue, however, that there are two uses of definite descriptions. The definition of denotation given by Russell is applicable to both, but in one of these the definite description serves to do something more. I shall say that in this use the speaker uses the definite description to *refer* to something, and call this use the "referential use" of a definite description. Thus, if I am right, referring is not the same as denoting and the referential use of definite descriptions is not recognized on Russell's view.

Furthermore, on Russell's view the type of expression that comes closest to performing the function of the referential use of definite descriptions turns out, as one might suspect, to be a proper name (in "the narrow logical sense"). Many of the things said about proper names by Russell can, I think, be said about the referential use of definite descriptions without straining senses unduly. Thus the gulf Russell thought he saw between names and definite descriptions is narrower than he thought.

Strawson, on the other hand, certainly does recognize a referential use of definite definitions. But what I think he did not see is that a definite description may have a quite different role – may be used nonreferentially, even as it occurs in one and the same sentence. Strawson, it is true, points out nonreferential uses of definite descriptions,[2] but which use a definite description has seems to be for him a function of the kind of sentence in which it occurs; whereas, if I am right, there can be two possible uses of a definite description in the same sentence. Thus, in "On Referring," he says, speaking of expressions used to refer, "Any expression of any of these class- es [one being that of definite descriptions] can occur as the subject of what would traditionally be regarded as a singular subject-predicate sentence; and would, so occurring, exemplify the use I wish to discuss."[3] So the definite description in, say, the sentence "The Republican candidate for president in 1968 will be a conservative" presumably exemplifies the referential use. But if I am right, we could not say this of the sentence in isolation from some particular occasion on which it is used to state something; and then it might or might not turn out that the definite description has a referential use.

Strawson and Russell seem to me to make a common assumption here about the question of how definite descriptions function: that we can ask how a definite description functions in some sentence independently of a particular occasion upon which it is used. This assumption is not really rejected in Strawson's arguments against Russell. Although he can sum up his position by saying, "'Mentioning' or 'referring' is not something an expression does; it is something that someone can use an expression to do,"[4] he means by this to deny the radical view that a "genuine" referring expres- sion *has* a referent, functions to refer, independent of the context of some use of the expression. The denial of this view, however, does not entail that definite descriptions cannot be identified as referring expressions in a sen- tence unless the sentence is being used. Just as we can speak of a function of a tool that is not at the moment performing its function, Strawson's view, I believe, allows us to speak of the referential function of a definite descrip- tion in a sentence even when it is not being used. This, I hope to show, is a mistake.

A second assumption shared by Russell's and Strawson's account of definite descriptions is this. In many cases a person who uses a definite description can be said (in some sense) to presuppose or imply that some- thing fits the description.[5] If I state that the king is on his throne, I presup- pose or imply that there is a king. (At any rate, this would be a natural thing to say for anyone who doubted that there is a king.) Both Russell and

Strawson assume that where the presupposition or implication is false, the truth value of what the speaker says is affected. For Russell the statement made is false; for Strawson it has no truth value. Now if there are two uses of definite descriptions, it may be that the truth value is affected differently in each case by the falsity of the presupposition or implication. This is what I shall in fact argue. It will turn out, I believe, that one or the other of the two views, Russell's or Strawson's, may be correct about the nonreferential use of definite descriptions, but neither fits the referential use. This is not so surprising about Russell's view, since he did not recognize this use in any case, but it is surprising about Strawson's since the referential use is that he tries to explain and defend. Furthermore, on Strawson's account, the result of there being nothing which fits the description is a failure of reference.[6] This too, I believe, turns out not to be true about the referential use of definite descriptions.

II

There are some uses of definite descriptions which carry neither any hint of a referential use nor any presupposition or implication that something fits the description. In general, it seems, these are recognizable from the sentence frame in which the description occurs. These uses will not interest us, but it is necessary to point them out if only to set them aside.

An obvious example would be the sentence "The present King of France does not exist," used, say, to correct someone's mistaken impression that de Gaulle is the King of France.

A more interesting example is this. Suppose someone were to ask, "Is de Gaulle the King of France?" This is the natural form of words for a person to use who is in doubt as the whether de Gaulle is King or President of France. Given this background to the question, there seems to be no presupposition or implication that someone is the King of France. Nor is the person attempting to refer to someone by using the definite description. On the other hand, reverse the name and description in the question and the speaker probably would be thought to presuppose or imply this. "Is the King of France de Gaulle?" is the natural question for one to ask who wonders whether it is de Gaulle rather than someone else who occupies the throne of France.[7]

Many times, however, the use of a definite description does carry a presupposition or implication that something fits the description. If definite descriptions do have a referring role, it will be here. But it is a mistake, I think, to try, as I believe both Russell and Strawson do, to settle this matter without further ado. What is needed, I believe, is the distinction I will now discuss.

III

I will call the two uses of definite descriptions I have in mind the attributive use and the referential use. A speaker who uses a definite description attributively in an assertion states something about whoever or whatever is the so-and-so. A speaker who uses a definite description referentially in an assertion, on the other hand, uses the description to enable his audience to pick out whom or what he is talking about and states something about that person or thing. In the first case the definite description might be said to occur essentially, for the speaker wishes to assert something about whatever or whoever fits that description; but in the referential use the definite description is merely one tool for doing a certain job – calling attention to a person or thing – and in general any other device for doing the same job, another description or a name, would do as well. In the attributive use, the attribute of being the so-and-so is all important, while it is not in the referential use.

To illustrate this distinction, in the case of a single sentence, consider the sentence, "Smith's murderer is insane." Suppose first that we come upon poor Smith foully murdered. From the brutal manner of the killing and the fact that Smith was the most lovable person in the world, we might exclaim, "Smith's murderer is insane." I will assume, to make it a simpler case, that in a quite ordinary sense we do not know who murdered Smith (though this is not in the end essential to the case). This, I shall say, is an attributive use of the definite description.

The contrast with such a use of the sentence is one of those situations in which we expect and intend our audience to realize whom we have in mind when we speak of Smith's murderer and, most importantly, to know that it is this person about whom we are going to say something.

For example, suppose that Jones has been charged with Smith's murder and has been placed on trial. Imagine that there is a discussion of Jones's odd behavior at his trial. We might sum up our impression of his behavior by saying, "Smith's murderer is insane." If someone asks to whom we are referring, by using this description, the answer here is "Jones." This, I shall say, is a referential use of the definite description.

That these two uses of the definite description in the same sentence are really quite different can perhaps best be brought out by considering the consequences of the assumption that Smith had no murderer (for example, he in fact committed suicide). In both situations, in using the definite description "Smith's murderer," the speaker in some sense presupposes or implies that there is a murderer. But when we hypothesize that the presupposition or implication is false, there are different results for the two uses. In both cases we have used the predicate "is insane," but in the first case, if there is no murderer, there is no person of whom it could be correctly said that we attributed insanity to him. Such a person could be identified (correctly) only in case someone fitted the description used. But in the second case, where the definite description is simply a means of identifying the person we want to talk about, it is quite possible for the correct identification to be made even though no one fits the description we used.[8] We were speaking about Jones even though he is not in fact Smith's murderer and, in the circumstances imagined, it was his behavior we were commenting upon. Jones might, for example, accuse us of saying false things of him in calling him insane and it would be no defense, I should think, that our description, "the murderer of Smith," failed to fit him.

It is, moreover, perfectly possible for our audience to know to whom we refer, in the second situation, even though they do not share our presupposition. A person hearing our comment in the context imagined might know we are talking about Jones even though he does not think Jones guilty.

Generalizing from this case, we can say, I think, that there are two uses of sentences of the form, "The ϕ is ψ." In the first, if nothing is the ϕ then nothing has been said to be ψ. In the second, the fact that nothing is the ϕ does not have this consequence.

With suitable changes the same difference in use can be formulated for uses of language other than assertions. Suppose one is at a party and, seeing an interesting-looking person holding a martini glass, one asks, "Who is the man drinking a martini?" If it should turn out that there is only water in the glass, one has nevertheless asked a question about a particular person, a question that it is possible for someone to answer. Contrast this with the use of the same question by the chairman of the local Teetotalers Union. He has just been informed that a man is drinking a martini at their annual party. He responds by asking his informant, "Who is the man drinking a martini?" In asking the question the chairman does not have some particular person in mind about whom he asks the question; if no one is drinking a martini, if the information is wrong, no person can be singled out as the person about whom the question was asked. Unlike the first case, the attribute of being the man drinking a martini is all-important, because if it is the attribute of no one, the chairman's question has no straight-forward answer.

This illustrates also another difference between the referential and the attributive use of definite descriptions. In the one case we have asked a question about a particular person or thing even though nothing fits the description we used; in the other this is not so. But also in the one case our question can be answered; in the other it cannot be. In the referential use of a definite description we may succeed in picking out a person or thing to ask a question about even though he or it does not really fit the description; but in the attributive use if nothing fits the description, no straightforward answer to the question can be given.

This further difference is also illustrated by commands or orders containing definite descriptions. Consider the order, "Bring me the book on the table." If "the book on the table" is being used referentially, it is possible to fulfill the order even though there is no book on the table. If, for example, there is a book *beside* the table, though there is none *on* it, one might bring that book back and ask the issuer of the order whether this is "the book you meant." And it may be. But imagine we are told that someone has laid a book on our prize antique table, where nothing should be put. The order, "Bring me the book on the table" cannot now be obeyed unless there is a book that has been placed on the table. There is no possibility of bringing back a book which was never on the table and having it be the one that was meant, because there is no book that in that sense was "meant." In the one case the definite description was a device for getting the other person to pick the right book; if he is able to pick the right book even though it does not satisfy the description, one still succeeds in his purpose. In the other case, there is, antecedently, no "right book" except one which fits the description; the attribute of being the book on the table is essential. Not only is there no book about which an order was issued, if there is no book on the table, but the order itself cannot be obeyed. When a definite description is used attributively in a command or question and nothing fits the description, the command cannot be obeyed and the question cannot be answered. This suggests some analogous consequence for assertions containing definite descriptions used attributively. Perhaps the analogous result is that the assertion is neither true nor false: this is Strawson's view of what happens when the presupposition of the use of a definite description is false. But if so, Strawson's view works not for definite descriptions used referentially, but for the quite different use, which I have called the attributive use.

I have tried to bring out the two uses of definite descriptions by pointing out the different consequences of supposing that nothing fits the description used. There are still other differences. One is this: when a definite description is used referentially, not only is there in some sense a presupposition or implication that someone or something fits the description, as there is also in the attributive use, but there is a quite different presupposition; the speaker presupposes of some *particular* someone or something that he or it fits the description. In asking, for example, "Who is the man drinking a martini?" where we mean to ask a question about that man over there, we are presupposing that that man over there is drinking a martini – not just that *someone* is a man drinking a martini. When we say, in a context where it is clear we are referring to Jones, "Smith's murderer is insane," we are presupposing that Jones is Smith's murderer. No such presupposition is present in the attributive use of definite descriptions. There is, of course, the presupposition that someone *or other* did the murder, but the speaker does not presuppose of someone in particular – Jones or Robinson say – that he did it. What I mean by this second kind of presupposition that someone or something in particular fits the description – which is present in a referential use but not in an attributive use – can perhaps be seen more clearly by considering a member of the speaker's audience who believes that Smith was not murdered at all. Now in the case of the referential use of the description, "Smith's murderer," he could accuse the speaker of mistakenly presupposing both that someone or other is the murderer and that also Jones is the murderer, for even though he believes Jones not to have done the deed, he knows that the speaker was referring to Jones. But in the case of the attributive use, he can accuse the speaker of having only the first, less specific presupposition; he cannot pick out some person and claim that the speaker is presupposing that that person is Smith's murderer. Now the more particular presuppositions that we find present in referential uses are clearly not ones we can assign to a definite description in some particular sentence in isolation from a context of use. In order to know that a person presupposes that Jones is Smith's murderer in using the sentence "Smith's murderer is insane," we have to know that he is using the description referentially and also to whom he is referring. The sentence by itself does not tell us any of this.

IV

From the way in which I set up each of the previous examples it might be supposed that the important difference between the referential and the attributive use lies in the beliefs of the speaker. Does he believe of some particular person or thing that he or it fits the description used? In the Smith murder example, for instance, there was in the one case no belief as to who did the deed, whereas in the contrasting case it was believed that Jones did it. But this is, in fact, not an essential difference. It is possible for a definite description to be used attributively even though the speaker (and his audience) believes that a certain person or thing fits the description. And it is possible for a definite description to be used referentially where the speaker believes that nothing fits the description. It is true – and this is why, for simplicity, I set up the examples the way I did – that if a speaker does not believe that anything fits the description or does not believe that he is in a position to pick out what does fit the description, it is likely that he is not using it referentially. It is also true that if he and his audience would pick out some particular thing or person as fitting the description, then a use of the definite description is very likely referential. But these are only presumptions and not entailments.

To use the Smith murder case again, suppose that Jones is on trial for the murder and I and everyone else believe him guilty. Suppose that I comment that the murderer of Smith is insane, but instead of backing this up, as in the example previously used, by citing Jones's behavior in the dock, I go on to outline reasons for thinking that *anyone* who murdered poor Smith in that particularly horrible way must be insane. If now it turns out that Jones was not the murderer after all, but someone else was, I think I can claim to have been right if the true murderer is after all insane. Here, I think, I would be using the definite description attributively, even though I believe that a particular person fits the description.

It is also possible to think of cases in which the speaker does not believe that what he means to refer to by using the definite description fits the description, or to imagine cases in which the definite description is used referentially even though the speaker believes *nothing* fits the description. Admittedly, these cases may be parasitic on a more normal use; nevertheless, they are sufficient to show that such beliefs of the speaker are not decisive as to which use is made of a definite description.

Suppose the throne is occupied by a man I firmly believe to be not the king, but a usurper. Imagine also that his followers as firmly believe that he is the king. Suppose I wish to see this man. I might say to his minions, "Is the king in his countinghouse?" I succeed in referring to the man I wish to refer to without myself believing that he fits the description. It is not even necessary, moreover, to suppose that his followers believe him to be the king. If they are cynical about the whole thing, know he is not the king, I may still succeed in referring to the man I wish to refer to. Similarly, neither I nor the people I speak to may suppose that *anyone* is the king and, finally, each party may know that the other does not so suppose and yet the reference may go through.

V

Both the attributive and the referential use of definite descriptions seem to carry a presupposition or implication that there is something which fits the description. But the reasons for the existence of the presupposition or implication are different in the two cases.

There is a presumption that a person who uses a definite description referentially believes that what he wishes to refer to fits the description. Because the purpose of using the description is to get the audience to pick out or think of the right thing or person, one would normally choose a description that he believes the thing or person fits. Normally a misdescription of that to which one wants to refer would mislead the audience. Hence, there is a presumption that the speaker believes *something* fits the description – namely, that to which he refers.

When a definite description is used attributively, however, there is not the same possibility of misdescription. In the example of "Smith's murderer" used attributively, there was not the possibility of misdescribing Jones or anyone else; we were not referring to Jones nor to anyone else by using the description. The presumption that the speaker believes *someone* is Smith's murderer does not arise here from a more specific presumption that he believes Jones or Robinson or someone else whom he can name or identify is Smith's murderer.

The presupposition or implication is borne by a definite description used attributively because if nothing fits the description the linguistic purpose of the speech act will be thwarted. That is, the speaker will not succeed in saying something true, if he makes an assertion; he will not succeed in asking a question that can be answered, if he has asked a question; he will not succeed in issuing an order than can be obeyed, if he has issued an order. If one states that Smith's murderer is insane, when Smith has no murderer, and uses the definite description nonreferentially, then one fails to say anything true. If one issues the order "Bring me Smith's murderer" under similar circumstances, the order cannot be obeyed; nothing would count as obeying it.

When the definite description is used referentially, on the other hand, the presupposition or implication stems simply from the fact that normally a person tries to describe correctly what he wants to refer to because normally this is the best way to get his audience to recognize what he is referring to. As we have seen, it is possible for the linguistic purpose of the speech act to be accomplished in such a case even though nothing fits the description; it is possible to say something true or to ask a question that gets answered or to issue a command that gets obeyed. For when the definite description is used referentially, one's audience may succeed in seeing to what one refers even though neither it nor anything else fits the description.

VI

The result of the last section shows something to be wrong with the theories of both Russell and Strawson; for though they give differing accounts of the implication or presupposition involved, each gives only one. Yet, as I have argued, the presupposition or implication is present for a quite different reason, depending upon whether the definite description is used attributively or referentially, and exactly what presuppositions or implications are involved is also different. Moreover, neither theory seems a correct characterization of the referential use. On Russell's there is a logical entailment: "The ϕ is ψ " entails "There exists one and only one ϕ." Whether or not this is so for the attributive use, it does not seem true of the referential use of the definite description. The "implication" that something is the ø, as I have argued, does not amount to an entailment; it is more like a presumption based on what is *usually* true of the use of a definite description to refer. In any case, of course, Russell's theory does not show – what is true of the referential use – that the implication that *something* is the ø comes from the more specific implication that *what is being referred to* is the ø. Hence, as a theory of definite descriptions, Russell's view seems to apply, if at all, to the attributive use only.

Russell's definition of denoting (a definite description denotes an entity if that entity fits the description uniquely) is clearly applicable to either use of definite descriptions. Thus whether or not a definite description is used referentially or attributively, it may have a denotation. Hence, denoting and referring, as I have explicated the latter notion, are distinct and Russell's view recognizes only the former. It seems to me, moreover, that this is a welcome result, that denoting and referring should not be confused. If one tried to maintain that they are the same notion, one result would be that a speaker might be referring to something without knowing it. If someone said, for example, in 1960 before he had any idea that Mr. Goldwater would be the Republican nominee in 1964, "The Republican candidate for president in 1964 will be a conservative," (perhaps on the basis of an analysis of the views of party leaders) the definite description here would *denote* Mr. Goldwater. But would we wish to say that the speaker had referred to, mentioned, or talked about Mr. Goldwater? I feel these terms would be out of place. Yet if we identify referring and denoting, it ought to be possible for it to turn out (after the Republican Convention) that the speaker had, unknown to himself, referred in 1960 to Mr. Goldwater. On my view, however, while the definite description used did *denote* Mr. Goldwater (using Russell's definition), the speaker used it *attributively* and did not *refer* to Mr. Goldwater.

Turning to Strawson's theory, it was supposed to demonstrate how definite descriptions are referential. But it goes too far in this direction. For there are nonreferential uses of definite descriptions also, even as they occur in one and the same sentence. I believe that Strawson's theory involves the following propositions:

(1) If someone asserts that the ø is ψ he has not made a true or false statement if there is no ø.[9]
(2) If there is no ø then the speaker has failed to refer to anything.[10]
(3) The reason he has said nothing true or false is that he has failed to refer.

Each of these propositions is either false or, at best, applies to only one of the two uses of definite descriptions.

Proposition (1) is possibly true of the attributive use. In the example in which "Smith's murderer is insane" was said when Smith's body was first discovered, an attributive use of the definite description, there was no person to whom the speaker referred. If Smith had no murderer, nothing true was said. It is quite tempting to conclude, following Strawson, that nothing true *or* false was said. But where the definite description is used referentially, something true may well have been said. It is possible that something true was said of the person or thing referred to.[11]

Proposition (2) is, as we have seen, simply false. Where a definite description is used referentially it is perfectly possible to refer to something though nothing fits the description used.

The situation with proposition (3) is a bit more complicated. It ties together, on Strawson's view, the two strands given in (1) and (2). As an account of why, when the presupposition is false, nothing true or false has been stated, it clearly cannot work for the attributive use of definite descriptions, for the reason it supplies is that reference has failed. It does not then give the reason why, if indeed this is so, a speaker using a definite description attributively fails to say anything true or false if nothing fits the description. It does, however, raise a question about the referential use. Can reference fail when a definite description is used referentially?

I do not fail to refer merely because my audience does not correctly pick out what I am referring to. I can be referring to a particular man when I use the description "the man drinking a martini," even though the people to whom I speak fail to pick out the right person or any person at all. Nor, as we have stressed, do I fail to refer when nothing fits the description. But perhaps I fail to refer in some extreme circumstances, when there is nothing that *I* am willing to pick out as that to which I referred.

Suppose that I think I see at some distance a man walking and ask, "Is the man carrying a walking stick the professor of history?" We should perhaps distinguish four cases at this point. (a) There is a man carrying a walking stick; I have then referred to a person and asked a question about him that can be answered if my audience has the information. (b) The man over there is not carrying a walking stick, but an umbrella; I have still referred to someone and asked a question that can be answered, though if my audience sees that it is an umbrella and not a walking stick, they may also correct my apparently mistaken impression. (c) It is not a man at all, but a rock that looks like one; in this case, I think I still have referred to something, to the thing over there that happens to be a rock but that I took to be a man. But in this case it is not clear that my question can be answered correctly. This, I think, is not because I have failed to refer, but rather because, given the true nature of what I referred to, my question is not appropriate. A simple "No, that is not the professor of history" is at least a bit misleading if said by someone who realizes that I mistook a rock for a person. It may, therefore, be plausible to conclude that in such a case I have not asked a question to which there is a straightforwardly correct answer. But if this is true, it is not because nothing fits the description I used, but rather because what I referred to is a rock and my question has no correct answer when asked of a rock. (d) There is finally the case in which there is nothing at all where I thought there was a man with a walking stick; and perhaps here we have a genuine failure to refer at all, even though the description was used for the purpose of referring. There is no rock, nor anything else, to which I meant to refer; it was, perhaps, a trick of light that made me think there was a man there. I cannot say of anything, "That is what I was referring to, though I now see that it's not a man carrying a walking stick." This failure of reference, however, requires circumstances much more radical than the mere nonexistence of anything fitting the description used. It requires that there be nothing of which it can be said, "That is what he was referring to." Now perhaps also in such cases, if the speaker has asserted something, he fails to state anything true or false if there is nothing that can be identified as that to which he referred. But if so, the failure of reference and truth value does not come about merely because nothing fits the description he used. So (3) may be true of some cases of the referential use of definite descriptions; it may be true that a failure of reference results in a lack of truth value. But these cases are of a much more extreme sort than Strawson's theory implies.

I conclude, then, that neither Russell's nor Strawson's theory represents a correct account of the use of definite descriptions – Russell's because it ignores altogether the referential use, Strawson's because it fails to make the distinction between the referential and the attributive and mixes together truths about each (together with some things that are false).

VII

It does not seem possible to say categorically of a definite description in a particular sentence that it is a referring expression (of course, one could say this if he meant that it *might* be used to refer). In general, whether or not a definite description is used referentially or attributively is a function of the speaker's intentions in a particular case. "The murderer of Smith" may be used either way in the sentence "The murderer of Smith is insane." It does not appear plausible to account for this, either, as an ambiguity in the sentence. The grammatical structure of the sentence seems to me to be the same whether the description is used referentially or attributively: that is, it is not syntactically ambiguous. Nor does it seem at all attractive to suppose an ambiguity in the meaning of the words; it does not appear to be semantically ambiguous. (Perhaps we could say that the sentence is pragmatically ambiguous: the distinction between roles that the description plays is a function of the speaker's intentions.) These, of course, are intuitions; I do not have an argument for these conclusions. Nevertheless, the burden of proof is surely on the other side.

This, I think, means that the view, for example, that sentences can be divided up into predicates, logical operators, and referring expressions is not generally true. In the case of definite descriptions one cannot always assign the referential function in isolation from a particular occasion on which it is used.

There may be sentences in which a definite description can be used only attributively or only referentially. A sentence in which it seems that the definite description could be used only attributively would be "Point out the man who is drinking my martini." I am not so certain that any can be found in which the definite description can be used only referentially. Even if there are such sentences, it does not spoil the point that there are many sentences, apparently not ambiguous either syntactically or semantically, containing definite descriptions that can be used either way.

If it could be shown that the dual use of definite descriptions can be accounted for by the presence of an ambiguity, there is still a point to be made against the theories of Strawson and Russell. For neither, so far as I can see, has anything to say about the possibility of such an ambiguity and, in fact, neither seems compatible with such a possibility. Russell's does not recognize the possibility of the referring use, and Strawson's, as I have tried to show in the last section, combines elements from each use into one unitary account. Thus the view that there is an ambiguity in such sentences does not seem any more attractive to these positions.

VIII

Using a definite description referentially, a speaker may say something true even though the description correctly applies to nothing. The sense in which he may say something true is the sense in which he may say something true about someone or something. This sense is, I think, an interesting one that needs investigation. Isolating it is one of the byproducts of the distinction between the attributive and referential uses of definite descriptions.

For one thing, it raises questions about the notion of a statement. This is brought out by considering a passage in a paper by Leonard Linsky in which he rightly makes the point that one can refer to someone although the definite description used does not correctly describe the person:

.... said of a spinster that "Her husband is kind to her" is neither true nor false. But a speaker might very well be referring to someone using these words, for he may think that someone is the husband of the lady (who in fact is a spinster). Still, the statement is neither true nor false, for it presupposes that the lady has a husband, which she has not. This last refutes Strawson's thesis that if the presupposition of existence is not satisfied, the speaker has failed to refer.[12]

There is much that is right in this passage. But because Linsky does not make the distinction between the referential and the attributive uses of definite descriptions, it does not represent a wholly adequate account of the situation. A perhaps minor point about this passage is that Linsky apparently thinks it sufficient to establish that the speaker in his example is referring to someone by using the definite description "her husband," that he *believe* that someone is her husband. This will only approximate the truth provided that the "someone" in the description of the belief means "someone in particular" and is not merely the existential quantifier, "there is someone or other." For in both the attributive and the referential use the belief that someone *or other* is the husband of the lady is very likely to be present. If, for example, the speaker has just met the lady and, noticing her cheerfulness and radiant good health, makes his remark from his conviction that these attributes are always the result of having good husbands, he would be using the definite description attributively. Since she has no husband, there is no one to pick out as the person to whom he was referring. Nevertheless, the speaker believed that *someone or other* was her husband. On the other hand, if the use of "her husband" was simply a way of referring to a man the speaker has just met whom he assumed to be the lady's husband, he would have referred to that man even though neither he nor anyone else fits the description. I think it is likely that in this passage Linsky did mean by "someone," in his description of the belief, "someone in particular." But even then, as we have seen, we have neither a sufficient nor a necessary condition for a referential use of the definite description. A definite description can be used attributively even when the speaker believes that some particular thing or person fits the description, and it can be used referentially in the absence of this belief.

My main point, here, however, has to do with Linsky's view that because the presupposition is not satisfied, the statement is neither true nor false. This seems to me possibly correct if the definite description is thought of as being used attributively (depending upon whether we go with Strawson or Russell). But when we consider it as used referentially, this categorical assertion is no longer clearly correct. For the man the speaker referred to may indeed be kind to the spinster; the speaker may have said something true about that man. Now the difficulty is in the notion of "the statement." Suppose that we know that the lady is a spinster, but nevertheless know that the man referred to by the speaker is kind to her. It seems to me that we shall, on the one hand, want to hold that the speaker said something true, but be reluctant to express this by "It is true that her husband is kind to her."

This shows, I think, a difficulty in speaking simply about "the statement" when definite descriptions are used referentially. For the speaker stated something, in this example, about a particular person, and his statement, we may suppose, was true. Nevertheless, we should not like to agree with his statement by using the sentence he used; we should not like to identify the true statement via the speaker's words. The reason for this is not so hard to find. If we say, in this example, "It is true that her husband is kind to her," *we* are now using the definite description either attributively or referentially. But we should not be subscribing to what the original speaker truly said if we use the description attributively, for it was only in its function as referring to a particular person that the definite description yields the possibility of saying something true (since the lady has no husband). Our reluctance, however, to endorse the original speaker's statement by using the definite description referentially to refer to the same person stems from quite a different consideration. For if we too were laboring under the mistaken belief that this man was the lady's husband, we could agree with the original speaker using his exact words. (Moreover, it is possible, as we have seen, deliberately to use a definite description to refer to someone we believe not to fit the description.) Hence, our reluctance to use the original speaker's words does not arise from the fact that if we did we should not succeed in stating anything true or false. It rather stems from the fact that when a definite description is used referentially there is a presumption that the speaker believes that what he refers to fits the description. Since we, who know the lady to be a spinster, would not normally want to give the impression that we believe otherwise, we would not like to use the original speaker's way of referring to the man in question.

How then would we express agreement with the original speaker without involving ourselves in unwanted impressions about our beliefs? The answer shows another difference between the referential and attributive uses of definite descriptions and brings about an important point about genuine referring.

When a speaker says, "The ø is ψ," where "the ø" is used attributively, if there is no ø, we cannot correctly report the speaker as having said of this or that person or thing that it is ψ. But if the definite description is used referentially we can report the speaker as having attributed ψ to something. And we may refer to what the speaker referred to, using whatever description or name suits our purpose. Thus, if a speaker says, "Her husband is kind to her," referring to the man he was just talking to, and if that man is Jones, we may report him as having said *of Jones* that he is kind to her. If Jones is also the president of the college, we may report the speaker as having said *of the president of the college* that he is kind to her. And finally, if we are talking to Jones, we may say, referring to the original speaker, "He said of you that *you* are kind to her." It does not matter here whether or not the woman has a husband or whether, if she does, Jones is her husband. If the original speaker referred to Jones, he said of him that he is kind to her. Thus where the definite description is used referentially, but does not fit what was referred to, we can report what a speaker said and agree with him by using a description or name which does fit. In doing so we need not, it is important to note, choose a description or name which the original speaker would agree fits what he was referring to. That is, we can report the speaker in the above case to have said truly of Jones that he is kind to her even if the original speaker did not know that the man he was referring to is named Jones or even if he thinks he is not named Jones.

Returning to what Linsky said in the passage quoted, he claimed that, were someone to say "Her husband is kind to her," when she has no husband, *the statement* would be neither true nor false. As I have said, this is a likely view to hold if the definite description is being used attributively. But if it is being used referentially it is not clear what is meant by "the statement." If we think about what the speaker said about the person he referred to, then there is no reason to suppose he has not said something true or false about him, even though he is not the lady's husband. And Linsky's claim would be wrong. On the other hand, if we do not identify the statement in this way, what is the statement that the speaker made? To say that the statement he made was that her husband is kind to her lands us in difficulties. For we have to decide whether in using the definite description here in the identification of the statement, we are using it attributively or referentially. If the former, then we misrepresent the linguistic performance of the speaker; if the latter, then we are ourselves referring to someone and reporting the speaker to have said something of that person, in which case we are back to the possibility that he did say something true or false of that person.

I am thus drawn to the conclusion that when a speaker uses a definite description referentially he may have stated something true or false even if nothing fits the description, and that there is not a clear sense in which he has made a statement which is neither true nor false.

IX

I want to end by a brief examination of a picture of what a genuine referring expression is that one might derive from Russell's views. I want to suggest that this picture is not so far wrong as one might suppose and that strange as this may seem, some of the things we have said about the referential use of definite descriptions are not foreign to this picture.

Genuine proper names, in Russell's sense, would refer to something without ascribing any properties to it. They would, one might say, refer to the thing itself, not simply the thing in so far as it falls under a certain description.[13] Now this would seem to Russell something a definite description could not do, for he assumed that if definite descriptions were capable of referring at all, they would refer to something only in so far as that thing satisfied the description. Not only have we seen this assumption to be false, however, but in the last section we saw something more. We saw that when a definite description is used referentially, a speaker can be reported as having said something of something. And in reporting what it was of which he said something we are not restricted to the description he used, or synonyms of it; we may ourselves refer to it using any descriptions, names, and so forth, that will do the job. Now this seems to give a sense in which we are concerned with the thing itself and not just the thing under a certain description, when we report the linguistic act of a speaker using a definite description referentially. That is, such a definite description comes closer to performing the function of Russell's proper names than certainly he supposed.

Secondly, Russell thought, I believe, that whenever we use descriptions, as opposed to proper names, we introduce an element of generality which ought to be absent if what we are doing is referring to some particular thing. This is clear from his analysis of sentences containing definite descriptions. One of the conclusions we are supposed to draw from that analysis is that such sentences express what are in reality completely general propositions: there is a ∅ and only one such and any ∅ is ψ. We might put this in a slightly different way. If there is anything which might be identified as reference here, it is reference in a very weak sense – namely, reference to *whatever* is the one and only one ∅, if there is any such. Now this is something we might well say about the attributive use of definite descriptions, as should be evident from the previous discussion. But this lack of particularity is absent from the referential use of definite descriptions precisely because the description is here merely a device for getting one's audience to pick out or think of the thing to be spoken about, a device which may serve its function even if the description is incorrect. More importantly perhaps, in the referential use as opposed to the attributive, there is a *right* thing to be picked out by the audience and its being the right thing is not simply a function of its fitting the description.

ACKNOWLEDGEMENTS

I should like to thank my colleagues, John Canfield, Sydney Shoemaker, and Timothy Smiley, who read an earlier draft and gave me helpful suggestions. I also had the benefit of the valuable and detailed comments of the referee for the paper, to whom I wish to express my gratitude.

NOTES

1. "On Denoting," reprinted in *Logic and Knowledge*, ed. Robert C. Marsh (London: 1956), p. 51.

2. "On Referring," reprinted in *Philosophy and Ordinary Language*, ed. Charles C. Caton (Urbana: 1963), pp. 162-163.

3. *Ibid.*, p. 162.

4. *Ibid.*, p. 170.

5. Here and elsewhere I use the disjunction "presuppose or imply" to avoid taking a stand that would side me with Russell or Strawson on the issue of what the relationship involved is. To take a stand here would be beside my main point as well as being misleading, since later on I shall argue that the presupposition or implication arises in a different way depending upon the use to which the definite description is put. This last also accounts for my use of the vagueness indicator, "in some sense."

6. In a footnote added to the original version of "On Referring" (*op. cit.*, p. 181) Strawson seems to imply that where the presupposition is false, we still succeed in referring in a "secondary" way, which seems to mean "as we could be said to refer to fictional or make-believe things." But his view is still that we cannot refer in such a case in the "primary" way. This is, I believe, wrong. For a discussion of this modification of Strawson's view see Charles E. Caton, "Strawson on Referring," *Mind*, LXVIII (1959), 539-544.

7. This is an adaptation of an example (used for a somewhat different purpose) given by Leonard Linsky in "Reference and Referents," in *Philosophy and Ordinary Language*, p. 80.

8. In "Reference and Referents" (pp. 74-75, 80), Linsky correctly points out that one does not fail to refer simply because the description used does not in fact fit anything (or fits more than one thing). Thus he pinpoints one of the difficulties in Strawson's view. Here, however, I use this fact about referring to make a distinction I believe he does not draw, between two uses of definite descriptions. I later discuss the second passage from Linsky's paper.

9. In "A Reply to Mr. Sellars," *Philosophical Review*, LXIII (1954), 216-231, Strawson admits that we do not always refuse to ascribe truth to what a person says when the definite description he uses fails to fit anything (or fits more than one thing). To cite one of his examples, a person who said, "The United States Chamber of Deputies contains representatives of two major parties," would be allowed to have said something true even though he had used the wrong title. Strawson thinks this does not constitute a genuine problem for his view. He thinks that what we do in such cases, "where the speaker's intended reference is pretty clear, is simply to amend his statement in accordance with his guessed intentions and assess the amended statement for truth or falsity; we are not awarding a truth value at all to the original statement" (p. 230).

The notion of an "amended statement," however, will not do. We may note, first of all, that the sort of case Strawson has in mind could arise only when a definite description is used referentially. For the "amendment" is made by seeing the speaker's intended reference. But this could happen only if the speaker had an intended reference, a particular person or thing in mind, independent of the description he used. The cases Strawson has in mind are presumably not cases of slips of the tongue or the like; presumably they are cases in which a definite description is used because the speaker believes, though he is mistaken, that he is describing correctly what he wants to refer to. We supposedly amend the statement by knowing to what he intends to refer. But what description is to be used in the amended statement? In the example, perhaps, we could use "the United States Congress." But this description might be one the speaker would not even accept as correctly describing what he wants to refer to, because he is misinformed about the correct title. Hence, this is not a case of deciding what the speaker meant to say as opposed to what he in fact said, for the speaker did not mean to say "the United States Congress." If this is so, then there is no bar to the "amended" statement containing any description that does correctly pick out what the speaker intended to refer to. It could be, e.g., "The lower house of the United States Congress." But this means that there is no one unique "amended" statement to be assessed for truth value. And, in fact, it should now be clear that the notion of the amended statement really plays no role anyway. For if we can arrive at the amended statement only by first knowing to what the speaker intended to refer, we can assess the truth of what he said simply by deciding whether what he intended to refer to has the properties he ascribed to it.

10. As noted earlier (note 6), Strawson may allow that one has possibly referred in a "secondary" way, but, if I am right, the fact that there is no ø does not preclude one from having referred in the same way one does if there is a ø.

11. For a further discussion of the notion of saying something true *of* someone or something, see section VIII.

12. "Reference and Referents," p. 80. It should be clear that I agree with Linsky in holding that a speaker may refer even though the "presupposition of existence" is not satisfied. And I agree in thinking this an objection to Strawson's view. I think, however, that this point, among others, can be used to define two distinct uses of definite descriptions which, in turn, yields a more general criticism of Strawson. So, while I develop here a point of difference, which grows out of the distinction I want to make, I find myself in agreement with much of Linsky's article.

13. Cf. "The Philosophy of Logical Atomism," reprinted in *Logic and Knowledge*, p.200.

WHAT METAPHORS MEAN

Donald Davidson

Metaphor is the dreamwork of language and, like all dreamwork, its interpretation reflects as much on the interpreter as on the originator. The interpretation of dreams requires collaboration between a dreamer and a waker,
even if they be the same person; and the act of interpretation is itself a work
of the imagination. So too understanding a metaphor is as much a creative
endeavor as making a metaphor, and as little guided by rules.

These remarks do not, except in matters of degree, distinguish
metaphor from more routine linguistic transactions: all communication by
speech assumes the interplay of inventive construction and inventive construal. What metaphor adds to the ordinary is an achievement that uses no
semantic resources beyond the resources on which the ordinary depends.
There are no instructions for devising metaphors; there is no manual for
determining what a metaphor "means" or "says"; there is no test for
metaphor that does not call for taste.[1] A metaphor implies a kind and
degree of artistic success; there are no unsuccessful metaphors, just as there
are no unfunny jokes. There are tasteless metaphors, but these are turns that
nevertheless have brought something off, even if it were not worth bringing
off or could have been brought off better.

This paper is concerned with what metaphors mean, and its thesis
is that metaphors mean what the words, in their most literal interpretation,
mean, and nothing more. Since this thesis flies in the face of contemporary
views with which I am familiar, much of what I have to say is critical. But I
think the picture of metaphor that emerges when error and confusion are
cleared away makes metaphor a more, not a less, interesting phenomenon.

The central mistake against which I shall be inveighing is the idea
that a metaphor has, in addition to its literal sense or meaning, another
sense or meaning. This idea is common to many who have written about
metaphor: it is found in the works of literary critics like Richards, Empson,

and Winters; philosophers from Aristotle to Max Black; psychologists from Freud and earlier, to Skinner and later; and linguists from Plato to Uriel Weinreich and George Lakoff. The idea takes many forms, from the relatively simple in Aristotle to the relatively complex in Black. The idea appears in writings which maintain that a literal paraphrase of a metaphor can be produced, but it is also shared by those who hold that typically no literal paraphrase can be found. Some stress the special insight metaphor can inspire and make much of the fact that ordinary language, in its usual functioning, yields no such insight. Yet this view too sees metaphor as a form of communication alongside ordinary communication; it conveys truths or falsehoods about the world much as plainer language does, though the message may be considered more exotic, profound, or cunningly garbed.

The concept of metaphor as primarily a vehicle for conveying ideas, even if unusual ones, seems to me as wrong as the parent idea that a metaphor has a special meaning. I agree with the view that metaphors cannot be paraphrased, but I think this is not because metaphors say something too novel for literal expression but because there is nothing there to paraphrase. Paraphrase, whether possible or not, is appropriate to what is *said*: we try, in paraphrase, to say it another way. But if I am right, a metaphor doesn't say anything beyond its literal meaning (nor does its maker say anything, in using the metaphor, beyond the literal). This is not, of course, to deny that a metaphor has a point, nor that that point can be brought out by using further words.

In the past those who have denied that metaphor has a cognitive content in addition to the literal have often been out to show that metaphor is confusing, merely emotive, unsuited to serious, scientific, or philosophic discourse. My views should not be associated with this tradition. Metaphor is a legitimate device not only in literature but in science, philosophy, and the law: it is effective in praise and abuse, prayer and promotion, description and prescription. For the most part I don't disagree with Max Black, Paul Henle, Nelson Goodman, Monroe Beardsley, and the rest in their accounts of what metaphor accomplishes, except that I think it accomplishes more and that what is additional is different in kind.

My disagreement is with the explanation of how metaphor works its wonders. To anticipate: I depend on the distinction between what words mean and what they are used to do. I think metaphor belongs exclusively to the domain of use. It is something brought off by the imaginative employment of words and sentences and depends entirely on the ordinary meanings of those words and hence on the ordinary meanings of the sentences they comprise.

It is no help in explaining how words work in metaphor to posit metaphorical or figurative meanings, or special kinds of poetic or metaphorical truth. These ideas don't explain metaphor, metaphor explains them.

Once we understand a metaphor we can call what we grasp the "metaphor-ical truth" and (up to a point) say what the "metaphorical meaning" is. But simply to lodge this meaning in the metaphor is like explaining why a pill puts you to sleep by saying it has a dormative power. Literal meaning and literal truth-conditions can be assigned to words and sentences apart from particular contexts of use. This is why adverting to them has genuine explanatory power.

I shall try to establish my negative views about what metaphors mean and introduce my limited positive claims by examining some false theories of the nature of metaphor.

A metaphor makes us attend to some likeness, often a novel or sur-prising likeness, between two or more things. This trite and true observation leads, or seems to lead, to a conclusion concerning the meaning of metaphors. Consider ordinary likeness or similarity: two roses are similar because they share the property of being a rose; two infants are similar by virtue of their infanthood. Or, more simply, roses are similar because each is a rose, infants, because each is an infant.

Suppose someone says "Tolstoy was once an infant." How is the infant Tolstoy like other infants? The answer comes pat: by virtue of exhibiting the property of infanthood, that is, leaving out some of the wind, by virtue of being an infant. If we tire of the phrase "by virtue of," we can, it seems, be plainer still by saying the infant Tolstoy shares with other infants the fact that the predicate "is an infant" applies to him; given the word "infant," we have no trouble saying exactly how the infant Tolstoy resembles other infants. We could do it without the word "infant"; all we need is other words that mean the same. The end result is the same. Ordinary similarity depends on groupings established by the ordinary mean-ings of words. Such similarity is natural and unsurprising to the extent that familiar ways of grouping objects are tied to usual meanings of usual words.

A famous critic said that Tolstoy was "a great moralizing infant." The Tolstoy referred to here is obviously not the infant Tolstoy but Tolstoy the adult writer; this is metaphor. Now in what sense is Tolstoy the writer similar to an infant? What we are to do, perhaps, is think of the class of objects which includes all ordinary infants and, in addition, the adult Tolstoy and then ask ourselves what special, surprising property the mem-bers of this class have in common. The appealing thought is that given patience we could come as close as need be to specifying the appropriate property. In any case, we could do the job perfectly if we found words that meant exactly what the metaphorical "infant" means. The important point, from my perspective, is not whether we can find the perfect other words but the assumption that there is something to be attempted, a metaphorical meaning to be matched. So far I have been doing no more than crudely sketching how the concept of meaning may have crept into the analysis of metaphor, and the answer I have suggested is that since what we think of as garden variety similarity goes with what we think of as garden variety meanings, it is natural to posit unusual or metaphorical meanings to help explain the similarities metaphor promotes.

The idea, then, is that in metaphor certain words take on new, or what are often called "extended," meanings. When we read, for example, that "the Spirit of God moved upon the face of the waters," we are to regard the word "face" as having an extended meaning (I disregard further metaphor in the passage). The extension applies, as it happens, to what philosophers call the extension of the word, that is, the class of entities to which it refers. Here the word "face" applies to ordinary faces, and to waters in addition.

This account cannot, at any rate, be complete, for if in these contexts the words "face" and "infant" apply correctly to waters and to the adult Tolstoy, then waters really do have faces and Tolstoy literally was an infant, and all sense of metaphor evaporates. If we are to think of words in metaphors as directly going about their business of applying to what they properly do apply to, there is no difference between metaphor and the introduction of a new term in our vocabulary: to make a metaphor is to murder it.

What has been left out is any appeal to the original meaning of the word. Whether or not metaphor depends on new or extended meanings, it certainly depends in some way on the original meanings; an adequate account of metaphor must allow that the primary or original meanings of words remain active in their metaphorical setting.

Perhaps, then, we can explain metaphor as a kind of ambiguity: in the context of a metaphor, certain words have either a new or an original meaning, and the force of the metaphor depends on our uncertainty as we waver between the two meanings. Thus when Melville writes that "Christ was a chronometer," the effect of metaphor is produced by our taking "chronometer" first in its ordinary sense and then in some extraordinary or metaphorical sense.

It is hard to see how this theory can be correct. For the ambiguity in the word, if there is any, is due to the fact that in ordinary contexts it means one thing and in the metaphorical context it means something else; but in the metaphorical context we do not necessarily hesitate over its meaning. When we do hesitate, it is usually to decide which of a number of metaphorical interpretations we shall accept; we are seldom in doubt that what we have is a metaphor. At any rate, the effectiveness of the metaphor easily outlasts the end of uncertainty over the interpretation of the metaphorical passage. Metaphor cannot, therefore, owe its effect to ambiguity of this sort.[2]

Another brand of ambiguity may appear to offer a better suggestion. Sometimes a word will, in a single context, bear two meanings where we are meant to remember and to use both. Or, if we think of wordhood as implying sameness of meaning, then we may describe the situation as one in which what appears as a single word is in fact two. When Shakespeare's Cressida is welcomed bawdily into the Grecian camp, Nestor says, "Our general doth salute you with a kiss." Here we are to take "general" two ways: once as applying to Agamemnon, who is the general; and once, since she is kissing everyone, as applying to no one in particular, but everyone in general. We really have a conjunction of two sentences: our general, Agamemnon, salutes you with a kiss; and everyone in general is saluting you with a kiss.

This is a legitimate device, a pun, but it is not the same device as metaphor. For in metaphor there is no essential need of reiteration; whatever meanings we assign the words, they keep through every correct reading of the passage.

A plausible modification of the last suggestion would be to consider the key word (or words) in a metaphor as having two different kinds of meaning at once, a literal and a figurative meaning. Imagine the literal meaning as latent, something that we are aware of, that can work on us without working in the context, while the figurative meaning carries the direct load. And finally, there must be a rule which connects the two meanings, for otherwise the explanation lapses into a form of the ambiguity theory. The rule, at least for many typical cases of metaphor, says that in its metaphorical role the word applies to everything that it applies to in its literal role, and then some.[3]

This theory may seem complex, but it is strikingly similar to what Frege proposed to account for the behavior of referring terms in modal sentences and sentences about propositional attitudes like belief and desire. According to Frege, each referring term has two (or more) meanings, one which fixes its reference in ordinary contexts and another which fixes its reference in the special contexts created by modal operators or psychological verbs. The rule connecting the two meanings may be put like this: the meaning of the word in the special contexts makes the reference in those contexts to be identical with the meaning in ordinary contexts.

Here is the whole picture, putting Frege together with a Fregean view of metaphor: we are to think of a word as having, in addition to its mundane field of application or reference, two special or supermundane fields of application, one for metaphor and the other for modal contexts and the like. In both cases the original meaning remains to do its work by virtue of a rule which relates the various meanings.

Having stressed the possible analogy between metaphorical meaning and the Fregean meanings for oblique contexts, I turn to an imposing
difficulty in maintaining the analogy. You are entertaining a visitor from
Saturn by trying to teach him how to use the word "floor." You go through
the familiar dodges, leading him from floor to floor, pointing and stamping
and repeating the word. You prompt him to make experiments, tapping
objects tentatively with his tentacle while rewarding his right and wrong
tries. You want him to come out knowing not only that these particular
objects or surfaces are floors but also how to tell a floor when one is in sight
or touch. The skit you are putting on doesn't *tell* him what he needs to
know, but with luck it helps him to learn it.

Should we call this process learning something about the world or
learning something about language? An odd question, since what is learned
is that a bit of language refers to a bit of the world. Still, it is easy to distinguish between the business of learning the meaning of a word and using the
word once the meaning is learned. Comparing these two activities, it is natural to say that the first concerns learning something about language, while
the second is typically learning something about the world. If your
Saturnian has learned how to use the word "floor," you may try telling him
something new, that *here* is a floor. If he has mastered the word trick, you
have told him something about the world.

Your friend from Saturn now transports you through space to his
home sphere, and looking back remotely at earth you say to him, nodding
at the earth, "floor." Perhaps he will think this is still part of the lesson and
assume that the word "floor" applies properly to the earth, at least as seen
from Saturn. But what if you thought he already knew the meaning of
"floor," and you were remembering how Dante, from a similar place in the
heavens, saw the inhabited earth as "the small round floor that makes us
passionate"? Your purpose was metaphor, not drill in the use of language.
What difference would it make to your friend which way he took it? With
the theory of metaphor under consideration, very little difference, for
according to that theory a word has a new meaning in a metaphorical context; the occasion of the metaphor would, therefore, be the occasion for
learning the new meaning. We should agree that in some ways it makes relatively little difference whether, in a given context, we think a word is
being used metaphorically or in a previously unknown, but literal way.
Empson, in *Some Versions of Pastoral*, quotes these lines from Donne: "As
our blood labours to beget / Spirits, as like souls as it can,... / So must pure
lover's soules descend...." The modern reader is almost certain, Empson
points out, to take the word "spirits" in this passage metaphorically, as
applying only by extension to something spiritual. But for Donne there was
no metaphor. He writes in his *Sermons*, "The spirits ... are the thin and
active part of the blood, and are a kind of middle nature, between soul and

body." Learning this does not matter much; Empson is right when he says, "It is curious how the change in the word [that is, in what we think it means] leaves the poetry unaffected."[4]

The change may be, in some cases at least, hard to appreciate, but unless there is a change, most of what is thought to be interesting about metaphor is lost. I have been making the point by contrasting learning a new use for an old word with using a word already understood; in one case, I said, our attention is directed to language, in the other, to what language is about. Metaphor, I suggested, belongs in the second category. This can also be seen by considering dead metaphors. Once upon a time, I suppose, rivers and bottles did not, as they do now, literally have mouths. Thinking of present usage, it doesn't matter whether we take the word "mouth" to be ambiguous because it applies to entrances to rivers and openings of bottles as well as to animal apertures, or we think there is a single wide field of application that embraces both. What does matter is that when "mouth" applied only metaphorically to bottles, the application made the hearer *notice* a likeness between animal and bottle openings. (Consider Homer's reference to wounds as mouths.) Once one has the present use of the word, with literal application to bottles, there is nothing left to notice. There is no similarity to seek because it consists simply in being referred to by the same word.

Novelty is not the issue. In its context a word once taken for a metaphor remains a metaphor on the hundredth hearing, while a word may easily be appreciated in a new literal role on a first encounter. What we call the element of novelty or surprise in a metaphor is a built-in aesthetic feature we can experience again and again, like the surprise in Haydn's Symphony no. 94, or a familiar deceptive cadence.

If metaphor involved a second meaning, as ambiguity does, we might expect to be able to specify the special meaning of a word in a metaphorical setting by waiting until the metaphor dies. The figurative meaning of the living metaphor should be immortalized in the literal meaning of the dead. But although some philosophers have suggested this idea, it seems plainly wrong. "He was burned up" is genuinely ambiguous (since it may be true in one sense and false in another), but although the slangish idiom is no doubt the corpse of a metaphor, "He was burned up" now suggests no more than that he was very angry. When the metaphor was active, we would have pictured fire in the eyes or smoke coming out of the ears.

We can learn much about what metaphors mean by comparing them with similes, for a simile tells us, in part, what a metaphor merely nudges us into noting. Suppose Goneril had said, thinking of Lear, "Old fools are like babes again"; then she would have used the words to assert a similarity between old fools and babes. What she did say, of course, was "Old fools are babes again," thus using the words to intimate what the simile

declared. Thinking along these lines may inspire another theory of the figurative or special meaning of metaphors: the figurative meaning of a
metaphor is the literal meaning of the corresponding simile. Thus "Christ
was a chronometer" in its figurative sense is synonymous with "Christ was
like a chronometer," and the metaphorical meaning once locked up in "He
was burned up" is released in "He was like someone who was burned up" (or
perhaps "He was like burned up").

There is, to be sure, the difficulty of identifying the simile that corresponds to a given metaphor. Virginia Woolf said that a highbrow is "a man
or woman of thoroughbred intelligence who rides his mind at a gallop across
country in pursuit of an idea." What simile corresponds? Something like
this, perhaps: "A highbrow is a man or woman whose intelligence is like a
thoroughbred horse and who persists in thinking about an idea like a rider
galloping across country in pursuit of ... well, something."

The view that the special meaning of a metaphor is identical with
the literal meaning of a corresponding simile (however "corresponding" is
spelled out) should not be confused with the common theory that a
metaphor is an elliptical simile.[5] This theory makes no distinction in meaning between a metaphor and some related simile and does not provide any
ground for speaking of figurative, metaphorical, or special meanings. It is a
theory that wins hands down so far as simplicity is concerned, but it also
seems too simple to work. For if we make the literal meaning of the
metaphor to be the literal meaning of a matching simile, we deny access to
what we originally took to be the literal meaning of the metaphor, and we
agreed almost from the start that *this* meaning was essential to the working
of the metaphor, whatever else might have to be brought in the way of a
nonliteral meaning.

Both the elliptical simile theory of metaphor and its more sophisticated variant, which equates the figurative meaning of the metaphor with
the literal meaning of a simile, share a fatal defect. They make the hidden
meaning of the metaphor all too obvious and accessible. In each case the
hidden meaning is to be found simply by looking to the literal meaning of
what is usually a painfully trivial simile. This is like that – Tolstoy like an
infant, the earth like a floor. It is trivial because everything is like everything, and in endless ways. Metaphors are often very difficult to interpret
and, so it is said, impossible to paraphrase. But with this theory, interpretation and paraphrase typically are ready to the hand of the most callow.

These simile theories have been found acceptable, I think, only
because they have been confused with a quite different theory. Consider this
remark by Max Black:

> When Schopenhauer called a geometrical proof a mousetrap, he
> was, according to such a view, *saying* (though not explicitly): "A

geometrical proof is *like* a mousetrap, since both offer a delusive reward, entice their victims by degrees, lead to disagreeable surprise, etc." This is a view of metaphor as a condensed or elliptical *simile*.[6]

Here I discern two confusions. First, if metaphors are elliptical similes, they say *explicitly* what similes say, for ellipsis is a form of abbreviation, not of paraphrase or indirection. But, and this is the more important matter, Black's statement of what the metaphor says goes far beyond anything given by the corresponding simile. The simile simply says a geometrical proof is like a mousetrap. It no more *tells* us what similarities we are to notice than the metaphor does. Black mentions three similarities, and of course we could go on adding to the list forever. But is this list, when revised and supplemented in the right way, supposed to give the *literal* meaning of the simile? Surely not, since the simile declared no more than the similarity. If the list is supposed to provide the figurative meaning of the simile, then we learn nothing about metaphor from the comparison with simile – only that both have the same figurative meaning. Nelson Goodman does indeed claim that "the difference between simile and metaphor is negligible," and he continues, "Whether the locution be 'is like' or 'is,' the figure *likens* picture to person by picking out a certain common feature...."[7] Goodman is considering the difference between saying a picture is sad and saying it is like a sad person. It is clearly true that both sayings liken picture to person, but it seems to me a mistake to claim that either way of talking "picks out" a common feature. The simile says there is a likeness and leaves it to us to pick out some common feature or features; the metaphor does not explicitly assert a likeness, but if we accept it as a metaphor, we are again led to seek common features (not necessarily the same features the associated simile suggests; but that is another matter).

　　Just because a simile wears a declaration of similitude on its sleeve, it is, I think, far less plausible than in the case of metaphor to maintain that there is a hidden second meaning. In the case of simile, we note what it literally says, that two things resemble one another; we then regard the objects and consider what similarity would, in the context, be to the point. Having decided, we might then say the author of the simile intended us – that is, meant us – to notice that similarity. But having appreciated the difference between what the words meant and what the author accomplished by using those words, we should feel little temptation to explain what has happened by endowing the words themselves with a second, or figurative, meaning. The point of the concept of linguistic meaning is to explain what can be done with words. But the supposed figurative meaning of a simile explains nothing; it is not a feature of the word that the word has prior to and independent of the context of use, and it rests upon no linguistic customs except those that govern ordinary meaning.

What words do do with their literal meaning in simile must be possible for them to do in metaphor. A metaphor directs attention to the same sorts of similarity, if not the same similarities, as the corresponding simile. But then the unexpected or subtle parallels and analogies it is the business of metaphor to promote need not depend, for their promotion, on more than the literal meanings of words.

Metaphor and simile are merely two among endless devices that serve to alert us to aspects of the world by inviting us to make comparisons. I quote a few stanzas of T. S. Eliot's "The Hippopotamus":

> The broad-backed hippopotamus
> Rests on his belly in the mud;
> Although he seems so firm to us
> He is merely flesh and blood.
>
> Flesh and blood is weak and frail,
> Susceptible to nervous shock;
> While the True Church can never fail
> For it is based upon a rock.
>
> The hippo's feeble steps may err
> In compassing material ends,
> While the True Church need never stir
> To gather in its dividends.
>
> The 'potamus can never reach
> The mango on the mango-tree;
> But fruits of pomegranate and peach
> Refresh the Church from over sea.

Here we are neither told that the Church resembles a hippopotamus (as in simile) nor bullied into making this comparison (as in metaphor), but there can be no doubt the words are being used to direct our attention to similarities between the two. Nor should there be much inclination, in this case, to posit figurative meanings, for in what words or sentences would we lodge them? The hippopotamus really does rest on his belly in the mud; the True Church, the poem says literally, never can fail. The poem does, of course, intimate much that goes beyond the literal meanings of the words. But intimation is not meaning.

The argument so far has led to the conclusion that as much of metaphor as can be explained in terms of meaning may, and indeed must, be explained by appeal to the literal meanings of words. A consequence is that the sentences in which metaphors occur are true or false in a normal, literal way, for if the words in them don't have special meanings, sentences don't have special truth. This is not to deny that there is such a thing as metaphorical truth, only to deny it of sentences. Metaphor does lead us to notice what might not otherwise be noticed, and there is no reason, I suppose, not to say these visions, thoughts, and feelings inspired by the metaphor, are true or false.

If a sentence used metaphorically is true or false in the ordinary sense, then it is clear that it is usually false. The most obvious semantic difference between simile and metaphor is that all similes are true and most metaphors are false. The earth is like a floor, the Assyrian did come down like a wolf on the fold, because everything is like everything. But turn these sentences into metaphors, and you turn them false; the earth is like a floor, but it is not a floor; Tolstoy, grown up, was like an infant, but he wasn't one. We use a simile ordinarily only when we know the corresponding metaphor to be false. We say Mr. S. is like a pig because we know he isn't one. If we had used a metaphor and said he was a pig, this would not be because we changed our mind about the facts but because we chose to get the idea across a different way.

What matters is not actual falsehood but that the sentence be taken to be false. Notice what happens when a sentence we use as a metaphor, believing it false, comes to be thought true because of a change in what is believed about the world. When it was reported that Hemingway's plane had been sighted, wrecked, in Africa, the New York *Mirror* ran a headline saying, "Hemingway Lost in Africa," the word "lost" being used to suggest he was dead. When it turned out he was alive, the *Mirror* left the headline to be taken literally. Or consider this case: a woman sees herself in a beautiful dress and says, "What a dream of a dress!" – and then wakes up. The point of the metaphor is that the dress is like a dress one would dream of and therefore isn't a dream-dress. Henle provides a good example from *Anthony and Cleopatra* (2.2):

> The barge she sat in, like a burnish'd throne
> Burn'd on the water

Here simile and metaphor interact strangely, but the metaphor would vanish if a literal conflagration were imagined. In much the same way the usual effect of a simile can be sabotaged by taking the comparison too earnestly. Woody Allen writes, "The trial, which took place over the following weeks, was like a circus, although there was some difficulty getting the elephants into the courtroom."[8]

Generally it is only when a sentence is taken to be false that we accept it as a metaphor and start to hunt out the hidden implication. It is probably for this reason that most metaphorical sentences are *patently* false, just as all similes are trivially true. Absurdity or contradiction in a metaphorical sentence guarantees we won't believe it and invites us, under proper circumstances, to take the sentence metaphorically.

Patent falsity is the usual case with metaphor, but on occasion patent truth will do as well. "Business is business" is too obvious in its literal meaning to be taken as having been uttered to convey information, so we look for another use; Ted Cohen reminds us, in the same connection, that no man is an island.[9] The point is the same. The ordinary meaning in the context of use is odd enough to prompt us to disregard the question of literal truth.

Now let me raise a somewhat Platonic issue by comparing the making of a metaphor with telling a lie. The comparison is apt because lying, like making a metaphor, concerns not the meaning of words but their use. It is sometimes said that telling a lie entails saying what is false; but this is wrong. Telling a lie requires not that what you say be false but that you think it false. Since we usually believe true sentences and disbelieve false, most lies are falsehoods; but in any particular case this is an accident. The parallel between making a metaphor and telling a lie is emphasized by the fact that the same sentence can be used, with meaning unchanged, for either purpose. So a woman who believed in witches but did not think her neighbor a witch might say, "She's a witch," meaning it metaphorically; the same woman, still believing the same of witches and her neighbor but intending to deceive, might use the same words to very different effect. Since sentence and meaning are the same in both cases, it is sometimes hard to prove which intention lay behind the saying of it; thus a man who says "Lattimore's a Communist" and means to lie can always try to beg off by pleading a metaphor.

What makes the difference between a lie and a metaphor is not a difference in the words used or what they mean (in any strict sense of meaning) but in how the words are used. Using a sentence to tell a lie and using it to make a metaphor are, of course, totally different uses, so different that they do not interfere with one another, as say, acting and lying do. In lying, one must make an assertion so as to represent oneself as believing what one does not; in acting, assertion is excluded. Metaphor is careless to the difference. It can be an insult, and so be an assertion, to say to a man "You are a pig." But no metaphor was involved when (let us suppose) Odysseus addressed the same words to his companions in Circe's palace; a story, to be sure, and so no assertion – but the word, for once, was used literally of men.

No theory of metaphorical meaning or metaphorical truth can help explain how metaphor works. Metaphor runs on the same familiar linguistic tracks that the plainest sentences do; this we saw from considering simile. What distinguishes metaphor is not meaning but use – in this it is like assertion, hinting, lying, promising, or criticizing. And the special use to which we put language in metaphor is not – cannot be – to "say something" special, no matter how indirectly. For a metaphor says only what shows on its face – usually a patent falsehood or an absurd truth. And this plain truth or falsehood needs no paraphrase – it is given in the literal meaning of the words.

What are we to make, then, of the endless energy that has been, and is being, spent on methods and devices for drawing out the content of a metaphor? The psychologists Robert Verbrugge and Nancy McCarrell tell us that:

> Many metaphors draw attention to common systems of relationships or common transformations, in which the identity of the participants is secondary. For example, consider the sentences: *A car is like an animal. Tree trunks are straws for thirsty leaves and branches.* The first sentence directs attention to systems of relationships among energy consumption, respiration, self-induced motion, sensory systems, and, possibly, a homunculus. In the second sentence, the resemblance is a more constrained type of transformation: suction of fluid through a vertically oriented cylindrical space from a source of fluid to a destination.[10]

Verbrugge and McCarrell don't believe there is any sharp line between the literal and metaphorical uses of words; they think many words have a "fuzzy" meaning that gets fixed, if fixed at all, by a context. But surely this fuzziness, however it is illustrated and explained, cannot erase the line between what a sentence literally means (given its context) and what it "draws our attention to" (given its literal meaning as fixed by the context). The passage I have quoted is not employing such a distinction: what it says the sample sentences direct our attention to are facts expressed by paraphrases of the sentences. Verbrugge and McCarrell simply want to insist that a correct paraphrase may emphasize "systems of relationships" rather than resemblances between objects.

According to Black's interaction theory, a metaphor makes us apply a "system of commonplaces" associated with the metaphorical word to the subject of the metaphor: in "Man is a wolf" we apply commonplace attributes (stereotypes) of the wolf to man. The metaphor, Black says, thus "selects, emphasizes, suppresses, and organizes features of the principal subject by implying statements about it that normally apply to the subsidiary subject."[11] If paraphrase fails, according to Black, it is not because the metaphor does not have a special cognitive content, but because the paraphrase "will not have the same power to inform and enlighten as the original.... One of the points I most wish to stress is that the loss in such cases is a loss in cognitive content; the relevant weakness of the literal paraphrase is not that it may be tiresomely prolix or boringly explicit; it fails to be a translation because it fails to give the insight that the metaphor did."[12]

How can this be right? If a metaphor has a special cognitive content, why should it be so difficult or impossible to set it out? If, as Owen Barfield claims, a metaphor "says one thing and means another," why should it be that when we try to get explicit about what it means, the effect is so much weaker – "put it that way," Barfield says, "and nearly all the tarning, and with it half the poetry, is lost."[13] Why does Black think a literal paraphrase "inevitably says too much – and with the wrong emphasis"? Why inevitably? Can't we, if we are clever enough, come as close as we please?

For that matter, how is it that a simile gets along without a special intermediate meaning? In general, critics do not suggest that a simile says one thing and means another – they do not suppose it *means* anything but what lies on the surface of the words. It may make us think deep thoughts, just as a metaphor does; how come, then, no one appeals to the "special cognitive content" of the simile? And remember Eliot's hippopotamus; there there was neither simile nor metaphor, but what seemed to get done was just like what gets done by similes and metaphors. Does anyone suggest that the *words* in Eliot's poem have special meanings?

Finally, if words in metaphor bear a coded meaning, how can this meaning differ from the meaning those same words bear in the case where the metaphor *dies* – that is, when it comes to be part of the language? Why doesn't "He was burned up" as now used and meant mean *exactly* what the fresh metaphor once meant? Yet all that the dead metaphor means is that he was very angry – a notion not very difficult to make explicit.

There is, then, a tension in the usual view of metaphor. For on the one hand, the usual view wants to hold that a metaphor does something no plain prose can possibly do and, on the other hand, it wants to explain what a metaphor does by appealing to a cognitive content – just the sort of thing plain prose is designed to express. As long as we are in this frame of mind, we must harbor the suspicion that it can be done, at least up to a point.

There is a simple way out of the impasse. We must give up the idea that a metaphor carries a message, that it has a content or meaning (except, of course, its literal meaning). The various theories we have been considering mistake their goal. Where they think they provide a method for deciphering an encoded content, they actually tell us (or try to tell us) something about the *effects* metaphors have on us. The common error is to fasten on the contents of the thoughts a metaphor provokes and to read these contents into the metaphor itself. No doubt metaphors often make us notice aspects of things we did not notice before; no doubt they bring surprising analogies and similarities to our attention; they do provide a kind of lens or lattice, as Black says, through which we view the relevant phenomena. The issue does not lie here but in the question of how the metaphor is related to what it makes us see.

It may be remarked with justice that the claim that a metaphor provokes or invites a certain view of its subject rather than saying it straight out is a commonplace; so it is. Thus Aristotle says metaphor leads to a "perception of resemblances." Black, following Richards, says a metaphor "evokes" a certain response: "a suitable hearer will be led by a metaphor to construct a ... system."[14] This view is neatly summed up by what Heraclitus said of the Delphic oracle: "It does not say and it does not hide, it intimates."[15]

I have no quarrel with these descriptions of the effects of metaphor, only with the associated views as to *how* metaphor is supposed to produce them. What I deny is that metaphor does its work by having a special meaning, a specific cognitive content. I do not think, as Richards does, that metaphor produces its result by having a meaning which results from the interaction of two ideas; it is wrong, in my view, to say, with Owen Barfield, that a metaphor "says one thing and means another"; or with Black that a metaphor asserts or implies certain complex things by dint of a special meaning and *thus* accomplishes its job of yielding an "insight." A metaphor does its work through other intermediaries – to suppose it can be effective only by conveying a coded message is like thinking a joke or a dream makes some statement which a clever interpreter can restate in plain prose. Joke or dream or metaphor can, like a picture or a bump on the head, make us appreciate some fact – but not by standing for, or expressing, the fact.

If this is right, what we attempt in "paraphrasing" a metaphor cannot be to give its meaning, for that lies on the surface; rather we attempt to evoke what the metaphor brings to our attention. I can imagine someone granting this and shrugging it off as no more than an insistence on restraint in using the word "meaning." This would be wrong. The central error about metaphor is most easily attacked when it takes the form of a theory of metaphorical meaning, but behind that theory, and statable independently, is the thesis that associated with a metaphor is a cognitive content that its author wishes to convey and that the interpreter must grasp if he is to get the message. This theory is false, whether or not we call the purported cognitive content a meaning.

It should make us suspect the theory that it is so hard to decide, even in the case of the simplest metaphors, exactly what the content is supposed to be. The reason it is often so hard to decide is, I think, that we imagine there is a content to be captured when all the while we are in fact focusing on what the metaphor makes us notice. If what the metaphor makes us notice were finite in scope and propositional in nature, this would not in itself make trouble; we would simply project the content the metaphor brought to mind onto the metaphor. But in fact there is no limit to what a metaphor calls to our attention, and much of what we are caused to notice is not propositional in character. When we try to say what a metaphor "means," we soon realize there is no end to what we want to mention.[16] If someone draws his finger along a coastline on a map, or mentions the beauty and deftness of a line in a Picasso etching, how may things are drawn to your attention? You might list a great many, but you could not finish since the idea of finishing would have no clear application. How many facts or propositions are conveyed by a photograph? None, an infinity, or one great unstatable fact? Bad question. A picture is not worth a thousand words, or any other number. Words are the wrong currency to exchange for a picture.

It's not only that we can't provide an exhaustive catalogue of what has been attended to when we are led to see something in a new light; the difficulty is more fundamental. What we notice or see is not, in general, propositional in character. Of course it *may* be, and when it is, it usually may be stated in fairly plain words. But if I show you Wittgenstein's duck-rabbit, and I say, "It's a duck," then with luck you see it as a duck; if I say, "It's a rabbit," you see it as a rabbit. But no proposition expresses what I have led you to see. Perhaps you have come to realize that the drawing can be seen as a duck or as a rabbit. But one could come to know this without ever seeing the drawing as a duck or as a rabbit. Seeing as is not seeing that. Metaphor makes us see one thing as another by making some literal statement that inspires or prompts the insight. Since in most cases what the metaphor prompts or inspires is not entirely, or even at all, recognition of some truth or fact, the attempt to give literal expression to the content of the metaphor is simply misguided.

The theorist who tries to explain a metaphor by appealing to a hidden message, like the critic who attempts to state the message, is then fundamentally confused. No such explanation or statement can be forthcoming because no such message exists.

Not, of course, that interpretation and elucidation of a metaphor are not in order. Many of us need help if we are to see what the author of a metaphor wanted us to see and what a more sensitive or educated reader grasps. The legitimate function of so-called paraphrase is to make the lazy or ignorant reader have a vision like that of the skilled critic. The critic is, so to speak, in benign competition with the metaphor-maker. The critic tries to make his own art easier or more transparent in some respects than the original, but at the same time he tries to reproduce in others some of the effects the original had on him. In doing this the critic also, and perhaps by the best method at his command, calls attention to the beauty or aptness, the hidden power, of the metaphor itself.

NOTES

1. I think Max Black is wrong when he says, "The rules of our language determine that some expressions must count as metaphors." He allows, however, that what a metaphor "means" depends on much more: the speaker's intention, tone of voice, verbal setting, etc. "Metaphor," in his *Models and Metaphors* (Ithaca, N.Y.: 1962), p. 29.

2. Nelson Goodman says metaphor and ambiguity differ chiefly "in that the several uses of a merely ambiguous term are coeval and independent" while in metaphor "a term with an extension established by habit is applied elsewhere under the influence of that habit"; he suggests that as our sense of the history of the "two uses" in metaphor fades, the metaphorical word becomes merely ambiguous (*Languages of Art*, Indianapolis, Ind.: 1968, p. 71). In fact in many cases of ambiguity, one use springs from the other (as Goodman says) and so cannot be coeval. But the basic error, which Goodman shares with others, is the idea that two "uses" are involved in metaphor in anything like the way they are in ambiguity.

3. The theory described is essentially that of Paul Henle. "Metaphor," in *Language, Thought and Culture*, ed. Henle (Ann Arbor, Mich: 1958).

4. William Empson, *Some Versions of Pastoral* (London: 1935), p. 133.

5. J. Middleton Murray says a metaphor is a "compressed simile," *Countries of the Mind*, 2d ser. (Oxford: 1931), p. 3. Max Black attributes a similar view to Alexander Bain, *English Composition and Rhetoric*, enl. ed. (London: 1887).

6. Black, *op. cit.*, p. 35.

7. Goodman, *op. cit.*, pp. 77-78.

8. Woody Allen, *New Yorker*, 21 November 1977, p. 59.

9. Ted Cohen, "Figurative Speech and Figurative Acts," *Journal of Philosophy* 72 (1975): 671. Since the negation of a metaphor seems always to be a potential metaphor, there may be as many platitudes among the potential metaphors as there are absurds.

10. Robert R. Verbrugge and Nancy S. McCarrell, "Metaphoric Comprehension: Studies in Reminding and Resembling," *Cognitive Psychology* 9 (1977): 499.

11. Black, *op. cit.*, pp. 44-45.

12. *Ibid.*, p. 46.

13. Owen Barfield, "Poetic Diction and Legal Fiction," in *The Importance of Language*, ed. Max Black (Englewood Cliffs, N.J. 1962), p. 55.

14. M. Black, "Metaphor," 41.

15. I use Hannah Arendt's attractive translation of "*σημαίνει*": it clearly should not be rendered as "mean" in this context.

16. Stanley Cavell mentions the fact that most attempts at paraphrase end with "and so on" and refers to Empson's remark that metaphors are "pregnant" (*Must We Mean What We Say?* New York: 1969, p. 79). But Cavell doesn't explain the endlessness of paraphrase as I do, as can be learned from the fact that he thinks it distinguishes metaphor from some ("but perhaps not all") literal discourse. I hold that the endless character of what we call the paraphrase of a metaphor springs from the fact that it attempts to spell out what the metaphor makes us notice, and to this there is no clear end. I would say the same for any use of language.

SOURCES

Austin, J.L. "Performative Utterances." *Philosophical Papers*. Ed. J.O. Urmson and G.J. Warnock. 3rd ed. Oxford: Oxford UP, 1979: 233-52.

Chomsky, Noam. *Knowledge of Language: Its Nature, Origin and Use*. Westport CT: Praeger, 1985. Reprinted with permission of Greenwood Publishing Group, Inc.

Davidson, Donald. "Truth And Meaning." *Synthese* 17 (1967): 304-23. Reprinted with kind permission of Kluwer Academic Publishers.

Davidson, Donald. "What Metaphors Mean." *On Metaphor*. Ed. Sheldon Sacks. Chicago: University of Chicago Press, 1978: 29-46. Copyright 1978, Donald Davidson. Reprinted with permission of the author.

Dennett, Daniel C. "Three Kinds of Intentional Psychology." *Reduction, Time and Reality*. Ed. R. Healy. Cambridge: Cambridge UP, 1981: 37-61. Reprinted with permission of Cambridge University Press.

Donnellan, Keith. "Reference and Definite Descriptions." *Philosophical Review* 75 (1966): 281-304. Copyright 1966, Cornell University. Reprinted by permission of the publisher.

Fodor, Jerry A. "Propositional Attitudes." *The Monist* 61 (1978): 501-23. Copyright 1978, The Monist, La Salle, Illinois 61301. Reprinted by permission.

Frege, Gottlob. "Ueber Sinn und Bedeutung." *Translations from the Philosophical Writings of Gottlob Frege*. Trans. Max Black. Ed. Peter Geach and Max Black. 3rd ed. Oxford: Basil Blackwell, 1980: 56-78. Reprinted with permission of the publisher. First published in *Zeitschrift für Philosophie und philosophische Kritik* 100 (1892).

Grice, H.P. "Logic and Conversation." *Syntax and Semantics*. Ed. Peter Cole and Jerry L. Morgan. Vol 3. New York: Academic Press, 1975: 41-58. Reprinted with permission of the publisher.

Grice, H.P. "Meaning." *Philosophical Review* 66 (1957): 377-88. Copyright 1957, Cornell University. Reprinted by permission of the publisher.

Kripke, Saul. "Identity and Necessity." *Identity and Individuation*. Ed. Milton K. Kunitz. New York: NYU Press, 1971: 135-64. Reprinted with permission of the author.

Quine, W.V. "Two Dogmas of Empiricism." *From A Logical Point of View*. 2nd ed. Cambridge MA: Harvard UP, 1961. Reprinted by permission of the publisher. Copyright 1953, 1961, 1980 by the President and Fellows of Harvard College.

Russell, Bertrand. "Descriptions." *Introduction to Mathematical Philosophy*. London: George Allen & Unwin, 1919: 167-80. Reprinted with permission of The Bertrand Russell Peace Foundation and the publisher.

Searle, John R. "What Is A Speech Act?" *Philosophy in America*. Ed. Max Black. Ithaca: Cornell UP, 1965: 221-39. Reprinted with permission of Routledge Ltd.

Strawson, P.F. "On Referring." *Mind* 59 (1950): 320-44. Reprinted with permission of Oxford University Press and the author.

Wittgenstein, Ludwig. *Philosophical Investigations*. Trans. G.E.M. Anscombe. 2nd ed. Oxford: Basil Blackwell, 1958. Reprinted with permission of the publisher.

AGMV MARQUIS

Québec, Canada
2000